Ethics, Business and Capitalism

T0309279

Ethics, Business and Capitalism
Thailand and Indonesia
in an Asian Perspective

Edited by
Janet Hunter, Patnaree Srisuphaolarn,
Pierre van der Eng and Julia S. Yongue

NUS PRESS
SINGAPORE

This publication is funded by the Shibusawa Eiichi Memorial Foundation.

© 2025 Janet Hunter, Patnaree Srisuphaolarn, Pierre van der Eng
and Julia S. Yongue

Published by:
NUS Press
National University of Singapore
AS3-01-02
3 Arts Link
Singapore 117569

Fax: (65) 6774-0652
E-mail: nusbooks@nus.edu.sg
Website: http://nuspress.nus.edu.sg

print ISBN 978-981-325-274-5 (paper)
ePDF ISBN 978-981-325-275-2

National Library Board, Singapore Cataloguing in Publication Data
Name(s): Hunter, Janet, 1948- editor. | Patnaree Srisuphaolarn, editor. | Eng,
    Pierre van der, editor. | Yongue, Julia S., editor.
Title: Ethics, business and capitalism : Thailand and Indonesia in an Asian
    perspective / edited by Janet Hunter, Patnaree Srisuphaolarn, Pierre van der Eng
    and Julia S. Yongue.
Description: Singapore : NUS Press, [2025] | Includes index.
Identifier(s): ISBN 978-981-325-274-5 (paperback) | 978-981-325-275-2 (ePDF)
Subject(s): LCSH: Business ethics--Thailand. | Business ethics--Indonesia.
Classification: DDC 330.9593--dc23

Cover: "Aerial photo of vehicles on road, Jakarta, Indonesia" by Tom Fisk, Pexels,
free to use photo.

Typeset by: Ogma Solutions Pvt Ltd
Printed by: Integrated Books International

Contents

v

List of Figures and Tables

Figures

Tables

List of Graphs and Diagrams

Graphs

Diagrams

Acknowledgements

This volume started as part of a project on historical and contemporary business ethics sponsored by Japan's Shibusawa Eiichi Memorial Foundation. Inspired by the ideas and approach to capitalism of Shibusawa Eiichi, often referred to as "the father of Japanese capitalism", the starting point of the project was the possibility that Shibusawa's ideas might be of relevance to business leaders in more recent late industrialising and middle-income economies, and that they could also help inform a broader exploration of business ethics and business structures in such economies.

This is the third of three volumes that have emerged from the project. The first, published in both English and Japanese, looked at the case of Japan from the mid-19th century, while the second analysed a range of aspects of Turkish business in comparative perspective through the 20th century up to the present time.

The editors of this third volume, which focuses on business and business ethics in Thailand and Indonesia—two of Southeast Asia's most important growing economies—would like to thank the Shibusawa Eiichi Memorial Foundation and its current managing director, Mr Takashi Iwanaga, for its ongoing support over a number of years, as well as the contributing authors. In particular, we would like to thank Mr Jun'etsu Komatsu, former managing director of the Foundation and Mr Jun Inoue, former director of the Shibusawa Memorial Museum, for their invaluable support and encouragement.

We appreciate the encouragement of Mr Masahide Shibusawa and his family over the period of this project. Our gratitude is also due to all the participants at the project conferences and workshops for their invaluable contributions and comments, in particular Geoffrey Jones, Patrick Fridenson and Takeo Kikkawa, who were present from the start of the project. Finally, we would also like to thank the editorial staff at NUS Press for taking on this volume and for their meticulous editorial care.

Chapter 1

Introduction: Rethinking Business Ethics in Thailand and Indonesia

Janet Hunter, Patnaree Srisuphaolarn,
Pierre van der Eng and Julia S. Yongue

Indonesia and Thailand are two of Asia's most important economies. With a population of 275 million, Indonesia is a member of G20, and by a clear margin, the largest economy in Southeast Asia. With 72 million people, Thailand is somewhat smaller, but in 2022, these countries were ranked third and fourth respectively in terms of gross national product among the emerging economies of Asia. However, neither Thailand nor Indonesia has experienced a smooth trajectory of economic growth over the last few decades, and on both countries, the Asian financial crisis of 1997 had dire effects. Thailand, the country where the crisis began, and whose economy had for a decade been experiencing growth rates in the region of 9 per cent per annum, was devastated by the withdrawal of foreign portfolio investors and the depreciation of the baht. A similar scenario was repeated in Indonesia. The chain of events culminated in both Indonesia and Thailand requiring support from the International Monetary Fund (IMF) to stabilise their currencies. That support came with mandatory regulatory reforms and it took several years for the national income of both countries to recover from the crisis. The financial crisis also generated policy changes. In Thailand, for example, there was an increased focus on the importance of the shareholder and finance capital.

The 1997 crisis, coming at a time when both Indonesia and Thailand were on the cusp of achieving middle-income status, was in some respects a turning point for the two economies. The experience offered the populations of both countries an opportunity for reflection—on the purpose of economic development, the kind of society that might be achieved in the process of recovery, and the role

1

of private companies in relation to stakeholders and society as a whole. Piling on top of growing concerns during the 1990s—in particular regarding the environment—were significant changes that followed the crisis, not least in the nature of corporate governance, where a key aim was to improve transparency for investors. Following the crisis, there were also indications of broader initiatives aimed at improving the social reputation and contributions of private companies. The book focuses on the consideration of the relationship between business and society, and what that might mean for economic development and business strategies in Thailand and Indonesia.

Twenty-five years on from the crisis, Indonesia is ranked by the World Bank as a lower middle-income country while Thailand is ranked as upper middle-income. Per capita GDP (gross domestic product) in Thailand in 2021 was over 60 per cent higher than that in Indonesia. Profound issues of economic inequality persist in both countries while corruption remains rampant across much of their economies. At the same time, there have been some significant changes, including in the ways in which businesses think about their position in society, and in turn how elites in the two societies expect businesses to behave, not least through the exercise of corporate social responsibility (CSR). The economic fortunes of the two countries continue to be of crucial importance for their own populations; for the wider Asian economy; and for what they might be able to tell us about the challenges to development in middle-income economies.

The papers in this volume offer in-depth analyses of the evolution of business, and of particular firms that have exemplified some of the features of economic growth in the two economies, locating them both in their specific historical and geographical context and within the parameters of late development and "catch-up" growth. Our analysis focuses in particular on the relationship of the private sector with its diverse stakeholders, who include shareholders, consumers, suppliers, workers, political actors and the broader community. This takes us beyond the study of business institutions and corporate structure, into the evolution of business ethics, business values and philanthropy. As noted, the 1997 financial crisis reinforced the need for thinking about the extent to which a private enterprise serves more than just the interests of its owners or shareholders; how it contributes to the broader development of economy and society; and how it in turn shapes that development. We have had to ask how far business enterprises in Thailand and Indonesia can be credited with a strategic vision that generates positive outcomes for different groups in society, or with promoting the common good, and what kinds of values and discourse underlie entrepreneurial activity in relation to diverse stakeholders. Can we see in either of these economies a remodelling of older ideas and/or of new and original understandings of the position of business in society? Considering the contribution of business to social welfare, and not just to economic growth, necessitates the consideration of major issues of sustainability, diversity, ethics and social responsibility.

Together, the papers in this volume highlight three key interrelated issues: the emergence of alternatives to existing models of shareholder capitalism; how a business conceives its responsibilities towards diverse stakeholders and society as a whole; and the relative importance of ethics and structural imperatives as drivers of business operation and in shaping the social responsibility of firms.

To start with, in thinking about alternatives to existing models of capitalism, it is apparent that the factors influencing the context for business in emerging economies such as Thailand and Indonesia differ considerably from those in their more developed counterparts. This of itself calls into question the validity of the existing Anglo-American model of shareholder capitalism as any kind of universal or ideal model—a questioning that was also associated with the economic growth of Japan in the 1970s–80s. We show here the importance of positing alternative strategies and institutions that are possibly more appropriate for emerging economies, and how such alternatives have been articulated and actualised by businesses and individuals in the two countries.

Second, the possibility of alternatives to the Anglo-American model has led us to consider the potential of business for promoting both the individual and the collective good, and more broadly how a business conceives its responsibilities towards its multiple stakeholders and society as a whole. We argue here that some businesses in Thailand and Indonesia have been influenced not only by their own traditions but also by ideas initially articulated elsewhere in Asia and beyond. Japanese entrepreneurs were not the only business actors whose views had a major resonance among their peers in other Asian countries, though they were perhaps more unusual in their articulating more explicitly the purposes of businesses discharging their perceived responsibilities to stakeholders and society, and the means by which to do so. Many Thai and Indonesian companies had significant exposure to Japanese direct investment, particularly in the manufacturing sector. Thailand had a conspicuously high proportion of partnerships between domestic and foreign firms (OECD 2021). In 2020, there were reported to be 2,362 Japanese subsidiaries operating in Thailand and 1,147 in Indonesia. These businesses employed over 620,000 workers in Thailand and over 380,000 in Indonesia, with a large majority of them being in manufacturing in both countries. Japan has been consistently the second largest foreign investor in Indonesia after Singapore, accounting for around 30 per cent of Indonesia's cumulative inward foreign direct investment (FDI) flows through the earlier decade, up to 2019 (OECD 2020). The stock of Indonesia's FDI from Japan in 2020 amounted to USD 25.5 billion, out of the country's total FDI stock of

USD 240.5 billion, and in Thailand, USD 94.9 billion, out of a total USD 289.3 billion. Faced by an increasing legal obligation to implement CSR policies, in both countries, stakeholder engagement policies have been formulated, targeted to respond to mounting concerns about sustainability, the climate, inequality and diversity. Some of this discourse and practice resonates not only with Western-influenced CSR policies, but also with earlier Japanese ideas relating to the social responsibilities of business. At the same time, however, new and distinct approaches to stakeholder engagement and social responsibility in the two countries have also drawn on traditional forms of philanthropy and pre-existing value systems, both religious and non- religious. For example, Chapter 10 (Reconstructing Business Ethics through Egodocuments: Non-Western Perceptions of Business Ethics in Indonesia, 1950s–2000s) by Farabi Fakih and Chapter 12 (Business in Indonesia since *Reformasi*: New Opportunities for CSR and Ethical Capitalism) by Pierre van der Eng show how, in Indonesia, recent approaches to business ethics and philanthropy have built on the historical legacy and on the value systems espoused by individual entrepreneurs based on Islamic beliefs or traditional Confucian philanthropy.

Third, our findings confirm that there is no consistent response among Thai and Indonesian businesses in the balance they choose to strike between structural imperatives and ethical considerations. As might be expected, businesses across the two countries are enormously diverse in their approaches, as well as the values that they articulate, and there is a range of outcomes in relation to the social responsibility of firms. As we show, consideration by businesses of ethical factors and philanthropy—or increasingly, corporate social responsibility—is far from new, only that the language may have changed; notwithstanding the novelty often claimed for CSR, well before the modern period, some businesses in both the West and Asia were already engaging with diverse stakeholders and articulating a broader understanding of social responsibility.

The term CSR has its own ambiguities and might potentially be interpreted as conforming to Western models of philanthropy and business ethics, but it has become the common currency of debates on the social role of businesses in both Indonesia and Thailand. A number of the chapters in this volume therefore explore the discourse and practice relating to CSR and how businesses seek to implement a societal role. The autobiographical writings of leading Indonesian entrepreneurs analysed by Fakih allow us to understand better how entrepreneurs seek to identify their roles in society, as well as the broader discourse on ethical values in business within a highly diverse national culture. Sari Wahyuni and Sely Haudy, in Chapter 7 (The Linkage between Stewardship, Competitive Advantage and Firm Performance: An Empirical Study of Indonesian Family Businesses), offer the concept of "stewardship" as an indicator of firms in Indonesia moving away from simple profit-maximisation as the core objective of their activities, underlining the conspicuous nature of family business philanthropy. Julia S. Yongue, in Chapter 3 (Siam Then, Thailand Now: Contextualising the Emergence of Thai Capitalism through Three Phases of Globalisation), argues that in Thailand, the re-emergence of the "Sufficiency Economy" occurred in the context of the 1997 crisis, also reflecting the dominant role of the Crown and the articulation of an alternative to free market capitalism. As shown in Chapter 11 (The Essence and Mechanism of Transformation to a "Sufficiency Economy") by Patnaree Srisuphaolarn and Nuttapol Assarut, there is an emphasis on human development—one that can offer more support to small producers, particularly in the agricultural sector. Their chapter focuses on two villages in which this alternative strategy has been implemented, emphasising the distinctive approach in terms of economic process, objectives and attitudes to resource use. The idea of the Sufficiency Economy has had a broader impact on how Thai businesses consider their ethical responsibilities. As Patarapong Intarakumnerd suggests in Chapter 6 (Entrepreneurship and Innovation of Thai Firms in Manufacturing Industries), CSR practices in Thailand have often been localised by their proximity to Sufficiency Economy ideas, as well as to Buddhism. This "greener", small scale approach to economic activity is to some extent matched by efforts in Indonesia, where there is evidence of the social enterprise with a basis in the local community.

Collectively, therefore, the chapters in this volume contribute to our understanding of economic development and business strategy in Indonesia and Thailand, thereby allowing us to better understand the business contexts of middle-income economies and the motives and strategies of businesses and entrepreneurs in a complex and imperfect business environment. We highlight the importance of foreign investment and multinationals as conduits for the transfer of technology and ideas. In particular, we focus much of our analysis on some of the ways in which entrepreneurs and businesses in Indonesia and Thailand realise their role in relation to society more broadly, and the strategies that they have devised in an attempt to discharge that role. Inevitably, these strategies are shaped by, and respond to, the particular contexts within which firms operate, not least their relationships with the State, the nature of existing institutions, the characteristics of business structures and the longstanding importance in business of significant ethnic minorities, in particular, a Chinese minority. The prevalence of family-owned conglomerates and diversified business groups in Southeast Asian business systems also required us to confront the question of the extent to which family-owned businesses may be conducive to stakeholder and social engagement, although in this case, our findings suggest no clear pattern.

In the post-1997 economic environment, spurred by the recovery of some private business groups, questions were raised about the real beneficiaries of private enterprise activity and how businesses might meet the needs of the broader regional and national communities. Revolving around the issue of how extensively models of large-scale private enterprises in Thailand and Indonesia serve merely their owners or shareholders, and whether it is possible to identify a more embracing model of capitalist enterprise serving a diversity of stakeholders, these debates that resulted are in line with our core research questions. Our evidence suggests that some new patterns of enterprises have emerged in response to perceived failings, though not necessarily on a sufficiently substantial scale, such as to undermine older patterns of operation.

Three major areas of scholarly investigation frame the approach that we have adopted, and these are discussed in the next part of this introduction. First, we briefly summarise the framework of alternative business history and note some key studies on Asian economic development that have informed much of the existing research on Indonesia and Thailand. Second, we discuss the significance of Japanese ideas relating to the social responsibilities of business, to which some businesses in the Southeast Asian region have been exposed. Third, we offer some comments on the broader links between business ethics and the societal role of businesses in emerging economies. The final part of the chapter provides an overview of some of the major features of recent economic development in Thailand and Indonesia, many of which are taken up in the individual chapters. We focus on three broad contextual issues that impact how companies in Thailand and Indonesia define their social obligations: namely the political environment and business-State relations; the dominance of family businesses, business groups and ethnic minority entrepreneurs; and the trends in ethical business practices and CSR, particularly in the context of the significant inflows of FDI associated with the operations of multinational enterprises (MNEs). These three contextual issues are critical if we are to understand better the activities of businesses in Thailand and Indonesia and the environment that has helped to shape them.

Historiographical and Scholarly Context of the Volume

Our framing of our subject matter is informed by what Gareth Austin, Carlos Dávila and Geoffrey Jones term "alternative business history" (2017). This approach emphasises the importance of considering new settings "when asking the established and familiar questions that concern business historians" (Austin, Dávila and Jones 2017, 538). Focusing on the development of the business sector in emerging markets, these authors argue that "the different institutional and other contexts of emerging markets drove business responses unlike those in the West" (Austin, Dávila and Jones 2017, 568). In other words, in such markets, a less than optimal context for business led to a path different from that followed by earlier developing economies. While the many differences between and within emerging economies are not ignored, Austin, Dávila and Jones argue for the existence of commonalities in the history of countries across Asia, Latin America and Africa as forming a sufficient basis that created new, distinct approaches. They summarise these commonalities as: being on the wrong side of the Great Divergence, colonial legacies, long periods of State intervention, institutional voids in capital, labour and other markets, and turbulence in the broader business environment (Austin, Dávila and Jones 2017, 538ff). These commonalities generated different business responses and outcomes:

> In this alternative business history world, entrepreneurs and their families counted more than managerial hierarchies; immigrants and diaspora were critical sources of entrepreneurship; illegal and informal forms of business were commonplace; diversified business groups rather than the M-form became the major form of large-scale business; corporate strategies to deal with turbulence were essential; and radical social-responsibility concepts were pursued, if not by the majority of businesses (Austin, Dávila and Jones 2017, 568).

The authors make little mention of either Thailand or Indonesia in their article, but our chapters make clear that both these countries share in many of the emerging market outcomes indicated by these authors. Yongue, for example, traces how the existence of entrepreneurs, ethnic minorities and diversified business groups helped to shape the context for business development in Thailand, while Chapter 8 (The Making of a Thai Consumer Goods Conglomerate: The Role of Dynamic Entrepreneurship and Social Capital) by Srisuphaolarn and Motoi Ihara shows how some big Thai business groups coped with institutional voids through the mobilisation of entrepreneurship and social capital. It is also apparent from our studies that the context in these emerging markets can affect the behaviour of multinational, as well as domestic enterprises. Of course, arguing that business and capitalism in emerging economies differ from their earlier forms in the West is far from new. Similar arguments can be found in research on Japan in the 1970s to the 1980s, highlighting the existence of both similarities, as well as very significant differences between Japanese and Western models of capitalism. What the alternative business history approach does provide, however, is a more coherent and consistent way of looking at the characteristics of how business unfolded, *and unfolds*, in emerging markets, particularly those characteristics that are distinct from the Anglo-American model. As such, they allow for deeper insights into both context and causal relationships.

Putting the economic and business development of Thailand and Indonesia in a transnational, as well as domestic context has led us to highlight the importance of locating them within studies on the economic development of the East Asia region more broadly—an area of scholarship in which Japanese scholars have been influential. Building on some of the ideas of Friedrich List, Kaname Akamatsu (1897–1974) articulated the "flying geese" paradigm, a stage-based approach to explain the economic catch-up process of late developing economies such as Japan. Subsequent versions of this paradigm sought to represent the comparative and hierarchical development of countries and industries across East and Southeast Asia (1961). Of particular relevance to this volume is the work of the economist Terutomo Ozawa, who has focused on adapting earlier "flying geese" theories to reflect the now dominant role of multinational corporations as key agents of structural change and growth across the globe. Ozawa's identification of MNEs as crucial vectors for the transplanting of industrial technologies and knowledge dissemination leads to a focus on the crucial nature of cross-border supply chains and the importance of a country's FDI strategy. Ozawa's argument that his revised model "zeroes in on the dynamics of intra-Asian (that is regionalised) economic integration and agglomeration" (2016, 11) underlines its importance for our focus on the transfer of technologies and ideas to Indonesia and Thailand through MNEs and FDI.

More recent work by Akira Suehiro has highlighted the importance of two factors that have been critical in both Thailand and Indonesia, and which also figure prominently in the studies in this volume. One is the concept of social capability, namely the ability of a latecomer nation to implement the institutions needed to enable firms to absorb the technologies they acquire and import from their competitors in forerunner nations. The other is innovative combinations, defined by Suehiro as "entrepreneurial spirit that seeks new synergies between existing management resources". By skilfully combining imported technologies with the existing advantage of a low-cost, well-educated labour force, and a number of disparate management strengths, it was possible to acquire, or create, new international competitiveness. This, in a nutshell, Suehiro has argued, has been the secret behind enterprises in various East Asian countries engaged in the strategic pursuit of the increased exports of specific manufactured products (2008, 58, 68). Suehiro extended his analysis to Thailand, and his work has been influential in studies on the emerging economies of Southeast Asia. The concepts of social capability and innovative combinations are equally fundamental to any analysis of Indonesian business development. Yuri Sato's Chapter 4 (Indonesian Business Groups from the Perspective of the Shibusawa Business Model) shows how William Soeryadjaya, founder of the Astra Group, built his business up through the careful combination of mobilising and fostering human resources and making the most of new knowledge and technologies. Clearly, these strategies have helped to make some large Indonesian and Thai business groups globally competitive exporters; some smaller businesses and business groups have also demonstrated entrepreneurial ability, although others may not have fared so well. Nevertheless, both economies have experienced persistent net growth following their recovery from the 1997 crisis, albeit not at the high GDP growth rate of the earlier newly industrialised economies (NIEs) such as South Korea, Taiwan and Singapore (see, for example Doner 2009).

Locating Indonesia and Thailand in the Asian context, both conceptually and historically, thus underlines the potential for comparison with the experiences of higher income Asian economies, including Japan. As the first Asian economy to achieve industrialisation, Japan's experience has impacted in diverse ways—both positively and negatively—companies in other Asian economies. Japanese firms are still looked to for inspiration in terms of management, production and the broader imperatives of industrialisation. We also know that technology transfers associated with foreign investment and technology tie-ups with Japanese firms, as well as access to the Japanese market, have been crucial to the efforts of some businesses in Thailand and Indonesia to develop their production and marketing potential, and to enhance their international comparative advantage. These interactions enabled a greater familiarity with the preconditions and requirements of industrialisation and manufacturing for export, particularly with the ways in which Japanese firms handled these aspects. Japanese companies remain crucial actors in business across Asia, as their intra-Asian investments reveal.

It should in no way be argued that any so-called "Japanese model" can serve as a template for today's emerging economies of Southeast Asia. The global environments of early 20th century Japan compared with early 21st century Southeast Asian economies are very different, as are the three countries' endowments and patterns of comparative advantage. However, previous scholarship has made clear that both Indonesia and Thailand face developmental constraints not dissimilar to those encountered by Japan over a century ago. We show that earlier debates in Japan about the broader role and responsibilities of businesses in society addressed issues that are highly germane to the attempts by the private sector in the two Southeast Asian economies to work out pragmatic solutions to problems of capital, information, technology and institutions, as well as offer insights into the broader relationship between business and society. With Japanese investment and bilateral collaboration acting as a conduit for the exchange of ideas, capital, knowhow and skills, it is clear that Japanese firms had a role in the evolution of the business sector in both Indonesia and Thailand.

At the heart of the early debates in Japan on the role of businesses in society was the entrepreneur Shibusawa Eiichi, often thought of as "the father of Japanese capitalism". Shibusawa played a pre-eminent role in the Japanese business market through the late 19th and early 20th centuries. Not only was Shibusawa involved in the founding and development of well over five hundred financial and commercial enterprises, he was also known for his intense involvement with a multiplicity of voluntary organisations, and for his views on the moral and ethical dimensions of business practice and the role of private enterprises in the economy. Advocating a form of capitalist business enterprise very different from the Anglo-American model, and with a vision of business stakeholders that embraced not only owners, shareholders and managers, but also employees, business contacts, consumers and the broader public, Shibusawa provoked discussions on what exactly capitalist enterprise was for and how it might serve the widest interest. His lectures and writings addressed: the role of business structures creating shared value, the necessity of morality, and the role of entrepreneurs, not only in building and managing businesses, but also in providing moral leadership and serving the interests of the community as a whole. As Chapter 2 (Management Philosophies and Economic Development in Emerging Countries: Learning from Shibusawa Eiichi and Matsushita Kōnosuke) by Masakazu Shimada and Kazuhiro Tanaka shows, there are clear similarities between Shibusawa's thinking and the much later ideas of Matsushita Kōnosuke, the founder of Panasonic, many of which were fed into Thailand and Indonesia through Panasonic's activities there.

When it comes to the social responsibilities of business, therefore, both in industrialising Japan and in emerging economies such as Thailand and Indonesia, the imperatives of later development impose particular constraints on the ability of businesses to consider the broader societal interest. Many questions arise from this: Are high standards of business ethics, or support by companies with active CSR practices, luxuries that can only be embraced once a certain level of income or stability has been achieved? Is generous business philanthropy always to be welcomed, even if it is based on unethically acquired profits? How do private enterprises view their responsibilities in terms of raising general income levels or ameliorating domestic inequalities? Are unethical or even illegal company behaviours inevitable when firms try to survive the competitive pressures that they face in the international factor and product markets in which they operate? And under what circumstances do unethical business practices or bribery impede economic growth; and under what circumstances might they promote it?

All these questions matter from a developmental perspective, and while we cannot claim to answer them all, they are addressed by a number of the chapters in this volume. Van der Eng shows in Chapter 12 how CSR has become a hot topic in contemporary Indonesia, and that the CSR practices of firms also build on policies and ideas articulated at an earlier stage in the country's economic development—what he in Chapter 9 terms the "antecedents" of CSR. Intarakumnerd's Chapter 6, while conceding the contribution of Sino-Thai business to economic and social development, argues that the concept and practice of CSR still need to be diffused more broadly in Thailand. Van der Eng also highlights the difficulty of tackling corruption in Indonesia despite the introduction in 2007 of state regulations, making corporate social and environmental responsibility compulsory. Understandably, the priority for most firms in emerging markets is sustainability and survival rather than ethics, but we also offer evidence that profit maximisation and social welfare need not necessarily be in direct conflict with each other. Indeed, the acquisition of profits, if not profit maximisation, has often been seen as important exactly because it has allowed a business to give more back to the community.

The Economic Context in Thailand and Indonesia

We make no claim that the two countries' shared location within Southeast Asia, or their status as "late industrialising" in any way suggest that these economies will necessarily follow a path similar to each other. Nor is there any reason to believe that they will in any way replicate the experience of earlier Asian industrialisers, not least because countries such as Japan and South Korea resorted to a labour-intensive industrialisation strategy, while both Thailand and Indonesia continue to possess a clear comparative advantage in terms of primary exports. The very abundance of agricultural and/or mineral resources raises the spectre of a "resource curse", as well as suggests the significance of the primary sector, agribusinesses and mineral processing in the development of the economy. It goes without saying that there are many differences between the business contexts of Thailand and Indonesia that have shaped their divergent responses. They have had different experiences of colonial domination and different levels of Japanese FDI, and there has been considerable divergence in policies towards the ethnic minority business community, trade, investment and the rural sector. The role of religion has been profoundly different. Common to both countries, however, is the presence of key factors identified in the alternative business history approach, including institutional voids, colonial or quasi-colonial legacies, extended periods of state intervention and occasionally turbulent business environments. Also shared are many of the responses to these impediments, not least the dominance of family businesses and diversified business groups; of immigrant and diaspora entrepreneurs, corporate strategies to deal with turbulence and the pursuit of radical social responsibility concepts, often informed by religious belief, by at least a minority of business actors. In both economies, illegal and informal forms of business have been commonplace, and major issues of economic inequality persist.

The State and the Private Sector

The coexistence of similarities and differences between the two countries is well demonstrated by the fact that since the mid-20th century, both economies have been constructed mainly on the basis of private enterprise, albeit with significant State involvement. The relationship between the State and the private sector in the two economies has taken a variety of forms over the modern period. At times, these structures have included State ownership and management, including by the military; and in Thailand, the Crown has retained a dominant role in much of the country's economic activity. The power of the State in the development of these two economies has been much debated. As in the case of early newly industrialised countries (NIEs), governments in Thailand and Indonesia used a range of economic policy tools, including financial, fiscal, monetary and industrial policies, as well as policies related to foreign trade. However, the effectiveness of this mix of policy tools varied significantly over time. Differences in effectiveness compared to the NIEs were also conspicuous, as were major differences between Indonesia and Thailand. What is not in doubt, however, is that on multiple occasions, policy combinations were significant in shaping the opportunities for and the direction of private sector development, and our research confirms that consideration of State policies and State attributes is integral to any analysis of private sector activity in Thailand and Indonesia, just as it is elsewhere.

While over recent years private enterprise has been broadly accepted as a more efficient mode of operation than State-run enterprises, nevertheless, in both Thailand and Indonesia, the role and responsibilities of the private sector have consistently been the subject of considerable debates—debates that were highlighted by the 1997 crisis and the course of recovery from it—as well as by the rise of China, which pushed the Association of Southeast Asian Nations (ASEAN) countries, including Indonesia and Thailand, towards greater cooperation to promote intra-regional trade and the internationalisation of the operations of their companies. Questions continue to be asked about the extent to which business groups and larger enterprises are really contributing to the public good; historical nationalism, we might suggest, is among the factors that have left a heritage of ambiguity about the relative contribution of the private sector to the broader national interest, as well as towards the role of the State and of multinational enterprises and policies towards inward direct investment. The extent of nationalist pressures has fluctuated over time, as has the power of any nationalist rhetoric, but both have been a critical element in the context within which businesses in these countries operate.

This ambiguity cannot be totally separated from the past limitations imposed on the political and economic independence of both countries by foreign dominance. Indonesia's experience of Dutch colonialism, up to The Netherlands' formal recognition of Indonesian sovereignty in 1949, would appear to stand in contrast to the position of Thailand through the 19th and early 20th centuries. While Thailand was never formally colonised, some of the country's economic activities, however, were heavily dominated by British and other European interests. In both cases, the effects of foreign domination on sectors of business were themselves often ambiguous; while there were in some cases detrimental impacts on the development and activities of indigenous businesses, the presence of foreign enterprises also opened up new markets and opportunities to local enterprises. There was certainly a widespread and powerful perception in post-war Indonesia that the presence of foreign enterprise had been detrimental to development, but it coexisted with policies that aimed to encourage some inward FDI and multinational enterprise activity, and the wholesale nationalisation of foreign companies came largely in response to particular disputes. The core issue, perhaps, is not so much colonialism, but rather the fact that the economic policies that were implemented favoured the business interests of some entrepreneurs over that of others. These policy leg-ups made a big difference for would-be private entrepreneurs and were a cause for resentment. Those who were advantaged by the policies were not ignorant of that and glossed it over by emphasising the nationalist streaks identified by Fakih (Chapter 10); as his chapter demonstrates, many Indonesian businessmen self-identified as freedom fighters and nationalists and not just entrepreneurs. Closely associated with this broader political context, therefore, have been fluctuations in the interests of different stakeholders within the economy and society, leading to a degree of political instability and some dramatic changes in policy. It is also integral to the existence of institutional voids, such as the delayed introduction of a business-friendly banking system. It is in responding to voids of this kind that entrepreneurs and businesses have been compelled to devise alternative strategies.

Family Businesses, Business Groups and Ethnic Minority Business

Both Thailand and Indonesia host a diversity of structures of business ownership and management. Within this diversity, however, family businesses account for a very high proportion of all enterprises—large, medium or small. In some instances, these family businesses have grown to become some of the largest business actors of the region, often evolving into diversified business groups rather than simply growing as single companies driven by the specialisation of economic activity. Business groups can be composed of both large- and medium-sized firms; the largest ones play a key role in the two countries' economies and their increasing globalisation. In both countries, the largest business groups continue to be controlled by business families even though the largest firms within a group may have been listed on the stock market and are financed by share capital. Unsurprisingly, this situation has led to the articulation of concerns relating to the corporate governance practices of firms, the rights of minority shareholders and other company stakeholders, and potentially dire consequences for business ethics. A number of the chapters in this book address these concerns by exploring the activities of family enterprises and diversified business groups. Gen Endo's Chapter 5 (What Significance does the Continuance of Family Business Groups have in Thai Society? A Case Study of the Central Group) analyses two of the major family business groups of Thailand, concluding that family businesses appear to be more focused on longer-term economic gains than their shareholder-driven counterparts. Yongue (Chapter 3) highlights changes in the cultures and business practices of large Thai family companies after the 1997 crisis, suggesting that those that were more willing to change were more successful over the longer term. Wahyuni and Haudy (Chapter 7) use a large sample of family businesses in Indonesia to explore issues of firm reputation, competitive advantage and firm performance—a study that leads them to observe that the benefits of such stewardship are insufficiently recognised in Indonesia.

In both countries, many of these large family business groups are owned by ethnic Chinese business people. In Thailand, there were large Indian and Muslim businesses, but they have played a far smaller role than the ethnic Chinese business groups. Adjustments in corporate governance made after the 1997 crisis have impacted family ownership structures, but many of the Thai-Chinese business groups have retained their dominance. The Chinese ethnic minority is a significantly larger proportion of the total population in Thailand than in Indonesia, but in both countries, business families of ethnic Chinese heritage have played major roles in the development of modern private enterprise, in some industries achieving a near-monopoly, or at least an oligopolistic position in certain sectors of business (Carney 2008). In Thailand, the ethnic Chinese minority have become increasingly socially integrated into Thai society—to an extent that is not mirrored in Indonesia—and account for a majority in business. Nevertheless, a range of ethnic Chinese entrepreneurs, and later their extended families, rose to prominence in business in Indonesia as well. Ethnic Chinese business offers an additional lens through which to explore issues of how business defines its responsibilities towards different stakeholder groups in society in relation to those immediately involved in the actual enterprise. The activities of ethnic Chinese origin entrepreneurs therefore loom large in a number of the chapters in this volume. For example, Intarakumnerd's (Chapter 6) analysis of entrepreneurship and innovation in three of Thailand's most important sectors—electronics, automotive and seafood—is largely focused on Chinese-Thai entrepreneurs, although he argues that Thailand needs more "opportunity-based" entrepreneurs prepared to take risks with innovation.

Foreign Direct Investment, Ethical Business and CSR

While leading Thai and Indonesian businesses began to involve themselves more in international markets only from the 2000s, their involvement with foreign firms through direct investment and joint ventures dates to a much earlier time. In Thailand, the introduction of new policies and the calming of internal tensions in the last decades of the 20th century helped to promote the country as a welcoming destination for FDI. From the 1980s, Japan replaced the United States as the largest foreign investor in Thailand, and apart from a couple of exceptional years, has retained that position (Brimble 2003; Bank of Thailand statistics). A number of the chapters in this book show how some European and North American firms have sought to establish wholly owned subsidiaries in Southeast Asian countries, including Indonesia and Thailand, while others, including many Japanese firms, have preferred to use joint ventures to negotiate the local business environment. Some of these joint ventures were with Chinese-Indonesian or Sino-Thai entrepreneurs, but as shown in the case of Panasonic, discussed by Shimada and Tanaka (Chapter 2), in some cases, the joint venture was with an Indonesian *pribumi* firm. Srisuphaolarn and Ihara's case study of the Sahapat conglomerate (Chapter 8) shows clearly how a joint venture with the Japanese Lion Corporation enabled an indigenous Thai firm to move from distribution into manufacturing, and to end up as one of the most successful consumer goods conglomerates in Southeast Asia. It also demonstrates how the firm's founder, Thiam, was significantly influenced by exposure to Japanese management and business strategies, suggesting that along with foreign interactions came foreign ideas and influences. Japanese firms have been particularly influential in terms of impacting models of production and labour management, as shown in the case of Matsushita's Panasonic, or the establishment of Toyota's production hub in Thailand.

While the term CSR is specific to recent decades, it is possible to trace in both countries what van der Eng refers to as the "antecedents" of CSR practices (Chapter 9). Indonesia's policies relating to worker welfare, as well as what might be called ethical business practices were implemented by firms in colonial Indonesia, not least to try and address various labour issues, some of which were mandated by obligations that came with colonial Indonesia's membership with the International Labour Organization. In both countries, ethnic Chinese communities established a range of charitable associations and other welfare facilities to which local Chinese companies contributed. Historians do not normally consider these activities to be a form of CSR, but rather a means of protecting and unifying the ethnic Chinese population and its business community in a context of persecution, as well as tensions within the Chinese community between different regional and linguistic groups. Charitable activities by Chinese businesses were a way of showing that members of the ethnic minority community were good citizens, and in the case of Thailand, fully worthy of the favour of the Thai monarchy. While CSR policies have more recently emerged in Thailand, what has been more conspicuous is the promotion of the sufficiency economy and the so called "middle way" by the late King Bhumibol; this strategy of arguing for greater self-sufficiency and more ethical business practices, with a view to benefiting society as a whole, is considered in more depth in the chapter by Srisuphaolarn and Assarut (Chapter 11). Although the sufficiency economy concept was influenced by aspects of Buddhism, the influence of religion has been more conspicuous in the practices of Indonesian businesses, for whom Islamic obligations have long been a reason for philanthropy and charitable donations, as van der Eng notes in Chapter 12.

Together, the chapters in this volume demonstrate that when it comes to their business activities, firms in Thailand and Indonesia are in various ways guided by their perceptions of morality in society and concerns about the environment. It is likely that foreign influences contributed to this development, for example through the expansion of Japanese subsidiary firms from the 1980s, or the spread of foreign articulations of the concept of CSR since the 2000s. Certainly, a degree of pragmatism in how companies developed these activities cannot be denied. Nevertheless, in many ways, the perceptions of morality in business that many entrepreneurs and companies in Thailand and Indonesia have formulated and adhere to are their own responses to the dynamic political, social and economic factors that have shaped the business environments of both countries.

Notes

[1] "World Economic Outlook Database", International Monetary Fund, October 2022 edition, accessed 9 January 2023, https://www.imf.org/en/Publications/WEO/weo-database/2022/October/select-countries?grp=2505&sg=All-countries/Emerging-market-and-

developing-economies/Emerging-and-developing-Asia. China was in top place, followed by India in second.

[2] Data at https://datahelpdesk.worldbank.org/knowledgebase/articles/906519-world-bank-country-and-lending-groups, accessed 27 February 2023.

[3] World Bank data shows Thailand's 2021 per capita GDP at US$7,066.2, compared with Indonesia's at US$4,332.7. See https://data.worldbank.org/?locations=TH-MY-ID-SG-PH-VN, accessed 10 January 2023.

[4] "Trade and Industry Annual Survey", Japan Ministry of Economy, accessed 9 March 2023, https://www.e-stat.go.jp/stat-search/files?page=1&layout=datalist&toukei=00550120&tstat=000001011012&cycle=7&year=20210&month=0&tclass1=000001023635&tclass2=000001165586&tclass3val=0.

[5] Much of the inward investment from Singapore into both Thailand and Indonesia originated elsewhere, not least because many multinational enterprises have regional headquarters in Singapore.

[6] ADB, Asia Regional Integration Center, Integration Indicators Database, accessed 9 March 2023, https://aric.adb.org/datacenter.

[7] The Great Divergence refers to the divergent growth paths of Northwest Europe (and North America) and the rest of the world—particularly Asia—that emerged from the mid-18th century.

[8] As suggested by Ravi Ramamurti, "Developing Countries and MNEs: Extending the Research Agenda", *Journal of International Business Studies* 35, no. 4 (July 2004): 278.

[9] For the ideas of Shibusawa Eiichi, see Patrick Fridenson and Takeo Kikkawa, ed., *Ethical Capitalism: Shibusawa Eiichi and Business Leadership in Global Perspective* (Toronto: University of Toronto Press, 2017); John H. Sagers, *Confucian Capitalism: Shibusawa Eiichi, Business Ethics, and Economic Development in Meiji Japan* (London: Palgrave Macmillan, 2018). The Shibusawa Eiichi Memorial Foundation has led the way in uniting business history scholars from Japan and elsewhere in raising important questions about the modern capitalist system from a comparative historical research perspective. Earlier findings have been published in Asli Colpan and Geoffrey Jones, *Business, Ethics and Institutions: The Evolution of Turkish Capitalism in Global Perspectives* (London: Routledge, 2021).

References

Akamatsu, Kaname. 1961. "A theory of Unbalanced Growth in the World Economy". *Weltwirtschaftliches Archiv* [Global Economy Archive] 86 (2): 196–217.

Asian Development Bank. n.d. "Integration Indicators Database". Asia Regional Integration Center. Accessed 9 March 2023. https://aric.adb.org/datacenter.

Austin, Gareth, Carlos Dávila and Geoffrey Jones. 2017. "The Alternative Business History: Business in Emerging Markets". *Business History Review* 91 (3): 537–69.

Bank of Thailand. n.d. "Bank of Thailand statistics". https://www.bot.or.th/English/Statistics/Articles/F45_report/IIPSurvey_47E.pdf; https://www.bot.or.th/English/Statistics/Economic AndFinancial/Pages/StatInternationalInvestmentPosition.aspx.

Brimble, Peter. 2003. "Foreign Direct Investment, Technology and Competitiveness in Thailand". In *Competitiveness, FDI and Technological Activity in East Asia*, ed. Sanjaya Lall and Shujiro Urata. Gloucestershire: Edward Elgar Publishing.

Colpan, Asli and Geoffrey Jones. 2021. *Business, Ethics and Institutions: The Evolution of Turkish Capitalism in Global Perspectives*. Abingdon: Routledge.

Carney, Michael. 2008. "Ethnic Chinese Business Groups in Southeast Asia: Social Capital and Institutional Persistence". In *Asian Business Groups: Context, Governance and Performance*, ed. Michael Carney. Oxford: Chandos.

Doner, Richard F. 2009. *The Politics of Uneven Development: Thailand's Economic Growth in Comparative Perspective*. Cambridge: Cambridge University Press.

Fridenson, Patrick and Takeo Kikkawa, ed. 2017. *Ethical Capitalism: Shibusawa Eiichi and Business Leadership in Global Perspective*. Toronto: University of Toronto Press.

International Monetary Fund. October 2022. "World Economic Outlook Database". World Economic and Financial Surveys. Accessed 9 January 2023. https://www.imf.org/en/Publications/WEO/weo-database/2022/October/select-countries?grp=2505&sg=All-countries/Emerging-market-and-developing-economies/Emerging-and-developing-Asia.

Japan Ministry of Economy. n.d. "e-Stat Trade and Industry annual survey". Accessed 9 March 2023. https://www.e-stat.go.jp/stat-search/files?page=1&layout=datalist&toukei=00550120&tstat=000001011012&cycle=7&year=20210&month=0&tclass1=000001023635&tclass2=000001165586&tclass3val=0.

Organisation for Economic Co-operation and Development (OECD). 2020. "OECD Investment Policy Reviews: Indonesia 2020, Trends and Impacts of Foreign Direct Investment in Indonesia". Accessed 15 February 2023. https://www.oecd-ilibrary.org/sites/c228dc2f-en/index.html?itemId=/content/component/c228dc2f-en.

————. 2021. "OECD Investment Policy Reviews: Thailand, Trends and Qualities of FDI in Thailand". Accessed 15 February 2023. https://www.oecd-ilibrary.org/sites/59874f17-en/index.html?itemId=/content/component/59874f17-en.

OECD/Economic Research Institute for ASEAN and Asia. 2018. *SME Policy Index: ASEAN 2018—Boosting Competitiveness and Inclusive Growth*. Paris: OECD Publishing; Jakarta: ERIA. Accessed 11 January 2023. https://www.oecd-ilibrary.org/sites/9789264305328-24-en/index.html?itemId=/content/component/9789264305328-24-en.

Ozawa, Terutomo. 2011. *The Rise of Asia: The "Flying-Geese" Theory of Tandem Growth and Regional Agglomeration*. Gloucestershire: Edward Elgar Publishing.

————. 2016. *The Evolution of the World Economy: The "Flying-Geese" Theory of Multinational Corporations and Structural Transformation*. Gloucestershire: Edward Elgar Publishing.

Ramamurti, Ravi. 2004. "Developing Countries and MNEs: Extending the Research Agenda". *Journal of International Business Studies* 35, no. 4 (July).

Sagers, John. 2018. *Confucian Capitalism: Shibusawa Eiichi, Business Ethics, and Economic Development in Meiji Japan*. London: Palgrave Macmillan.

Suehiro, Akira. 2008. *Catch-Up Industrialization: The Trajectory and Prospects of East Asian Economies*. Singapore: NUS Press.

World Bank. 2022. *Thailand Rural Income Diagnostic: Challenges and Opportunities for Rural Farmers*. Washington DC: World Bank, 2022.

Chapter 2

Management Philosophies and Economic Development in Emerging Countries: Learning from Shibusawa Eiichi and Matsushita Kōnosuke

Masakazu Shimada and Kazuhiro Tanaka

Introduction

Japanese companies have made a major imprint on the Southeast Asian economic sphere, especially in Thailand and Indonesia. Numerous Japanese firms have filled local markets with popular products, established local distribution and manufacturing sites, and made a sizable impact on local employment. While some Japanese-affiliated companies had met with occasional backlashes and animosity as they expanded into the region, the current climate is generally favourable: more often than not, local communities see entrants from Japan less as adversaries or targets for exclusion and more as partners or actual drivers of economic development.

One of the first Japanese companies to break into the Southeast Asian market relatively quickly after World War II, and which started connecting directly with people in the region through products and local production was Panasonic [formerly Matsushita Electric Industrial Co., Ltd. (Matsushita Electric Industrial)]. With an extensive track record in local production, Panasonic has considerable experience in providing local employees with an understanding of its corporate philosophy—an undertaking the company embraces wholeheartedly. Panasonic's founder, Matsushita Kōnosuke, molded his corporate-management

19

philosophy—which was rooted in strong, deep-seated principles—into a systematic framework that aligned with his focus on a company's role in society at large and established firm roots in the company organisation. This chapter first explores that construct. After a brief historical overview of how Panasonic has expanded into Southeast Asia, we examine the basic philosophy forming the backdrop for the process—the aspiration to realise mutual harmony and benefit for both the destination country and society as a whole.

In the same context, we also discuss Shibusawa Eiichi, the pre-war Japanese business leader who helped create and develop a profusion of major Japanese firms that still thrive today. Stepping away from the process of laying building blocks for individual companies, Shibusawa shifted toward carving out an image of what a company means in the larger social picture, enrooting specific patterns of behaviour for Japanese companies to follow. We focus on Shibusawa in this chapter for two main reasons. First, is the applicability of his philosophy and methods: in our view, the ideas and practices that shape Shibusawa's legacy are brimming with insights into finding a fruitful balance between sustained growth and stability—a key challenge for virtually every emerging country—through the pursuit of economic, political and social ideals. (The second section examines those themes in detail.) The second reason: Shibusawa's philosophy and practical approaches—those elements that molded Japanese management across the board in the pre-war context—share deep, organic commonalities with those of Panasonic's Matsushita, whose ideas have left such a salient impact in modern-day Thailand and Indonesia. In the final section, we look at those common philosophical threads linking the two business luminaries. We also probe those conceptual frameworks to locate certain Japanese management principles and behavioural standards that may be capable of helping Southeast Asia make further developmental strides.

Before we begin our discussion, however, it merits mention that today's Japanese companies are actually losing sight of those very underpinnings, resulting in stagnation in the corporate sphere. Under these circumstances, the discussion of Matsushita's and Shibusawa's philosophies can also serve as a self-reproaching critique of contemporary Japan's struggles to provide a useful model for the world.

Panasonic's Entry into Southeast Asia

Panasonic's history dates back to 1918, when Matsushita Electric Industrial (the company's predecessor) launched operations. The company set up a trade department (later the Matsushita Electric Trading Company) as early as 1932, prior to World War II, making it one of the few manufacturers in existence at that time to export products directly to foreign markets without going through a trading company. After establishing the Matsushita Dry Battery Co., Ltd. Shanghai Factory in 1939, Matsushita Electric Industrial eventually saw its organisation grow to include production sites in 39 locations, mostly in Asia, during World War II; every step of the expansion effort was on military orders under Japan's wartime economic framework. Japan's defeat in the war resulted in the complete dismantling of the company's foreign network; the countries where the sites were located confiscated every facility (Matsushita Electric Industrial 2008a, 90; 2008b, 30).

Matsushita Electric Industrial proceeded to head back overseas in the post-war years in hopes of "expanding its operations on a global scale", a policy that Matsushita championed. Besides launching exports on a larger scale, in 1961, the company also began providing technical assistance to targets abroad and established a growing collection of foreign production sites. That same year, Matsushita Electric Industrial created its first overseas production company of the post-war era: this was National Thai Company (in which Matsushita held a 60 per cent share), which drew on technical assistance from its parent company and served as a local production hub for dry-cell batteries. In 1962, Matsushita Electric Industrial established Matsushita Electric (Taiwan) to manufacture radios and other appliances. Subsequent years, especially from 1965 onward, saw a flurry of similar activity; foreign production sites popped up in areas as diverse as Latin America, the Philippines, Malaysia, and Australia. By 1980, the company had a whopping total of 39 manufacturing companies in 23 countries (Matsushita Electric Industrial 1968, 309–10; Matsushita Electric Industrial 2008a, 90–1; 2008b, 29–32). As noted, Matsushita Electric's first foreign foray after World War II was in Thailand. That initial production site was the beginning of the company's diversifying activities in Thailand, where it would go on to start producing radios, black-and-white television sets, electric fans, storage batteries, and in 1970, colour television sets (Matsushita Electric Industrial 1968, 309–10; 2008b, 126).

The Asian region was a popular destination for contemporary Japanese companies looking to reach beyond Japan's borders. In the 1970s, with the value of the Japanese yen rising, firms homed in on Asian newly industrialised economies (NIEs)—especially Singapore and Malaysia—as production sites for exports. That geographical scope grew in the ensuing decade, as the Association of Southeast Asian Nations (ASEAN) community joined Asian NIEs as go-to locations for expanding companies. Producing everything from finished consumer goods to semiconductors and other parts, local manufacturing sites in the region grew in terms of both number and scope.

When one examines the progression of Matsushita Electric's expansion into Southeast Asia, the case of PT National Gobel emerges as a particularly representative example of the company's approach. A joint venture in home electronics manufacturing, the company began operations in 1970. The president of the partner company that joined with Matsushita Electric Industrial, Thayeb Mohammad Gobel, was a *pribumi* Indonesian—a person with indigenous roots; this fact is an essential piece in understanding Matsushita's management philosophy and delineating how that mindset found acceptance in foreign settings. Thayeb Mohammad's first meeting with Matsushita was in 1957—a full 13 years prior to the creation of the joint venture—when he visited Japan as part of a delegation representing then Indonesian president, Sukarno. According to narratives of the company's history, Thayeb Mohammad "recalled that he agreed to merge with Matsushita Electric Industrial when he learnt about the company's philosophy. Executive Advisor (then president) Matsushita spoke to him about 'the mindset of serving the general public through work and the importance of embodying an identity that every employee can understand and accept', and Advisor (then executive director) Takahashi Aratarō laid out the philosophical essence at the heart of Matsushita Electric Industrial's identity" (Matsushita Electric Industrial 1978, 222–3). Matsushita Electric Industrial began providing Thayeb Mohammad's factories with technical assistance in 1960. While political turmoil in Indonesia led to a temporary break in the assistance, the relationship between the two companies remained strong and eventually resulted in the birth of PT National Gobel in 1970.

Basic Policies of Founder Matsushita Kōnosuke in the Process of Overseas Expansion

In its overseas expansion into both Asia and elsewhere, Matsushita Electric Industrial adhered to a basic policy of "doing a service to the destination country" and sought the ideal of "mutual harmony and benefit"[1] with the countries in which it established operations. Matsushita verbalised that commitment:

> At Matsushita Electric Industrial, we do a lot of exporting. We run factories abroad, too. Still, everything we do overseas comes down to how our local operations can both further our aims and do a service to the destination country—a pattern of mutual harmony and benefit. That spirit, which we instill in our local teams, is what puts the company on the best path to success (Sato 2013, 42).

The ideas of doing "a service to the destination country" and striving for "mutual harmony and benefit", both central to the above quote, capture Matsushita's core tenets of utility—as a company and a business pursuit—as well as horizontal relations with stakeholders, in this case, the destination country and local community. By embodying such ideals, Matsushita said, the company could secure its footing on the "best path to success". From this, we can see that he focused not only on public interest but also on private profit, aiming to realise both. Without that dual emphasis, a company would lack the dynamics it needed to thrive. (Horizontal relations and the balance between public interest and private profit will be discussed in more detail later).

Matsushita practiced what he preached both at home and abroad. In Southeast Asia, the activities of Matsushita Electric Industrial clearly reflected its founder's business stance. Kinoshita Hajime, the senior Matsushita official who served as National Gobel's second-ranking executive under president Thayeb Mohammad, remembers what Matsushita told him as the joint venture was about to get off the ground:

> When you do business overseas, you have to work to benefit the country and serve the local community. Our relationship with Mr Gobel began in 1960, when we started offering technical assistance. The ten years since have been something of an engagement period—we've been betrothed to each other, in a way. Now, it's finally time for the wedding, so to speak. Think of yourself as Gobel's wife. Commit to that relationship, just like a wife devotes herself to her husband. Focus on the marriage—you don't have to worry about Matsushita Electric Industrial back home (Sato 2013: 71).

In Indonesia, Matsushita engaged in joint ventures with Thayeb Mohammad who had studied in Japan, and there is evidence that both Thayeb Mohammad, and his son who succeeded him, were influenced by Matsushita's ideas in defining their firm's corporate culture. Articulated by Thayeb Mohammad as his "banana tree" philosophy, the culture of the firm was based on the production of high-quality products that would serve the needs of people in society—that is, a company must look to the benefit of the community (Hadimadja 1994; Ali and Ahmad 1998). Together, Matsushita and Thayeb Mohammad, in 1979, established a charitable foundation—the Matsushita Gobel Foundation—whose support of projects generating social benefits foreshadowed the idea of CSR. To Matsushita, establishing operations abroad obviously required a deep-seated "devotion" to the destination country.

Matsushita's choice of venture partner was intriguing. As noted above, Thayeb Mohammad was a *pribumi* Indonesian. In 1970, the Indonesian population included a minority of overseas Chinese, who, despite their comparatively small numbers, represented a dominant force in the local economy: "nine out of ten joint ventures in Indonesia were with overseas Chinese partners", Kinoshita explains.[2] Teaming up with an overseas Chinese entrepreneur would almost certainly have given Matsushita a stronger advantage in the market, but

Matsushita made a conscious decision to join forces with a *pribumi*. "Matsushita was firm in his belief that any overseas venture had to benefit the country and make the local population happy", Kinoshita says, "or else there would be no way for the business to succeed". For Matsushita, "doing business in Indonesia meant doing a service to the people of the land—and that meant joining up with the *pribumi*, the native Indonesians who had been the victims of exploitation ever since Dutch colonial rule".[3]

In 1974, anti-Japanese demonstrations in Indonesia made Japanese joint ventures with overseas Chinese entrepreneurs frequent targets of animosity. Angry protesters often pelted Japanese establishments with rocks and even set fire to the buildings. Matsushita Electric Industrial, however, was never a target. The fact that the company escaped harm was likely a sign of understanding and acceptance—it seems likely that Matsushita's priority of benefiting the people of the country made a strong impression on the community.[4] Doing a "service to the destination country" was the staunch, unswerving policy that Matsushita sought to embody in his overseas ventures.[5] The management of joint ventures abroad, too, was local. In virtually all cases, Panasonic appointed people with strong local ties (in Indonesia's case, Thayeb Mohammad) to serve as the company president, and organised a host of functions, such as morning meetings, to strengthen lines of communication with local employees. In that approach are clear signs of Matsushita's "horizontal" management, a conscious effort to create a setup in which Matsushita Electric Industrial would not be abusing its position of power.

The management philosophy at the core of Matsushita Electric Industrial's value framework was a firm cornerstone, to be sure, but the company occasionally adapted elements of its principles to facilitate local reception and better align with the values characterising overseas environments. If the philosophy ever conflicted with local religious beliefs, for example, Matsushita would make the necessary adjustments so that interpretations of the principles would fit within the public consciousness. Attendees at morning meetings would often recite the company's "Seven Principles", the last of which is "gratitude". In Japan, the "gratitude" principle implies being thankful to the company's customers and other stakeholders. In Indonesia, where Muslims account for a significant part of the population, the company shifted the object of gratitude from stakeholders to God.[6]

While minor adjustments were not unusual, the central components of Matsushita's management principles and basic philosophy enjoyed nearly universal acceptance in every country in which Matsushita Electric Industrial launched operations. In many respects the same is true for Panasonic today. Matsushita and Panasonic have made continuous efforts to disseminate that founding vision across the entirety of their global reach through a so-called "Basic Business Philosophy" (BBP), an English translation of their "Basic Management Objective", "Company Creed", and "Seven Principles". At overseas locations that hold morning meetings, employees often recite the BBP. Panasonic also makes the BBP a centrepiece of its in-house human-resource development (Sato 2013, 60). In September 2018, we had the opportunity to visit a morning meeting at a Panasonic (Thailand) office, where, sure enough, the employees recited the BBP in Thai. We also paid a visit to a BBP training session at Panasonic Appliances Cold-Chain (Thailand). There, a team of Thai instructors guided dozens of employees through a series of different activities geared towards deepening their interest in and understanding of the company's core philosophy, as well as nurture a sense of ownership within them. The enthusiasm was palpable; watching the instructors and trainees go back and forth exchanging ideas and discussing concepts left quite an impression on us.

The Genesis and Practice of Shibusawa Eiichi's Management Philosophy

Most people in Japan today identify the name Shibusawa Eiichi with his reputation as an industrialist, manager and "economic man"—a business figure who focused primarily on the economic morality and management ethics espoused in his "principle of harmony between morality and the economy" and his book *Rongo to Soroban* (The Analects and the Abacus). With history also remembering Shibusawa as the "father of Japanese capitalism", he is often seen as having made morality and the Confucian spirit the foundation for Japanese economic progress. Although these popular conceptions have some merit, they are in some respects misleading. The image of Shibusawa leads people to believe that he was a man of pure greatness and an unflappable and infallible leader of men devoted to pursuing the ideal form of capitalism. These notions, however, can cloud a proper understanding of Shibusawa's close involvement in the introduction and establishment of Japan's capitalist system.

After travelling to France at the end of the Edo period, experiencing the modern world that Napoleon III had helped forge, and studying modern economies, Shibusawa returned to Japan—a country that had few systems or capitalist framework for modern economic activity—and promptly went to work on building those structures, launching a modern banking industry and introducing the joint-stock system for modern manufacturing and the railroad and other industries that demanded large amounts of capital. Shibusawa played a vital role in laying the groundwork for modern economics in Japan, all the while dealing with the pressure the advanced major powers wielded over the rest of the world and the availability of their top-quality products. He also made it his mission to "bring an end to revering public officials and despising the common people"—a slogan that chanelled his determination to make Japan's economic development a private sector-driven endeavour instead of a government-led project.[7] Encompassing all of these beliefs and modes of conduct was what Shibusawa termed the "*gapponshugi* ideal", a key concept that has remained on the fringes of his image in the public eye.

Observers have long equated the term *gapponshugi* with the idea of the "joint-stock company system", but a deeper look reveals that *gapponshugi* actually covers a conceptual and philosophical range that extends far beyond the simple introduction and use of the joint-stock company system; the scope is so large, in fact, that the Analects and morality only constitute parts of the idea. In concise terms, *gapponshugi* refers to "the idea of ensuring public good by gathering together the optimal human resources and capital in the effort to drive business" (Kimura 2015, 72). By elucidating the mechanisms of modern economics under the *gapponshugi* philosophy, we will discuss how Shibusawa contributed to Japan's development and show how those contributions have a universal character that transcends time and place.

In 1871, while employed at the Ministry of Civil Affairs (Minbushō), Shibusawa condensed many of his experiences in Europe into *Ryūkai Ryakusoku* (Summary Rules of Companies), a manual on the implementation of corporate organisations. In this publication, Shibusawa explained that while any given company or organisation is a private entity, they both serve to bring profits to participating individuals, while also pursuing public good—a notion that eventually became the "*gappon*" (joint-stock) concept (Shibusawa 1871, 29–32). Both Fridenson and Suzuki have suggested that the views of French theorist Henri de Saint-Simon helped shape Shibusawa's *gappon* philosophy (Kikkawa & Fridenson 2017; Suzuki 2014). Shibusawa continued to allude to the *gappon* idea in various settings. Speaking about why he saw the need for "*gappon*", for example, Shibusawa said "A single wealthy individual does not make the country more prosperous. To elevate the low status of people engaged in commerce and industry, we must make improvements to the whole by helping the joint-stock company organisations take root". In other words, individual wealth would not guarantee national strength. To elevate the status of commerce and industry, Shibusawa argued, Japan would have to improve the prosperity of society as a whole by establishing a firm foundation for the joint-stock company system. Japan's late-developer status meant that modernising industry on a nationwide scale necessitated improving the traditionally low status of those involved in commerce and industry. Shibusawa considered the *gappon* approach the best way of taking up that initiative (Shibusawa 1909, 5).

Shibusawa also addressed the issue of corporate organisation, likening it to "a form of republicanism, with shareholders as the citizens". For Shibusawa, corporate organisations, which comprised many members and a wide breadth of viewpoints, required management standards that were "governed by reason rooted in the Analects of Confucius". He used the Analects because it was an accepted discourse on logic and reason that represented common ground for members of the company (Shibusawa 1909, 6–7). Prolific management author Peter F. Drucker (1909–2005) professed his admiration for Shibusawa in many of his publications. The achievements of Shibusawa and Iwasaki Yatarō (founder of Mitsubishi), he argued, "were a good deal more spectacular than those of Rothschild, Morgan, Krupp, or Rockefeller". Shibusawa and Iwasaki alone "founded something like two-thirds of Japan's enterprises in manufacturing and transportation. No other two men in any economy have had a similar impact" (Drucker 1969, 159).

Adhering to his basic philosophy, Shibusawa helped found an incredible number of companies. In 1898, he ranked 18th in total income received in the Tokyo/Yokohama area, 25th in a nationwide survey of major shareholders in 103 major corporations, and first among a total of 31 leadership positions in corporations and other organisations (Shimada 2007). In 1909, Shibusawa declared that he would be withdrawing from the front line of the business world and left most of his leadership positions as well as his posts at a few companies and banks. However, a closer look at Shibusawa's involvement in Japan's leading major corporations [coal, transportation, electricity, and gas companies ranked by total assets (total capital employed)] in 1911—probably the period when Shibusawa had his biggest direct impact on the industry—reveals that he still either managed or owned 8 of the top 10 companies and 23 of the top 50 companies. Shibusawa still had a hand in roughly half of the most powerful industrial players in Japan (Shimada in Kikkawa and Fridenson 2014, 5–9).

The companies that Shibusawa was involved in share several characteristics. First of all, many of the companies operated in sectors that incorporated brand-new Western knowledge and technologies that Japan had never seen, like Japan Brick Manufacturing, Tokyo Rope Manufacturing, Artificial Fertilizer Manufacturing Company of Tokyo, Tokyo Marine Fire Insurance Company, Ishikawa Shipyard, Ōji Paper Mill, Tokyo Gas, and Sapporo Beer. Second, Shibusawa was active in companies like the Nippon Railway Company, Hokuetsu Railway, Wakamatsu Harbour Construction, and Iwaki Coal—firms that helped build the infrastructure for a modern economy through railways, harbours, coal mining, and more (Shimada 2007, 20).

The Gappon Company in Theory and Practice

Shibusawa constructed his joint-stock company model for implementation in Japan around the market-type model that he had seen in France and other countries during his visit to Europe. Under this European model, in which the pursuit of individual profit dictated shareholder behaviour, companies procured large amounts of funding via wide-open market dealings. Corporate management was purportedly dictated by the rational decision-making logic and reasoning of Western Europe, while shareholder interests were guaranteed by democratic proceedings (majority rule). This model, which equates to the so-called "Anglo-Saxon model", assigned to corporate executives and bankers, levels of social status and fame equalling those of nobles and kings.

The *gappon* capitalism envisioned by Shibusawa, while operating within the European framework, also contained elements of its designer's unique invention. For Japan, which trailed Western countries like the United Kingdom, the United States, France and Germany in the quest for modernisation, failing to modernise would immediately put the country at risk of colonisation. Japan needed to implement the appropriate political and legal systems to achieve modernity. It also needed to fuel the growth of modern industry and develop the economic prowess needed to keep up with Western powers. Providing the framework for that effort were the capitalist and joint-stock systems, which had to attract private funding and human resources for Japan to make the necessary progress. To win support for these structures among the Japanese community, Shibusawa needed to not only maintain an emphasis on the pursuit of private profit, but also adapt the approach to the unique conditions of Japan. In this context he advocated a "public interest first" philosophy, but the management principles within the *gapponshugi* system reconceived "public interest" as the "attainment of *long-term* profits", thereby allowing for a wider range of approaches (Tanaka 2014; Tanaka in Kikkawa and Fridenson 2014). In order to attract as many people as possible to business and thereby elevate the social standing of business, this approach prioritised profit-seeking business activity. Shibusawa believed, the only viable source of common interests for uniting different stakeholders was not the maximisation of short-term profits—which carried with it the risk of bankruptcy—but rather the *gappon* system's promise of long-term stability that would allow people to launch businesses under potentially precarious, uncertain conditions. Seeking long-term profits made it possible for multiple parties to pursue and secure gains, creating an environment in which profits could acquire a public and "communal" character.

General meetings of shareholders assumed supreme importance in Shibusawa's philosophy, reflecting principles that he held dear. To deter specific large-scale shareholders from going after purely short-term gains, Shibusawa worked to eliminate the principle of majority rule in favour of thorough explanations and discussions that continued for as long as necessary. Although the desire for long-term profits applied to all shareholders, regardless of their specific interests, morals and logic played crucial roles in locating the value and worth of long-term gains. Morals, by definition, are what people consider to be "common sense". In order to unite all classes and all generations in a shared understanding of the "private-public" framework, Shibusawa thus utilised the *Rongo* or Analects, which were traditional teachings that virtually every citizen was familiar with. His logical conclusion was the inseparability of morality and economic rationality—a construct that was at once moral in its beliefs and grounded in Western economic thought, making it acceptable and agreeable to a broad range of people. Through this framework, Shibusawa strove to help shareholders across the board recognise their common interests and cultivate an awareness among companies receiving investments that being a "collective" meant being a public entity (Shimada 2014).[8] What distinguishes *gapponshugi*, therefore, is its commitment toward securing both "private profit" and "public profit". Building on the premise of Western capitalism, Shibusawa incorporated his own views on ethics and commonality using the *Rongo* as his foundation and added the formation of stable, long-term interests. By calling for a moral perspective to forge bonds among stakeholders, as well as a prescribed order to regulate competition among companies, Shibusawa's philosophy marked a clear departure from conventional capitalist thought.

How, then, did a company function under Shibusawa's *gappon* philosophy of stable operations and commonality? We focus on two perspectives: (1) the personal network operations of management groups and (2) the selection of company structures for optimal funding. Personal network operations were crucial for keeping businesses solvent. The level of Shibusawa's legal responsibilities in multiple corporate directorial and presidential roles reached its peak around 1907, when he was active in as many as 30 companies at the same time. A look at the directors serving on the Boards that Shibusawa was involved in, however, shows little evidence of a "Shibusawa inner circle"—that is, managers who consistently showed up on the Boards of many companies with ties to Shibusawa. Rather, Shibusawa managed his companies with a diverse mix of different executives (Shimada 2007, Ch. 5). Most of the companies with which Shibusawa was involved were "non-*zaibatsu*" firms, which had no affiliations with business conglomerates like Mitsubishi and Mitsui and thus needed to secure funding and managers independently. Due to their lack of *zaibatsu* ties, these types of enterprises tended to procure funding from wealthy nobility, merchants and landowners, and tended to concentrate primarily on short-term profits. Shibusawa thus had to fill his boards of directors with managers who were receptive to focusing on stable, long-term profits and who could bring in large investments. Examples of managers who fit this mold included venture managers like Asano Sōichirō and Ōkura Kihachirō, and Mitsui *zaibatsu* officials such as the Masuda brothers, Takashi and Katsunori, and Magoshi Kyōhei and the directors of the First National Bank (later the Dai-ichi Bank from 1896, and now Mizuho Bank), which was essentially Shibusawa's own institutional bank.

In order to maintain the operations of all the companies he helped get off the ground, Shibusawa also needed a support staff of managers and managing directors to monitor the day-to-day operations so that he could tend to all of his other obligations. Filling those roles were young managers whom Shibusawa had selected and trained, such as Uemura Chōzaburō, who worked at Sapporo Beer and other companies, and career managers at the First National Bank. Identified via various means, these assistants gained the practical experience they needed to build careers as professional managers (Shimada 2007, Ch. 4).

Shibusawa would not have been able to engage in such a diverse mix of business activities if not for his wide-ranging circle of managerial connections. So, what were the incentives for private profit-seeking managers who brought in sizeable investments, such as Asano and Ōkura, and public profit-oriented managers, such as Uemura? For private profit-seeking managers, the main motivators for getting involved were risk diversification, asset portfolios and opportunities for investments in what Shibusawa termed "next-generation priority investment" businesses—such as, for example, electric and chemical industries in the later half of the Meiji period. On the other hand, managers who focused on the public good could leverage the positions that Shibusawa gave them to get into higher-ranking positions at other companies, enjoy opportunities for career advancement, and secure better pay. In taking charge of businesses, managers developed a sense of responsibility for their companies and derived an enhanced public character— the tenet of Shibusawa's philosophy—for their companies (Shimada 2007, Ch. 5). Drucker lauded Shibusawa's ability to cultivate personal abilities—in other words, his expertise in human resource development and support for what Drucker called "human resource supremacy". "Shibusawa himself, for almost fifty years, acted as an unofficial and unpaid 'management development centre'. He counselled and guided hundreds of young civil servants, businessmen, and executives", Drucker explained, praising Shibusawa for paralleling Iwasaki's monetary capital formation with the vital element of human resources (Drucker 1969, 158–9).

When it came to funding, Shibusawa was neither the heir to a family of large landowners nor a member of the nobility, but rather a former retainer to the shogun, which was a position that did not necessarily give him a particularly strong influence to wield, be it political or financial. How then was Shibusawa, a person without any easy access to massive amounts of money, able to found a steady stream of giant corporations? With an asset management strategy that focused on ensuring balance by adjusting his assets through the sale of held stock. Shibusawa sold off appropriate numbers of shares in companies that had settled into a healthy growth pattern (blue-chip stocks), then used that income to reinvest in the next promising business, and thereby steered the stock market along (Shimada 2007, Ch. 8). We looked at the 40-year period between 1891 and 1931 (the year of Shibusawa's death) and analysed the companies which Shibusawa was involved in. The companies in which he invested differed widely, from anonymous partnerships to joint-stock companies, and our analysis revealed a different image of Shibusawa from the popular widely held perception of him as a promoter and nurturer of joint-stock companies. For companies with a strong public-utility character requiring large amounts of capital, he used the joint-stock company structure; for high-risk, high-return ventures, he set up limited partnerships; small individual businesses were established as ordinary partnerships. By combining these with anonymous partnerships, he was able to limit the risks borne by investors. Thus, rather than consider the joint-stock company as the only appropriate business form, he chose what he considered an appropriate form of organisation, depending on the scale and goals of the enterprise. In particular, when establishing ordinary partnerships, he combined them with anonymous partnerships—whose origins can be traced back to the Edo period—making it easier for outside investors to participate, since they were not subjected to unlimited liability.

Instead of mandating that every company adopt a joint-stock structure across the entire organisation, the *gappon* approach to operations allowed administrators to apply optimal organisational schemes in light of the business risk in play. For businesses that prioritised private gains, for example, this reduced the immense risk that would be generated by implementing a limited partnership under the principles of unlimited liability and kept a manageable level of risk.

The Management Philosophies of Shibusawa Eiichi and Matsushita Kōnosuke: Some Commonalities

Few would take exception to the argument that Shibusawa and Matsushita respectively represent the defining managers of Japan's pre-war and post-war eras. In Japan today, Matsushita's presence—in terms of visibility and influence, among other aspects— seems to overshadow Shibusawa's. Part of the gap in the contemporary consciousness likely stems from the simple fact that Matsushita lived in a time closer to the present day. Another important factor is Matsushita's enthusiastic embrace of publicising his views; always eager to convey his personal philosophy, Matsushita founded the PHP Institute (which has a publishing arm) and penned numerous works that presented his ideas in plain, straightforward language.[9] Most pivotal, of course, is Matsushita's pervasive, almost universal recognition as the person behind the development and growth of Matsushita Electric Industrial—a corporate hallmark of post-war Japan. The indelible link between Matsushita and his company in popular perception has an immediacy largely absent from Shibusawa's reputation. The gap in visibility between Shibusawa and Matsushita is even more evident abroad. Whereas Matsushita has gained a considerable amount of name recognition thanks to the prominence of Panasonic in the global market, at least until recently, Shibusawa has perhaps had less name recognition outside scholarly circles and some segments of the professional population.

Going beyond simple name recognition and into the sphere of management philosophy, however, one might assume that Matsushita's vision would probably also be another virtual unknown overseas; people might know of him, but be much less likely to be well-versed in Matsushita's approach to business. Nevertheless, foreign audiences *are*, in fact, familiar with Matsushita's philosophy. At the very least, his ideas are common knowledge at foreign Panasonic subsidiaries—a reality that came about in part due to Matsushita's emphasis on training employees in his founding principles. The process of educating local-subsidiary employees in a parent company's vision only succeeds if the employees in the field embrace the ideas, of course; when a company pushes a philosophy that fails to resonate with the workforce, regardless of how earnestly the company tries, the audience may feel that the company is trying to enforce a particular mindset, which could alienate the target audience. A look at the Panasonic subsidiaries in other locations abroad shows that, especially in emerging Asian countries, the company has avoided that pitfall; Matsushita's business philosophy has found receptive audiences and laid solid roots (albeit with some region-to-region disparity). The spread of Matsushita's management ideals in emerging countries has rarely extended beyond the Panasonic umbrella, but the audience it has reached, more often than not, comprises people born and raised in the local community. Seeing how it can cross borders and resonate with non-Japanese audiences suggests that Matsushita's philosophy has significant potential for connecting with people outside the Panasonic family (if not all people) and society at large.

Although Matsushita and Shibusawa occupy different places in the popular consciousness, their philosophies actually share numerous commonalities. The fact that Matsushita's vision has found a positive reception in emerging countries suggests that Shibusawa's ideas could have a similar pull. While Shibusawa may be virtually unknown among these populations, his ideas have the potential to make an impression on local audiences and, by extension, make valuable contributions to their developing economies. With that basic perspective in place, we now delve into the essential commonalities linking the management philosophies of Shibusawa and Matsushita in three areas: business activities, profit and stakeholder relations.

The first common thread is in how the two men perceived the "company" concept and what they valued in business—which were the two issues at the heart of management. If we consider the prevailing concept of the company in the Anglo-American sphere, a company in the capitalist economic system is normally seen as a private entity that engages in commercial activity. It thus resides in the private sector, working to expand the private assets of its investing shareholders. In Japan, however, the general school of thought sees the company as more of a public entity. Members of the Japanese business community began championing that idea when the country began importing the company system from the West in the early Meiji period, and influential corporate executives have continued to sustain the idea through the pre-war and post-war periods.

As noted, it was Shibusawa who introduced the company system to Japan in the early years of the Meiji era. His manual, *Ryūkai Ryakusoku*, explained that the people gathering into a company needed to be "individuals who apply their minds toward the public interest of the country as a whole". Even in the earliest days of the company system in Japan, Shibusawa had already conceived of the "company"—an organisation that would by definition normally serve private interests—to have a public dimension; the *gapponshugi* concept, at its origin, held the utility of the company as its core ideal.[10]

Looking at Matsushita, we find that he echoed Shibusawa's conception of the company, writing:

> Business management, in its basic sense, is a matter not private, not personal, but public. A company is fundamentally a public institution.
>
> You should never think about the direction of your company—be it even a private enterprise—based on your own personal perspective or convenience. Whatever the situation may be, weigh every matter and make every decision based on how it will affect community life and whether it will be a benefit or detriment to others (Matsushita 1978, 26).

The idea of the company as a public entity was thus a common current running through the philosophies of both Shibusawa and Matsushita. Both highlighted the public nature of everything a company does. This focus was closely tied to a common philosophical thread in relation to their interpretation of profitmaking. Both men believed that corporate "business" had a social utility in and of itself, and both argued that companies should make realising that utility their first priority rather than simply seeking profits. For Shibusawa, the central mission of a company was to improve and enrich people's lives through business activities.[11] That, in large part, explains why he wanted to tie corporate activity so closely to meeting Japan's dire need for "new Western knowledge and technologies that have no precedent in Japan" and "a viable infrastructure for a modern economy". In his eyes, doing business through a company (*gappon* organisation) was equivalent to "leading the nation with virtue". Clearly, Shibusawa was a firm believer in the idea that business activities were of a thoroughly public nature.

Matsushita, meanwhile, also discussed the fundamental character of business activities:

> ... The mission of business management—and the company itself—lies in developing a constant stream of high-quality products that benefit people's lives, selling the results at fair, reasonable prices, and providing a stable supply in just proportion.... The ideal of using business itself to help make life better for the community at large applies to every company of every kind. No company can truly excel in business without recognising that fundamental mission (1978, 25).

Here, the crucial element is the fact that Matsushita was not simply advocating "using business itself to help make life better" and idealising a "fundamental mission" as lofty aspirational concepts. Rather, he saw that fundamental mission as essential to "truly excel[ling] in business". The ideals had a practical application, not just a nice theoretical ring to them.

One potential criticism of this mode of thought might contend that an emphasis on the public nature of a given business pursuit tends to gloss over the business's profitability. Companies could potentially use the "public nature" of their business activities to legitimise lacklustre profits or justify not even making a concerted effort toward pursuing profits in the first place. That would be an oversimplification, however. Matsushita and Shibusawa consistently underscored the importance of generating reasonable profits from business activities. No matter how much utility a given business had, Shibusawa knew that it needed to produce enough profits to keep itself going and growing, and he made that necessity clear to his fellow entrepreneurs. "A business that never produces a profit will never succeed, regardless of its benefits to the national society" (2010, 144). The first of Shibusawa's four ground rules for starting a business was to have a clear, organised plan for generating profits. Only if a company managed to survive, grow, turn profits, pay out dividends, and pay its taxes could it achieve the primary goal of *gapponshugi* or prosperity for all as a nation. Shibusawa also recognised that business profits played a crucial role as resources for incentivising the individuals actually doing business.[12] He never condemned the human desire to make money outright; he saw desire as a powerful engine capable of stirring people into action; a useful motivator as long as it stayed within a certain scope.

Matsushita's thoughts on profits bear a strong resemblance to Shibusawa's. For Matsushita, profits were important because they kept businesses alive and expanding. When those business profits turned into dividends and tax payments, they also served to enrich society at large.

> To me, securing reasonable profits—proper earnings— is an extremely important part of our everyday business activities. Those reasonable profits are what enable us to develop our firms and benefit more people; without earnings, we would never be able to do that. A majority of the profits turn into national tax resources as well, which go toward enriching society on a countrywide scale. In that sense, turning reasonable profits is a noble obligation that we bear as citizens—a responsibility to our country (Matsushita 2001, 86–7).[13]

When it came to human desire, Matsushita took a non-judgmental stance. "Desire is by no means an inherently sinful, vile thing or some indecent source of evil", he wrote, "rather, desire is an expression of human vitality, a manifestation of a person's will to live ... [human desire] in and of itself is neither good nor bad ... in other words, it has the capacity for good and the capacity for evil" (Matsushita 2009, 104–5). For Matsushita, the moral character of desire depended on "whether the act of fulfilling that desire fosters—or ruins—mutual prosperity, peace, and happiness" (Matsushita 2009, 105–6).

> Take, for instance, the desire to make money. In and of itself, there is nothing in the least wrong with that desire. If you know how to satisfy that desire properly, you seek those profits through honest, diligent work, provide the fruits of your labor in the forms of services to others, and reap the rewards accordingly. Through that process, you not only bring happiness to people but also derive your own satisfaction (Matsushita 2009, 109).

Like Shibusawa, Matsushita saw individual human desire as a trait that could be a virtue—if, of course, the pursuit of the desire helped the community prosper and promoted human well-being.

As their statements suggest, both Shibusawa and Matsushita thus believed that business activities could promote public welfare *and* serve personal interests at the same time. We touched on Shibusawa's beliefs earlier in this chapter;[14] Matsushita echoed his predecessor's thoughts on the dual nature of business, writing:

> To some, the phrase "corporate profits" has negative connotations—something about the idea rubs them the wrong way. The problem is that those critics are interpreting the whole concept the wrong way.... The mission of contributing to the betterment of society through business and the process of generating reasonable profits through business are by no means mutually exclusive (Matsushita 1978, 33).

For both Shibusawa and Matsushita, the acquisitive pursuit of self-interest was a vital asset—not an anathema—in that it played a crucial role in motivating the people active in the business venture. As both men emphasised, employee motivation often ties into monetary compensation and incentives. However, the company-employee relations they envisioned were about far more than money and transcended mere contractual connections. We therefore need to examine those relationships between companies and employees (including managers) in closer detail, and then expand the discussion to include another type of corporate relations—"competitor relations"—to paint a fuller picture of how Shibusawa and Matsushita shared similar views on the bonds linking companies and their stakeholders.

Shibusawa and Matsushita adopted similar views on the relationships between companies and employees—a type of stakeholder—in many ways, but the most important common feature is their shared view of "horizontal labour relations". Labour relations often come down to an uneven power struggle: the employer, protected by a superior position, against the employees, exploited and oppressed. The imbalance can go both ways, too. When a union on the labour side gains momentum, the employees might brandish their newfound power by battering their employer with unreasonable demands or vilifying their managers. Either way, one side seeks to use its power and rights to put itself above the other; one faction becomes the subjugator at the top and the other the subjugated at the bottom. That common pattern amounts to "vertical" labour relations, an arrangement of which both Shibusawa and Matsushita were extremely critical. Instead, they advocated the opposite: "horizontal" labour relations. While vertical relations inevitably have a winner aiming to use its power and rights to grab the upper hand and keep the loser down, horizontal relations aim for a win-win situation characterised by mutual respect for the other's position and character.

Shibusawa envisaged that level playing field—a true harmony between management and labour—as the product of three essential components: (1) capitalists and labourers acting with the same noble virtue;[15] (2) a mutual awareness of the need to have aligned interests in a business; and (3) always possessing mutual compassion (Shibusawa 2008, 232). In that vision, Shibusawa was aspiring toward a form of labour relations under which management and labour would respect one another and work together for mutual harmony and benefit, with both sides seeking their own interests, and in doing so, never depending on the other. When Shibusawa participated in the founding of the Kyōchōkai (Harmony Society)[16] in 1919, that was the very vision that he was hoping to fulfil.

The idea of management-labour relations is one area where the parallels between Shibusawa and Matsushita are particularly striking. For Matsushita, conflicts of interest between companies and their employees were "natural byproducts of their respective roles". At the same time, however, the development of the company naturally benefits both sides. "Companies and labor unions", Matsushita asserted, "should always be in *constant opposition and harmony*" (1978, 90–1) (emphasis added).

> Ultimately, companies and unions have their sights set on the same end goal—the only difference is their focus in pursuing that objective. If they stand in opposition with each other on the points where they differ, but cooperate in harmony on the points where they agree, both sides benefit (1978, 92).

The key was "horizontal" labour relations, the literal opposite of their "vertical" counterpart:

> Management and labor are like the two wheels of a cart. If one wheel is bigger than the other, the cart will only be able to lurch clumsily forward; progress will be a challenge. The wheels need to be the same size for the cart to move the right way. *If one side of the management-labor relationship is ever too powerful, the ideal response is for the dominant side to help the other side grow.* A balanced power arrangement that situates management and labor in a collaborative relationship not only fosters fruitful labor relations—it also helps the company mature and improves employee welfare (Matsushita 1978, 93) (emphasis added).

The italicised phrase embodies the idea of respecting the other in a fair, conscientious way. Matsushita's philosophy stood in stark contrast to the competitive nature of "vertical" relations, where both sides jump on any opportunity to gain an edge over the other.

Matsushita and Shibusawa thus agree that harmonious labour relations are realised objectively by a community of interest, and subjectively by mutual respect between management and employees. The key point here is not simply that harmony leads to favourable results. What generates those results, according to Shibusawa and Matsushita, is the process by which both sides *work toward* harmony *in spite of* their conflicting standpoints or tense relations. Disingenuous relations that look to circumvent that delicate balance, like collusions between management and labour or paternalistic approaches from the management side (a line that Shibusawa specifically warned against crossing), might show signs of "harmony" (or something resembling it) on the surface, but will never produce true results. That view of labour relations—a combination of conflict and harmony—also applied to competitor relations, as we will see next.

Shibusawa and Matsushita both held the belief that without competition in markets for products and services, there would be no development. They also believed that without harmony, on the other hand, there would be no lasting value. As Takeo Kikkawa explains, Shibusawa's *gapponshugi* embodied a traditional capitalist principle by "aiming for an open economic system built on market mechanisms, which marked a departure from the closed economic system created by the *zaibatsu*". However, Shibusawa also advocated a "certain degree of order in the competition among different firms" (Kikkawa 2014, 247). He understood the value of competition, but he also recognised the perils of extremes. His writings on the topic make frequent reference to "good competition" and "bad competition". The "good" variety entails "pursuing one's own profits without doing any harm to others"—the "source of thriving business" and a precondition for social progress and prosperity. "Bad competition", conversely, corresponds to "pursuing nothing but one's own profits, oblivious to the harm it does to others". When companies engage in bad competition, they "inevitably inhibit the prosperity of their own firms sooner or later, thereby ruining the credibility of the firms involved". The single-minded hunt for their own profits also leaves companies "vulnerable to defeat at the hands of others and, in the final analysis, dooms them to mutual destruction, leaving nothing but a needless trail of malice in its wake". If a "victor" emerges from bad competition (even only temporarily), the industry will "be the winner's to monopolise ... and the resulting catastrophe will be society's to bear. Such is not the path to national prosperity", argued Shibusawa. It follows that "industrial and commercial competition must be good competition". The process of good competition hinges on striving for mutual harmony and benefit, an ideal that companies can realise by simultaneously competing and "working toward joint progress in as synergistic and disciplined a manner possible". While Shibusawa emphasised the need for a collaborative attitude, he also made it clear that competition should never subside or grow too friendly. "If the heat of competition were to die away ... competitors would lose their desire to learn, and the wheels of progress and enlightenment would cease to turn" Shibusawa warned. "That would not be a happy outcome". For Shibusawa, promoting joint progress did not simply mean colluding with fellow competitors. What he championed was the pursuit of "mutual harmony and benefit through moderate [inter-firm] competition" (Shibusawa Seien Memorial Foundation, Ryūmonsha 1986, 83–5, 101–3).

Matsushita again echoed Shibusawa's philosophy. Competition, for Matsushita, was vital in "helping competitors push one another to the next level, enhancing their own activities, and contributing to the betterment of both the industry and society as a whole" (Matsushita 2001, 131).

> ... because of competition, companies tap into their ingenuity and make concerted efforts to keep pace with their rivals. Out of that process come higher-quality products, better cost rationalisation, and more balanced operations. We often witness that without competition, markets see quality stagnate and costs rise.

> ... Competition itself, therefore, is something to embrace—a necessary element in business (Matsushita 1978, 46).

The logic is relatively straightforward: every individual company strives to enrich and enhance its own activities, which in turn "contributes to the betterment of both the industry and society as a whole". It would be an oversimplification to assume that competition is all it takes for companies and society to improve however. As Matsushita wrote:

> The point to understand is that competition itself is not the be-all and end-all. What comes *out* of that competition is the important thing. For me, the true value of competition lies in its power to secure benefits common to the entire industry, protect benefits for society at large, and bear the fruits of mutual harmony and benefit for the entire population of the country (2001, 131–2).

With every "good" comes a "bad" of course, and Matsushita saw excessive, cutthroat conflict as the worst form of bad, inherently fruitless competition.

> Excessive competition is a form of competition devoid of any reasonable profits. In extreme cases, some firms even resort to selling their products with no concern whatsoever for profitability, just to thwart their fellow competitors.... Therefore, excessive competition ... plunges industries into chaos and threatens the well-being of society. If those relentless battles prevent competitors from securing reasonable profits, moreover, tax revenues dwindle—and national society thus feels the detrimental effects. I think it would be safe to say that excessive competition does nothing but harm (1978, 46–7).

Operating from that perspective, Matsushita urged companies, especially industry leaders, to be aware of their circumstances and take responsibility for their roles in the competitive environment.

> Large corporations and industry leaders with substantial financial resources need to be especially cautious about [engaging in excessive competition]. As long as the leaders in the industry maintain proper moderation in competition, the industry should be able to withstand occasional bursts of excessive competition from smaller rivals ... [But] if front-running companies take the lead in initiating excessive competition ... they will throw the industry into disarray, sap its energy and destroy its credibility (1978, 47–8).

Matsushita's advice for avoiding that trap is virtually identical to Shibusawa's: "A company cannot think only of its own standing.... A company should base all its decisions and actions on how it can propel society forward and what the right thing to do is" (2001, 133). Again, that was what Matsushita expected of leading companies in particular.

Central to Matsushita's thoughts on competition was the idea of "simultaneously valuing competition and creating mutual harmony and benefit"—a clear analogy to his view on labour relations, which emphasised "constant opposition and harmony".

> Companies must thus commit to competing in the proper sense of the term and establishing an orderly form of opposition. Within that competitive conflict, however, they can find amity. Engaging in constant opposition and harmony is how companies can ensure mutual well-being and contribute together toward building trust in the industry as a whole, which I believe to be a vital process (2001, 76).

Taking a broader look at Matsushita's philosophy as an integral whole, one can see how his idea of "horizontal labour relations" overlapped with his stance on competition. In the labour sphere, he advocated for horizontal relations involving employers and employees to "respect one another in a fair, conscientious way"; when it came to competition, he urged major industry leaders to strive for mutually respectful and mutually beneficial relations with competitors instead of abusing their dominant positions in the market.

The Philosophies of Shibusawa and Matsushita in Emerging Countries and Contemporary Context

We argue, in this chapter, that an exploration of these past business philosophies can be a revealing window on what the economics and corporate management of today's Japan need to learn from and improve on. Following the example that Shibusawa set long ago, Matsushita's legacy illuminates another need: for strong groups capable of sensing exactly what society is looking for at a particular moment and immediately responding to those insights. These same kinds of needs apply to economic development in emerging countries. In that sense, the management philosophies of Shibusawa and Matsushita have a universal quality. Given the commonalities in the views of Shibusawa and Matsushita on business pursuits, profits, and stakeholder relations, we propose two basic conclusions. First, both Shibusawa and Matsushita emphasised the public nature of a company and focused on the utility of business activities. At the same time, they appreciated the values inherent in the private gains of business (rather than seeing them as conflicting with public utility) for three main reasons: (1) the pursuit of self-interest is essential in sustaining and expanding business; (2) the dividends and taxes resulting from private profits turn the gains into benefits for society at large; and (3) the promise of self-profit creates incentives for the individuals involved in the business and thus helps maximise their energies. Second, in their views on stakeholder relations, Shibusawa and Matsushita extolled the process of "seeking mutual harmony and benefit" while (or more accurately, *by*) "maintaining a certain amount of tension between the parties". Never should a company try to control others, do harm (out of its own self-interest), attempt to eliminate the opposing party or fall into patterns of collusion with the other side. Labour relations were also one area where companies needed to focus on mutual benefit; even if the power balance tilts in management's favour, the company needs to respect and empower (and thereby motivate) the labour side instead of unfairly leveraging its position. That way, both management and labour can benefit from the relationship and the company can thus survive and flourish. The same basic philosophy applies to competitor relations. If a company were to find itself at the top of the market, Shibusawa and Matsushita would urge the firm to avoid abusing its power or taking cut-throat means to overpower rivals. Instead, the company should focus on the larger scheme of things and adhere to fair, honest competition with its counterparts, which is the key to better products, higher-quality services, a stronger industry and by extension, healthier economic progress for the community and the nation.

Overall, to a varying degree, many of the ideas shared by Shibusawa and Matsushita have become a relatively common foundation for corporate management throughout Japan's high growth period. By explaining those tenets in simple, intuitive, impassioned terms, Matsushita effectively cemented his status as Japan's most popular and most respected corporate leader—a reputation he has continued to maintain for more than half a century. Given the numerous ways in which Matsushita's views coincided with those of Shibusawa, one can certainly make the case that Shibusawa's philosophy was essentially a prototype for the thinking behind Matsushima Electric Industrial and later Panasonic. A prototype is just an initial embodiment, however. Matsushita never (one can assume, at least) learnt directly from Shibusawa; he did not simply lift Shibusawa's model out of the past and transplant it into his contemporary context. What transpired was a coincidental consequence of two insightful executives, both active in Japan during formative periods in the country's growth, finding their ways to similar conclusions by way of intuition and reasoning. This leads to an important conclusion in the context of this book. Namely that the commonalities between Shibusawa and Matsushita and the ideas that constituted the philosophical core of Shibusawa's principles, which were shared—or at least sympathised with—by much of Japan during the country's high-growth period, have many implications for emerging countries that are experiencing similar high and rapid growth. We will therefore conclude by discussing the significance of *gapponshugi* for emerging countries and how Shibusawa's position and view on management might apply in the contemporary context.

Several observers of capitalism in the modern-day setting have noted the many problems with "faceless" fund shareholders in global markets trying only to maximise shareholders' value. *Gappon*-related concepts that might help reshape and improve global capitalism include ideas like fairness, morality, happiness, and shared value, but all involve certain concerns about their practical relevance. However, in *Gapponshugi in Global Perspective: Debating the Responsibility of Capitalism*, Harvard University's Professor Geoffrey Jones underscores the practical relevance of Shibusawa's ideas:

> The global significance of Shibusawa Eiichi and *gapponshugi* is that he laid out many of the challenges of combining capitalism and societal responsibility, and suggested solutions that are still relevant today. There remain wide variations as to what responsibility means, and even wider variations in the relationship between rhetoric and practice, but Shibusawa stands out as a pioneer who helped start the journey towards making capitalism sustainable (Kikkawa and Fridenson 2017, 164).

The *gappon* system should enhance global capitalism with a sense of morality, a deeper awareness of sharing and long-term stability, and enable emerging countries to develop that awareness as early as possible in order to avoid interfering with progress. Currently, however, the idea of applying Shibusawa's *gapponshugi* concept to the present can only go as far as the medium term. Any attempt to translate Shibusawa's concept into modern-day terms would entail formulating rules for long-term, stabilising operations in the joint-stock framework, building a public-oriented relationship among stakeholders, and establishing rules for distributing profits according to that structure. We argue that Shibusawa's framework would require some modification to create a form of capitalism that places a stronger emphasis on the joint-stock system and which focuses on avoiding unmanageable hidden risks. When it comes to controlling risk, much can be learnt from invoking the company types that Shibusawa selected according to risk level (joint-stock company, limited partnership, or general partnership plus anonymous partnership) to give firms a choice of different company formats, helping them to avoid the risks of market instability and credit uncertainty.[17]

One of the crucial points is the idea of "responsibility", a concept to which Shibusawa made frequent reference. Managers need to exercise responsibility in their managerial duties, of course, but responsibility goes further than giving shareholders returns on their investments. Considering that a company represents a public institution in society and thereby contributes to the creation of the public good, there also needs to be a system that companies can use to make decisions on improving their "private-sector" capabilities in a way that is both principled and rational. Shareholders, on the other hand, take responsibility for their investments not in terms of speculation but rather as investors; this means that the *gappon* system for the modern context needs to have a mechanism through which shareholders assume responsibility for relatively long-term holdings. Issues specific to emerging countries also require close attention. A remarkable amount of the business in emerging countries tends to follow the family business model, leaving companies vulnerable to the dangers of models under which *zaibatsu*-type and family-business-only structures hold significant clout (Suehiro 2014, Ch. 5). Figure 2.1 below represents a stylised representation of the features and definitions of capitalist systems in various countries. The horizontal axis represents the power relationship between the government and the private sector, while the vertical axis corresponds to the power relationship between marketability/competition and monopoly/*zaibatsu* control.

Figure 2.1: Matrix for *"gappon"* capitalism

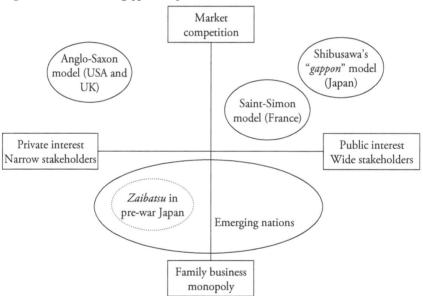

In mapping the various items on the matrix, the orientation of the vector—indicating direction and energy—is more important than exactly where each item lies on the matrix. This representation is premised on the hypothesis that emerging nations generally tend to be under the influence of the Government and family-operated businesses, limiting the strength of the market and private sector. The most distinctive feature of the *gapponshugi* model in pre-war Japan, however, was that it included both the nation and *zaibatsu* in its market model. In Meiji-period Japan, the *zaibatsu*—with their closed capital and closed organisations—were mighty corporate groups. They served as powerful engines of modernisation by recruiting elite college graduates who had studied in the West and absorbed the advantages of modern education. Company startup capital was supplied by the *zaibatsu* and their respective families, never through general funding.

At first glance, Shibusawa's market-based model and the *zaibatsu* model that kept both capital and the organisation closed appear to be completely incompatible, not to mention, they were indeed formidable rivals in various industries. A closer look, however, reveals that many *zaibatsu* executives took part in Shibusawa's market-based model, while Shibusawa himself worked with *zaibatsu* organisations. The two models thus had some common elements, in terms of both capital and the people involved. This, too, may be instructive for emerging economies. We, therefore, hope that the experiences of Japan's economic development and the management philosophies behind those transformations can help provide a foundation for fostering new economic societies in Southeast Asia, in which Japanese-style business has a pervasive presence and nations share numerous commonalities. Matsushita's aspiration was that Panasonic's investments should be of service to the destination country, but his broader ideas, as well as those of Shibusawa, also have the capacity to inform business activity in the two Southeast Asian economies that are the focus of this volume.

Notes

[1] *Kyōzon kyōei* in Japanese, sometimes also translated as "co-existence and co-prosperity".
[2] Kinoshita Hajime, interview with the authors, 6 August 2018. We would like to thank Mr Kinoshita for this interview. Kinoshita also played a role in the founding of PT National Gobel, where he later served as president. According to Kinoshita, "At the time, overseas Chinese accounted for just 3 to 4 per cent of the population but represented around 80 per cent of the economy".
[3] The first quote is from the authors' interview with Kinoshita Hajime, 6 August 2018; the second is from Kinoshita Hajime, as quoted in Watanabe (2013, 72).
[4] In the interview with Kinoshita Hajime on 6 August 2018, he said: "Matsushita's reputation in Indonesia was so different from anyone else's because he'd chosen to do business with a *pribumi* [at the height of the anti-Japanese protests].... We were the only Japanese company that rioters never threw rocks at or tried to burn down. I'm sure it had a lot to do with the fact that we were working with Gobel—a company with *pribumi* roots".
[5] The policy was also evident in Matsushita Electric Industrial's foray into the Thai market in 1961, which established the company's first overseas production site in the post-war era, as confirmed in our interview with Panasonic (Thailand) Co., Ltd's then deputy managing director, Itō Shūichi, on 28 September 2018. We also interviewed then assistant general manager, Ōta Keisuke, who said that the training session he participated in prior to relocating

to Thailand also emphasised the need to "do service to the country and benefit the people there". We would like to thank Mr Itō and Mr Ōta for the interviews and for arranging the company visits in Thailand.

[6] Kinoshita Hajime, interview with authors, 6 August 2018.

[7] In fact, Japan's industrialisation process during the second half of the Meiji period shifted significantly away from being a top-down, government-driven process, and instead became increasingly dominated by the private sector.

[8] See especially, Chapter 3 of Masakazu Shimada's book for discussions of shareholders' general meetings at Kyushu Railway and the Hokkaido Colliery and Railway Company.

[9] As of February 2019, one of Matsushita's most famous publications, *Michi o Hiraku* [The Path], had sold over 5.2 million copies since its release in 1968, making it the second-highest-selling book in post-war Japan.

[10] Shibusawa himself made countless references to the public nature of his own companies. In 1879, for example, he addressed the 13th general meeting of shareholders at the First National Bank (where he was president), saying, "This bank does not operate solely for the purpose of gaining profits. We must pay careful heed to how investments affect the nation at large and, if an investment is sure to produce a gain for the nation as a whole—even if it should come at the expense of the interest on the loan—the bank should finance the effort.... To put it simply, I want to see this bank serve not just its own interests but also industry across the nation" (Shibusawa Seien Memorial Foundation, Ryūmonsha 1955, 397).

[11] See Tanaka (2017).

[12] "If a person knows that his work is entirely for the sake of others, that his efforts have no bearing on his own personal interests, that the gains of others will not produce gains for himself, or that the losses of others will bring no harm to him in any way, he will never pour himself into his work.... If the work does affect his personal interests, however, he will want to carry that work forward—and he will follow that inspiration in doing so. This is an uncontestable fact" (Shibusawa 2008, 126).

[13] See Matsushita (1978, 35–41) for more on Matsushita's conception of profit.

[14] See also Tanaka (2014) and Tanaka (2017).

[15] Here, "with noble virtue" is synonymous with "in an ethical way". Thus, in Shibusawa's view, capitalists and labourers are to respect one another in an ethical way.

[16] The Kyōchōkai was a quasi-government body aiming to bring labour and management together in the case of disputes.

[17] Looking at the issues from this standpoint, Yoshitaka Suzuki has touted the usefulness of Shibusawa's anonymous partnership format and other systems in the contemporary context in helping small businesses struggling to recover from the industrial devastation of the Great East Japan Earthquake and tsunami (Suzuki 2014, 272–34).

References

Ali, Fachry and Ahmad Imam. 1998. *Gobel, Budaya dan Ekonomi: Tentang Wirausaha, Manajemen, dan Visi Industri Thayeb M. Gobel* [Gobel, Culture and Economics: About Entrepreneurship, Management and Industrial Vision of Thayeb M. Gobel] Jakarta: LP3ES.

Chō, Yukio. 1964. *Jitsugyō no Shisō* [Business Thought]. Tokyo: Chikuma Shobō

_____. 1984. "Kaisetsu" [Commentary]. In *Amayogatari: Shibusawa Eiichi Jiden* [The Autobiography of Shibusawa Eiichi], annotated by Yukio Chō. Tokyo: Iwanami Shoten.

Drucker, Peter. 1969. *The Age of Discontinuity: Guidelines to Our Changing Society.* New York: Harper & Row Publishers.

Fridenson, Patrick and Takeo Kikkawa, ed. 2017. *Ethical Capitalism: Shibusawa Eiichi and Business Leadership in Global Perspective.* Toronto: University of Toronto Press.

Hadimadja, Ramadhan Karta. 1994. *Gobel: Pelopor Industri Elektronika Indonesia dengan Falsafah Usaha Pohon Pisang* [Gobel: Pioneer of the Indonesian Electronics Industry with the Banana Tree Business Philosophy]. Jakarta: Pustaka Sinar Harapan.

Hashimoto, Jurō and Nishino Hajime. 1998. "Sengo Nihon no Kigyōsha Kigyō Keieisha: Matsushita Kōnosuke" [Post-war Japanese Entrepreneurial Management: Matsushita Kōnosuke]. In *Kigyōka no Gunzō to Jidai no Ibuki* [Leagues of Entrepreneurs and the Atmospheres of the Times], ed. Itami Hiroyuki et al. Tokyo: Yuhikaku.

Hattori, Shisō and Irimajiri Yoshinaga, ed. 1955. *Kindai Nihon Jinbutsu Keizai-shi, Jōkan* [An Economic History of Modern Japanese Leaders, Volume 1]. Tokyo: Tōyō Keizai.

Hirschmeier, Johannes. 1964. *The Origins of Entrepreneurship in Meiji Japan.* Massachusetts: Harvard University Press.

Hirschmeier, Johannes and Yui Tsunehiko. 1981. *The Development of Japanese Business, 1600–1980.* Second edition. London: George Allen & Unwin.

Itami, Hiroyuki. 2010. *Honda Sōichirō.* Kyoto: Minerva Shobō.

Jones, Geoffrey. 2007. *Kokusai Keiei Kōgi: Takokuseki Kigyō to Gurōbaru Shihonshugi* [Multinationals and Global Capitalism: From the 19th to the 21st Century]. Tokyo: Yuhikaku.

Kikkawa, Takeo. 2013. "Shibusawa Eiichi no Hitozukuri ni Chūmoku suru Riyū: Kōhatsukoku Kōgyōka e no Shisa to Shihonshugikan no Saikōchiku" [Explaining the Focus on Shibusawa Eiichi's Human Resource Development: Insights into Industrialization in Late-developing Countries and the Reconfiguration of Views on Capitalism]. In *Shibusawa Eiichi to Hitozukuri* [Shibusawa Eiichi and Human Resource Development], ed. Takeo Kikkawa, Masakazu Shimada and Kazuhiro Tanaka. Tokyo: Yuhikaku.

_____. (2014). "Shihonshugi-kan no saikōchiku to Shibusawa Eiichi no gapponshugi" [The Reconfiguration of Views on Capitalism and the Gapponshugi of Shibusawa Eiichi]. In *Global Shihonshugi no naka no Shibusawa Eiichi* [Gappon Capitalism: The Economic and Moral Ideology of Shibusawa Eiichi in Global Perspective], ed. Takeo Kikkawa and Patrick Fridenson. Tokyo: Tōyō Keizai Shinpōsha.

_____. 2017. "Shihonshugi-kan no saikōchiku to Shibusawa Eiichi no gapponshugi" [The Reconfiguration of Views on Capitalism and the Gapponshugi of Shibusawa Eiichi]. In *Ethical Capitalism: Shibusawa Eiichi and Business Leadership in Global Perspective*, ed. Takeo Kikkawa and Patrick Fridenson. Toronto: University of Toronto Press.

Kikkawa, Takeo and Patrick Fridenson, ed. 2014. *Global Shihonshugi no naka no Shibusawa Eiichi* [Gappon Capitalism: The Economic and Moral Ideology of Shibusawa Eiichi in Global Perspective]. Tokyo: Tōyō Keizai Shinpōsha.

Kikkawa, Takeo and Patrick Fridenson, ed. 2017. *Ethical Capitalism: Shibusawa Eiichi and Business Leadership in Global Perspective.* Toronto: University of Toronto Press.

Kikkawa, Takeo, Masakazu Shimada and Kazuhiro Tanaka, ed. 2013. *Shibusawa Eiichi to Hitozukuri* [Shibusawa Eiichi and Human Resource Development]. Tokyo: Yuhikaku.

Kimura, Masato. 2015. "Shibusawa Eiichi Kenkyū no Gurōbaruka: Gapponshugi, *Rongo to Soroban*" [The Globalization of Scholarship on Shibusawa Eiichi: Gapponshugi and The Analects and the Abacus]. In *Shibusawa Kenkyū* 27 [Shibusawa Research 27].

Matsushita Electric Industrial. 1968. *Matsushita Denki Gojū-nen no Ryakushi* [The Brief History of Fifty Years of Matsushita Electronic Industrial]. Osaka: Matsushita Electric Industrial.

_____. 1978. *Shashi, Matsushita Denki: Gekidō no Jūnen, Showa 43–53* [The History of Matsushita Electric Industrial: A Decade of Turbulence, 1968–1978]. Osaka: Matsushita Electric Industrial.

_____. 2008a. *Shashi, Matsushita Denki: Henkaku no Sanjū-nen, 1978–2007* [The History of Matsushita Electric Industrial: Thirty Years of Transformation, 1978–2007]. Osaka: Matsushita Electric Industrial.

_____. 2008b. "History of Matsushita Electric Industrial's Overseas Business", appendix. In *Shashi, Matsushita Denki: Henkaku no Sanjū-nen, 1978–2007* [The History of Matsushita Electric Industrial: Thirty Years of Transformation, 1978–2007]. Osaka: Matsushita Electric Industrial.

Matsushita, Kōnosuke. 1978. *Jissen Keiei Tetsugaku* [Practical Management Philosophy]. Kyoto: PHP Institute.

_____. 2001. *Keiei Kokoroe-chō* [Business is People]. Kyoto: PHP Institute.

_____. 2009. *Matsushita Kōnosuke no Tetsugaku* [The Philosophy of Matsushita Kōnosuke]. Kyoto: PHP Institute.

Mitsui, Izumi, ed. 2013. *Ajia Kigyō no Keiei Rinen: Seisei, Denpa, Keishō no Dainamizumu* [The Management Philosophies of Asian Companies: The Dynamics of Formation, Propagation, and Succession]. Tokyo: Bunshindō Publishing.

Miyamoto, Matao, ed. 2002. *Nihon o Tsukutta Kigyōka* [The Entrepreneurs Who Made Japan]. Tokyo: Shinshokan.

Morikawa, Hidemasa. 1976. "Shibusawa Eiichi: Nihon Kabushikikaisha no Sōritsusha" [Shibusawa Eiichi: The Creator of the Japanese Joint-stock Company]. In *Nihon no Kigyō to Kokka* [Japanese Companies and the State], ed. Hidemasa Morikawa. Tokyo: Nikkei.

Nakamura, Muneyoshi. 2014. "Imēji no Shūren to Kōsan: Tayōka suru Media to Shibusawa-zō" [The Convergence and Diffusion of Image: Diversifying Media and Perceptions of Shibusawa]. In *Kioku to Kiroku no naka no Shibusawa Eiichi* [Shibusawa Eiichi in Memories and Records], ed. Hirai Y. and Takada T. Tokyo: Hosei University Press.

Ōshima, Kiyoshi, Toshihiko Katō and Tsutomu Ōuchi, ed. 1976. *Meiji Shoki no Kigyōka (Jinbutsu, Nihon Shihon-shugi 3)* [Early Meiji Entrepreneurs (People in Japanese Capitalism, Volume 3)]. Tokyo: University of Tokyo Press.

Sasaki, Satoshi, ed. 2001. *Nihon no Sengo Kigyōka Shi* [A History of Entrepreneurs in Post-war Japan]. Tokyo: Yuhikaku.

Satō, Teijirō. 2013. "Matsushita Kōnosuke no Keiei Rinen to Kaigai Tenkai e no Kihon Shisei" [Matsushita Kōnosuke's Management Philosophy and Basic Stance on Overseas

Expansion]. In *Ajia Kigyō no Keiei Rinen: Seisei, Denpa, Keishō no Dainamizumu* [The Management Philosophies of Asian Companies: The Dynamics of Formation, Propagation, and Succession], ed. Izumi Mitsui. Tokyo: Bunshindō Publishing.

Shibusawa, Eiichi. 1871. *Ryūkai Ryakusoku* [The Elements of Company Formation]. Tokyo: Ministry of Finance. Reprinted by the Investigation Bureau of the Bank of Japan in 1956 in *Nihon Kin'yū Shi Shiryō: Meiji/Taishō-hen, Dai 5-kan, Meiji Jidai no Kin'yū ni kansuru Ronchō* [Resources on the History of Japanese Finance: Meiji/Taisho Periods, Volume 5: Papers on Finance in the Meiji Period]. Ministry of Finance. Reference is to the reprint.

————. 1909. "Seien-sensei Kungen" [The Precepts of Dr Seien]. In *Ryūmon Zasshi* No. 249. Reprinted in 1937 by the Shibusawa Seien Memorial Foundation, Ryūmonsha as "Seien-sensei Enzetsu Senshū" [Collection of Lectures by Dr Seien], *Ryūmon Zasshi* No. 590.

————. 2008. *Rongo to Soroban* [The Analects and the Abacus]. Tokyo: Kadokawa Publishing. Originally published in 1916.

————. 2010. *Shibusawa Hyakkun* [Shibusawa's One Hundred Stories]. Tokyo: Kadokawa Publishing. Originally published under the title *Seien Hyakuwa* [Seien's One Hundred Stories] in 1913.

Shibusawa Seien Memorial Foundation, Ryūmonsha. 1955. *Shibusawa Eiichi Denki Shiryō*, Volume 4 [Biographical Material of Shibusawa Eiichi]. Tokyo: Shibusawa Seien Kinenzaidan Ryūmonsha.

————. 1986. *Shibusawa Eiichi Kungen-shū* [Collection of Shibusawa Eiichi's Precepts]. Tokyo: Kokusho Kankōkai.

Shimada, Masakazu. 2007. *Shibusawa Eiichi no Kigyōsha Katsudō no Kenkyū* [The Entrepreneurial Activities of Shibusawa Eiichi]. Tokyo: Nihon Keizai Hyōronsha.

————. 2014. *Shibusawa Eiichi no Messēji* [The Message of Shibusawa Eiichi]. Tokyo: Iwanami Shoten.

————. (2014). "Shibusawa Eiichi ni yoru Gapponshugi" [Shibusawa Eiichi's Gapponshugi]. In *Global Shihonshugi no naka no Shibusawa Eiichi* [Gappon Capitalism: The Economic and Moral Ideology of Shibusawa Eiichi in Global Perspective], ed. Takeo Kikkawa and Patrick Fridenson. Tokyo: Tōyō Keizai Shinpōsha.

Shimokawa, Kōichi et al., ed. 1980. *Nihon no Kigyōka (4): Sengo-hen* [Japanese Entrepreneurs (4): The Post-war Years]. Tokyo: Yuhikaku Shinsho.

Suehiro, Akira. 2009. *Tai: Chūshin-koku no Mosaku* [Thailand: Exploring a Newly Industrialized Country]. Tokyo: Iwanami Shoten.

————. 2014. *Shinkō Ajia Keizairon* [Emerging Asian Economies]. Tokyo: Iwanami Shoten.

Suehiro, Akira and Makoto Nanbara. 1991. *Tai no Zaibatsu* [Zaibatsu in Thailand]. Tokyo: Dōbunkan.

Suzuki, Yoshitaka, ed. 2014. *Sōsharu Entapuraizu Ron* [On Social Enterprise]. Tokyo: Yuhikaku.

Tanaka, Kazuhiro. 2014a. "Prioritising Public Interest: The Essence of Shibusawa's Doctrine and Its Implications for the Re-invention of Capitalism". Paper presented at the annual conference of the Association for Asian Studies. Philadelphia, Pennsylvania, March 2014.

_____. 2014b. *Ryōshin kara Kigyō Tōchi o Kangaeru* [The Concept of "Conscience" in Corporate Governance]. Tokyo: Tōyō Keizai Shinpōsha.

_____. 2014c. "Dōtoku Keizai Gōitsu Setsu" [The Unity of Morality and Economics]. In *Global Shihonshugi no naka no Shibusawa Eiichi* [Gappon Capitalism: The Economic and Moral Ideology of Shibusawa Eiichi in Global Perspective], ed. Takeo Kikkawa and Patrick Fridenson. Tokyo: Tōyō Keizai Shinpōsha.

_____. 2017. "Harmony between Morality and Economy". In *Ethical Capitalism: Shibusawa Eiichi and Business Leadership in Global Perspective*, ed. Takeo Kikkawa and Patrick Fridenson. Toronto: University of Toronto Press.

Teranishi, Jurō. 2018. *Nihon-gata Shihonshugi: Sono Seishin no Minamoto* [Japanese-style Capitalism: The Source of the Spirit]. Tokyo: Chūō Kōron Shinsha.

Tsuchiya, Takao. 1931. *Shibusawa Eiichi Den* (*Kaizōsha Ijin Den Shū* 14) [Biography of Shibusawa Eiichi (Kaizōsha Biographies of the Greats, Volume 14)]. Tokyo: Kaizōsha.

_____. 1939. *Nihon Shihonshugi Shijō no Shidōshatachi* [Leaders in the History of Japanese Capitalism]. Tokyo: Iwanami Shoten.

_____. 1959. *Nihon no Keieisha Seishin* [The Spirit of Japanese Managers]. Tokyo: Keizai Ōraisha.

_____. 1967. *Zoku Nihon Keiei Rinen Shi* [History of Japanese Managerial Principles, Part 2]. Tokyo: Nikkei.

Udagawa, Masaru, ed. 2004. *Sengo Nihon no Kigyōka Katsudō* [Entrepreneurship in Post-war Japan]. Tokyo: Bunshindō Publishing.

Watanabe, Yūsuke. 2013. "Matsushita Denki no Ajia Shinshutsu to Keiei Rinen no Denpa: Indoneshia, Taiwan, Chūgoku no Jirei" [Matsushita Electric Industrial's Advance into Asia and the Spread of its Philosophy: The Cases of Indonesia, Taiwan, and China]. In *Ajia Kigyō no Keiei Rinen: Seisei, Denpa, Keishō no Dainamizumu* [The Management Philosophies of Asian Companies: The Dynamics of Formation, Propagation, and Succession], ed. Izumi Mitsui. Tokyo: Bunshindō Publishing.

Yui, Tsunehiko and Daitō Eisuke, ed. 1995. *Daikigyō Jidai no Tōrai* [Arrival of the Age of the Large Firm]. Tokyo: Iwanami Shoten.

Chapter 3

Siam Then, Thailand Now: Contextualising the Emergence of Thai Capitalism through Three Phases of Globalisation[1]

Julia S. Yongue

Origins, Institutions and Actors

To grasp the dynamics of Thai business development in the context in which it occurred, one must examine the origins and evolution of its institutions, values and norms, as well as crises and opportunities. One outstanding feature of Thai business development is how it was punctuated by external shocks that range from clashes with Western imperialism in the late 19th century—which opened Siam as it was known then until 1939—to international trade, and to a series of global crises, the most devastating of which occurred in 1997. Internal shocks such as military coups and mass demonstrations also shaped the course of business development. Context is influenced by multiple actors, and to understand business development in Thailand, one must take into account the most prominent ones: (1) kings and the Crown Property Bureau (once the Privy Purse Bureau); (2) Chinese and Western capitalists; and (3) politicians, bureaucrats, and other government officials, as well as military during some periods. These actors are noteworthy, as their choices directly affected the allocation and use of natural resources, investments in infrastructure and technology, the treatment of the environment and so on. Other groups and individuals also merit examination, such as civil society organisations, non-ethnic Chinese minority businesses and female entrepreneurs, who in 1932 became the first women in Asia to receive the right to vote. Though less visible, these actors also had a significant impact on the course of Thailand's business development and the features of its particular brand of capitalism.

This chapter analyses the context for Thai business development over three distinct phases. In the first phase, from the 1850s to the mid-1950s, Thailand became fully integrated into the global economy. Features of the second phase, from the late 1950s to the mid-1980s, include a surge in foreign direct investments and the introduction of new marketing approaches, mainly from Japan. The third phase, from the late 1980s to 2008, was a watershed for business, triggered by the 1997 financial crisis with Thailand at the epicentre.

"Unequal Treaties", Early Capitalists and Economic Nationalism (1850s to Mid-1950s)

Arguably the most important agreement in Thailand's diplomatic and economic history before 1960, the Bowring Treaty, was concluded in 1855 between the representative of the British Government, Sir John Bowring, and King Mongkut or Rama IV (1804–68). With the signing of this treaty, Siam entered the realm of free trade and global commerce. Similar commercial agreements, referred to collectively as the "unequal treaty system", were signed in countries across Asia with two distinct differences. First was their reception: Siam's progressive king viewed the treaty as a positive development and means to better the nation. According to James Ingram (1971), "… Siam, unlike Japan, came within Western influence largely because her monarch desired change … and was convinced that his country would benefit from cultural and commercial contact with the West". As an absolute monarch, King Mongkut played an active role in diplomacy and new business creation. One example was the expansion of rice production, achieved by incentivising growers through a reduction in their rice tax burden (Manarungsan 1989, 62). One should not underestimate King Mongkut's role and that of his successors in enacting changes that had a strong and direct impact on the economy, society and the context for business.

Second was the long-term effects of the agreement on the development of capitalism. Import duties were fixed at 3 per cent, the lowest of all Asian nations, making foreign goods cheaper and more competitive than those produced domestically. No duties were levied on opium, which was banned for the Thai people's use. Opium, spirits and gambling were under the control of Chinese from an early date (Skinner 1957). Westerners enjoyed special privileges, including the right to extraterritoriality, land purchase and travel within the kingdom

(Hewison 1989, 40). Thanks to the changes in Britain's relationship with China, the ethnic Chinese residing in Siam became British subjects, meaning that they could also take advantage of the same privileges. The treaties had a lasting impact as the full renegotiation was only achieved in 1927, much later than Japan, whose tariff autonomy occurred in 1911 (Suehiro 1999; Skinner 1957).

Assessments of this period paint a dismal picture of indigenous business development. Somboon Siriprachai wrote that the Thai economy "had stagnated for at least 100 years (1855–1949)" (Siriprachai 2009). Sompop Manarungsan (1988) asserts that little actual economic growth occurred before 1950. Some 70 per cent of trade in the 1930s was with Britain and 95 per cent of Thailand's modern industries were under foreign—chiefly British—ownership (Siriprachai 2012). This long period of foreign domination fostered a collective psychology of submissiveness, which hindered indigenous entrepreneurship. According to Ingram, "Thailand has been a sort of passive entity, adapting to changes and market influences originating in the world economy. Few innovations have originated from within, and most of the adaptive response to external influence has taken place along traditional lines" (1971). The nation's diplomatic situation obstructed the growth of indigenous industries—both traditional and modern. Given the low import duties levied on foreign goods and indigenous handicrafts such as pottery could not compete with European and Chinese imports. Infant industries such as sugar refining were also hampered by foreign competition, while existing spinning, smelting and iron production also declined. By the 1920s, the cotton weaving industry was forced to stave off competition from not only Western but also Japanese firms (Hewison 1989; Suehiro 1999). While the circumstances were generally unfavourable to business development, a small number of prominent Siamese enterprises emerged, one of which was Siam Cement, which was founded in 1913. This firm would grow to become Siam Cement Group, one of Thailand's largest business groups. Others included: Bangkok (leather) Industry (1917), Siam (1925) and Surasindu (1927) Ice Works and Boon Rawd Brewery (1933). Though British interests dominated the early Siamese economic landscape in trading, mining and banking, there was also a notable Greek, Dutch, Australian, and Swedish presence. The Danes, founders of the powerful conglomerate, the East Asiatic Company, however, were Britain's strongest competitors (Eggers-Lura 1993). Foreign industries, particularly shipping, were essential to the expansion of global trade and developed in tandem with and in large part thanks to the opening of Asian markets.

While Western capitalists helped to finance infrastructure projects, they were often slow to turn the control over to indigenous managers. Similarities were witnessed in the banking sector: Siam Commercial Bank, the first major Thai bank, was established in 1906 by the Privy Purse Bureau (later the Crown

Property Bureau), but was run by Europeans, mainly British, until 1941 (Eggers-Lura 1993; Falkus 1989). Colonial banks also have a long history of operations. The first modern bank to operate in Thailand was Hong Kong Shanghai Banking Corporation, founded in 1888, followed by the British Chartered Bank (1894) and the Banque d'Indochine (1897). The lack of a domestic banking sector, though essential to the foundations of capitalism, was a long-term bottleneck for the Siamese economy. According to British consular and budgetary reports, cowrie shells remained in use until the 1860s; even after 1900, the most common currencies used in the north were Indian rupees, and in the south, Mexican and Straits dollars (Falkus 1989). Though Siamese commercial banks were established in Bangkok in the late 19th century, the circulation of bank notes remained limited, even over a decade after their founding (Manarungsan 1989).

During this period of Western domination, Siam's main commodities were rice, tin ore, teakwood and rubber. International trade expanded; however, as foreign interests controlled Siam's exports, the benefits of commerce accrued mainly to foreign, namely British, imperial territories (Falkus 1989). As Siam lacked a strong banking system and an indigenous business class to absorb foreign managerial capabilities, capital left the country and domestic businesses were slow to take root. In contrast to banking, King Mongkut, followed by his son, King Chulalongkorn or Rama V (1853–1910)—who is known as the father of the modern railway system—strove to retain control of the railways. Unlike the banking sector, where foreign investment was permitted, the railways were financed indigenously. While ownership was maintained, in the long term, the industry yielded fewer opportunities for business expansion compared to the same in other developing nations, like for example Japan, where railway transportation became foundational to economic growth. This aspect may serve as a factor for explaining why Thailand's logistics management sector remained less competitive through the 1950s.

Attempts were also made to confine tin mining by foreigners to the southern provinces. Nonetheless, during the 1850s to the 1950s period, Thailand's trajectory from subsistence to barter, then to a money economy, was not easily traversed (Ingram 1971). Economic backwardness did however provide some advantages. The absence of a national metal currency system may have been more effective in preventing Westerners from making inroads into the distant provinces than the Government's protectionist responses. Thus, institutional voids—though in some contexts perceived as having a negative impact on economic development—may have actually worked in Siam's favour by shielding the economy and businesses from total foreign domination (Falkus 1989).

The rice economy was essential to Thailand's early business development and was formed through a division of labour based on ethnicity. The indigenous population residing primarily in farming villages entered traditional professions such as rice growing, handicraft production, boat construction and fishing, while the migrant population—comprised mainly of ethnic Chinese—engaged in non-traditional vocations such as shopkeepers, retailers and middlemen (Falkus 1989). Middlemen performed an important role in Siam's early economy as the links between the farming villages and the urban economy. Some managed to rise in social status thanks to their role as tax collectors for Siamese aristocrats. However, the largest concentration of ethnic Chinese resided in Bangkok. According to an analysis of population surveys compiled by Skinner (1957), it is likely that over half of the population of Bangkok in the first half of the 19th century was Chinese.

While the Bowring Treaty weakened ethnic Chinese capitalists' relationship with the crown, their local knowledge, language skills and networks enabled them to dominate the nation's main export commodity—rice—despite the formidable legal, capital and technological disadvantages they faced. The economy and labour force remained highly dependent on the rice trade long after the renegotiation of the unequal treaties. On the eve of World War II, rice accounted for 60 per cent of exports, while four out of five Thais worked in the supply chain—be it in cultivation, transportation, milling, or trading (Phongpaichit and Baker 1998). The growing rice trade fostered new business opportunities in sectors such as banking and finance. Between 1904 and 1908, three Chinese banks and three rice trading family businesses—Bulasuk, Lamsan and Wanglee—were established. To support their activities, Chinese middlemen created a system of credit for farmers to purchase seeds and other necessities, as well as to transport their harvests and other merchandise from the paddies in the provinces to Bangkok. The Chinese were gradually able to gain a stronghold in the export of rice and another key sector—during the World War I period, they also made inroads into the rubber industry. While Europeans and Chinese competed for control of the rice sector, there is evidence of a certain degree of complementarity existing between the two groups. In the retail arena, the European trading houses dealt mainly in high-end value-added luxury goods catering to affluent consumers, while the Chinese traders targeted average consumers who preferred to purchase their everyday household essentials in small shops (Endo 2013; Vilaithong 2006).

Thai business history is replete with "rags to riches" stories of Chinese migrants who, despite having arrived with only a "mat and pillow", managed to amass great fortunes in a single generation (Phongpaichit and Baker 1998). Business opportunities facilitated the rapid upward mobility of those who took advantage of them. Agribusinesses, essential to Thailand's economic development—both in the past and present—formed during this period. CP Group is one of Asia's largest business groups whose roots can be traced back to the vegetable seed shop, Chia Tai, which opened in Bangkok in 1921 (Pananond 2001). The growing wealth of Chinese capitalists eventually led to tensions after the death of King Chulalongkorn, particularly during the reign of his Oxford-educated son, King Vajiravudh (Rama VI, 1880–1925). King Vajiravudh, though credited as the father of the first Thai nationalist movement, is perhaps best known for his sharp critique of ethnic Chinese, whom he characterised in 1914 as "the Jews of the Orient". The political, social and economic context for King Vajiravudh's article has deep historical roots, and his grievances against the Chinese population reflect a more general concern over the changing political climate in China and its implications for Siam's status vis-à-vis the West, particularly Britain (Wongsurawat 2016).

In the early 20th century, the ethnic Chinese population did not constitute a unified community with a shared identity. Before World War I, violence between different language groups had produced deep rifts. However, the same changes in the political climate that preoccupied the king were also impacting the Chinese diaspora's connections to their homeland. Heightened instability at home fostered greater social cohesion among the Chinese who were residing abroad. This was witnessed in the establishment of a hospital in 1906 in Bangkok's Chinatown, with a rotating chairmanship from among the five main language groups. In 1908, the first Chinese chamber of commerce was founded, followed by mutual aid funds and a benevolent society (Skinner 1957). While these developments could be interpreted as gestures of social responsibility, it is likely that they were carried out as a means of safeguarding and promoting the interests of the Chinese community.

The Siamese monarchy had long given Chinese traders a free reign in their commercial activities as this mutually benefitted both parties, which meant that the economy was largely under Chinese control (Endo 2013). Despite growing tensions under the reign of King Vajiravudh, Siamese elites—many of whom had Chinese ancestry—welcomed Chinese businesses, much more so than in other parts of Southeast Asia, including the Philippines. (Chinese and Indians were expelled from Burma; pogroms targeting Chinese took place in Indonesia in 1965). The 1911 Nationality Act, based on birthright citizenship (*jus soli*), is symbolic of this stance. According to the act, anyone born in the country could become a Siamese citizen regardless of parentage. According to Phongpaichit and Baker (1998), "The kings emphasi[s]ed that 'being Thai' was not an ethnic definition but a cultural act. An immigrant who learnt the Thai language, became Buddhist, honoured the king, and *acted like a Thai*, could become a Thai" (emphasis added). Thus, the ethnic Chinese were more easily integrated into Thai society than in Malaysia or Indonesia where religious differences became a source of tension.

However, the situation for the ethnic Chinese began to evolve in the 1930s during the transition from an absolute to a constitutional monarchy. Change was sparked during the 1932 coup by fascist military leader, Field Marshall Plaek Phibunsonkhram or Phibun (1887–1964), who served as prime minister from 1938 to 1944, and from 1948 to 1957. Under Phibun, economic nationalism, as reflected through his "Thai-ification" policies, dominated the political landscape. His government aimed to enact a shift in the control of the business sector. Some of his measures could be interpreted as beneficial, since they encouraged the participation of indigenous Thais, the majority of whom had until then performed primarily unskilled work. Some measures included the creation of vocational schools, which burgeoned during 1947 to 1954.

Other measures, however, were designed to wrench control of the economy from the Chinese by expanding the role of the State. The Phibun Government founded some 100 State enterprises, whose Boards were filled with bureaucrats; though in some cases, they were Chinese managed (Suehiro 1999). The restrictions introduced in 1948 were clearly discriminatory, as they limited the freedom of the Chinese to open and operate their own business. A series of Occupation Restriction Acts barred Chinese from engaging in numerous skilled professions, such as barber/hairdresser, dressmaker, taxi driver, as well as makers of salt, umbrellas, charcoal and monastic goods; in 1952, measures were enacted to limit remittances to China and the Chinese immigration (Skinner 1957). Despite the repressive environment, the 1940s were a propitious period for Thai businesses. During World War II, imports from European countries ceased, providing an opportunity for the emergence of light industries and commercial banks. The gradual growth of a manufacturing sector, which would take off during the following period, aided in the formation of business groups, the founders of which were often the children of Chinese migrants. This second generation was born and educated in Thailand, as well as in China and/or Hong Kong. Unlike their parents, they were able to enjoy the advantages of having both local and global knowledge.

By the 1940s and 1950s, commercial banks began to play a major role in supporting economic and business development. Thai banks fulfilled their conventional function as suppliers of capital, while also operating in similar ways as investment houses, consultancies and chambers of commerce by collecting information and matching potential investors with entrepreneurs (Phongpaichit and Baker 1998). Though commercial activities had hitherto been Bangkok-centered, the situation evolved from the 1940s to the 1960s. One example is Chin Sophonpanich, founder of Thailand's largest bank, Bangkok Bank, who began expanding his services into parts of the country where the only sources of financing had been moneylenders and pawnshops. Chin's most notable contribution to business development, however, was the alliance he forged with military governments during this period, or what Phongpaichit and Baker (1998) refer to as the "politico-financial axis", which formed after the 1947 military coup. This alliance was sealed when Chin succeeded in persuading the military generals to transfer a large amount of government funds to Bangkok Bank rather than establish their own banking institution. Shortly afterwards, military officers began joining the bank's Board. Thanks to this alliance, when the decision was made to privatise State enterprises in the 1950s, members of the Bangkok Bank group were able to acquire important sectors of the economy that had previously been under State control. The relationship between Chinese capitalists in the banking sector and military governments remained a feature of Thai business until the early 1970s, despite numerous changes in political leadership (Phongpaichit and Baker 1998; Polsiri and Wiwattanakantang 2004). Such alliance-based business practices were widespread and also occurred in other sectors.

Continuity and Change in a Thai Context (Late 1950s to Mid-1980s)

> The relatively slow emergence of a manufacturing sector, in comparison to some other latecomer economies in the Asian region can be traced to Thailand's specific development context. As shown above, the lack of tariff autonomy prevented the introduction of measures to foster domestic industries. Overseas demand for agricultural commodities (rice) and primary materials (teak, tin and rubber) discouraged the development of other sectors. During this period, however, the situation evolved. Thus, Thailand's development model diverged significantly from those of other Asian nations, since it was agribusinesses and not manufacturing that led the way. This environment was propitious for the rise of family-owned business groups, which became dominant players in the domestic economy, but which were not encouraged to establish overseas operations until 1989 (Suehiro 1999).

In the first period, a single commodity—rice—occupied the central position in the Thai economy. As such, Thailand became the world's largest rice exporter in 1962, a position it would retain until 2012. At the same time, the Government encouraged crop diversification and fostered high-value-added food processing industries by promoting the construction of mills for sugar refining and cassava processing, canning factories for agricultural products and seafood and equipment purchases for aquiculture. The transition from a mono-crop dominated economy to one focusing on sophisticated agribusinesses was a success from an economic standpoint. One example was Thailand's sugar industry, which in 1991 became the world's largest exporter (Yoshihara 1994).

Other industries in which Thai exports captured a top position included rubber, cassava, canned pineapple, prawns, soy and frozen seafood[2] (Intarakumnerd 2016). The contribution of agrobusinesses to long-term economic growth is significant: by the mid-1990s, Thailand was the world's fifth largest food exporting nation (Muscat 1994).

This was achieved thanks to assistance from the public and private sectors. To incentivise farmers to diversify, the Government invested in large-scale irrigation projects while simultaneously raising taxes on rice. This encouraged farmers to clear lands for cultivation and diversify their crops. Private enterprise contributed both to agribusiness development and technology transfer through joint ventures with foreign enterprises. From an environmental standpoint, however, the downsides to this development model were evident, as the clearing of large tracts of land caused great environmental damage. According to Phongpaichit and Baker (2008), "… the economy grew by chopping down trees, putting more land under crops, damming rivers for hydropower, mining more minerals, exploiting the sea, and pulling people away from a semi-subsistent existence in the villages". Moreover, it was counterproductive: expanding the area of land for cultivation without adopting measures to modernise and upgrade farming techniques was inefficient and did little to improve yields (World Bank 1970, cited by Muscat 1994, 265).

Notable changes occurred in Thailand's trading partners. While Britain had been the key investor in the first period, during the Vietnam War, the United States took its place. The new relationship with Thailand stemmed from the geopolitical interests of the US in the Southeast Asian region (Randolph 1979). As its ally, Thailand received sizeable financial support through United States Agency for International Development[3] (USAID) projects. With the US as its patron, infrastructure for power generation and transportation, namely the construction of airstrips and roads in economically under-developed areas of the country, improved. One symbol of this relationship was the Friendship Road or Mittraphap Thanon from Bangkok to Nongkai, the first "all weather" highway made from asphalt and concrete. Such US investments had positive spillovers for the domestic construction industry (Dixon 1998). New urban areas proliferated around military bases in the remote northeast, helping to draw the most underdeveloped areas into the market economy. By the 1980s, supermarkets and department stores appeared (Vilaithong 2006; Ihara 2013). The US presence in Thailand sparked urbanisation and the emergence of a service sector led by tourism, catering to off-duty soldiers and personnel.

The key figure in forging the US-Thai relationship was Field Marshall Sarit Thanarat (1908–63). Having overthrown his predecessor Phibun in a coup, Sarit promulgated a new constitution, granting himself absolute authority to suppress opposing dissent. From the initial military takeover in 1947 to the popular uprising, known as the October 14 Revolution of 1973, military capitalists dominated the economic landscape. Sarit, who served as prime minister from 1957 until his death in 1963, is credited with modernising business and making economic development a policy priority, though much of the groundwork had been built under Phibun (Dixon 1998; Muscat 1994). Until the end of the Vietnam War and closing of the bases in 1976, the US Government supported the Thai economy and exercised direct influence on policymaking. One example is the adoption of a US-inspired free market model of capitalism, which relied on private- rather than public-sector investment. With some notable exceptions, such as infrastructure, public utilities (electricity and water) and a small number of manufacturing industries (tobacco, sugar and glass), all of Phibun's State-owned enterprises (SOEs) were privatised. At the same time, Sarit created new SOEs, such as Thai Airways. Sarit also replaced Phibun's bank-centered politico-financial axis with a triple alliance uniting the military, bureaucracy and businesses, resulting in military officers and bureaucrats joining their corporate boards. SOEs have served multiple functions in Thai business development: under Phibun, they were a source of income that could be used to garner the support of politicians, mainly from the military, while under Sarit, they served as the foundations for a new business infrastructure. Under Thaksin, a new wave of SOE privatisation occurred as a means to further modernise Thai business.

Another noteworthy development was the growing prominence of the monarchy in Thai politics. Thailand's later ruler, King Bhumibol (Rama IX, 1927–2016), who had supported Sarit's efforts to overthrow Phibun, returned from overseas to a long reign in which he initiated numerous infrastructure projects through the monarchy's investment arm, the Crown Property Bureau, particularly in the most remote parts of the country (Ouyyanont 2015). Thus, the monarchy played a key role in provincial economic development and in nation-building by strengthening a sense of national unity among the Thai people.

New Institutions of Business and Economic Planning

The year that Sarit took office was the year that the World Bank launched its first mission to Thailand, which prescribed the introduction of economic plans that were strongly influenced by US ideology (Suehiro 1999). Based on their recommendations, the Thai Government introduced a series of five-year economic plans. While some economists have argued that the Thai State was "soft" or "weak" in comparison to its Asian counterparts, the existence of economic planning illustrates an active role in policy formulation (Siriprachai 2012). According to Phongpaichit and Baker (1998), "Government has always played a large role in shaping the economy. In the 1960s and 1970s, it looked very 'passive' to economists interested in urban growth because it was focusing on something else—namely agriculture. Since the early 1980s, the Government has learnt very quickly how to manage export industriali[s]ation and has played a large role...."

Another illustration of the State's involvement in business is the founding of key institutions. The NEDB (National Economic Development Board, later renamed the National Economic and Social Development Board or NESDB in 1972) was created in 1959 to oversee the national and regional economies, while the Board of Investment (BOI), founded through the Industrial Promotion Act of 1966, continues to play vital roles in attracting foreign investment. Other institutions included the Budget Bureau and the Office of Fiscal Policy. Of note is the fact that the directors of these institutions were technocrats, many of whom had studied at US universities on government scholarships. Their free market-oriented policies provided a favourable environment for private enterprises.

Another key institution was the Bank of Thailand (BOT), initially created in 1942. Sarit appointed a highly respected economist as its head, Puey Ungphakorn, known in Thailand as the father of modern banking. During his 1959 to 1971 term as governor, Puey strove to maintain the bank's autonomy and independence by shielding it from the pressures of various stakeholders. His sound macroeconomic policies and personal integrity earned him a high reputation (Tasker 1999; Muscat 1994). The Commercial Banking Act, introduced in 1962, systematised the banking system, and in 1979, a second act made banking regulations more rigorous. The Thai stock market opened in 1962 but was replaced in 1975 by the Securities Exchange of Thailand (SET). Using the stock market as a vector for raising capital, however, would not take off until the boom years described below (Yoshihara 1994).

All of these institutions were vital in fostering strong and sustained economic growth in the long term and helped to attract FDI (Doner and Ramsay 2000). Thus, Thailand's policy-makers succeeded in providing a more welcoming environment for private ownership and foreign capital than its Southeast Asian neighbours, particularly Malaysia and Indonesia, where a State capitalism model prevailed (Yoshihara 1994). Multinational enterprises (MNEs) operating in Thailand enjoyed numerous privileges: Sarit's Government allowed them to remit profits and purchase land. Through the Labour Act of 1956, which made unions illegal, Sarit ensured that firms would not be encumbered by labour disputes. Economic concentration was also encouraged. According to Muscat (1994), "the objective of public policy was to promote the accumulation of private capital, not to constrain the process". Economic nationalism was also at play: the Promotion of Industrial Investment Act required a majority Thai ownership in joint ventures. However, given the US Government's patronage, it was revised in 1961 to allow a special exemption for American MNEs. The same act provided tax exemptions to firms that imported such items as machinery and parts. The cumulative effects of these measures made Thailand one of the most attractive foreign investment locations in all of Southeast Asia (Yoshihara 1994).

Domestic industries benefited from legislative measures. A new tariff regime was put in place to protect infant industries. Entrepreneurship was also encouraged through a policy to restrict public enterprises from entering certain sectors that would compete with private ones (Suehiro 1999). In general, Thai policies towards business tended to be measured and pragmatic. For the service, distribution and low-tech manufacturing industries, and commercial banking and insurance sectors for example, lobbying from domestic interests was successful in influencing policy-makers' decisions to introduce protective legislation. In the manufacturing sector, however, such maneuvering was less effective. This can be explained by the fact that the State's objective was to encourage joint ventures with MNEs for the purpose of introducing new technologies. Though not an official policy objective, this enabled the speedy introduction of a '"modern business culture" to Thailand (Muscat 1994).

Though it can be disputed whether corruption should be included as one of the key institutions of Thai business, there is little doubt that for entrepreneurs in many latecomer economies, the level and types of corruption are important investment considerations. In Thailand, various forms of illegal behaviour were rampant during this period, to the point that some might consider them institutions of business. As Doner and Ramsay point out in their study on the Thai textile industry, Thailand's form of clientelism benefitted rather than impeded economic growth and entrepreneurial opportunity. This is due to Thailand's specific context, in which a *competitive* rather than a *monopolistic* form of clientelism emerged between businesses and their political patrons.

> The presence of rapid economic growth in Thailand, despite extensive clientelism, corruption and rent-seeking suggests that these phenomena can have different effects upon growth in different settings.... Thai clientelism facilitated new entrants because of the relative insecurity of its patrons, on the one hand, and the stable macroeconomic context in which Sino-Thai businesses operated and prospered, on the other. Various public, private, and mixed public-private institutional arrangements enabled Thailand to overcome collective action problems that hampered sustained economic growth in many other less developed countries ... the particular type of clientelism in Thailand tended to expand, rather than restrict opportunities" (Doner and Ramsay 2000).

During this period, circumstances discouraged the monopolisation of power and wealth. However, the dominance of competitive clientelism weakened by the 1990s, due in part to frequent changes in government and the instability this engendered. The 1997 crisis dealt the final blow to this system, which was followed by the new prime minister, Thaksin, the founder of Shin Corporation, who awarded privileges to his family and supporters, thus causing the "monopoli[s]ation of opportunities" by a select few (Phongpaichit and Baker 2009).

A New Climate for Entrepreneurship

The political context changed after the fall of the military government and the return to civilian rule in 1973. The withdrawal of US troops, whose presence had boosted investor confidence, had a negative effect on new FDI in Thailand. Global factors also contributed to the relative decline: the first oil shock brought inflation and a drop in commodity prices, impacting Thai agribusinesses. The Government responded by introducing import substitution industrialisation (ISI) policies from 1971 to 1980. However, in the early 1980s the Prem Tinsulanonda Government changed course by implementing measures to devalue the Thai baht (TB) and shift from ISI to export-oriented industrialisation (EOI). Prem's market-oriented policies differed from previous administrations, where business strategies had been State-led and successful in ushering in a period of high growth.

Prem also strove to attract FDI by reducing the corporate tax burden and simplifying administrative procedures (Yoshihara 1994). Among the macroeconomic measures introduced, those relating to the exchange rate were particularly effective in stimulating investments. The devaluation of the TB, which had been pegged to the US dollar, sparked demand from foreign businesses in search of new locations with low labour costs. In particular, Japanese investment grew during this period (Phongpaichit 1989).

Unlike Western MNEs that often opted for fully-owned operations, Japanese firms preferred joint venture arrangements established with assistance from general trading companies or *sōgō shōsha* that were known for their extensive overseas experience. This strategy enabled the internationally inexperienced Japanese to limit risk, and was equally beneficial to Thai investors as it facilitated knowledge acquisition of manufacturing processes and management practices. The Japanese had three main investment targets: (1) areas where there was little or no existing production (such as automobiles and electric/electronic household products); (2) areas with low efficiency/productivity due to a lack of modern machinery (such as cotton weaving and spinning); and (3) areas where production was ongoing but lacked technological expertise (such as synthetic spinning and fibre) (Yoshihara 1994). In 1961, Matsushita Electric Industrial became the first Japanese firm to establish a joint venture with a Thai partner, and in 1957, Toyota was the first to open a subsidiary in Thailand. (Kawabe 2013). Both consumer electronics and automobiles were key growth sectors in Thai business.

While Japanese investment aided Thai business development, it was not always welcomed. In the early 1970s, the surge of Japanese FDI sparked a large-scale student-led protest which erupted during the visit of Prime Minister Tanaka Kakuei. Nonetheless, in general, there has been little backlash against FDI—Japanese or otherwise—since then (Muscat1994). The 1985 Plaza Accord caused a steep rise in the Japanese yen, marking a watershed for Japanese investments, which soon surpassed that of US. As Japanese FDI increased, Thailand became a key production hub for goods that were sold not only in the Thai market but also in the US, European and Japanese home markets (Yoshihara 1994).

Sino-Thai commercial activities were also promoted, a move that sparked the ascent of a central actor in the Thai economy: business groups defined as large-scale, family-owned entities, whose governance structure provided little separation between ownership and management. In the 1960s, they tended to join the commercial banking and general importing sectors. The latter lacked investment capital and often expanded through partnerships with Japanese firms, so as to take advantage of the import substitution incentives provided under Sarit. In addition to family-ownership, Thai business groups have also been known for their high degree of diversification into unrelated sectors, which can be partially explained by their ownership structure—such that intergenerational and/or interfamily family rivalries are avoided by entry into new areas.

The fundamental features of Thai business groups are: (1) Chinese dominance; (2) low economic concentration; (3) initial capital accumulation through trading; (4) shared ownership; (5) Bangkok rather than provincial-based development; (6) dependence on foreign capital and technology; and (7) reliance on political patronage (Phipatseritham and Yoshihara 1983). One can identify three main types of Thai business groups during this period. The first—the financial type—is comprised of four main commercial banks. By 1979, this group had established some 295 companies in trade, finance and manufacturing (Wailerdsak and Suehiro 2010). The second group type is industrial. The formation of this group got underway during World War II, but during the 1960s, it focused on manufacturing to take advantage of the ISI policy. The third group type is agribusiness. This category formed in the late 1970s and contributed to Thailand's transition from ISI to EOI. Diversification took place from primary product exportation to agribusiness, followed by (forward and backward) vertical integration into other sectors such as insurance and transportation, including shipping, warehouse storage businesses and so on. (Phongpaichit and Baker 1998). In addition to political patronage, these groups strengthened their bargaining power through relationships such as marriages, cross-shareholding and community welfare associations. While the ownership of business groups resides mainly with Sino-Thai families, there is one notable exception, the Crown Property Bureau. Indo-Thai business groups also have a long history of operations and are well assimilated as prominent players in the Thai economy (Esho 2013; Suehiro and Wailerdsak 2004).

Business groups have served an important purpose in economic development, particularly in developing countries, as Michael T. Rock (2000) asserts: "… large business groups can help developing countries acquire industrial competence, internali[s]e external economies and overcome shortages of entrepreneurial talent, but can also lead to substantial economic inefficiency". It is clear that Thai business groups have made a vital contribution to economic development and the expansion of trade. After 1986, Thai business groups began to engage in outward globalisation, a trend that accelerated after 1990 due to financial liberalisation (Pananond 2008).

Thai Business during the Boom, Bust and Recovery (1986 to 2008)

Of the many developments in the economy that occurred during the third phase, two are particularly significant to understanding the Thai business context. First, the top contributor to GDP (gross domestic product) shifted from agriculture to manufacturing. An important factor for this shift was the growth in Japanese investment after 1985, especially in the automobile and automotive parts industries. So vital had Thailand become to Japan's global supply chain that some have referred to it as the "Detroit of Asia" (Kawabe 2013). As the manufacturing sector developed, so did the sophistication of the goods that Thai factories produced. Thailand became the world's second largest exporter of hard drives. Other non-agricultural sectors that made sizeable contributions to GDP were tourism and financial services.

Table 3.1: Value added percentage of GDP in the agriculture and manufacturing industries, 1960–2017

Year	Agriculture	Industry
1960	36.4	12.5
1965	31.9	14.1

Table 3.1 (*cont'd*)

Year	Agriculture	Industry
1970	25.9	15.9
1975	26.8	18.6
1980	23.2	21.5
1985	15.8	21.9
1990	12.5	27.2
1995	9.0	26.4
2000	8.5	28.5
2005	9.1	29.7
2010	10.5	31.0
2015	8.9	27.5
2017	8.6	27.0

Source: World Bank data.

Second, from 1987 to 1996, Thailand witnessed an unprecedented economic boom, making it the world's fastest growing economy. Thanks to its sustained and robust economic growth, the World Bank categorised it as a *middle-income nation*. The economic boom yielded two new forms of entrepreneurship. The first could be seen among the business groups: a younger generation, having studied management at business schools in the West, began creating spinoffs in new fields. The second type was provincial entrepreneurship: some of these entrepreneurs achieved financial success through land speculation, and others through resource exploitation; the profits were used to enter new businesses, including in the telecommunications, hotel and retail industries (Phongpaichit and Baker 1998, 6). During the boom years, the World Bank economists were optimistic about Thailand's prospects, as can be seen in their 1996 report entitled, "Thailand's Macroeconomic Miracle: Stable Adjustment and Sustained Growth".[4] The timing of this pronouncement, however, was in retrospect premature. The Asian financial crisis of 1997 caused growth rates to plunge from 5.7 per cent in 1996 to a record low of –7.6 per cent in 1998 (World Bank n.d.).

Structural Adjustments and a New Post-crisis Form of Thai Capitalism

Thailand's remarkable economic expansion influenced long-term policymaking. In 1990, the Thai Government decided to prepare for a new stage in the country's development by adhering to the clauses in Article VIII of the International Monetary Fund's Articles of Agreement, which calls for the liberalisation of capital markets through the lifting of tariffs and other restrictions on the flow of funds across borders (Bank of Thailand 2019). In 1992, the Anand Government introduced reforms to liberalise the banking sector by allowing financial institutions to borrow funds offshore. The ultimate goal was to make Bangkok a regional financial hub. Given the favourable business environment and the stability of the TB, which was pegged to the US dollar, Thailand was becoming an increasingly attractive market for investment as well as speculation (Sharma 2002). A surfeit of borrowed money flowed into Thailand, much of which was channeled into overpriced real estate assets. The crash, which was initially triggered in February 1997 by the defaults of several large property developers, sent shockwaves through stock markets worldwide. Foreign investors grew increasingly pessimistic about the Thai economy and began converting their TB to US dollars. The BOT responded by buying TB, thus depleting foreign reserves. While interest rates were raised in an effort to discourage investors from withdrawing their funds, all countermeasures proved futile.

The BOT then made the momentous decision on 2 July 1997 to float the TB. This was the catalyst for the crash: the immediate effect of this decision was a 15 to 20 per cent fall in the value of the TB in foreign currency markets. In just 5 months, its value halved, while the value of debt doubled. Foreign lenders withdrew their loans en masse (Phongpaichit and Baker 2008). The Asian financial crisis (1997–99) became, according to Peter Warr (2009), "the most serious global financial crisis since the Great Depression of the 1930s". Though one could trace it to the above, Laurids S. Lauridsen (1998) asserts that the root cause was neither foreign investor behaviour nor policy failure, but the private sector's "careless lending/borrowing and the accumulation of non-performing loans in the financial sector". In the midst of the crisis, the IMF (International Monetary Fund) offered the Thai Government a bailout plan which was conditional on a number of macroeconomic policy commitments—one being to maintain high interest rates. This particular recommendation—as the IMF would later admit—was a grave error as it increased the corporate debt burden and led to a slew of bankruptcies. US policymakers, who also provided advice, simply advocated for the adoption of a more Anglo-Saxon model of capitalism. In their assessment, the dominance of family enterprises, characterised by a lack of accounting transparency and cronyism, was an urgent problem. According to Natenapha Wailerdsak, however, the US prescription was essentially to let "creative destruction" run its course and encourage the selling off of Thai businesses to foreign buyers and bankruptcies (Wailerdsak 2008).

The crisis had a number of enduring effects on the Thai business sector, in particular making room for a much greater foreign presence. Post-crisis annual inflow of FDI nearly tripled from the level it had reached during the boom years (Pavida 2006, cross-referenced in Wailerdsak 2008). To avoid bankruptcies among the joint ventures that the Government had endeavored to promote during the second period, policies were amended to allow foreign partners to own a majority stake, swap debt for equity and/or fully acquire businesses. The commercial banks survived chiefly through government assistance and reductions in the share of family ownership. The business owners in the property, construction, retail and service sectors—all of which had become heavily indebted—had little choice but to sell off their assets—in most cases to large foreign MNEs whose presence in terms of capital investments and number of subsidiaries increased exponentially between 1988 and 2000 (Wailerdsak 2008). Though drastic, these policies were effective. By 2003, the laggards had been weeded out and healthier businesses recovered and GDP rates eventually rebounded to higher levels than before the crisis.

Figure 3.1: Thai GDP per capita

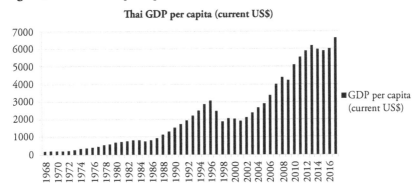

Source: World Bank data.

The crisis affected Thai firms in different ways. Those hardest hit were the financial and real estate sectors. Even Siam Cement Group, part of the Crown Property Bureau, incurred debts of US$6 billion, meaning that some of its companies became "technically bankrupt". Viewed in the long term, the downturn had little effect on the top-ranking firms. Those ranked below the top 200, however, were the most negatively impacted. Between 1997 and 2004, approximately 100 firms were de-listed, 53 due to bankruptcies (Wailerdsak 2008). Despite the severity of the crisis, however, many large, family-owned firms survived and continue to dominate the Thai business landscape. According to Wailerdsak (2008), four main types of family businesses overcame the crisis. Their principal features are summarised below. With the exception of authoritarian family conglomerates, these family firms found ways to modernise their management practices and adjust to the new business climate.

Table 3.2: Comparison of the post-crisis responses of selected family firms

Type	Example(s)	Management
Authoritarian family conglomerate	Thai Petrochemical	(1) No/few outside managers; (2) managed by family patriarch/eldest son
Unreformed single business	Boonrawd Group	Same as (1) and (2) above; closely tied to banks; created new businesses via cross-shareholding among family firms
Modernised single business	Sahapat; Saha Union; Shin Group	Little diversification; use of outside managers while still retaining family control; less foreign debt
Modernised family conglomerate	CP Group; Kasikorn Group	Highly diversified; hired outside managers while still retaining family control

Changes in firm structure and management practices were key determinants for survival: in general, firms that were dominated by a patriarch, with operations that lacked transparency, fared worse than those with outside managers. After the crisis, firms also depended less on commercial banks for raising capital. Large business groups secured investment opportunities in new fields like media, entertainment and telecommunications, as well as old ones like real estate (Wailerdsak 2008).

Capitalism in Moderation: From Thaksinomics to a "Middle Way"

Overseeing the recovery was Thailand's richest businessman-turned-politician, Thaksin, who served as prime minister from 2001 to 2006. Different versions of his family history exist, though they all share common features with the "rags to riches" stories of the Chinese migrants of the first period. According to one version, Thaksin's great-grandfather left Guangdong Province in the 1860s before working as a tax farmer and moving to Bangkok, and then to Chiang Mai. The Shinawatras became one of Thailand's richest families, thanks to a government concession which provided them with a major stake in the telecommunications sector. As Phongpaichit and Baker (2009) point out, "In Thailand, the coincidence of political leadership and commercial leadership is absolutely traditional". This statement held true in the first period when Chinese migrants were able to win favours from Siamese aristocrats as tax collectors, and in the second when politicians and bureaucrats were invited to join corporate boards. Under Thaksin, this tradition persisted with one notable difference: business leaders began taking a proactive approach to political participation. By entering politics and becoming prime minister, Thaksin could not only influence policies and regulations, he could create them.

The timing of Thaksin's political ascent is noteworthy as it took place when the country was struggling to cope with the aftershock of the financial crisis. Before rebranding himself as a populist to win a second term, Thaksin emphasised his successes as a CEO and spoke of the need to "manage" a country the same way as a business—an approach he termed *Thaksinomics*. Thais' needs, he asserted, would be best served by abandoning East Asian development models which relied on economic growth through exports (Amsden 2003). He advocated instead, employing indigenous sources of innovation and entrepreneurship.

Thaksin introduced stimulus packages to boost consumer spending and raise the average Thai income as he believed that higher levels of disposable income would stimulate the demand for domestically produced goods. This provided funding for social programmes, his centrepiece policy being a universal healthcare scheme. He also encouraged firms to reduce their dependence on the commercial banking system and to rely instead on the stock market for capital. In 2003, he hired Harvard Business School professor, Michael Porter, to assess Thailand's competitive advantages and propose a new national strategy for its industries (Porter/NESDB 2003). His Government also invested in projects to expand regional business opportunities in Association for Southeast Asian Nations (ASEAN) countries. While some of his policies were commendable from a business perspective, his critics noted that his stimulus packages had significantly raised the levels of both public debt and the corruption used to finance them. One example is the privatisation of State enterprises, which were sold to his family members and close political supporters (Phongpaichit and Baker 2009). By combining populism with corruption, Thaksin divided more than unified the Thai population. Irreconcilable divisions eventually led to violent demonstrations and his forced flight into exile.

Running counter to Thaksin's pro-capitalist/pro-globalist agenda was a wholly different approach to economic development—one that was initially articulated by King Bhumibol in the mid-1970s, but which was reiterated in the throes of the Asian financial crisis.

> Recently, so many projects have been implemented, so many factories have been built, that it was thought Thailand would become a little tiger, and then a big tiger. People were crazy about becoming a tiger.... Being a tiger is not important. The important thing for us is to have a sufficient economy ... to have enough support ourselves.... Those who like modern economics may not appreciate this. But we have to take a careful step backwards" (UNDP 2017; see also Grossman and Faulder 2012).

King Bhumipol's staff, academics and officials met to devise a manifesto based on his philosophy, which was founded on three guiding principles: (1) moderation, (2) wisdom or insight and (3) resilience in the face of internal and external shocks (UNDP 2007). This is known as the "just-enough" or "sufficiency economy" (*sekkhakit pho phiang*), which is also discussed in Chapter 11 (The Essence and Mechanism of Transformation to a "Sufficiency Economy") of this volume. Reminiscent of the ideas articulated much earlier by Shibusawa Eiichi, the sufficiency economy prescribes a moral and ethical approach to capitalism (Fridensen and Kikkawa 2017; Unger 2009). According to Danny Unger (1999), "the king calls for people to recogni[s]e that their own self-interest necessarily is linked to the welfare of their communities", which is a notion that is remarkably similar to Shibusawa's *gapponshugi* or "ethical capitalism".

What, then, led to the formulation of this philosophy? During his lifetime, King Bhumibol frequently travelled outside Bangkok; he was devoted to improving the lives of Thais living in the provinces, often through infrastructure projects. During his sojourns, he undoubtedly witnessed a darker side of capitalism as exemplified by environmental devastation that widened economic and social inequalities and prompted the dissolution of rural communities. Whether or not the "just-enough" economy is compatible with today's model of global capitalism is a matter of debate. There is little doubt, however, that in today's increasingly turbulent economic environment, the Thai business sector will one day face new shocks. When they arise, taking "a careful step backwards" to consider Thailand's past might provide some useful lessons.

Conclusions

The context for the Thai business sector shaped, and was shaped, by many factors, including policies and institutions, forms of ownership and governance, and innovation and entrepreneurship. These factors have in turn influenced its formation and transformation over time. It is hoped that a better understanding of the business history of Thailand can open up new debates on the rise of global capitalism from multiple perspectives, as well as proffer an opportunity to re-examine a large body of business history scholarship, which is mainly Western- or Japan-focused. This chapter has provided one interpretation of three highly complex phases by weaving together numerous secondary literature sources on Thailand's economic history and political economy. While it offers a starting point for discussion, its scope is limited. It principally examined large- as opposed to small- and medium-sized businesses; urban as opposed to provincial and/or regional commerce; male rather than female entrepreneurship; and successful rather than unsuccessful operations. By concentrating on Thai business history's most prominent actors and events, this study is more mainstream than it is alternative. Further research on the areas not covered in this chapter is therefore necessary to fully understand all the complexities and characteristics of the development of Thai capitalism.

Among the questions that future studies should address are the following: Why are Thai women more entrepreneurial than their counterparts in the same region or even in many developed nations? How have Muslim and other minority-owned businesses influenced indigenous Thai or Sino-Thai businesses? How have companies dealt (or not dealt) with the ravages of capitalism, namely environmental issues, and how has this changed over time? Finally, as the trade and traffic between Southeast Asian nations increase and deepen through their ASEAN ties, another, perhaps more urgent, question emerges: What implications does the context for Thailand's business history have for its neighbours in the same region? To answer this question and others, many new Asian alternative business histories need to be told.

Throughout its history, Thailand experienced shocks that laid bare unethical and corrupt behaviour as well as institutional weaknesses; however, these jolts also provided society with new opportunities to reflect and challenge the Western-style capitalism model. Thailand's assimilation of ethnic minorities, who supported its economic development while also espousing the common values of being Thai, offer an alternative approach to consider for other societies struggling with low growth and demographic decline.

Notes

[1] The title "Siam Then, Thailand Now", and some of the chapter's themes were borrowed from the discussions that took place during a workshop hosted by Thammasat Business School on 13–14 July 2013. The purpose of the gathering was to exchange views on the features of Thai capitalism and to encourage the study of business history as one of the tools for understanding its evolution; Julia S. Yongue, "The First Asian Business History Conference in Bangkok, Thailand", *The Business History Review* 88, no. 2 (Summer 2014): 373–7.

[2] The writer found a typographical error in the original text: "frozen sugar" rather than "frozen seafood" was listed as one of the products. After confirming the error with the text's author, the writer modified the passage accordingly.

[3] The United States Agency for International Development (USAID) was created in 1961 during the Kennedy administration. Its activities in nations such as Thailand were designed to promote economic growth, build new infrastructure and foster social welfare through partnerships with the host government as well as other organisations.

[4] Peter G. Warr and Bhanupong Nidhiprabha, "Thailand's Macroeconomic Miracle: Stable Adjustment and Sustained Growth", World Bank Publications, accessed on 3 May 2024, https://elibrary.worldbank.org/doi/abs/10.1596/0-8213-2654-6

References

Achavanuntakul, Sarinee, N. Rakkiattiwong and W Direkudomsak. 2008. "Inequality, the Capital Market, and Political Stocks". In *Thai Capital after the 1997 Crisis*, ed. Pasuk Phongpaichit and C. Baker. Chiang Mai: Silkworm Books.

Akamatsu, Kaname. 1961. "A Theory of Unbalanced Growth in the World Economy". *Weltwirtschaftliches Archiv*. Bd: 86.

Amsden, Alice H. 2003. *The Rise of "The Rest": Challenges To The West From Late-Industrializing Economies*. Oxford: Oxford University Press.

Austin, Gareth, Carlos Dávila and Geoffrey Jones. 2017. "The Alternative Business History: Business in Emerging Markets". *Business History Review* Volume 91, A special issue on methodologies (Autumn): 1–33.

Bank of Thailand. 2019. "Bank of Thailand History". Accessed 6 February 2019. https://www.bot.or.th/th/about-us/history.html.

Bardhan, Pranab. 1997. "Corruption and Development, A Review of Issues". *Journal of Economic Literature* 35, no. 3 (Sept): 1320–46.

Baumol, William J. 1990. "Entrepreneurship: Productive and Unproductive, and Destructive". *Journal of Political Economy* 98, no. 5, part 1 (Oct).

Christensen, Scott et al. 1993. *Thailand: The Institutional and Political Underpinnings of Growth (The lessons of East Asia)*. World Bank Publication.

Dixon, Chris. 1998. *The Thai Economy: Uneven Development and Internationalisation*. London: Routledge.

Doner, Richard F. 2009. *The Politics of Uneven Development, Thailand's Economic Growth in Comparative Perspective*. Cambridge: Cambridge University Press.

Doner, Richard F. and A. Ramsay. 2000. "Rent-Seeking and Economic Development in Thailand". In *Rents and Rent-Seeking and Economic Development: Theory and the Asian Evidence*, ed. M. Khan and K. S. Jomo, 145–80. Cambridge: Cambridge University Press.

Eggers-Lura, A. 1993. "The Danes in Siam: Their Involvement in Establishing of the Siam Commercial Bank Ltd., At the End of the Last Century". *Journal of the Siam Society* 81 (2): 131–40.

Endo, Gen. 2013. *Diversifying Retail and Distribution in Thailand*. Chiang Mai: Silkworm Books.

Esho, Hideki. 2013. "A Brief Note on Indian Business Groups in Thailand: Transformation from Diaspora to Global Business Players". IDE-JETRO. January. https://www.ide.go.jp/library/Japanese/Publish/Download/Seisaku/pdf/201301_esho.pdf#search=%27Indian+families+in+Thailand%27.

Falkus, Malcolm. 1989. "Early British Business in Thailand". In *Early British Business in Asia Since 1860*, ed. R. P. T. Davenport-Hines and G. Jones. Cambridge: Cambridge University Press.

Fridensen, Patrick and Takeo Kikkawa. 2017. *Ethical Capitalism: Shibusawa Eiichi and Business Leadership in Global Perspective*. Toronto: University of Toronto Press.

Gerschenkron, Alexander. 1962. *Economic Backwardness in Historical Perspective: A Book of Essays*. Belknap Press/Harvard University Press.

Gerybadze, Alexander. 2018. "Industrial Development Strategies in Asia: The Influence of Friedrich List on Industrial Evolution in Japan, South Korea, and China". In *Economic Thought of Friedrich List*, ed. H. Heigemann, S. Seiter and E. Wedler, 223–44. London: Routledge.

Grossman, Nicolas and D. Faulder. 2012. *Bhumibol Adulyadej: A Life's Work*. Editions Didier Millet.

Hewison, Kevin. 1989. *Bankers and Bureaucrats: Capital and Role of tThe State in Thailand*. Connecticut: Yale University Press.

Ihara, Motoi. 2013. "Impact of Hypermarkets on Consumption and Distribution in Rural Areas: Case Study of Ubon Ratchathani in Northeastern Thailand". *International Review of Retail, Distribution, and Consumer Research* 23 (2): 174–88.

Ingram, James C. 1971. *Economic Change in Thailand, 1850–1970*. California: Stanford University Press.

Intarakumnerd, Patarapong. 2016. "Upgrading in the Global Value Chains: The Cases of High, Mid, Low, Technology Sectors in Thailand". *Asian Journal of Innovation and Policy* 6 (3): 332–53.

International Monetary Fund. n.d. "Articles of Agreement of the International Monetary Fund". https://www.imf.org/external/pubs/ft/aa/index.htm.

Iversen, Martin Jes. 2013. "H.N. Andersen – An Imperialistic Entrepreneur? On the Relationship between Modernization, Imperialism, and Innovation in Bangkok, 1880–1920". Paper presented at conference *Siam Then, Thailand Now: Creating Thai Capitalism during Two Eras of Globalization*, Thammasat Business School, 13–14 July 2013. http://www.bus.tu.ac.th/uploadPR/TBHC_program.pdf.

Kawabe, Nobuo. 2013. "Roles of Multinational Companies in Self-Sustenance of the Thai Automobile Industry: The Case of Toyota Motor Thailand". *Waseda Shōgaku* 438 (December): 415–662.

Khanna, Tarun and K.G. Papelu. *Winning in Emerging Markets: A Roadmap for Strategy and Execution*. Massachusetts: Harvard Business Press.

Kikkawa, Takeo. 2011. "Beyond the Product Lifecycle and Flying Geese: International Competitiveness of East Asian Region and the Japanese Position Within". *Hitotsubashi Journal of History and Management* 45, no. 1 (October): 89–97.

Lathapipat, Dilaka. 2016. "Inequality in Education and Wages". In *Unequal Thailand: Aspects of Income, Wealth, and Power*, ed. Pasuk Phongpaichit and Chris Baker. Singapore: NUS Press.

Lauridsen, Laurids S. 1998. "The Financial Crisis in Thailand: Causes, Conduct, and Consequences". *World Development* 26 (8): 1575–91.

List, Friedrich. 1909. *National System of Political Economy*. Ttranslated from German by Sampson S. Lloyd. London: Longmans Green & Company.

Manarungsan, Sompop. 1989. "Economic Development of Thailand, 1850–1950, Responses to the Challenge of the World Economy". Doctoral dissertation, Rijksuniversiteit Groningen.

Muscat, Robert J. 1994. *The Fifth Tiger: A Study of Thai Development Policy*. Helsinki: United Nations University Press.

North, Douglass C. 1991. "Institutions". *Journal of Economic Perspectives* 5, no. 1 (Winter).

Ouyyanont, Porphant. 2008. "The Crown Property Bureau in Thailand and the Crisis of 1997". *Journal of Contemporary Asia* 38 (1): 166–89.

———. 2015. "The Founding of the Siam Commercial Bank and the Siam Cement Company: Aspects of Historical Context and Historiography". *SOJOURN* 30 (2): 255–496.

Ozawa, Terutomo. 2009. *The Rise of Asia: The "Flying-Geese" Theory of Tandem Growth and Regional Agglomeration*. Gloucestershire: Edward Elgar Publishing.

Pananond, Pavida. 2001. "The Making of Thai Multinationals: A comparative Study of the Growth and Internationalization Process of Thailand's Charoen Pokpand and Siam Cement Groups". *Journal of Asian Business* 17 (3): 41–70.

———. 2006. "Foreign Direct Investment and the Development of Thai Business: A Case Study of the Electronics Industry". Proceedings of the Thai Economy in the Changing Global Economy and Society seminar of the Faculty of Economics, Thammasat University, Bangkok, held annually.

———. 2008. "Finding Some Space in the World: Thai Firms Overseas". In *Thai Capital After the 1997 Crisis*, ed. Pasuk Phongpaichit and Chris Baker. Chiang Mai: Silkworm Books.

Phipatseritham, Krirkkiat and Yoshihara K. 1983. "'Thai Business Groups". Research Notes and Discussion Papers 41, Institute of Southeast Asian Studies, Singapore.

Phongpaichit, Pasuk. 1989. *The New Wwave of Japanese Investment in ASEAN*. Singapore: ASEAN Economic Research Unit, Institute of the Southeast Asian Studies.

Phongpaichit, Pasuk and Chris Baker. 1998. *Boom and Bust*. Chiang Mai: Silkworm Books.

———, ed. 2008. *Thai Capital After the 1997 Crisis*. Chiang Mai: Silkworm Books.

———. 2009. *Thaksin*. Chiang Mai: Silkworm Books.

———. 2016. *Unequal Thailand: Aspects of Income, Wealth, and Power*. Singapore: NUS Press.

Polsiri, Piruna and Y. Wiwattanakantang. 2004. "Business Groups in Thailand: Before and After the East Asian Financial Crisis". Working Paper Series 2004-13, Center for Economic Institutions, 1–43. Institute for Economic Research, Hitotsubashi University, Tokyo, Japan.

Porter, Michael and National Economic and Social Development Board (NESDB). 2003. "Preliminary Findings: Thailand's Competitiveness: Creating the Foundations for Higher Productivity", 4 May 2003. Accessed 7 February 2019. https://www.nesdb.go.th/article_attach/data14.pdf.

Ramamurti, Ravi. 2004. "Developing Countries and MNEs: Extending the Research Agenda". *Journal of International Business Studies* 35, no. 4 (July).

Randolph, R. Sean. 1979. "The Limits of Influence: American Aid to Thailand, 1965–70". *Asian Affairs* 6, no. 4 (March–April): 243–66.

Rock, Michael T. 2000. "Thailand's Old Bureaucratic Polity and its New Semi-Democracy". In *Rents and Rent-Seeking and Economic Development: Theory and the Asian Evidence*, ed. M. Khan and K. S. Jomo, 183–206. Cambridge: Cambridge University Press.

Senghaas, Dieter. 1991. "Friedrich List and the Basic Problems of Modern Development". *Review (Fernand Braudel Center)* 14, no. 3 (Summer): 451–67.

Sharma, Shalendra D. 2002. "Thailand's Financial Crisis: From Irrational Exuberance to the IMF's Star Pupil". *Crossroads: An Interdisciplinary Journal of Southeast Asian Studies* 16 (1): 49–99.

Siriprachai, Somboon. 2009. "Structural Changes and Challenges Ahead". *Thammasat Economic Journal* 27, no. 1 (March).

————. 2012. *Industrialization with a Weak State*. Chicago: University of Chicago Press Economics Books.

Skinner, G. William. 1957. *Chinese Society in Thailand: An Analytical Study*. New York: Cornell University Press.

Suehiro, Akira. 1999. *Capital Accumulation in Thailand, 1855–1995*. Chiang Mai: Silkworm Books.

————. 2008. *Catch-up Industrialization: The Trajectory and Prospects of East Asian Economies*. Singapore: NUS Press.

Suehiro, Akira and Natenapha Wailerdsak. 2004. "Family Business in Thailand: Its Management, Governance and Future Challenges". *ASEAN Economic Bulletin*, April.

Unger, Danny. 2009. "Sufficiency Economy and Bourgeois Views". *Asian Affairs: An American Review* 39 (3): 139–56.

United Nations Development Programme (UNDP). n.d. "Sufficiency Economy and Humanitarian Development". Thailand Human Development Project. http://www.unesco.org/new/fileadmin/MULTIMEDIA/HQ/Rio20/images/Sufficiency%20Economy%20and%20Human%20Development.pdf.

Vilaithong, Villa. 2006. "A Cultural History of Hygiene Advertising in Thailand, 1940s to Early 1980s". PhD thesis, December, Australian National University.

Wailerdsak, Natenapha. 2008. "Companies in Crisis". In *Thai Capital After the 1997 Crisis*, ed. Pasuk Phongpaichit and Chris Baker. Chiang Mai: Silkworm Books.

Wailerdsak, Natenapha and Akira Suehiro. 2010. "Business Groups in Thailand". In *The Oxford Handbook of Business Groups*, ed. A. Colpan, T. Hikino and J. R. Lincoln. London and New York: Oxford University Press.

Warr, Peter. 2009. "Thailand's Crisis Overload". In *Southeast Asian Affairs*, 334–54. Singapore: Institute of Southeast Asian Studies. https://www.degruyter.com/view/book/9789812309471/10.1355/9789812309471-020.xml.

Wongsurawat, Wasana. 2016. "Beyond Jews of the Orient: A New Interpretation of the Problematic Relationship between the Thai State and its Ethnic Chinese Community". *Positions: East Asia Cultures Critique* 24, no. 2 (May).

World Bank. 1970. *Current Economic Position and Prospects of Thailand*, Volume 1. Washington DC.

_____. 1993. *The East Asian Miracle, Economic Growth and Public Policy.* Washington DC: Oxford University Press.

_____. n.d. "GDP Growth (Annual %) – Thailand". World Bank National Accounts Data and OECD National Accounts Data Files. Accessed 26 October 2022. https://data.worldbank.org/indicator/NY.GDP.MKTP.KD.ZG?locations=TH.

Yongue, Julia S. 2014. "Conference Report, The First Asian Business History Conference, Bangkok, Thailand". *Business History Review* 88 (Summer): 373–77.

Yoshihara, Kunio. 1994. *The Nation and Economic Growth: The Philippines and Thailand.* Oxford: Oxford University Press.

Chapter 4

Indonesian Business Groups from the Perspective of the Shibusawa Business Model

Yuri Sato

Introduction

This chapter discusses business groups in Indonesia from the perspective of social entrepreneurship, which is also the core concept in the business ideas of Shibusawa Eiichi and considered by a number of the papers in this volume. Let me start by introducing the "Shibusawa business model".

There is a well-known episode regarding a dispute between Shibusawa Eiichi and Iwasaki Yatarō, the founder and top manager of the Mitsubishi Group, which later became one of Japan's largest business groups or *zaibatsu*. One day, Shibusawa was invited to a get-together organised by Iwasaki. The two men at first enjoyed their conversation about Japan's development prospects, but then got into a fierce dispute over how business should be managed. Shibusawa criticised Iwasaki's principles as presented in the 1875 regulations of Mitsubishi Steamship Company, namely that "the company was totally the business of the family, all things should be decided by the president and profits should return solely to the president himself". Iwasaki believed that the power and the risks should be concentrated into the person who was company president. Shibusawa on the contrary was firmly convinced that wide mobilisation of human resources and capital from society was the essence of business management—something that was seen by Iwasaki as a case of "too many cooks spoil the broth" (Mitsubishi Group; Kimura 2017, 124–5).

This disagreement epitomises a remarkable contrast between Shibusawa's business thoughts and those of business groups in general, including Japanese *zaibatsu*. Shibusawa started his career as a government officer of the Tokugawa Government, got ahead as a senior bureaucrat in the Ministry of Finance of the new Meiji Government, and plunged into the private sector at the age of 33.[1] He was involved in the ownership and/or management of at least 178 companies and around 600 organisations during his life (Shimada 2017, 57, 162). As discussed in Chapter 2 (Management Philosophies and Economic Development in Emerging Countries: Learning from Shibusawa Eiichi and Matsushita Kōnosuke), his guiding principle of *gapponshugi* can be defined as "the principle of developing a business by assembling the best possible people and funding to achieve the mission and aim of pursuing the public good" (Kikkawa 2017; Kimura 2017). To put it concisely, Shibusawa's business model featured the following key aspects: (a) Many companies that Shibusawa created were engaged in new industries that had never existed in Japan (such as banking, bricks, steel, fertilizer, marine insurance, shipbuilding, paper, gas/fuel and beer brewing); (b) his focus was on infrastructure development for the modern economy (such as banking, railroads, ports, shipping and coal mining); (c) he took on major managerial positions in "a single company in each industry" in principle, seeking fair competition; (d) he collaborated with different managers in each of his companies, with a limited number of managers taking multiple posts; (e) he played a prominent role in ensuring the presence of core managers sharing his values in start-up companies, and in training young managers for daily operations; (f) he supported the establishment and management of educational institutions to foster managerial talent; (g) his ownership shares were generally low, at 10–30 per cent in the companies where he continuously served as chairman, and lower than that where he was a director, auditor or chairman for a limited period; (h) he promoted the use of the joint-stock company form in large-scale public-utility businesses, while he set up limited partnerships for high-risk, high-return ventures, and anonymous partnerships—or *tokumei kumiai*, which is a partnership between anonymous investors with limited liability and managers operating businesses[2]—for small individual businesses; and (i) he was deeply involved in creating the first bank in Japan and promoting the banking system to make money work as capital for the benefit of all and the enrichment of the country (Shimada 2011; Shimada 2017, 21–9; Kimura 2017).

These features are quite different from those of ordinary business groups, which are generally characterised by concentrated ownership held by a small number of owners, a grip on multiple managerial posts taken by a small number of top managers and pursuit of a dominant position in each industry in which the group is engaged. The *zaibatsu* which emerged in pre-war Japan, such as with Mitsui, Mitsubishi, Sumitomo and Yasuda, were an extreme case of such business groups. The *zaibatsu* were characterised by three key elements (Yasuoka 1976; Morikawa 1973, 20): exclusive family control—that is, both ownership and management; diversified business; and oligopolistic positions of group companies in each of their industries. In addition, the majority of *zaibatsu*-affiliated companies in the pre-war period took the form of closed private companies.

The Shibusawa business model is so unique that it is very hard to find any comparable examples of business groups, not only in Japan but also in other countries. For the purpose of practical analysis in this chapter, I deconstruct the uniqueness of the Shibusawa business model into three elements: (1) a philosophy of social entrepreneurship that places priority on the contribution to national development and the creation of public good through doing business—represented by points (a) to (c) above; (2) open mobilisation of human resources through wide networks and talent fostering efforts—points (d) to (f); and (3) open mobilisation of capital through banking and the joint-stock company system—points (g) to (i). From the perspective of these three elements, I examine Indonesian business groups to explore how they have thought and acted for the creation of public good through doing business.

The purpose of this chapter, therefore, is to revisit Shibusawa's business model, reviewing it through the context of Indonesia, or conversely, to rethink Indonesia's capitalist development from the perspective of social entrepreneurship. For this purpose, I take the following approach. First, I look at big businesses, that is, business groups, to capture the main current of the development of capitalism in Indonesia. A business group here is defined as "a set of legally separate firms bound together in persistent formal and/or informal ways" as defined by Granovetter (2005), and then I consider the element of "under common ownership". The period of observation ranges from the 1970s up to the present time, with a special focus on the beginnings of capitalist development under the Soeharto regime, which is equivalent to the period of Shibusawa's activities in Japan. Second, I review the Astra Group as the most relevant example bearing semblance to the Shibusawa business model and analyse the group in light of the three elements stated above, comparing Astra with other Indonesian business groups and with the Shibusawa model itself. Third, I discuss what factors have given rise to the differences between the Astra Group and other groups, in what respects the Astra Group is similar to or different from the Shibusawa model, and how we can understand the nature of social entrepreneurship in Indonesia.

The three sections that follow deal respectively with the three elements of
the Shibusawa business model noted above—that is, the philosophy of social
entrepreneurship, the open mobilisation of human resources and the open
mobilisation of capital, using these elements to conduct a comparative analysis
of the Astra Group. The last section concludes the discussion.

Philosophy of Social Entrepreneurship

Brief Profile of the Astra Group[3]

The Astra Group is one of Indonesia's leading business groups. It ranked top
in terms of group sales from 2010 to 2018, and ranked second after the Salim
Group during the 1980s and the 1990s, before the Asian financial crisis. This
ranking is based on an estimation derived from the annual special issues of
Warta Ekonomi, a local magazine, for the period 1987 to 1996, and 2008, as
well as *GlobeAsia*, for the period 2009 to 2018; no ranking was available for
the period 1997 to 2007 due to the turmoil of the prolonged crisis. The Astra
Group's current sales amounted to IDR 237 trillion (USD 22 billion) as of
2019, covering seven sectors: automotive, financial services, heavy equipment/
mining/construction/energy, agribusiness, infrastructure/logistics, information
technology and property.

The founder of the Astra Group, William Soeryadjaya, set up PT Astra
International Inc. (PT Astra International) in 1957. He was an Indonesian-born
ethnic Chinese, a so-called *peranakan*, whose family had lived in Indonesia for
generations and had already lost their Chinese sociocultural background. PT
Astra International began business with the sale of daily goods and the export
of primary products. It later got involved in the automotive industry in the late
1960s, at the dawn of industrialisation under the Soeharto regime. Seizing the
opportunity to be sole agent and assembler of Toyota Motor Co. (Japan) in the
early 1970s, the company rapidly grew to hold and manage multiple companies,
becoming known as the Astra Group by the end of the 1970s.

In 1992, William was forced to dispose of all the family-held shares in
PT Astra International due to the failure of a bank run by his older son. The
Astra Group, however, weathered successive shocks from the founder family's
divestiture, the Asian financial crisis, and the collapse of the Soeharto regime.
In 2000, after many twists and turns, its major owner became the British-Hong
Kong business group, Jardine Matheson. Since then, the Astra Group has
become a business group owned by foreign capital, but which is still managed
by Indonesians, with a business operations base in Indonesia.

To Be an Asset of the Nation

The Astra Group formulated its own corporate philosophy at the end of 1982 and publicly announced it in 1983 (AI 1983, 12(1): 5; Pambudi and Djatmiko 2012, 379–411). It was still rare at that time in Indonesia for business groups to formally create the group's philosophy. The Astra Group's philosophy, which was later referred to as *Catur Dharma* (literally meaning four principles in Sanskrit), was provided not only in Bahasa Indonesia but also English, and consisted of four principles as follows:
1. To be an asset of the nation;
2. [Extend] best service to customers;
3. Respect for the individual and development of teamwork; and
4. To strive for excellence.

The original ideas of this corporate philosophy can be traced back to 1975, when William had talked as follows in the group's in-house magazine, *Astra*: "We have maintained one philosophy all the time since the founding of Astra International up to the present. That is, the company can grow and develop toward success if all personnel are hardworking, cooperative with each other, and have 'a sense of belonging' to the company, and if all the personnel, the society and the shareholders can perceive and enjoy the fruits of the company's success" (AI 1975, 4(4): 18).

It is said that an incident in early 1982 triggered the formulation of Astra's corporate philosophy. One day, taking a coffee break with the executives, William expressed his mind. "You young guys, you are the future of Astra. I feel sad. I set up Astra for our nation to prosper. I've never thought about doing business for myself or my own family. I want our company to become the place for many people to live their lives.... I want to prosper with the nation. But I'm sad, as this Astra is said to be a Chinese company because I'm a Chinese descendant ... I've never thought of myself as Chinese. I am a child of Majalengka, born in Majalengka [a town of West Java].... At the time of Malari [an anti-Japan riot in January 1974], we were said to be the minions of Japan. Everyone, please think out how we can make this Astra become, firstly, not to be regarded as egoistic, thinking only of ourselves. Secondly, I want this company to prosper, all of you to prosper, but not for ourselves. Prosper with the nation" (Pambudi and Djatmiko 2012, 386). In the process of drawing up the corporate philosophy that began after this incident, William's favourite phrase, "prosper with the nation" (*sejahtera bersama bangsa*), was given high priority and in the end became stylised into the first principle: "To be an asset of the nation" (translated as *Menjadi milik yang bermanfaat bagi bangsa dan negara* in Indonesian, literally meaning "'To become a possession beneficial for the people and the nation").

Astra and Shibusawa as Creating Shared Value

It is notable that the Astra Group was conscious of making a contribution to society and the nation from an early stage of its development. The spirit of William resembles that of Shibusawa, in that importance is placed on the business's contribution to national development and the creation of social good (through business in the private sector). The point here is that both men believed that the operational aspects of the core business itself—for example, pioneering new industries, introducing new technologies, creating employment, building infrastructure and so on—was able to produce benefit for the nation's economy and society.

This belief is conceptually closer to creating shared value (CSV) or social entrepreneurship, than to corporate social responsibility (CSR) or philanthropy. CSV, as Porter and Kramer (2011) argue, is the concept of creating economic value and social value concurrently, where companies enhance the competitiveness of their core businesses by solving social problems. CSR, on the other hand, is the concept of responsibility, where companies should fulfill their responsibilities towards their stakeholders by creating social value through volunteering or ethically oriented activities related to or in conjunction with their core business. This is the conventional understanding of CSR. The concept of CSR, according to some literature, including Visser (2010), is evolving into a new CSR, which may be more similar to CSV. [For discussion on CSR in Indonesia, see also Chapters 9 (Antecedents of Corporate Social Responsibility in Indonesia, 1900s–1950s) and 12 (Business in Indonesia since *Reformasi*: New Opportunities for CSR and Ethical Capitalism) of this volume]. The Astra Group, like Shibusawa, intended its core business to create value that could be shared by society.

As suggested by William's words, the emphasis on Astra as being an asset to the nation can be considered to relate to the distinctive characteristics of the group. First, the founder and the then owner-cum-top manager, William, was *peranakan*. Although he and his family were seen as ethnic Chinese, they had totally lost their Chinese identity, language, culture, and linkages with their old Han home region in Southeast China, all of which first-generation Chinese-Indonesians (*totok*) mostly maintained. For the Astra Group, there was no way to live other than being accepted as an Indonesian company. Second, the Astra Group was taken as symbolising a partner to foreign capital, as it had joint ventures with Toyota, Honda, Daihatsu, Peugeot, Renault, Komatsu, Fuji-

Xerox and other companies by the mid-1970s. While the foreign joint ventures helped Astra to introduce new technologies into Indonesia, Astra also came to be regarded as a proxy of foreigners. The Astra Group therefore needed to be recognised as a national company whose roots were in Indonesia.

Limited Manifestation of Social Entrepreneurship in Indonesia

While most business groups in present-day Indonesia publicly announced their Vision, Mission, and CSR before the 1990s, it was not usual for them to declare their corporate philosophies, let alone to articulate the concept of the creation of social good through their core business, as we have observed with the Astra Group. Why then did that happen? And how should we understand the inconspicuous situation of private capitalists' social entrepreneurship in Indonesia?

The first possible explanation would be that the overwhelming role of the State in leading the development of capitalism, especially during the 1970s to the 1990s, under the Soeharto administration may have limited the room for any manifestations of private sector initiatives. For instance, in introducing pioneer industries, it was the prerogative of the State to allocate investment permits to allow low-interest loans from State banks and to regulate imports to protect infant industries. The State allowed pioneer industrialists to become oligopolistic, rather than be subjected to excessive competition in the small domestic market. In developing infrastructure such as railways, ports, electric power and mining, SOEs (State-owned enterprises) were a central player. Even in inter-firm linkage development, the State-led system was introduced, such as the *Bapak Angkat* (foster father) System,[4] according to which large private companies and SOEs were requested to support MSMEs (micro, small and medium enterprises) as their *anak angkat* (adopted children) in procurement and marketing. The leading role of the State has also been widely observed in late-starter industrialising countries in Europe and Asia (Gerschenkron 1962; Wade 1990; Suehiro 2008), including in relation to Japan's Meiji Government. However, Indonesia under Soeharto's rule is regarded as one of the most outstanding cases of such a State role in light of the State's dominance over private business.

The second explanation would be that some business groups actually undertook some kind of social contribution, but did not publicise these activities before the 2000s, when CSR became popular in Indonesia and across the world. One example of such activities is donations to overseas Chinese associations by *totok* business group owners. Two of the four core co-owner-managers of the Salim Group, Soedono Salim (Liem Sioe Liong) and Djuhar Sutanto (Liem Oen Kian), were *totok* born in Fuqing (or Futsing) County, Fujian Province, China, and emigrated to Kudus, Central Java, in the 1930s. In Kudus, they belonged to and were supported in early times of difficulty by the Futsing Association (Futsing Hai). They later returned the favor with large donations to the Singapore Futsing Association (Futsing Huay Kuan) as Chinese associations based in Indonesia were banned in 1965. Both men assumed its lifetime honorary chairmanship (SFA 1988). Hendra Rahardja (Tan Tjoe Hien), the founder of the Harapan Group, was also among Indonesian donors who made contributions to the same association. Whatever the case, such social contributions were not related to the core business.

Although any manifestation of business groups' social entrepreneurship through their business has been generally limited in Indonesia, there was one exceptional event that drew public attention in 2010. CT Group, the service-industry-based business group founded by Chairul Tanjung in 1987, acquired 40 per cent of shares of the largest retailer in Indonesia, PT Carrefour Indonesia. The public loudly applauded Chairul, a *pribumi* (native ethnic Malay) businessman of the new generation, who became the single largest owner of this French giant's operation in Indonesia. With its remarkably rapid expansion, Carrefour Indonesia had been seen as a symbol of foreign oppression over local MSMEs, as it opened large stores in the centre of cities and required local producers to supply goods at bedrock prices set by the French headquarters (KPPU 2008). Soon after the acquisition, Chairul opened spaces in all Carrefour stores dedicated to selling the products of MSMEs and farmers (Tanjung 2012, 318–9). This is a special example of social entrepreneurship manifested by a *pribumi* Indonesian business group aimed at bringing pride to the nation and saving MSMEs from foreign giants.

Open Mobilisation of Human Resources

Professional Managers, Talent Training and Value Chain Promotion

The Astra Group is the exception in Indonesia in that it has been able to maintain its unity and survive as a business group even after the exit of the founding family. When asked why, Theodore Permadi Rachmat, commonly addressed as Teddy Rachmat, the then president director of PT Astra International, stated that this was because Astra was professional with regard to human resources, and they had kept the whole group transparent, in addition to the solidity of the group's core businesses as market leaders in each industry.[5]

Teddy Rachmat was the key person not only for Astra's survival, but also in terms of the employment of professional managers. He was a manager and also William's blood-relative, being William's nephew (as the son of William's elder sister), but he had no ownership in PT Astra International. The holding company was exclusively owned by William and his four children. Teddy Rachmat was thus a non-owner manager in Astra, while he and his wife owned their own side businesses outside Astra. It was the existence of this non-owner top manager who was related to the founder that bonded all Astra managers in support of the group's survival, and concurrently led to Astra inheriting the founder's spirit (Sato 1996, 268–9, 279–80). Teddy Rachmat graduated from the Bandung Institute of Technology (ITB), Indonesia's top university in science and technology, and joined Astra in 1969. While William had entrusted day-to-day operation to managers from the beginning, it was Teddy Rachmat who invited ITB graduates to be the next-generation of Astra's professional managers (Pambudi and Djatmiko 2012, 322–4, 432). To reproduce subsequent generations of professional managers, the group established the Astra Executive Training Center in 1989, which was renamed Astra Management Development Institute (AMDI) in 1993.

Apart from managerial talent development, the Astra Group has exercised initiative in promoting technological talent since the early years of its development. More correctly, this initiative was a focus not only on technology, but on training, with a skill set standard for sectors like technology, production management, marketing and financing. In 1980, William established a foundation named Yayasan Dharma Bhakti Astra (YDBA), with the aim of fostering MSMEs in line with his philosophy of social contribution. YDBA set up Klinik Industri (KI: Industrial Clinic), later renamed Unit Informasi Usaha Kecil dan Koperasi (UIUKK) or the Information Unit for Small Enterprises and Cooperatives, in the form of on-site MSME training units, first in Jakarta then expanding to rural clusters in Java and outer Java. The uniqueness of Astra's initiative lay in the combination of training with value chain promotion, where small manufacturers were encouraged to become suppliers to Astra Group companies if they could improve technological capabilities. It took YDBA over 10 years to attain this uniqueness. In the first stage (1980–87), its activities were of a charitable nature with minimum training effects. In the second stage (1987–90), YDBA started to select target MSMEs, taking into account how far they were related to Astra's value chain. After 1990, it shifted its focus in its training services to quality rather than quantity, so as to enhance talent development.[6] As at 1997–98, MSMEs in Ceper, a metal-casting cluster in Central Java, evaluated the assistance provided to them by UIUKK as more effective than government and foreign assistance—including the *Bapak Angkat* System—as UIUKK had also provided business incentives (Sato 2000, 154–7). Ten metal-working MSMEs at the Pulogadung Industrial Estate for Small Industry in Jakarta, with facilitation by UIUKK, formed a joint company in 1992 in order to receive UIUKK training, gain orders from Astra group companies and collectively obtain bank loans (Sato 1998, 137–40). Having taken that opportunity, some MSME members had grown to become first-tier component suppliers to the Astra-Honda motorcycle assembler. Of all business groups in Indonesia, the Astra Group is the one most deeply rooted in the machinery industry, and this has helped Astra develop the technological talent of MSMEs through subcontracting linkage (or value chain) creation.

Educational Institutions for the Broader Society

As a populous developing country, human resource development has been a major interest in Indonesia for the Government, as well as for the business sector for some time. The Astra Group is unique in its reproduction of professional managers—in the sense of ensuring a separation of ownership and management—and talent development through value chain promotion; AMDI was set up mainly for in-house training. More generally, some other business groups have put their efforts into human resource development by establishing educational and/or training institutions for the broader society. One pioneering example is the Gobel Group. In 1979, Thayeb Mohammad Gobel, the *pribumi* founder of the group, established a foundation named Yayasan Matsushita Gobel (YMG), in conjunction with his longtime senior partner in the electrical industry, Matsushita Kōnosuke, the founder of the Matsushita Group (Panasonic Group at present)—this is also discussed in Chapter 2. As a human resource development institute, YMG started a wide variety of training programmes ranging from technology, manufacturing, management, on-the-job discipline and work ethics to foreign languages. This was not only for in-house employees but also for MSME businesspersons (YMG n.d.; Ramadhan 1994).

At almost the same time, a movement was initiated, where around 70 ethnic-Chinese business group owners collected contributions and set up a foundation (1980) and opened a school of business and economics (1982). The foundation and the school (now university) were called Prasetiya Mulya, meaning "noble-minded promise", a name that was developed by President Soeharto himself. Salim Group's Liem Sioe Liong, who was the proposer coordinating the business group owners and mediating with the president, and Astra Group's William Soeryadjaya were elected as top leaders of the foundation, probably because they were the owners of the two largest business groups and represented the *totok* and *peranakan* business leaders respectively. Prasetiya Mulya can be regarded as a collective effort by ethnic Chinese-Indonesian business groups to contribute to the nation through education, and also a kind of political strategy born out of consideration of the growing antipathy in society against the rise of ethnic-Chinese big businesses (Soedarmanta 2014, 92–5).

Education as Business

In the 1990s, education started to become one of the major business pillars for some business groups. The Ciputra Group, one of the leading property development business groups, established Universitas Ciputra in Surabaya, the capital of East Java Province, in 1990. It obtained formal status as a higher education institution in 2006. The university focuses on entrepreneurial education embodying the motto "Creating world class entrepreneurship", in line with the firm belief of Ciputra, the group's founder, keyed toward emphasising the importance of strengthening entrepreneurship among younger generations in Indonesia (Ciputra 2009).

The Lippo Group is probably the most outstanding example of developing education as a purely private business. In 1994, the group established Universitas Pelita Harapan (UPH) as an international-level Christian university offering liberal arts in English in Lippo Karawaci, a satellite city that the group had developed 35 kilometres west of Jakarta in 1992. Targeting the emerging upper middle class, the Lippo Group succeeded in expanding UPH to Surabaya and Medan (North Sumatra), and in opening 45 K-12 schools (enrolling levels from kindergarten to 12th grade) by 2019 (Lippo Group n.d.). The founder of the group, Mochtar Riady, built up his career as a leading banker, but he decided to shift his focus to service industries targeted at emerging markets, integrating activities in areas such as education, healthcare, retail, IT and urban development, consciously moving away from banking, which carried high liability risks.[7] After the 2000s, more business groups, including Sampoerna, Bakrie, Sinar Mas, Bosowa and MNC set up universities or colleges bearing their group's name.

Variety in "Open" Mobilisation

When it comes to Indonesian business groups' activities in the development of human resource, we can observe a spectrum that ranges from the mobilisation and fostering of talent for one's own busines and the fostering of talent for the broader society, to education as a business, leaving aside more common philanthropic activities, including the offering of scholarships.

In relation to talent mobilisation for their own businesses, some business groups have shown what might be called "open" mobilisation, but the manner of openness is varied. The Astra Group has an internal reproduction mechanism for professional managers and this mechanism has been "open", regardless of ethnicity, to both ethnic Chinese and *pribumi*. Marseno Wirjosaputro, a first-generation *pribumi* professional who had graduated from ITB, and who was in charge of human resource development, was often told by William that "it is no matter whether he or she is *pribumi* or non-*pribumi* [meaning mainly ethnic Chinese]. What is important is the person".[8] Marseno later played a key role in developing YDBA as its first chairman. Another *pribumi* manager, Mochamad Teddy Thohir, who had moved to Astra from the American-affiliated Union Carbide in 1968, was entrusted by William with various tasks ranging from relations with State banks to management of the warehouse and the agro-businesses (Pambudi and Djatmiko 2012). Building on his longtime experiences in Astra, Thohir became known after the 2000s as the owner of a leading business group, TNT (Trinugraha Thohir) Group, which he had initially founded as a side business along with his older son, Garibaldi Thohir, in 1990 (Ministry of Justice n.d.; TBN 1990, 5206). Among the second-generation professionals, Teddy Rachmat and his six colleagues were called "the Seven Samurai" in the 1980s, and two of them were *pribumi* (Pambudi and Djatmiko 2012, 198, 324).

Ciputra, by contrast, created an "open" structure of talent mobilisation, which might be most similar to a Shibusawa-type business model among Indonesian business groups.[9] As of the mid-1980s, Ciputra functioned as the pivotal figure in three cooperating business groups, each with its own respective managers, before he shifted his main activities after the 1990s to the Ciputra Group, a family business with his wife and four children. The three groups, led by Ciputra, were the components of what was often called the Jaya Group. The first of these three groups was the Pembangunan Jaya Group, which worked on the development of Jakarta city, and in which the Jakarta regional government held 60 per cent of holding shares. Ciputra became president director with an 8 per cent shareholding in 1968, and operated around 20 subsidiaries in association with 5 managers, all of whom were new graduates from the top national universities. The second was Metropolitan Group, whose origin can be traced back to a partnership between Ciputra and two of his schoolmates, Budi Brasali and Ismail Sofjan; all three had majored in architecture at ITB together. The three students set up a design office in Bandung in 1957, expanded their office in Jakarta after graduation with support from the Jakarta Government in 1962, and finally in 1970, established PT Metropolitan Development, which was owned fifty-fifty by Budi and Ismail, and with Ciputra as non-owner president director. The third of these groups was the CMC (Capital Mutual Corporation) Group, which started in 1973 with another set of three owner-managers, supported by two out of the five managers of the Pembangunan Jaya Group. All the managers of the three groups, that is, Jaya Group collectively, whether *pribumi* or ethnic Chinese (Ciputra himself was *peranakan* born in Central Sulawesi), had similarly highly qualified educational backgrounds and expertise in the field of urban development and related business, such as building material production, equipment leasing and communication services.

Open Mobilisation of Capital

Listing the Holding Company

Business groups have complex ownership structures, and even if group companies are listed, they tend to be the blue-chip operating companies not the holding company. Listing on the stock market is a good way of mobilising capital from society, and it concurrently enhances the governance of the company concerned. On the other hand, a listed company is required to disclose information and assume accountability towards society. That is why most business groups avoid listing the holding company as this would necessitate a massive streamlining of ownership and the total disclosure of the group's business. Only very few business groups have dared to take this step, which has, in these rare cases, been driven by its underlying philosophy.

The Astra Group is one of the very few of such examples in Indonesia. PT Astra International went public on the Jakarta stock market in 1990 as the group's single holding company at the apex of a pyramidal ownership structure. With this IPO (initial public offering), the Astra Group became a totally transparent business entity holding 72 subsidiaries in 7 divisions—identified as automotive, financial services, heavy equipment, wood-based industries, agribusiness, electronics and other industries—as of 1990, demarcating the group's boundary from the founder family's private non-core business (AI 1990, 19(1); Sato 1996). The purpose of this IPO was fourfold, as PT Astra International officially revealed: (1) To penetrate international markets, (2) to expand investments for job creation, (3) to strengthen the group's financial position and (4) to give society an opportunity to participate in shareholding. William himself stressed that the IPO was for the sake of realising the Astra Group's first principle: "to be an asset of the nation", especially in relation to stimulating more employment (AI 1990, 19(1): 24–5). Behind this memorable event, however, lay several years of struggle by Edwin Soeryadjaya, William's second son and the then vice president director, and by professional managers, to streamline the intra-group shareholding structure and improve financial balances. They had considered William's inexhaustible energy in investing in as many as 170 companies throughout the 1980s as so risky that the group needed market exposure to make its financial management more solid (Pambudi and Djatmiko 2012, 497–522).

Another case was the Bakrie Group, which in some respects looks similar to the Astra Group, but differs in structure. One year before PT Astra International's IPO (in 1989), the Bakrie Group listed its holding company, PT Bakrie & Brothers, on the Jakarta stock market. PT Bakrie's IPO was led by Abrizal Bakrie, the second-generation president director, who had just succeeded to the post in 1988 on his father's death. The founder, Achmad Bakrie, a *pribumi* trader born in Lampung, Sumatra, set up a predecessor company—NV Bakrie & Brothers—in 1942 to export primary products, went into wire and steel pipe manufacturing in 1957–59, and had formed the Bakrie Group by the early 1980s. Achmad Bakrie had once stated: "I want this company to live hundreds of years.... Times are changing, so it would not be appropriate if the company remains owned by a person or a family. It must become a public company. Family shares will be only 40, 30 [or] 20 per cent, but it's large enough because the company is large. I just only want the name to remain [as] Bakrie" (Hardjoseputro 1987). Abrizal realised his father's dream by listing PT Bakrie & Brothers. For this purpose, however, he created another two holding companies, sorting the group's business into three categories: PT Bakrie & Brothers—for the business that was going public, PT Bakrie Nusantara Corporation (BNC)—for the business not going public and PT Bakrie Investindo—for family ventures. He left five profit-making steelmaking subsidiaries under PT Bakrie & Brothers and sold all other subsidiaries to BNC before the IPO and then bought back some subsidiaries in agribusiness and telecommunications from BNC for PT Bakrie & Brothers by the mid-1990s.[10] Abrizal's strategy of splitting the group into public and non-public segments, as well as the subsequent intra-group acquisition between the two segments was presumably regarded as more practical than the Astra Group's overall IPO, and was later imitated by other business groups.

Investing in Small Business

Returning to the Astra Group, it is worth noting one device developed by the group to invest capital on behalf of society, in addition to mobilising capital from society through the stock market. In 1991, Palgunadi Tatit Setyawan, PT Astra International's then vice president director who had just become the second chairman of YDBA, proposed to William that YDBA's talent development efforts for MSMEs should be complemented by capital financing facilities—just like the two wheels of a car. Soon after, the Astra Group decided to establish PT Astra Mitra Ventura (AMV), with Palgunadi as its president director. The initial fund of AMV was IDR 5 billion, 1 per cent of the net profits of PT Astra International, to which William added a special private subscription of IDR 20 billion (Pambudi and Djatmiko 2012, 421–7). This new company became a pioneer of private sector venture capital in Indonesia.

AMV has provided three types of capital investment: equity participation, convertible bonds and productive financing. In the initial stage, it started mainly with the first two, but after a few years, put greater importance on the third type, which was applicable to cooperatives and other non-stock-company enterprises. It also helped motivate investees to accelerate repayment as ratios of profit sharing with AMV decreased. Under productive financing, AMV provided capital investment for 3 to 7 years and investees shared their net profit with AMV in line with specified ratios of the outstanding balance. As of 1997, the number of AMV investees was 115 enterprises, 73 per cent of which utilised productive financing; 70 per cent was associated with the Astra Group's value chain.[11]

Partnership with Co-owners

The dispersed business group ownership structure of the Shibusawa business model, in which even a central owner has a minority shareholding in most of the group's companies, is in general rarely observed. La Porta, Lopez-de-Silanes and Shleifer (1999) found that concentrated ownership was rather common around the world, and dispersed ownership was prevalent only in the United States and the United Kingdom. Regarding Indonesia, a World Bank study showed that in 1996, 72 per cent of 178 listed companies were subject to concentrated ownership by an individual or family, 15 per cent were under concentrated ownership by a private corporation and only 5 per cent were characterised by dispersed ownership with no shareholders controlling over 20 per cent. (Claessens, Djankov and Lang 1999). In the case of concentrated ownership, however, the controlling shareholder is not always an individual or a family, but can be a partnership of plural individuals. Studies on the ownership structure of Indonesian business groups found that, firstly, controlling shareholders consisted of a central owner/family and co-owners, who respectively held 36 per cent and 20 per cent of the aggregate value of equity capital of business groups in 1985; secondly, the percentages of central owner/family shareholding had risen to 48 per cent in both 1996 and 2000, while those of co-owners had fallen to 7 per cent and 4 per cent in 1996 and 2000 respectively (Sato 1993a; 2004).[12]

The existence of non-family co-owners—though their percentages are decreasing—is a unique characteristic of Indonesian business groups, as most of their counterparts in Asia—such as those in South Korea, India, Thailand and the Philippines—as well as those in Latin America are more family centric. Partnership between a central owner/family and non-family co-owners, in most cases co-founders, accounted for 6 out of the 20 largest business groups in

1985, while closed family control accounted for 4 groups, and the remaining 10 were characterised by open family ownership in cooperation with domestic and foreign investors (Sato 1993a). The partnership type of ownership has been considered an organisational device, whereby a business group can mobilise business resources that cannot be obtained from the central owner/family, and has been especially effective in doing so before the next-generation family members have grown up. The business resources that were mobilised include equity investment, expertise in specific fields and the relationship with the State. For instance, the Jaya Group was a typical partnership type group, where expertise in urban development was mobilised from the co-owner-managers of its sub-groups, as earlier stated. Salim Group's core co-owner-managers, referred to as the "quartet" (*empat serangkai*), is another example of partnerships through which *totok* and *pribumi* were able to draw on their reciprocal resources. Two of the quartet were *pribumi*: Sudwikatmono—who as President Soeharto's cousin represented the president's authority and served as president director in many group companies, and Ibrahim Risjad—who was responsible for daily operations as director in those companies (Sato 1993a; 1993b).

It should be noted that both partnership- and family-type ownership/ management in Indonesian business groups can be flexibly transformed over time. As the second generation of co-owners grew up, the family-owned Ciputra Group and Brasali Group spun out from the Jaya Group. Salim Group moved into Sioe Liong's family ownership, and the two *pribumi* co-owners generated new family-type groups: Sudwikatmono's Subentra Group and Ibrahim's Risjadson Group respectively. After the death of Sudwikatmono, however, his family's second generation created the partnership-type Indika Group in conjunction with a non-family co-owner.

Conclusion

This chapter has examined Indonesian business groups, with a special focus on the Astra Group from the perspective of the three elements of the Shibusawa business model: philosophy of social entrepreneurship, open mobilisation of human resources and open mobilisation of capital. We have said that Shibusawa's philosophy of social entrepreneurship was to contribute to national development and the creation of social good through business in the private sector. The belief that the core business can itself create shared value for society— which can in present terms be referred to as CSV—has been rarely observed among Indonesian business groups. In this sense, the Astra Group, which has held such a belief from the early stages of its development and formulated it as its philosophy, can be regarded as unique. That private initiatives in social entrepreneurship were generally inconspicuous was partly due to the dominance over private businesses of the State-led system, particularly under the Soeharto regime. Now that the concept of CSR prevails, most business groups publicise their ethical activities, but these take the form more of philanthropy and the fulfillment of responsibilities associated with their business, rather than creating value through the core business. Astra's uniqueness can be regarded as relating to its strong anxiety for recognition as a national enterprise of Indonesia, given that the founder was *peranakan* and the group had many foreign partners. As an emerging *pribumi* business group, CT Group is seen to have demonstrated its social entrepreneurship through its heroic action of acquiring a foreign giant which dominated small local businesses.

Human resource development is an area in which Indonesian business groups have actively worked, and in various ways—whether through talent mobilisation and talent fostering for their own business or more broadly, for society or for education, purely as a business. The Astra Group has shown distinctive features in relation to talent mobilisation and fostering for its own businesses, generating professional managers regardless of ethnicity from the initial stages of its development, which later enabled the Astra Group to survive as a larger whole despite the founder-owner's sudden divestiture. The group has also fostered MSMEs by providing not only on-site training in technology and management, but also the opportunity of transactions with the Astra Group's businesses, which has been valued as effective in motivating MSMEs. The Astra Group's philosophy: "To be an asset of the nation", seems to have underlain these features. It is hard, however, to find open mobilisation in Indonesian business groups that is to the extent of that of the Shibusawa business model with its collaboration between the different managers of each group company. The closest example to this was the Jaya Group, where Ciputra had a partnership with several co-managers in each of the three sub-groups. The ties that connected these co-managers were their shared, highly qualified educational background and expertise in urban development.

The Astra Group is also notable in its open mobilisation of capital. While business groups generally prefer listing operating companies to a holding company, The Astra Group listed its single holding company on the stock market, making the entire group business transparent to the public. The Astra Group's total disclosure is also considered to have been backed by its social entrepreneurship philosophy. In addition to mobilising capital from the public, it had also invested in society—MSMEs in particular—combining this with training while promoting their participation in the Astra Group's value chains. In the corporate sector in Indonesia, the dispersed ownership of the Shibusawa business model is rarely observed; concentrated ownership is more widespread, including in the Astra Group. Concentrated ownership, however, is not necessarily family centric. One interesting phenomenon in Indonesian business groups is the coexistence of family-type and partnership-type ownership and their transformation. A partnership between a central owner and non-family co-owners functions as an effective device for mobilising capital and other useful business resources. As the owners' second generation grows up, the partnership-type group often splits into plural family-type groups. Jaya Group and Salim Group, which started as partnership-type groups underwent such a transformation in the 1990s. Some of the spin-off family-type groups in the second generation were then transformed back to a partnership-type group with new non-family co-owners. This flexible transformation, like cell division and fusion, shows Indonesia's dynamism in mobilising capital and talent, though not in the form of the Shibusawa model's open, dispersed ownership.

From the perspective of social entrepreneurship—in the sense of creating public value through business along the lines suggested by Shibusawa—not many Indonesian business groups have explicitly followed this path in the realisation of their business philosophy. The few outstanding examples where groups have exhibited their contribution to the nation have embraced a second factor: the owners' own ethnic backgrounds, which is a key to understanding the socio-economic context of Indonesia. In that respect, this chapter has shown that, for Indonesian business groups, human resource development is one area in which it is easier to pursue a variety of approaches in order to contribute to society regardless of an owner's background and business fields, and to link this contribution effectively with a group's core business activities.

Notes

[1] For Shibusawa's profile in English, see Gil Latz, ed., *Rediscovering Shibusawa Eiichi in the 21st Century* (Tokyo: Shibusawa Eiichi Memorial Foundation, 2014) and Patrick Fridenson and Takeo Kikkawa, ed., *Ethical Capitalism: Shibusawa Eiichi and Business Leadership in Global Perspective* (Toronto: University of Toronto Press, 2017).

[2] The form originated in the *commenda* in medieval Italy, and was a prototype of company organisations in Japan which can be traced back to the Edo era (Shimada 2017, 26).

[3] For the Astra Group, information as well as downloadable annual reports of PT Astra International is available at the company's website, https://www.astra.co.id/; Literature focusing on the group and/or the founder includes: Chowdhury (1983), Daulay et al. (1993), Sato (1996), Butler (2002) and Pambudi and Djatmiko (2012). A direct interview with the founder is available at "Wawancara: William Soeryadjaya" [Interview: William Soeryadjaya], *Eksekutif* [Executive] No. 7, January 1980, 8–16, 80.

[4] The legal basis for the introduction of this system lay in the Industry Law No. 5 of 1984, which emphasised the Government's role. Article 11 stipulated that the Government should guide industrial companies in organising and developing mutually beneficial cooperation.

[5] Based on the author's interview with Teddy Rachmat, 2 May and 3 June 2010, Jakarta, Indonesia.

[6] Based on the author's interview with Aminuddin, Head of Public Relations Division, PT Astra International Inc., 15 October 1997, Jakarta, Indonesia.

[7] Based on the author's interview with Mochtar Riady, 23 April 2012, Lippo Karawaci, Indonesia.

[8] "*Wawancara*: William Soeryadjaya" [Interview: William Soeryadjaya], *Eksekutif* [Executive] No. 7, January 1980.

[9] This paragraph is based on Sato (1993, 89–99), the articles of association of concerned companies in the Ministry of Justice Official Gazette Supplement [*Tambahan Berita Negara* (TBN)], the annual reports of PT Pembangunan Jaya (various years) and Ciputra (1986).

[10] Based on information from local magazine articles, including Friedland (1989); "Ambisi Bisnis Bakrie di Tahun 2000" [Ambition of Bakrie's Business in 2000], *Warta Ekonomi* [Economic News] 3, no. 37 (10 February 1992); "Mekarnya Saudara Muda" [The Bloom of the Younger Brother], *Prospek* [Prospect], 18 September 1993.

[11] Based on the author's interview with Krisni Murti, Director, PT Astra Mitra Ventura, 24 October 1997, Jakarta, Indonesia.

[12] The 1985 study was based on articles of association (Ministry of Justice) contained in TBN data on 630 companies (mostly unlisted) affiliated to the 20 largest business groups. The 1996 and 2000 studies were based on data on the 100 largest companies listed on the Jakarta stock market (ECFIN 1997; 2001), focusing on business-group-affiliated companies—54 and 37 companies respectively. The earlier and later studies are not strictly comparable due to the difference in sample, but are sufficient to indicate the direction of change.

References

PT Astra International (AI) Inc. *Astra* (the Astra Group's in-house magazine), 1972–various months.

Butler, Charlotte. 2002. *Dare to Do: The Story of William Soeryadjaya and PT Astra International*. Singapore: McGraw-Hill Education.

Chowdhury, Amitabha. 1983. "Corporate Leader of the Year: William Takes Astra Back to Grassroots". *Asian Finance* (Hong Kong) 9, no. 11 (15 November): 104–14.

Ciputra. 1986. "Pengalaman 25 Tahun sebagai Modal Pembangunan Masa Depan" [25 Years Experiences as a Capital of Future Development]. In *25th Anniversary Report of PT Pembangunan Jaya*. Jakarta: PT Pembangunan Jaya [The Jaya Group].

_____. 2009. *Ciputra Quantum Leap: Entrepreneurship Mengubah Masa Depan Bangsa dan Masa Depan Anda* [Ciputra Quantum Leap: Entrepreneurship Changes Future of the Nation and Your Future]. Jakarta: Elex Media Komputindo.

Claessens, S., S. Djankov and L. Lang. 1999. "Who Controls East Asian Corporations?" *World Bank Policy Research Working Paper No. 2088*. Washington DC: World Bank.

Daulay, A.H. et al. 1993. *William Soeryadjaya: Kejayaan dan Kejatuhannya* [William Soeryadjaya: His Glory and Fall]. Jakarta: Bina Rena Pariwara.

Fridenson, Patrick and Takeo Kikkawa Takeo, ed. 2017. *Ethical Capitalism: Shibusawa Eiichi and Business Leadership in Global Perspective.* Toronto: University of Toronto Press.

Friedland, Jonathan. 1989. "Indonesia's Bakrie and Brothers to List Holding Company: Stepping Out in Public". *Far Eastern Economic Review*, 6 July 1989.

Gerschenkron, Alexander. 1962. *Economic Backwardness in Historical Perspective.* Massachusetts: Harvard University Press.

Granovetter, Mark. 2005. "Business Groups and Social Organization". In *Handbook of Economic Sociology.* Second edition, ed. Neil Smelser and Richard Swedberg, 429–50. Oxford: Russell Sage Foundation; Princeton: Princeton University Press.

Hardjoseputro, H. 1987. *Berjaya Karena Wiraswasta: Buku Penuntun Karir Wiraswasta Indonesia: Simak Liku-Liku H. Achmad Bakrie dengan Bakrie & Brothers Group* [Victory because of Entrepreneurship: A Guide Book on Indonesian Entrepreneurial Career: Listening to Twists and Turns of H. Achmad Bakrie with Bakrie & Brothers Group]. Jakarta: Galaxy Puspa Mega.

Institute for Economic and Financial Research (ECFIN). *Indonesian Capital Market Directory.* Jarkarta: ECFIN, published annually.

Kikkawa, Takeo. 2017. "Introduction". In *Ethical Capitalism: Shibusawa Eiichi and Business Leadership in Global Perspective*, ed. Patrick Fridenson and Takeo Kikkawa, 3–14. Toronto: University of Toronto Press.

Kimura, Masato. 2017. "Shibusawa Eiichi's View of Business Morality in Global Society". In *Ethical Capitalism: Shibusawa Eiichi and Business Leadership in Global Perspective*, ed. Patrick Fridenson and Takeo Kikkawa, 121–43. Toronto: University of Toronto Press.

Komisi Pengawas Persaigan Usaha (KPPU) (Indonesia Competition Commission). 2008. *Saran Pertimbangan terhadap Rancangan Peraturan Presiden tentang Penataan dan Pembinaan Usaha Pasar Modern dan Usaha Toko Modern* (Recommendations for Draft of Presidential Regulation on Structuring and Guiding Modern Market Business and Modern Store Business]. Jakarta: KPPU, 2008.

La Porta, R., F. Lopez-de-Silanes and A. Shleifer. 1999. "Corporate Ownership Around the World". *Journal of Finance* 54 (2): 471–517.

Latz, Gil, ed. 2014. *Rediscovering Shibusawa Eiichi in the 21st Century.* Tokyo: Shibusawa Eiichi Memorial Foundation.

Lippo Group. n.d. "We Educate Indonesia's Future Leaders". Business. Education. https://lippogroup.com/businesses/education/.

Ministry of Justice, Republic of Indonesia. *Tambahan Berita Negara* (*TBN*) (Official Gazette Supplement). Jakarta: Ministry of Justice, Republic of Indonesia, various issues.

Mitsubishi Group. n.d. "Iwasaki Yatarō, Volume 22: Shibusawa Eiichi to Yatarō" [The Story of Iwasaki Yataro, Volume 22: Shibusawa Eiichi and Yataro]. Profile. History. Series. https://www.mitsubishi.com/ja/profile/history/series/yataro/22/.

Morikawa, Hidemasa. 1973. *Nihon Keiei no Genryū* [The Origin of Japanese-style Management]. Tokyo: Toyo Keizai Shinposha.

Pambudi, Teguh Sri and Harmanto Edy Djatmiko. 2012. *Man of Honor: Kehidupan, Semangat, dan Kearifan William Soeryadjaya* [Man of Honor: Life, Spirit, and Wisdom of William Soeryadjaya]. Jakarta: Gramedia Pustara Utama.

PT Pembangunan Jaya [The Jaya Group]. *Annual Report*, Jakarta: PT Pembangunan Jaya, various years.

Porter, Michael E. and Mark R. Kramer. 2011. "Creating Shared Value". *Harvard Business Review* 89 (1)/(2): 62–77.

Ramadhan, K.H. 1994. *Gobel: Pelopor Industri Elektronika Indonesia dengan Filsafah Usaha Pohon Pisang* [Gobel: A Pioneer of Indonesian Electronic Industry with the Business Philosophy of Banana Tree]. Jakarta: Pustara Sinar Harapan.

Sato, Yuri. 1993a. "Indoneshia ni okeru Kigyō Grūpu no Shoyū to Keiei: 'Paatonaashippu-gata' Kigyō Gurūpu o Chūshin ni" [Ownership and Management of Indonesian Business Groups: Focusing on 'Partnership-type' Business Groups]. In *Hatten Tojōkoku no Bijinesu Grūpu* [Business Groups in Developing Countries], ed. Kenji Koike and Takeo Hoshino, 73–128. Tokyo: Institute of Developing Economies (IDE).

_____. 1993b. "The Salim Group in Indonesia: The Development and Behavior of the Largest Conglomerate in Southeast Asia". *The Developing Economies* 31 (4): 408–41.

_____. 1996. "The Astra Group: A Pioneer of Management Modernization in Indonesia". *The Developing Economies* 34 (3): 247–80.

_____. 1998. "The Machinery Component Industry in Indonesia: Emerging Subcontracting Networks". In *Changing Industrial Structures and Business Strategies*, ed. Yuri Sato, 107–48. Tokyo: IDE.

_____. 2000. "Linkage Formation by Small Firms: The Case of a Rural Cluster in Indonesia". *Bulletin of Indonesian Economic Studies* 36 (1): 137–66.

_____. 2004. "Kigyō Gabanansu Kaikaku to Kigyō no Shoyū Keiei" [Corporate Governance Reform and Corporate Ownership and Management]. In *Indoneshia no Keizai Saihen: Kōzō, Seido, Akutaa* [Reorganizing the Indonesian Economy: Structure, Institutions, and Actors], ed. Yuri Sato, 205–60. Chiba: IDE.

Shimada, Masakazu. 2011. *Shibusawa Eiichi: Shakai Kigyōka no Senkusha* [Shibusawa Eiichi: Pioneer of Social Entrepreneurship]. Tokyo: Iwanami Shoten.

_____. 2017. "Tensions between the Open Market Model and the Closed Zaibatsu Model". In *Ethical Capitalism: Shibusawa Eiichi and Business Leadership in Global Perspective*, ed. Patrick Fridenson and Takeo Kikkawa, 14–34. Toronto: University of Toronto Press.

Singapore Futsing Association (SFA). 1988. *Xinjiapo Futsing Huay Kuan sanqing jinian tekan* [Futsing Association Triple Celebration Souvenir Magazine]. Singapore: SFA.

Soedarmanta, J.B. 2014. *Mempertahankan Cita-Cita, Menjaga Spirit Perjuangan: Refleksi 80 Tahun Harry Tjan Silalahi* [Retaining Ideal, Maintaining Spirit of Struggle: A Reflection of 80 Years Old Harry Tjan Silalahi]. Jakarta: Yayasan Pustaka Obor Indonesia.

Suehiro, Akira. 2008. *Catch-Up Industrialization: The Trajectory and Prospects of East Asian Economies*. Singapore: NUS Press.

Tanjung, Chairul. 2012. *Chairul Tanjung: Si Anak Singkong* [Chairul Tanjung: A Cassava Child]. Jakarta: Kompas Media Nusantara.

Universitas Prasetiya Mulya. n.d. "Background". Home. https://sbe.prasetiyamulya.ac.id/en/home/background.

Visser, Wayne. 2010. "The Age of Responsibility: CSR 2.0 and the New DNA of Business". *Journal of Business Systems, Governance and Ethics* 5 (3): 7–22.

Wade, Robert. 1990. *Governing the Market: Economic Theory and the Role of Government in East Asian Industrialization.* New Jersey: Princeton University Press.

Yasuoka, Shigeaki. 1976. "Nihon Zaibatsu no Rekishiteki Ichi" [The Historical Position of Japanese Zaibatsu]. In *Nihon no Zaibatsu* [Zaibatsu in Japan], ed. Shigeaki Yasuoka. Tokyo: Nihon Keizai Shinbunsha.

Yayasan Matsushita Gobel (YMG). n.d. About, History. http://www.mgf.or.id/history-of-mgf/

Chapter 5

What Significance does the Continuance of Family Business Groups have in Thai Society? A Case Study of the Central Group

Gen Endo

Introduction

As noted earlier, in the early phase of the development of capitalism in Japan—that is, in the early Meiji era—Shibusawa Eiichi advocated what he termed *gapponshugi* or ethical capitalism, which was an alternative model of capitalism deemed suitable for Japan at a time when it lacked the preconditions for the establishment of a modern joint-stock company system (Fridenson and Kikkawa 2017). In terms of institutional "immaturity", latecomers such as Southeast Asian countries may have had business conditions that were similar—in some respects—to those of Japan in the early Meiji era. However, the global environment that was faced by late 19th- to early 20th-century Japan, and that was faced by late 20th- to early 21st-century Southeast Asian countries was very different. Moreover, some Southeast Asian countries, including Thailand and Indonesia, are unlike Japan in terms of the extraordinary role played by ethnic minority businesses since the 1960s, when a full-scale industrialisation policy was implemented in these countries.

Taking the context of Southeast Asian countries into consideration, this chapter will discuss the significance of family business groups in the evolution of capitalism in Thailand, particularly in terms of ownership and control, as well as social responsibility. The major issues addressed here are: how large-scale family businesses have changed the structure of ownership and control in the age of economic globalisation, and, in the case of persistence of the structure, how family business groups can contribute to public benefit.

These research questions arise for the following reasons. First, transactions in markets inevitably have transaction costs owing to factors such as bounded rationality, opportunism and information asymmetry. As Williamson (1975) indicated, one means of reducing costs is to form an internal organisation characterised by hierarchical monitoring and command through integration, that is, a business group or conglomerate. In developing countries where economic institutions and market conditions are relatively immature, such business groups are more likely to emerge. Second, most of the local business groups that have witnessed remarkable growth in Thailand can be characterised as family businesses (Suehiro 1989).[1] In Thailand, as in other Southeast Asian countries, business groups originating from a family business have largely retained the features of a family business even after the business has grown large and diversified. This is due to the fact that most of these founders were from an ethnic minority background, particularly Thai-Chinese. The immature labour market induced them to rely more on their family members. "If mutual trust does not exist between workers and management, the cost of monitoring and enforcing the workers' efforts would become very large" (Hayami 1997, 246). Hierarchical organisations, that is, business groups in this chapter, are likely to fall into functional disorder with a high incidence of moral hazard, unless the community mechanism of co-operation is incorporated in some form or the other (Hayami 1997, 246). In such a situation, the workers in whom business leaders can place the most trust are likely to be their family members. Thai-Chinese or Chinese-Thai business leaders tended to attach greater importance to their family members because they had undergone many hardships during the period of nationalism lasting from the 1930s to 50s. Third, family business groups in Thailand have never been static organisations. They have so far adapted themselves to the changing environment (Suehiro 2006). Particularly, during the current phase of globalisation, how these family business groups have reformed themselves is an important issue that needs to be explored. The primary points of concern in this chapter are thus how and to what extent the structure of ownership and management of family business groups have changed given that exclusive control over ownership and management is a prerequisite for them.

Here, there is another point to be added. Even in a context similarly characterised by latecomers, institutional immaturity and the predominance of family business groups of Chinese origin—as Colpan and Jones (2020) have also argued—every business group does not always react in the same way.

Although a firm or business group cannot behave at will without any contextual constraints, it can to some extent react independently in a given context. Any case study therefore needs a comparative viewpoint. This chapter chooses the Central Group, a leading Chinese-Thai family business group, for the case study, while keeping the CP Group, another leading Chinese-Thai group, in mind for comparison. The American business magazine *Forbes* (September 2012) featured the Jiarawanon family, who founded the CP Group, as Thailand's richest, with assets totalling USD 9 billion, while the Jirathiwat family, who set up the Central Group, was ranked second, with a total net worth at USD 6.9 billion [*Prachachat Thurakit* (hereafter *PRCT-TK*), 4–6 February 2013]. As will be explained in greater detail in subsequent sections, the Central Group is regarded as a representative of family business groups in Thailand, while the CP Group has fewer family business characteristics.

However, the Central Group has recently announced a drastic restructuring of management (*Bangkok Post*, 13 October 2016; *PRCT-TK*, 17–19 October 2016). The group brought in a number of key professionals who are non-family members to assume top management positions. This is the first time the group has recruited professionals from outside to run the group's operations. Some newspapers reported that the Central Group had renounced its family-run business style as the family members by themselves could no longer manage the expanded businesses [*Than Setthakit* (hereafter *TNSK*), 15 June 2017; *Nikkei Asian Review*, 14 September 2017]. Has the Central Group, the archetypal family business group in Thailand, actually carried out a "separation of ownership and control" in conformity with Berle and Means's 1932 thesis? If, however, the Central Group still retains the basic elements of a family business, does it mean that the group is not treading a desirable path? Berle and Means (1932) categorised corporate control into five types: control through almost complete ownership, majority control, control through a legal device without majority ownership, minority control and management control. They then argued that corporate control would evolve in order from the first type—that is, control through almost complete ownership—to the fifth type—that is, management control. This suggests that a family business which belongs to the first type would shift finally to a modern corporation characterised by a separation of ownership and control as a business grows larger. Some studies have regarded family business groups in Asia, particularly conglomerates, as a backward and inferior form of enterprise. The World Bank (1998) attributed the 1997 Asian financial crisis partly to Asian-specific institutional vulnerability and criticised diversified conglomerates as being responsible for that vulnerability due to a lack of good corporate governance. But are family business groups really in a backward and inferior position compared to non-family business groups? In fact, we will see that family businesses are possibly in a superior position because of their prompt decision making and long-term goals because they are not bothered by demanding and shortsighted shareholders. The last section of this chapter discusses the possibility of family businesses contributing to public welfare in the same way as non-family-run firms.

Two Leading Business Groups in Thailand

The CP Group

Founder Family and Business Development[2]

We will start by looking at our comparator, the CP Group. The founder of the CP Group, Chia Ek Chow, emigrated from Swatow (Shantou) in southern China around 1920. He opened his store, Chia Tai, selling vegetable seeds in Bangkok's Chinatown, importing seeds from Swatow via Hong Kong, for sale not only in Thailand, but also other parts of Southeast Asia. With his younger brother, Chia Shiao Hui, on board, the business branched off into fertilizers and pesticides as well. When the founder's first and second sons, Jaran and Montri, had finished their studies in China and returned to Bangkok, they too joined their father's business. In 1953, Jaran launched an animal feed business to expand the scope of the family business, calling his company Charoen Pokphand Store. *Charoen* is a Thai word that translates to prosperity, while *pokphand* means farm produce and goods for the masses. After the Communist Party took power in China in 1949, the Chinese Government's relationship with the anti-communist Thai Government deteriorated. Thailand's government urged those of Chinese descent born in Thailand to change their Chinese names to something more Thai-sounding. Thus, the family name was changed to Jiarawanon.

Over time, their businesses became multiple companies and the Charoen Pokphand Group or CP Group was formed. As the CP Group steadily grew larger, Ek Chow's next generation (the second generation), at the initiative of Thanin, the fourth son of the founder, decided to bring in outside experts to turn the family business into a corporate organisation. On top of that, he prohibited the children of the Jiarawanon family from entering the CP Group's core business, which was agribusiness.[3] In 1969, Thanin became the president of the CP Group. In 1971, the CP Group launched a joint venture with Arbor Acres, the largest broiler breeding company in the United States, to raise chicks. The CP Group adopted a contract production system in which feed companies contracted out the raising to farmers. Under this system, the CP Group arranged funding for farmers, acting as their intermediary with banks, doing everything from providing guidance on building chicken coops to supplying feed. In 1973, the CP Group built a facility for incubating eggs and constructed a feed plant and a factory for processing broilers into meat. It also established a company for building chicken coops and another for transporting broilers. In this way, the CP Group created a vertically integrated structure that handled every step of the chicken production process within Thailand, from the upstream operation of feed supply to the downstream operation of meat processing. The same kind of vertical integration system was employed in the group's hog and shrimp farming businesses. Soon the CP Group began exporting frozen chicken, introducing rapid freezing equipment from Japan.

From the end of the 1980s until the mid-1990s, Thailand experienced rapid economic growth brought about by huge inflows of foreign direct investment (FDI). The CP Group expanded its business horizontally during this period. It moved into retail and distribution (cash-and-carry, hypermarkets, supermarkets and convenience stores), property development, telecommunications and petrochemicals. In addition, it diversified its business in China in the 1980s, extending its interests into motorbike manufacture and sales, property development (shopping centres), retail (hypermarkets), TV programme production and the pharmaceutical industry, as well as the agribusiness that the group had already started in the 1970s. In other words, the CP Group became a conglomerate characterised by the combination of many firms operating in entirely different industries within one corporate group.

However, the 1997 Asian financial crisis caused a drastic change in Thailand's industry (Phongpaichit and Baker 2008). The retail industry was no exception. Owing to financial problems, some major Thai retailers were obliged to sell off their new retail-format businesses to foreign retailers who were seeking investment opportunities in Southeast Asia (Endo 2013, 76–80). The CP Group sold most of its retail businesses, except for the convenience store business (Seven-Eleven), to foreign retail groups. The group also sold stakes in several of its non-core businesses, focusing its resources on its three core sectors—agribusiness, communications and retail.

By the mid-2000s, the CP Group had fully overcome the negative impact of the financial crisis and resumed profitable growth. It subsequently established a joint venture with SAIC Motor, China's leading automotive maker, to produce cars in Thailand, and also acquired Tops Foods, a Belgian ready-to-eat meal company, to get advanced technology for its food business. The CP Group also repurchased a cash-and-carry business (Makro) in 2013. In 2015, it formed a capital tie-up with the Itōchū Corporation, one of Japan's largest trading houses, and the Citic Group, one of China's largest State-owned conglomerates. As of 2018, the CP Group had sales of more than USD 60 billion and business bases in Southeast Asia and China to Europe and the United States. Today, the CP Group is one of the largest multinational conglomerates in Southeast Asia.

Ownership and Management Structure

The CP Group listed stocks of two of its affiliated companies on the stock market in Thailand in 1984; it was relatively early in doing so. It subsequently listed the stocks of its core companies, including Charoen Pokphand Feedmill, which was established in 1978. Because of the 1997–98 financial crisis, the group merged Charoen Pokphand Feedmill with three other affiliates——all agriculture-related companies——that had also been listed on the stock market, to create Charoen Pokphand Foods Plc. In addition, the CP Group launched new businesses during the investment boom in the late 1980s and early 90s and, thereafter, also listed the stocks of two other main group companies: True Corporation (formerly Telecom Asia) and CP ALL (formerly CP Seven-Eleven). Even though these non-financial companies were listed on the stock market, members of the founder-family and family-run companies remained their largest shareholders. The overall holdings of the family in 2019 were 54 per cent in Charoen Pokphand Foods, 36 per cent in CP ALL and 50 per cent in True Corporation.

The most important family-run company in the CP Group is the Charoen Pokphand Group (CPG). As the group's non-listed holding company, CPG controls the other companies in the CP Group and is almost entirely owned by members of the founder-family, who held an 88 per cent stake in 2015. It should be noted, however, that a certain percentage of the company's shares has been transferred to the group's senior non-family partners who had contributed much to its development (Suehiro 2006, 93, 150–1).

Table 5.1 shows the management structure of the main holding company and listed companies in the CP Group. Thanin, the group leader, took office as chairperson of the holding company, CPG, in 2015 and a majority of the board of directors in CPG were second-generation members of the Jiarawanon founding family. In 2017, there was a handover across generations at CPG, that is, at the top of the CP Group. Thanin's first son, Suphakit, and third son, Suphachai, were appointed as the group's chairperson and CEO respectively (Wannakon 2018, 24). Although non-family members now occupy an overwhelming majority on the board of directors and executive committee in the listed companies, the founding family's third generation members hold the position of chairperson in each company. This suggests that the CP Group has, on the one hand, been proactively seeking outside funds and human resources beyond the family, while on the other hand, it has been firmly keeping the most important positions, such as chairperson, within the family. In other words, the CP Group still retains some characteristics of a family business group, but is quite different from a traditional one.

Table 5.1: Management structure of the CP Group as of 2019

Name of company		Charoen Pokphand Group Co., Ltd.	Charoen Pokphand Foods Plc		CP ALL Plc		True Corporation Plc	
Category of business		Holding company	Agribusiness and food business		Retail and distribution business		Telecommunications	
Year of establishment/ year of stock listing		1976/non-listed	1978/1987		1988/2003		1990/1993	
Name of person	Relation among the Jiarawanon family	Board of directors	Board of directors	Executives committee	Board of directors	Executives committee	Board of directors	Executive committee
(Second generation)								
Jaran	s1 Ek Chow	D						
Montri	s2 Ek Chow	D						
Sumet	s3 Ek Chow	D						
Thanin	s4 Ek Chow	Chairperson						
Wulalop	s2 Shiao Hui	D						
Phongthep	s5 Shiao Hui	D	Vice Chairperson					
Prasoet Phungkuman	d1 Shiao Hui's husband	D						
(Third generation)								
Suphakir	s1 Thanin		Chairperson		Chairperson			
Narong	s2 Thanin		D		D		D	
Suphachai	s3 Thanin		Vice Chairperson		Vice Chairperson		Chairperson	CEO

(cont'd overleaf)

Table 5.1 (cont'd)

Name of company		Charoen Pokphand Group Co., Ltd.	Charoen Pokphand Foods Plc		CP ALL Plc		True Corporation Plc	
Category of business		Holding company	Agribusiness and food business		Retail and distribution business		Telecommunications	
Year of establishment/ year of stock listing		1976/non-listed	1978/1987		1988/2003		1990/1993	
Name of person	Relation among the Jiarawanon family	Board of directors	Board of directors	Executives committee	Board of directors	Executives committee	Board of directors	Executive committee
Chatchawan	s3 Sumet						D	
Kachorn	a third-generation member of founder-family							D
Family's sub total		7	3	0	3	0	3	2
Non-family		4	12	10	12	9	13	14
Total		11	15	10	15	9	16	16

Note: The data of Charoen Pokphand Group Co., Ltd. is of 2015.
"D" means director.
Ek Chow is the founder of the CP Group. Thanin is the fourth son of Ek Chow, and Shiao Hui is Ek Chow's younger brother.
"s1", "s2" and "d1" mean the first son, second son and first daughter, respectively.
Charoen Pokphand Foods' formaer name was Charoen Pokphand Feedmill.
True Corporation's former name was Telecom Asia Corporation.
Sufficient data on Phongthep is not available; Kachorn's kinship within the family is unknown.
Source: CP Group's 2019 directors list of the non-listed company and annual reports of the listed companies.

The Central Group

Founder Family and Business Development[4]

The founder of the Central Group, Tiang Jirathiwat (Chirathivat), emigrated from Hainan Island in southern China at the end of the 1920s. Tiang and his first son, Samrit, established a small shop named Central Trading in Bangkok for import and sales business in 1947. In 1956, they opened their first department store—Central Department Store—in Chinatown, at the time an emerging commercial district in Bangkok. It was the first department store in Thailand but quite different from those seen today. In 1964, Daimaru, a leading Japanese department store chain, opened an overseas branch in Bangkok and introduced the modern style of management to Thailand's retail industry. Central Department Store adopted this style to evolve into a modern department store. In 1972, the Central Group established the Central Garment Factory to manufacture various branded garments for Central Department Store branches, with the aim of dealing with the rise of economic nationalism and participating in the ongoing movement against foreign goods.

Tiang had 26 children from his three marriages.[5] He attached great importance to his descendants' education, particularly stressing on English and retail-related practical branches of learning. After Tiang's death in 1968, Samrit took over as the leader and chairperson of the group. Under Samrit's leadership, the Central Group endeavored to expand its department store business. In 1973, it opened its flagship Chit Lom branch and in 1983, it opened Central Plaza Lat Phrao, its first large-scale commercial facility (or shopping centre) at a suburban location in Bangkok. With the success of this project, the Central Group established three new business divisions: hotel and resorts, fast food and real estate development. By adding these three divisions to the two existing ones of retail and manufacturing and wholesale, the group now had five business divisions. Real estate development, in particular shopping centre development, was closely related to the department store business. After, whenever the property development division opened a new Central Plaza shopping centre, it always included a branch of the group's department store chain. The fast food business was also regarded as an integral part of the shopping centres; the hotel and resort business contributed to the group's retail business as well because tourists, including foreigners, were important customers. Despite this diversification, the group continued to devote itself to the expansion of retail-related businesses. In other words, the group did not deviate from its traditional core business, making it very different from the CP Group's pursuit of a conglomerate-type development.

In 1989, Wanchai, the second son of the founder (Tiang), succeeded Samrit after the latter faced health problems. Under the leadership of Wanchai, the Central Group divided the responsibility for its businesses among the second generation of the founder-family as follows: Sutthichat, the fifth son, was responsible for the retail business; Sutthitham, the eighth son, handled the real estate development business, focusing mainly on commercial complex development; Sutthikiat, the fourth son, oversaw the hotel and resort business, as well as the fast food business; and Sutthisak, the seventh son, took on the manufacturing and wholesale businesses. This clear division indicated that the group had made a drastic shift from the traditional leader-led management system to a professional management system (Saengthongkham et al. 2003, 216). The earlier professional managers were, however, all members of the founder-family who had acquired a professional education in Thailand and/or abroad, and when it came to decision making, the CEOs of the five business divisions regularly discussed important matters at the group board or the family council. (The next section explains this in greater detail).

The investment boom and rapid economic growth in Thailand from the end of the 1980s until the mid-1990s were followed by a consumption boom. This in turn stimulated competition to expand the retail business. In 1995, the Central Group effectively took over the Robinson Department Store, its former rival in Thailand's department store sector. On top of that, the Central Group, as well as the CP Group, rapidly developed various kinds of modern retail businesses, such as discount stores, hypermarkets, supermarkets, convenience stores and specialty stores; some of these were launched as joint ventures with foreign partners. The expansion of their business, as well as the successive introduction of new retail formats caused fierce competition between the Central Group and CP Group (Endo 2013, 40–3).

During the 1997 Asian financial crisis, many businesses in Thailand were severely affected. However, except for its Robinson Department Store,[6] the Central Group was relatively less affected owing to its conservative corporate behaviour. The Central Group's diversification strategy was based on "economies of scope". It was also very conservative in raising funds.[7] Nevertheless, in the post-crisis period, the Central Group decided to sell off to its foreign partners all or most of the shares it held in the hypermarket, supermarket and convenience store businesses, which were not the traditional businesses of the group. On the other hand, the Central Group firmly maintained its traditional core business—Central Department Store—and its related businesses, including the commercial complex development business. After recovering from the crisis, the Central Group repurchased shares in the supermarket and convenience store businesses in 2004 and 2012 respectively. In 2017, the group chalked sales of more than USD 10 billion (*Nikkei Asia*, 5 March 2018).

Ownership and Management Structure

The Central Group has three main holding companies: Harng Central Department Store Co., Ltd. (HCDS), Central Retail Corporation (CRC), and Central Holding Co., Ltd. All of these have been exclusively owned by the members of the founder-family. The first two companies are the holding companies of the retail business division, which is the core of the Central Group. Although HCDS had been a non-financial company since its establishment, and operated some branches of the Central Department Store chain, it was reorganised together with Central Department Store Co. Ltd. as a holding company in 1998. The reorganisation resulted from the incorporation of the Robinson Department Store in 1998, its former competitor in the department store industry. Simultaneously, the Central Group also established another holding company, CRC, to alleviate possible difficulties from the incorporation (Endo 2002, 275). Among the the group's various department store businesses, only Robinson Department Store had been a public limited company listed on the Stock Exchange of Thailand, that was until 2019.[8] Central Department Store, the founder-family's traditional core business, has been exclusively owned by the Jirathiwat family. However, even the Robinson Department Store eventually came to be owned by the family in 2018, holding a 62 per cent stake.

The manufacturing and wholesale business (Central Marketing Group) is also owned exclusively by the Jirathiwat family. The other divisions of the group—that is, the real estate development business, including commercial complex development (Central Pattana Plc), the hotel and resort business (Central Plaza Hotel Plc), and the fast food and restaurant business (Central Restaurants Group)—are also ultimately owned by the family, with individuals and the group's holding companies having a majority shareholding, even though Central Pattana and Central Plaza Hotel are listed companies.[9]

The shares of the group's holding companies have been transferred across the different generations of the Jirathiwat family. HCDS, the most important holding company of the Central Group, in terms of its position in the group's business structure, as well as the amount of registered capital, is one example. In 1986, the group's then chairperson, Samrit, and the second chairperson, Wanchai, respectively held 14 and 10 per cent of HCDS shares; these percentages were much higher than those held by other family members. However, HCDS was at that time a non-financial company. In 1999, when HCDS was reorganised purely as a holding company, Sutthichai, who was appointed as the first group CEO, personally held more than 20 per cent of HCDS shares, giving him a much higher percentage of shareholding than other members. However, in 2013, when the Jirathiwat family's third-generation succeeded to top management, the shares of HCDS seemed to become more evenly held among the family members than before. This shows that the concentration of shareholding among specific individuals was no longer observed, even though the holding company continued to be owned exclusively by the founder-family. In addition, the second-generation of the family still held some shares, resulting in the total number of shareholders increasing to 63 in 2015. Thus, unlike the situation that prevailed during the leadership of the founder and the second chairperson, the Central Group now seems to be keen on avoiding an excessive concentration of power in the hands of the group's chairperson.

Table 5.2 lists the directors of the Central Group's main non-listed companies. As mentioned above, HCDS, CRC and Central Holding, the main holding companies of the Central Group, have been exclusively owned by the Jirathiwat family. Similarly, all or most of the board directors of the three holding companies in 2015 were members of the founder-family. This is also true of Central Department Store, the most important non-financial company of the Central Group. Family members continue their exclusive hold over board director positions, as well as shares at the Central Department Store.

Table 5.2: List of directors of the main non-listed companies of the Central Group as of 2015

Name of company	Relation among the Jirathiwat family	HCDS	CRC	Central Holding	Central Department Store
Category of business		Holding company	Holding company	Holding company	Department store
(Second generation)					
Sutthiphon	s3 Tiang	D			D
Sutthikiat	s4 Tiang	D	D		D
Sutthichat	s5 Tiang			D	D
Sutthichai	s6 Tiang	D	D	D	D
Sutthisak	s7 Tiang	D	D		
Sutthitham	s8 Tiang	D	D	D	
Sutthilak	s11 Tiang	D	D	D	D
Sukanya	d5 Tiang	D			D
Jariya	d12 Tiang	D		D	D
(Third generation)					
Kriangsak	s1 Samrit				D
Parin	s2 Samrit	D	D	D	D
Thot	s3 Samrit	D	CEO	D	D
Yuwadi	d3 Samrit				CEO

Table 5.2 (*cont'd*)

Name of company	Relation among the Jirathiwat family	HCDS	CRC	Central Holding	Central Department Store
Category of business		Holding company	Holding company	Holding company	Department store
Nitsini	d5 Samrit				D
Siriket	d6 Samrit				D
Wat	s1 Wanchai				D
Narongrit	s1 Sutthiphon	D	D	D	D
Sukunya	d1 Mukda	D	D	D	D
Family's sub total		12	9	9	16
(Non-family)		0	1	0	0
Total		12	10	9	16

Note: "D" means director.
      Tiang is the founder of the Central Group. Samrit is the first son of Tiang, Wanchai the secon, Sutthiphon the third and Mukda the second daughter.
      "s1", "s2", "d1" and "d2" mean the first son, second son, first daughter and second daughter, respectively.
Source: The Central Group's 2015 directors lists of the non-listed companies.

Table 5.2 highlights three other interesting facts. First, many second-generation family members remain directors of the companies though third-generation family members have taken initiative in running Central Department Store, by virtue of being in the executive committee. This allocation of roles among family members preserves its special characteristics as a family business. Second, gender and seniority within the same generation are not always accorded top priority. Thot, the CEO of CRC, is the third son of Samrit and Yuwadi; the CEO of Central Department Store is the third daughter of Samrit.[10] Third, no son-in-law or daughter-in-law has been included in this list, or even in the shareholders list. This suggests that the Central Group is looking to establish a kind of competition—based on meritocracy—between the family members, although it resolutely remains a family-run business.[11]

Similar findings can to some extent be observed in the group's listed companies. According to Table 5.3 (page 113), as of 2019, the Jirathiwat family has a majority of the Board in Central Pattana Plc (property development) and Central Plaza Hotel Plc (hotel and resort, and fast food and restaurant), though it had only one-third of the Board in Robinson Department Store Plc. This may be due to the fact that Robinson Department Store was taken over from a competitor which had not been a family business. Even here, though, the

Jirathiwat family occupies important positions, particularly that of chairperson and the like.

In the listed companies, the board of directors is organisationally separated from the executive and management committees. The members of the founder-family have a majority of the Board, while posts on the executive and management committees are more evenly distributed between family members and non-family members. This suggests that the group's listed companies seek to have a separation of responsibilities, as well as a balance of power in their operations. However, the separation is actually imperfect because family members also assume important positions in management.

Comparative Analysis

As mentioned above, the CP Group has three distinguishing features. First, while the CP Group has expanded its business into areas in the agroindustry since its establishment, it has also diversified into non-related areas as well. It has thus adopted a conglomerate style of diversification. Second, the group has proactively not only introduced new technology and know-hows, but also brought in professional managers from outside whenever it lacked managerial resources. Third, the group has listed even its core businesses on the stock market. In other words, the CP Group seems to have relatively fewer characteristics of being traditional family businesses. The Central Group differs greatly from the CP Group in several respects. First, retail has remained the core business of this group since its establishment: the group's diversification has been into areas in retail-related businesses. In other words, the group has so far adopted a non-conglomerate diversification style. Second, the group has never listed its main business—Central Department Store—on the stock market. Third, the top management of its main companies has been controlled almost completely by family members. It can be said, therefore, that the Central Group has been more representative of Thailand's family business groups.

However, the two groups have some points in common. In both cases, their main holding companies are non-listed companies that are exclusively (or almost exclusively) owned by the members of the founder-family.[12] These companies are at the apex of each group and the chairperson of each company is a member of the founder-family. Moreover, even in the listed companies of the two groups, the ultimate owners are the founder-families. Thus, the CP Group and the Central Group still maintain the characteristics of a family business in some respects or another.

Table 5.3: Management structure of the listed companies of the Central Group as of 2019

Name of company		Central Pattana Plc			Central Plaza Hotel Plc		Robinson Department Store Plc	
Category of business		Property development			Hotel and restaurant		Department store	
Year of establishment/ year of stock listing		1980/1995			1983/1990		1979/1992	
Name of person	Relation among the Jirathiwat family	Board of directors	Executive committee	Management committee	Board of directors	Executives of management group	Board of directors	Executive committee
(Second generation)								
Suthikiat	s4 Tiang	D			Chairperson			
Sutthichat	s5 Tiang							
Suthichai	s6 Tiang	Chairperson	Chairperson		Vice Chairperson			
Suthisak	s7 Tiang	D	D		D		Chairperson	
Sutthitham	s8 Tiang	D	D		D	D	Vice Chairperson	Chairperson
Sutthiphak	s13 Tiang			SEVP		SEVP		
Suphattra	d6 Tiang							
Wanlaya	d10 Tiang			Deputy CEO				
Natthaya	d11 Tiang			EVP				
(Third generation)								
Parin	s2 Samrit	D	D		D	D	D	D
Yuwadi	d3 Samrit						D	D
Kopchai	s2 Wanchai	D						
Thirayut	s2 Surthikiat				D	CEO		

(cont'd overleaf)

Table 5.3 (*cont'd*)

Name of company		Central Pattana Plc			Central Plaza Hotel Plc		Robinson Department Store Plc	
Category of business		Property development			Hotel and restaurant		Department store	
Year of establishment/ year of stock listing		1980/1995			1983/1990		1979/1992	
Name of person	Relation among the Jirathiwat family	Board of directors	Executive committee	Management committee	Board of directors	Executives of management group	Board of directors	Executive committee
Thirakiat	s3 Sutthikiat					EVP		
Family's sub total		6	5	3	6	5	4	3
Non-family		5	0	6	5	11	7	3
Total		11	5	9	11	16	11	6

Note: The data of Robinson Department Store is of 2018.

"D" means director.

SEVP and EVP mean Senior Executive Vice President and Executive Vice President, respectively.

CEO and president of Central Pattana is a non-family member.

President of Robinson Department Store is a non-family member.

Tiang is the founder of the Central Group. Samrit is the first son of Tiang, Wanchai the second and Mukda the second daughter.

"s1", "s2", "d1" and "d2" mean the first son, second son, first daughter and second daughter, respectively.

Source: Central Group's 2019 annual reports of the listed companies

Will the Central Group become a Non-family Business?

Overseas Expansion and E-commerce

Some external and internal events could cause the Central Group to undergo a major transformation. The external events relate to overseas expansion and new businesses, while the internal ones pertain to a drastic change in top management. In 2013, Sutthichai, the sixth son of the founder, Tiang, succeeded Wanchai as the chairperson of the Central Group. Thot, the third son of Samrit, was appointed as president of the group. Under Thot's leadership, the Central Group has proactively expanded its retail business overseas. It purchased long-established department stores in large European cities: these include La Rinascente in Milan and Rome, Italy, Illum in Copenhagen, Denmark, and in Germany, KaDeWe in Berlin, Alsterhaus in Hamburg and Oberpollinger in Munich. The Central Group has also endeavoured to invest in neighbouring countries in expectation of market expansion in the ASEAN Economic Community established at the end of 2015. As a result, overseas business accounted for 30 per cent of the Central Group's total sales in 2015 (*Bangkok Post*, 13 October 2016).

Unlike a manufacturer, a retailer needs to be deeply familiar with the consumer market of the country in which it invests. It will thus inevitably be confronted with greater difficulties in overseas business. A quick glance at the many cases of world-class retail firms failing to achieve success in emerging markets makes this clear. Even though the Central Group has so far built an overwhelming advantage in Thailand's retail industry, it is unlikely to always be successful in foreign markets. Investing in European countries, as well as in neighbouring countries in Asia, will be a big challenge for the Central Group. Moreover, the Central Group is enthusiastic about e-commerce (EC) and has successively incorporated EC businesses, such as online shopping and an online payment system into the group's retail business division. The Central Group also established a joint venture with JD.com, one of the largest EC companies in China, in 2017. As it was integrating its online and offline channels into a single "omni-channel", the Central Group was also building an online network of world-class department stores in European cities, as well as its flagship branch, Central Department Store, in Bangkok. The fact that the new information and communications technology (ICT) and online businesses are very different from the group's traditional business makes these a challenging proposition for the Central Group.

Separation of Ownership and Control?

According to various Thai newspapers, the Central Group's management reform in 2016 was an epochal one in its business history. This was done to cope with globalisation, as well as digitalisation. Thot Jirathiwat, CEO of the Central Group, in his interviews with Thai newspapers, said the following:

> Online marketing is very important. Our 70-year expertise in the Thai retail business is not applicable to the changing retail industry today. We have to learn many new things to overcome the challenges in the next decade. (*Bangkok Post*, 2 March 2017)
>
> …
>
> Electronic commerce is playing an increasingly important role at present. We need to renovate our mindset by independence from successes experienced in the past. We need to newly learn everything of online business [from other people] (*PRCT-TK*, 6–8 November 2017).

Along with the organisational transformation in 2016, the Central Group invited several non-family professional managers and experts to join the group's top management (*TNSK*, 25 September 2016). With the new top management, Thot and non-family professional managers have been cooperating with one another to build the most efficient digital platform in Thailand. Does this mean that the family-business style of the Central Group has evolved into that of a modern business group, in which ownership and management are clearly separated?

A comparison of the ownership and management structures in 2015 and 2019 would lead to a better understanding of the transformation. No change can be seen in the ownership structure of the group's main companies, irrespective of their listing status. Thus, in 2019, the non-listed holding companies were still exclusively owned by founder-family members, while around 50 per cent of the listed companies' shares were held by members of the founder-family and/or the family holding companies. Likewise, little change can be found in the composition of the senior management of the group's companies as of 2019. This holds true both of the boards of directors and of the executive and management committees of the listed companies. By contrast, a noteworthy change can be observed in the Central Group's board of directors and Central Group's executive board, as shown in the next section.

Family Council and the Group Board

The Central Group's board of directors, or the group board, originated from the family council established around 1990, under the leadership of Wanchai, the then group leader; it was in fact based on an idea of Samrit, Wanchai's predecessor and older brother.[13] The family council consisted of 10 members, who were elected from among the Jirathiwat family; however, 2 non-family professional managers were invited as advisers. The term of office of the council was 4 years and the group leader assumed the position of chairperson. The purpose of the family council was to constitute the highest decision-making body of the group, as well as to clearly divide the business divisions among the family members (Saengthongkham et al. 2003, 92–4). The family council required each business sector within the group to prepare an annual report for the council.[14] However, there was an almost complete overlap of family council members with representatives of the board of directors and the executive and management committees in each business division. Although the Central Group was divided into several business divisions in adopting a policy to modernise the business group, the ultimate decision-making authority still resided with several leading members of the family. Therefore, the family council seemed to exist for the sake of "maintenance of ownership and control" rather than the "separation of ownership and control". The family council subsequently developed into the group board and group executive board. After a drastic reform in 2016, the Central Group invited five professional managers from outside to join the group's executive board to handle overseas investment and digitalisation (*PRCT-TK*, 17–19 October 2016).

The following explanation by one of the third-generation members of the family demonstrates that both the group board and group executive board play a crucial role in the Central Group:

> The group board of directors is a new organisation that has taken over and intensified the function of the family council. The group board consists of only the members of the founder-family, and most are from its second generation. The present chairperson is Mr Sutthichai, who is the group leader. Under the supervision of the group board, we have the group executive board as the apex of executive and management body of the group. The group executive board is virtually the highest decision-making body of the group. Its meeting is held at least once a month. Although the present group executive board consists of an almost equal number of family members and non-family professional managers, most of the important positions, including that of the CEO, are occupied by the family members, particularly those from the third generation. The CEO has control over the appointment of non-family members.[15]

This suggests that the Central Group still firmly maintains itself as a family business, even after its "epoch-making management reform". Thus, it can be said that the newspaper reports have overestimated the change.

Is the Central Group Treading the Right Path?

As stated in the preceding section, the Central Group has been carrying out various management reforms since 1990 to regulate the group businesses that began diversifying in the 1980s. As part of the reforms, the Central Group listed its affiliated companies on the stock exchange. Simultaneously, the group achieved a functional separation of the board of directors from the executive boards of the listed companies. The Central Group also established the group board and group executive board to regulate the group's diversified businesses. These were new organisations that replaced the previous family council; further, unlike the unitary management system of the family council, they were functionally separated. In addition, the Central Group has also more recently invited non-family professional managers to join the group executive board. At first glance, the Central Group, which used to be representative of Thailand's family business groups, seems to have been transforming itself into the "managerial enterprise" first conceptualised by Chandler (1990). However, founder-family members still occupy the most important positions, including that of chairperson, directors of the group board and CEO of the group executive board. Although non-family professional managers do play an important role, it seems to be complementary. At most, it can be said that the Central Group aims to build a system based on the cooperation between the founder-family managers and non-family professional managers, instead of replacing all managers of the former type with the latter. Besides, the leading members of the founder-family concurrently hold important positions in several affiliated companies and/or directorship and executive officer posts within the same company.

According to Williamson (1975, 148), "the multidivisional structure is thoroughly corrupted when the general management involves itself in the operating affairs of the divisions in an extensive and continuing way" and "the separation between strategic and operating issues is sacrificed in the process". We must therefore ask whether the structure at the Central Group, based on overlapping positions, will inevitably bring about a negative result for the group business. Nevertheless, the steady growth of the Central Group suggests that its structure will not necessarily cause the group organisation to fall into functional disorder. An efficient monitoring system could avoid any structure-associated problems. In this respect, the present group board and group executive board can play a critical role, as did the previous family council, by making use of the community mechanism of cooperation that is embedded in a family. As explained in the preceding section, the Central Group has secured a certain kind of competition based on meritocracy among the family members, which ensures a relatively inexpensive and efficient monitoring system, thereby enabling the group to save on agency costs. It also seems likely that as long as the family elements work well, it is possible for a family business group to run the business from a long-term perspective, as well as to achieve prompt decision making without being influenced by short-term profit-oriented shareholders. This can be a positive aspect of a family business. However, we need to ask whether the persistence of family business groups can be compatible with the interests of stakeholders, in the broad sense as well as with regards to public benefit.

Family Business and Corporate Social Responsibility (CSR)

Family Business and CSR

CSR has become a key concept in considering relationships between the corporation and society. "While many believe CSR is a Western invention, there is ample evidence that CSR in developing countries draws strongly on deep-rooted indigenous cultural traditions of philanthropy, business ethics, and community embeddedness" (Visser 2008, 480–1). Robertson (2009) raised the question of the nature of CSR in different countries, as well as the factors external to the firm that influence CSR. Based on the integrative social contract theory, Robertson undertook a comparative study covering Singapore, Turkey and Ethiopia. In the analysis, she paid attention to four institutional factors: firm ownership structure, corporate governance, openness of the economy to international investment and the role of civil society. Robertson's case study of the three countries showed that Turkey's business situation was similar to that of Thailand, particularly in firm ownership structure and corporate governance. In Turkey, a clear separation of ownership and control could not be observed in the vast majority of large-scale firms, in which the controlling shareholder was a holding company controlled by a family. In Robertson's words, "This structure of family ownership has a significant effect on CSR in Turkey. Turkey's present model of CSR as corporate philanthropy seems well-suited to the family ownership structure" (Robertson 2009, 622). She went on to argue that as a result, current CSR activities in Turkey were less organised/planned and were very much individual-based.

However, it is also possible for a family business group to work hard on CSR activities. Currently, there are many family business groups in Thailand that emphasise CSR—both the CP Group and Central Group are examples of this.[16] This behaviour may be due to the fact that both groups have affiliated companies listed on the stock exchange, and a public limited company needs to consider the interests of its shareholders. However, another fact stated previously that needs to be considered here is that a significant percentage of the total shares of those listed companies is still held by the founder-family, and both groups still remain family businesses. Despite being family businesses, why then do these groups proactively engage in CSR activities? At least two factors should be considered in the context of Thailand—the internationalisation of family businesses and long-term orientation for economic gain. Internationalisation is a relatively new phenomenon for Thailand's family businesses. Thailand's family business groups, such as the CP Group and the Central Group, have established many joint ventures with foreign partners and, more recently, have proactively invested overseas. These experiences are conducive to the adoption of CSR. It is the latter, however, that is fundamentally more important for family businesses. Family business groups are much less influenced by shareholders seeking short-term profits and have a higher affinity for long-term economic gain. Thus, they can more easily engage in non-profitable activities without having to consider short-term returns. Further, even family business groups must be increasingly responsive to stakeholders in a broader sense because civil society is growing in Thailand. They have to attach greater importance to appealing to stakeholders and preserving a good reputation in society to not only achieve long-term gain but also continue to exist as a family business.

The Central Group's CSR Activities

According to the former leader of the Central Group, Samrit:

> Our success grew out of our determination to bring Thailand into the modern world. We are committed to contributing to its prosperity and enhancing the quality of life of its people (Central Group n.d.).

Acting on this idea, the Central Group has practiced various kinds of CSR activities. In this section, I will focus on the group's rural community-based business development project, which is one of its large-scale CSR activity. The Central Group set up the Central Community Development Volunteers project in 2012, in line with the Thai Government's policy on public-private partnerships (PPPs) to promote community development and growth. According to Thot, a total of 123 communities in 49 provinces, making more than 1,500 products, have been able to realise a combined income of more than THB 637 million (about USD 18 million) in the 7 years since the start of the project (*PRCT-TK*, 13 February 2017).

The "Green Market" project in Phetchabun Province in northeast Thailand is a representative example. The Central Group supported the establishment of four agricultural cooperatives in the province—where none had existed before—and the construction of an air-conditioned packing house.[17] The Central Group has also become involved in product-development planning for every production process of the cooperatives. In concrete terms, this includes the skill development of farmers by providing knowledge on organic farming, farm management, crop selection based on the soil in a given area and crop planning in line with market demand, as well as creating a production-region brand and arranging distribution through branches of the group's supermarket chain (*The Nation*, 4 February 2017). The Central Group has also encouraged farmers to apply for Good Agricultural Practice (GAP) certification, as well as established farmer's markets in the group's shopping centers, where farmers can directly sell their produce.[18]

The vice president of Central Food Retail, a Central Group affiliate operating a nationwide supermarket chain, explains this step as follows:

> All these projects are nonprofitable for the Central Group. Farmers in the Green Market project are allowed to sell their produce to anyone. We have no trading contracts. Yet, if we support the establishment of agricultural cooperatives, the farmers can be our trading partners, which might be beneficial to our company in the long term.[19]

Up to now, the involvement of Thai supermarket chains in the production-distribution process for fresh produce has not been effective in making profit (Endo 2014). Thus, the Central Group practises these CSR activities with the objective of long-term economic gain rather than short-term profit. The CEO of the Central Group has also mentioned the aim of creating a Thai hub for toxin-free vegetables in the near future by comprehensively developing farm produce (*The Nation*, 4 February 2017). This long-term gain can benefit not only the Central Group and farmers, but also other stakeholders in a broader sense, because the provision of safer vegetables for the consumer market ultimately improves their quality of life. Those nonprofitable activities can be more smoothly carried out from the viewpoint of long-term gain, and in this respect, family business groups enjoy an advantage.

Conclusion

The preceding empirical analysis leads us to the following conclusions. First, the Central Group carried out one of the most epochal management reforms in the group's business history in 2016. This was to cope with globalisation as well as digitalisation—that is, a full-scale international expansion of the business and the incorporation of ICT and online businesses; the group has not been very open about either of these in the past. Along with its organisational revamp, the Central Group invited several non-family professional managers to join the top management of the group. Second—judging from the analysis of the details of the group's management structure—we find that the Central Group seems to be aimed toward building a system based on the cooperation between the founder-family and non-family managers, instead of replacing the former with the latter. Third, the ownership structure of the Central Group remains unchanged. The non-listed holding companies are still exclusively owned by the members of the founder-family, and even the public listed companies are ultimately controlled by the family through majority shareholding. Considered together, these three points indicate that the Central Group has no intention of renouncing its family-business style. In fact, the Central Group should be regarded as having transformed itself into the "hybrid-type" family business group proposed by Suehiro (2006).[20] In other words, not all family businesses in Thailand will transform into a modern-style firm or business group characterised by a complete separation of ownership and control, as conceptualised by Berle and Means (1932). One important institution that enabled the Central Group to maintain its organisation, even in the age of globalisation and digitalisation, was possibly the Jirathiwat family council and—in the past and in current times— the Central Group's current board of directors and executive board.

Theory suggests that an extensive and continuing involvement of the Board in the executive and management committees should lead to the malfunctioning of the organisation (Williamson 1975, 148–50), and that the separation between strategic and operating issues is of critical importance. So, does the family-led group board system inevitably mean a negative result for the Central Group? In fact, the highly stable business performance of the group, even after the 1997 crisis suggests that this system has some positive features. Family business groups can naturally manage the business from a long-term perspective because the directors are not influenced by shareholders seeking short-term profit. Strong leadership by the chairperson enables the businesses to make rapid decisions and carry out drastic reforms. It is true that any family business group is likely to have to confront difficulties arising from the lack of managerial resources, particularly human resources, as it expands its businesses. Rapid globalisation and technological evolution, such as digitalisation, may also make the situation of a family business much more precarious. Judging from the analysis above, however, it appears that the Central Group's family-led group board system can effectively reduce these difficulties.

The Central Group's CSR initiative, described in the preceding section, indicates that family business groups can also more smoothly engage in nonprofitable activities without considering short-term returns. They are much less influenced by shareholders seeking short-term profit; thus, they have a higher affinity for long-term economic gain. For this reason, family businesses can serve the interests of their owners and shareholders, besides contributing to the broader development of the economy and society. This suggests that there is a possible relationship between the ideas of Shibusawa and the role of family businesses in Thailand. Shibusawa's idea of *gapponshugi* has been defined as the principle of developing a business by assembling the best possible people and funding to achieve the mission and aim of pursuing public good (Kikkawa 2017, 3). In sharp contrast with this principle, modern, large-scale firms or managerial enterprises are obliged to focus on increasing corporate value by listing the firm on the stock market. The increased profit is divided only among the shareholders who are usually oriented towards short-term profits. Naturally, such a modern joint-stock company system may more easily conflict with the practice of ensuring public good advocated by Shibusawa. In contrast, family business groups can more smoothly carry out the aim of pursuing a social contribution from a long-term perspective. The analysis in this chapter suggests that the Central Group is a good example of this.

Notes

[1] That is, business groups in which a specific family (in many cases, a founder-family) has exclusive control in terms of ownership and management over the diversified businesses; at least one of which has an oligopolistic status within its business sector.

[2] Except where cited otherwise, information on the CP Group in this section is based on Wannakon (2018), Sapphaibun (2000) and Jiarawanon (2016).

[3] In 2019, however, Thanin's first son and third son respectively assumed the office of chairperson and vice chairperson of CPF Plc, the group's core agribusiness, in accordance with his resignation from the chairmanship (Charoen Pokphand Foods Plc 2020).

[4] Except where cited otherwise, information on the Central Group in this section is based on Jirathiwat (1992), Sapphaibun (2000) and Saengthongkham et al. (2003).

[5] Tiang had five sons and three daughters with his first wife, who migrated with him from China. After her death, he had eight sons and five daughters with his second wife, who was of Chinese-Thai heritage. After the second wife's death, he had one son and four daughters with his third wife, who was Thai.

[6] Robinson Department Store fell into a state of insolvency owing to a heavy currency exchange loss.

[7] The Central Group depended mainly on its subsidiaries and affiliated companies for financing. When borrowing money from banks and finance companies, it had a very conservative attitude towards foreign currency borrowing, in marked contrast to the approach of many other Thai companies and business groups during the investment boom (Endo 2002, 290–1).

[8] CRC made a tender for all securities of Robinson Department Store Plc (Robinsons Plc) and delisted the shares of Robinsons Plc from being a listed company on the Stock Exchange of Thailand in December 2019 (Central Retail Corporation Plc 2020).

[9] Central Holding Co., Ltd., and members of the Jirathiwat family altogether hold approximately 54 per cent of the total shares in Central Pattana Plc and 66 per cent of shares in Central Plaza Hotel Plc respectively.

[10] Thot has been playing a leading role as the CEO of CRC since 2002 (Phujatkan Rai-duan 2004).

[11] The internal competition system is backed by the Jirathiwat Family Constitution to prevent possible conflicts among the family members (Saengthongkham et al. 2003, 166–7).

[12] Although CRC, one of the Central Group's main holding companies, converted into a public company limited in February 2020, HCDS, another main holding company of the group, remains the largest shareholder of CRC. Moreover, the majority of the positions on the board of directors is held by the founder-family members (Central Retail Corporation Plc 2020).

[13] The strong family ties among members of the Central Group led to the establishment of the family council. One of the means of promoting these ties can be observed in their choice of residences. Although all the family members were not engaged in their family businesses, most of them lived together at mainly four locations in Bangkok (Saengthongkham et al. 2003, 169–72). This "community-style of living" was regulated as an article of the Jirathiwat Family Rule that was made under the leadership of Samrit, who succeeded the founder (Jirathiwat 1992, 114–5).

[14] Author's interview (in collaboration with Akira Suehiro) with Mr Sutthiphan Jirathiwat, one of the founder-family's second generation, 7 August 2000, Bangkok, Thailand.

[15] Author's interview with Mr Phong Sakuntanak, one of the founder-family's third generation, 7 August 2018, Nonthaburi, Thailand.

[16] They had already been practicing certain social responsibility activities before the CSR concept was introduced into Thai society. See for example, Jirathiwat (1992), Sapphaibun (2011) and Jiarawanon (2016). In this respect, the founder's philosophy and the tradition of business ethics should be further studied.

[17] Author's interview with Mr Somnuk Yotdamnoen, Vice President (in charge of buying produce), Central Food Retail Co., Ltd., 15 August 2018, Nonthaburi, Thailand.

[18] Ibid.

[19] Author's interview with Somuk Yotdamnoen, 15 August 2018, Nonthaburi, Thailand.

[20] Suehiro (2006, 295–9) argued on the evolution of Thai family business groups as follows: most of the family business groups in Thailand have not shifted to a managerial enterprise but to a hybrid-type one, in which the founder-family internally promoted staff, and professional managers recruited from the outside are combined for the purpose of cooperation, while shareholding is decentralised.

References

Berle, Adolf A. Jr. and Gardiner C. Means. 1932. *The Modern Corporation and Private Property*. New York: Palgrave Macmillan.

Central Group. n.d. "Central Group". Accessed 15 May 2024. https://www.centralgroup.com/en/home

Central Pattana Plc (CPN). *Central Pattana Plc Annual Report*. Bangkok, Thailand, CPN, published annually.

Central Plaza Hotel Plc. *Central Plaza Hotel Plc Annual Report*. Bangkok, Thailand, Central Plaza Hotel, published annually.

Central Retail Corporation Plc (CRC). *Central Retail Annual Report*. Bangkok, Thailand, CRC, 2020.

Chandler, Alfred D. Jr. 1990. *Scale and Scope: The Dynamics of Industrial Capitalism*. Massachusetts: Harvard University Press.

Charoen Pokphand Foods Plc (CPF). *Charoen Pokphand Foods Plc Annual Report.* Bangkok, Thailand, CPF, published annually.

Colpan, Asli M. and Geoffrey Jones. 2020. "Business, Ethics and Institutions: The Evolution of Turkish Capitalism in a Comparative Perspective". In *Business, Ethics and Institutions: The Evolution of Turkish Capitalism in Global Perspectives,* ed. Asli M. Colpan and Geoffrey Jones. London: Routledge.

CP ALL Plc. *CP ALL Plc Annual Report.* Bangkok, Thailand, CP ALL, published annually.

Endo, Gen. 2002. "Kouri-gyō no Kōzō Henka to Ryūtsū Shihon no Saihen: Gaishi no Taitō to Sentoraru Gurūpu no Taiō" [Structural Change in the Retail Industry and Reorganization of the Distribution Business: The Rise of Foreign Capital and Restructuring of the Central Group]. In *Tai no Seido Kaikaku to Kigyō Saihen: Kiki kara Saiken e* [Institutional Reform and Corporate Restructuring in Thailand: From Crisis to Recovery], ed. Akira Suehiro, 255–312. Chiba: Institute of Developing Economies (IDE).

――――――. 2013. *Diversifying Retail and Distribution in Thailand.* Chiang Mai: Silkworm Books.

――――――. 2014. "The Key Role of Intermediaries in Thailand's Fresh Food Distribution System". *The International Review of Retail, Distribution and Consumer Research* 24 (5): 544–63.

Fridenson, Patrick and Takeo Kikkawa, ed. 2017. *Ethical Capitalism: Shibusawa Eiichi and Business Leadership in Global Perspective.* Toronto: University of Toronto Press.

Hayami, Yujiro. 2001. *Development Economics: From the Poverty to the Wealth of Nations.* Second edition. Oxford: Oxford University Press.

Jiarawanon, Thanin. 2016. "My Personal History". *Nikkei Asian Review,* 1–30 September 2016.

Jirathiwat, Samrit. 1992. *Nangsu Anuson nai Ngan Phraratchathan Phaloeng Sop Nai Samrit Jirathiwat,* 3 Phrutsajikayon 2535 [A Crematorium Book of Remembrance for Mr. Samrit Jirathiwat, 3 November 1992].

Kikkawa, Takeo. 2017. "Introduction". In *Ethical Capitalism: Shibusawa Eiichi and Business Leadership in Global Perspective,* ed. Patrick Fridenson and Takeo Kikkawa, 3–13. Toronto: University of Toronto Press.

Phongpaichit, Pasuk and Chris Baker, ed. 2008. *Thai Capital after the 1997 Crisis.* Chiang Mai: Silkworm Books.

Phujatkan Rai-duan, ed. 2004. "The Great Challenge". *Phujatkan Rai-duan* [Manager Monthly] 22 (244): 90–104.

Robertson, Diana C. 2009. "Corporate Social Responsibility and Different Stages of Economic Development: Singapore, Turkey, and Ethiopia". *Journal of Business Ethics* 88 (supp 4): 617–33.

Robinson Department Store Plc. *Robinson Department Store Plc Annual Report.* Bangkok, Thailand, Robinson Department Store, published annually.

Saengthongkham, Wirat, Pandop Tangsiwong and Somsak Damrongsunthonrachai. 2003. *70 Pi Jirathiwat Central Ying Su Ying To* [The Growing Jirathiwat Family and Central Group for 70 Years]. Bangkok: Manager Media Group.

Sapphaibun, Thanawat. 2000. *55 Trakun Dang Phak 1* [55 Well-Known Families Volume 1]. Bangkok: The Nation Publishing.

————. 2011. *Khit Phut Tham Thanin Jiarawanon* [Words and Deeds of Thanin Jiarawanon]. Bangkok: Animate Group.

Suehiro, Akira. 1989. *Capital Accumulation in Thailand 1855–1985.* Tokyo: The Center for East Asian Cultural Studies.

————. 2001. "Family Business Gone Wrong? Ownership Patterns and Corporate Performance in Thailand". *ADB Institute Working Paper 19.*

————. 2006. *Famirii Bijinesu Ron* [A Theory of Family Business]. Nagoya: Nagoya University Press.

True Corporation Plc. *True Corporation Plc Annual Report.* Bangkok, Thailand. True Corporation, published annually.

Visser, Wayne. 2008. "Corporate Social Responsibility in Developing Countries". In *The Oxford Handbook of Corporate Social Responsibility*, ed. Andrew Crane et al., 473–9. Oxford: Oxford University Press.

Wannakon, Aphiwat. 2018. *Jao Sua Son Ruai* [A Multi-millionaire]. Bangkok: Kao Raek.

Williamson, Oliver E. 1975. *Markets and Hierarchies: Analysis and Antitrust Implications.* New York: The Free Press.

World Bank. 1998. *East Asia: The Road to Recovery.* Washington DC: World Bank.

Newspapers

Bangkok Post
Nikkei Asia (formerly, Nikkei Asian Review)
The Nation
Prachachat Thurakit (PRCT-TK)
Than Setthakit (TNSK)

Lists of shareholders and corporate officers of the non-listed companies that are included in company documents compiled by the Department of Business Development, Ministry of Commerce, Thailand

Central Group –
Central Department Store Co., Ltd.
Central Group Co., Ltd.
Central Holding Co., Ltd.
Central Retail Corporation Co., Ltd. (CRC)
Harng Central Department Store Co., Ltd. (HCDS)

CP Group –
Charoen Pokphand Group Co., Ltd.

Chapter 6

Entrepreneurship and Innovation of Thai Firms in Manufacturing Industries

Patarapong Intarakumnerd

Introduction

Thailand's economy grew at an average annual rate of 7.5 per cent during the boom years of 1960 to1996 and at an average rate of 5 per cent in the years 1999 to 2005 following the Asian financial crisis. In the early 2000s, its annual growth was around 5 per cent and slowed to rates closer to 3 per cent up to the time before the Covid pandemic (OECD 2021). The economy has become more diversified and the contribution of the aquiculture sector to gross domestic product (GDP) has significantly reduced from 44 per cent in 1951 to 8 per cent in 2019, while the share of manufacturing increased markedly from 13 per cent to 25 per cent in the same period (NESDB 2020). Nonetheless, in terms of exports, while the role of primary products has reduced in relation to that of manufacturing, agriculture has diversified remarkably as Thailand has become one of the world's largest exporters of a wide range of primary products, namely rice, rubber, sugar, cassava, prawns, canned pineapple, soy and frozen seafood. Coincidentally, the growth and diversification of manufactured exports in sectors ranging from textiles to automobiles and parts, and to electronic and electrical components has also been extraordinary. For example, the export shares of electronic/electrical and automotive products increased from 0.04 per cent and 0.25 per cent respectively in the year 1970 to 14.30 per cent and 15.29 per cent in the year 2019 (Bank of Thailand 2020).

However, unlike Western countries, Japan and the first-tier East Asian newly industrialised economies (NIEs), the Thai economy grew by overcoming its bottlenecks with foreign technology and capital without making serious efforts to increase its own savings or upgrade its technology. The country experienced a major economic crisis in 1997. After that, the economic growth rates decreased substantially to 3–4 per cent per year on average. The country's once labour-intensive and prominent sectors like textiles, garments, toys and shoes have lost their competitive advantages to lower-wage countries. These triggered growing concerns among Thai policymakers, and among the general public, that Thailand had moved into the middle-income trap.

In this paper, I will go beyond the above macro picture to explore the entrepreneurship and innovations that have taken place in Thailand's manufacturing sector, particularly in three industrial sectors that are the top exporting sectors of the country: electronics, automotive and seafood. We will then discuss the contribution of entrepreneurship to the broader economic and social development of the country. The analysis offers insights into how businesses and entrepreneurs think about their responsibilities towards their diverse stakeholders, as well as insights on the relative significance of structural imperatives and concepts of social responsibility on business operation, demonstrating how the concept of corporate social responsibility (CSR) has increasingly become adapted to local conditions.

An Overview of Entrepreneurship and Innovation in Thailand

There has not really been a class of indigenous big business entrepreneurs in Thailand. Even smaller businesses in Bangkok, especially in retail, are mostly owned and operated by Sino-Thais (East Asian Analytical Unit 1995, 78). The dominance of family-owned enterprises established by immigrant Chinese entrepreneurs in Thailand has long been rooted into Thai business norms and cultures. Therefore, historically and culturally, entrepreneurship in Thailand is not much different from that in Chinese-dominated countries like Taiwan.

In terms of trust, Chinese-owned businesses tend to be built as family-affiliated corporations that are ownership- and kinship-led rather than operate along skill-based management approaches. This "family-ownership-control-type business" (Suehiro 1992, 392), characterised by low stock ownership diffusion and more family-related CEOs has led to business and joint investment cooperation among different companies within the same family affiliates *but only a few* instances of cooperation between the various enterprises of different families (Suehiro 1992, 390; East Asian Analytical Unit 1995, 78). Although many Chinese-run firms have grown into big conglomerates covering a variety of business sectors, the founding family still keeps the ultimate rein. Nevertheless, firms under the same family umbrella overlap and compete, leading to intra-family conflicts. In sum, cooperation is less likely to occur in inter-family businesses, and in intra-family enterprises, cooperation often draws family complexity and contention.

There are two contrasting views on the effect of Chinese-Thai entrepreneurship on attitudes towards the acceptance of failure. The first view sees Sino-Thai influence as a threat towards innovation, owing to its low acceptance of failure and lack of merit-based management, while the second view regards the Chinese-Thai business culture as a positive factor— as being one that tolerates the risky ventures needed for long-term planning and investment. Due to the fact that Chinese-run enterprises expand their businesses for the main purpose of the "total fortune of the family" (Suehiro 1992, 403), they initially advanced into areas such as finance and real estate, a strategy that suggests their risk-averse characteristics in doing business. The upfront profit from trading and property businesses is far more attractive than expensive technology-intensive manufacturing that will only earn longer-term gains. As a result, technological deepening or long-term sustainability has not been much of a concern. In this case, political capability, in terms of gaining access to lucrative oligopolistic sectors, seems more important than technological capability.

The structural and political context has also affected the behaviour of Sino-Thai firms. Most of the domestic expansion and diversification rationale comes from the fact that Sino-Thai firms take advantage of the Government's industrial promotion policies and other tax incentives, while diversifying into foreign ventures for scale and scope purposes, given the limited domestic market and intensive local competition (Suehiro 1992, 400). Therefore, the liberalisation and high industrial growth of the 1980s, together with many favourable external conditions unrelated to the fundamental capability of Thai industries, allured the Thai conglomerates into new diversifications technologically unrelated to their original businesses. In order to do that, these firms actually accumulated an underlying capability; it was the capability to establish and maintain political connections with government authorities rather than have any kind of technological and innovation capabilities (see Intarakumnerd, Chairatana and Tangjitpiboon 2002).

The second view, however, offers a more positive perspective on Chinese-Thai entrepreneurship. The fact that "Sino-Thai families traditionally were reluctant to relinquish ownership and management of their companies ..." (East Asian Analytical Unit 1995, 80) allows each of them to create a long-term vision for their very own family businesses. While some list their assets on the stock market, many still prefer to raise capital conservatively, through loans and offshore bonds in the hope of benefiting from different international interest rates. The continuity of vision from fathers to children protects them from short-term concerns over stock prices or the threat of acquisition. A deep-rooted corporate culture and the tacit learning of family members constitute a well-qualified decision base for risky projects (Intarakumnerd 2000, 16). These family conglomerates are therefore capable of creating risky ventures in the expectation of future success without being distracted by their stockholders.

Entrepreneurship in Thailand has experienced a number of interesting changes. Attitude and behavioural changes towards entrepreneurship in Thailand have come from exposure to modernism, innovative culture and the new technologies of the West, all of which have been filtered in through the overseas education experienced by the predecessors of the newer generation. This is where the two contrasting views towards the Sino-Thai business culture indicated above finally merge. The combination of rapid decision-making traits and the long-term planning of assets is creating conditions that allow Thai businesses to grow both horizontally and vertically, and it will likely create a business structure that, while remaining a family-run type, becomes increasingly innovative and adaptive to the changing environment. The attitude that favours kinship rather than managerial skills has also started to change. The professionalism of management has been growing despite tight family control (see Intarakumnerd 2000), allowing a better prospect for competency building and technology development.

The above description is likely to be true for large and established enterprises, but knowledge-intensive start-up companies (newly emerged and fast-growing ventures aiming to meet marketplace needs by developing or offering innovative products, processes or services) may tell a different story. According to GEM, Bangkok University and BUSEM (2013), Thailand has a high rate of entrepreneurial activity. However, while there is plenty of "necessity-based" entrepreneurship—that is, people become entrepreneurs because they need to survive economically, such as in the case of street vendors—it is doubtful whether there is a critical mass of "opportunity-based" entrepreneurs who seize and execute risky opportunities through innovations. This opportunity-based entrepreneurship is usually an important characteristic of successful start-up companies. Innovation surveys show that the level of willingness to take risks is rather low among Thai entrepreneurs, although it has improved in recent surveys. Thai traditional wisdom places more emphasis on conforming to existing societal values and the ideas of those in positions of seniority rather than challenging them. To become opportunity-based entrepreneurs, two characteristics are required: (1) the perception of opportunity and (2) perceived capabilities. The perception of opportunity (opportunity perception) reflects the percentage of individuals who believe that there are opportunities to start a business in the area where they live. On the other hand, perceived capabilities reflect individuals who believe that they have the necessary skills, knowledge and experience to start a new venture. For opportunity-based perception, among the Southeast Asian countries that were surveyed, Thailand ranked third (45.3 per cent) behind the Philippines (47.9 per cent) and Indonesia (46.7 per cent). Thailand ranked fourth (44.4 per cent) in perceived capabilities, significantly lower than the Philippines (68.4 per cent), Indonesia (62.0 per cent) and Vietnam (48.7 per cent) (GEM, Bangkok University and BUSEM 2013, 27). In order to have a deeper understanding of this situation, we will examine three leading Thai manufacturing sectors: electronics, automotive and seafood.

Electronics

Thailand is one of the major manufacturing bases of the global electronics industry. The majority of firms are small- and medium-sized enterprises, with a substantial representation of transnational corporations (TNCs) in both assembly and parts supplying domains. The TNCs dominate the assembly activity with extensive control over the supply chain of parts and components. The central and eastern regions of Thailand are among the most favourable locations for this industry, followed by north-eastern and northern regions. After the financial crisis, the total export of electrical and electronic products increased drastically from USD 23 billion in the year 2000 to USD 36 billion in the year 2019 (Bank of Thailand 2020). Most of the international trade in this sector is in intermediate goods, that is, electrical and electronics parts and components. According to the Ministry of Labour, the workforce in the industry stood at around 545,000 strong in 2018, with an observable representation of migrant workers from Cambodia, Laos and Myanmar (Ministry of Labour 2018).

Subsidiaries of TNCs in Thailand have achieved considerable technical acquisition and upgrading since the 1980s, but R&D activities for new products or process innovation are still mainly conducted outside Thailand (Hobday and Rush 2007). Research and innovation activities in large Thai firms are not that high, but have also increased, especially in relation to integrated circuits (ICs) and appliance design (Intarakumnerd, Chairatana and Chaiyanajit 2016). Most small to medium enterprises (SMEs) in the electronics industry are original equipment manufacturers (OEMs) for TNCs, and the number of firms making innovations is low. Among those firms, process innovation is higher than production innovation, and the number of innovative Thai-owned firms is more or less the same as the number of innovative joint ventures (with foreign partners). When it comes to expenditure on innovation-related activities, we find that these innovating firms spent much more on the acquisition of machinery and external knowledge than they did on internal R&D. This reflects the nature of latecomer firms—namely that most of the knowledge for their innovations comes from outside; they learn from knowledge already generated elsewhere. However, they may also simultaneously make their own efforts in internal R&D to generate their own innovations and increase their capacity for absorbing this external knowledge.

In general, in Thailand, the sector still lags behind other countries in the designing and testing of ICs, transistors, capacitors, resistors, diodes and so on. Key inputs like wafers and bonding wire are mainly imported from abroad, although there is some local input of lead frames. Nonetheless, there are a few exceptional cases of local firms in the upstream segments of the semiconductor sub-sector, as shown in the following examples.

Stars Microelectronics Thailand

Stars Microelectronics Thailand (SMT) is a locally owned OEM operating in computer, electronic equipment, automobile, communications, safety equipment, and entertainment businesses. It is also a subcontractor and an electronics product designer. Its co-founders are an investor with a background in the rice milling industry and a university professor specialising in industrial engineering. The company headquarters is located in Bangpa, in the industrial estate, in Ayutthaya, Thailand, and it has sales offices in Japan, Germany, United States and Taiwan.

SMT was founded in 1995 and earned public company status in 2004, prior to being listed on the Stock Exchange of Thailand (SET) in 2009. It was among the first listed companies to enjoy the privileges of the free trade zone granted by the Board of Investment of Thailand (BOI). The firm had a registered capital of THB 730 million (USD 21 million) in 2016. SMT is actively engaged in the upstream mass production of microelectronics module assembly (MMA) and IC packaging, and has a 25,500-square-metre factory space. The company expanded its production capacity in MMA to 100 million units per year and IC packaging to 1.2 billion units, with a total of 1,450 employees, including more than 120 engineering staff in 2016.

SMT's core competency is in advanced electronics manufacturing services (EMS) for MMA, IC packaging and testing based on the on-site and solution-based practice provided by its local engineering teams. Another core factor is its operation space management, which provides secure and dedicated spaces where clients' intellectual properties and designs are not exposed. SMT executives recognise the importance of innovation, but it is not considered a priority for leveraging the firm's competitiveness. Process innovation can be observed from its investment in new machines and technologies. However, once a large amount of capital has been invested in a machine or an assembly line, it limits SMT's production capability as one machine can only produce a certain range of products and not others. Therefore, in this context, process innovation is more common in a bid to improve production processes, production controls and troubleshooting capabilities. In contrast, product innovation is less evident due to the limited nature of EMS or contract manufacturers, that is, they produce to order. Its production capability is also constrained by path-dependence[1] that occurs because of the machines it has invested in. Its influence over product modification is very limited and often only found at the later stages of the production line.

The external sources of innovation constitute suppliers and clients. SMT often requests machine specifications from machine suppliers, coorperating often and consistently with them through communication and technical support provided by their sales representatives and research teams. One example is when they were developing a new wire bonder. Engineers from the production line provided feedback that the old wire bonder had a short life span as the machine operator had to stop the machine often and change the wire bonder. This issue was effectively addressed and with the new wire bonder, production increased and costs were reduced. However, in contrast, in the hard disk drive sector, although SMT is located in the same Free Trade Zone as its customers in the industry, cooperation has been rare. SMT had to increase its capabilities on its own to meet the increasing demands of these customers. With new business opportunities, like the rise in demand for ultra-high radio frequency identification (RFID) chips, SMT was also given a chance to co-design new products. This has allowed SMT to cooperate with its clients through its on-site skills in manufacturing and process engineering. The company has also learnt to integrate new machinery into its manufacturing processes in line with its clients' orders, which has been a major learning event and opportunity (Intarakumnerd, Chairatana and Chaiyanajit 2016).

Silicon Craft Technology

Silicon Craft Technology (SIC) was a start-up company established in 2002 by five Thai co-founders with engineering and IC design backgrounds. SIC is a leading Thai knowledge-intensive business enterprise that values innovation and intelligence as the driver of growth. It aims to deliver high-quality products compatible with world standards and regulations. The firm was the prime mover in IC design in Thailand, and had the ambition of making itself a showcase for local technopreneurship, encouraging locals into the IC design business. The managing director and a co-founder, Manop Thamsirianunt, used to work as analogy design engineer and IC design manager for semiconductor firms in Silicon Valley in the US. Through a reverse brain drain scheme, he returned to Thailand in 2001 and became the head of Thailand IC Design Incubator (TIDI), a unit of the National Electronics and Computer Technology Centre (NECTEC). Some of the other co-founders have doctoral degrees in engineering, as well as university professorships.

SIC's business ranges across state-of-the-art, customised and standard microchip design for RFID applications. Its core competence resides in its experience and expertise in the design and development of a world-class foundry for the manufacturing of semiconductors for linear and mixed-signal ICs. Today, SIC has more than 20 international customers in chip design and solutions from Australia, the US, Europe and Japan. The majority of its employees have engineering or related degrees from leading Thai and international universities. At 25 July 2013, the company had 65 active employees, almost half of whom had a master's or PhD degree (Manop Thamsirianunt, personal communication with author, 25 July 2013). SIC has also provided scholarships to potential students in the microelectronics department of leading universities and later recruited them as employees.

In the early stage of the firm's establishment, the idea of IC design in Thailand was still considered high risk and a far-fetched ambition. It was very difficult for co-founders to persuade local investors to jump into the business. Thus the strategy that was adopted was individual spin-offs from research organisations to become technopreneurs. Manop therefore decided to leave NECTEC and set up his own IC design company with other co-founders, some of whom continued their work as university professors, while others worked as full-time directors at SIC. In the first 6 months, the new company had hardly any customers, as potential customers were unfamiliar with and lacked trust in the concept of a Thai IC design company. The second strategy was therefore to get Thai technological and IC design capabilities recognised in domestic and international markets. The company painstakingly focused only on IC design to develop chip products that could be sold to reputed international customers. This strategy proved successful. SIC developed application-specific IC chips used in electronic devices, and RFID chips, that were sold in many countries, leading to the company becoming internationally recognised as a chip provider.

The public procurement from NECTEC to develop a smart RFID chip used for animal identification—for example, for microchipping pets, which SIC claimed to be the world's tiniest and lowest priced chip—can be seen as an important "learning event" for the company in gaining technological and innovative capabilities. SIC also received financial investment from One Asset Management, a leading Thai venture capitalist, for this IC design development. Strategically, SIC conducts its technology road mapping for segmenting new technologies and markets based on performance, application, and users. The company has continued to benchmark its products' performance against those of world IC manufacturers like Philips, Texas Instruments and EM Microelectronics. As of 2016, all of the company's chip products were exported, but after a long period of marketing efforts, local customers have also begun to show interest (Intarakumnerd, Chairatana and Chaiyanajit 2016).

Automotive Sector

The automotive industry in Thailand started in the early 1960s, under an import substitution policy and revision of the investment promotion law to encourage automotive assembly. Since 2001, the automotive industry has contributed considerably and increasingly to the Thai economy in terms of value-add and employment. Thailand is the strongest automotive production base in Southeast Asia, benefiting from a sufficient pool of qualified engineers and technicians, and an extensive supplier network, thereby enabling integrated production. Approximately 750,000 people worked in the industry in 2018 (Ministry of Labour 2018).

Companies in the industry can be grouped into three broad categories as of 2018: 19 car assemblers; approximately 523 1st-tier suppliers; and 1,667 2nd- and 3rd-tier suppliers, including supporting companies (Thailand Automotive Institute 2019). Most are small- and medium-sized firms, while most assemblers are subsidiaries of TNCs. These are led by Japanese TNCs, together with the entry of the "big three" US car companies, namely Daimler Chrysler, General Motors (GM) and Ford, whose main goal is the production and export from Thailand of one-ton pickups.

Before the 2000s, these car manufacturers only had production bases in Thailand, while more sophisticated activities like design and R&D were carried out in their home countries. Starting around the 2000s, however, TNCs' investment strategies began to change, as many firms designated Thailand to be their regional or global export hub. In order to secure better coordination between the production phase and the development phase, these companies started to invest in Thailand in more technologically sophisticated activities than just simple assembly—such as in advanced engineering, process and product design, and advanced testing and validation. Several important automotive TNCs (mainly Japanese) founded technical centres in Thailand, separate from their normal production plants, like Toyota Motor Asia Pacific Engineering and Manufacturing Co., Ltd., Nissan Technical Centre Southeast Asia Co., Ltd., Isuzu Technical Centre Asia Co., Ltd., and Honda R&D Asia Pacific Co., Ltd. The R&D activities of these firms started by focusing on modifying the design of existing products to match local demands and to exploit local advantages, for example, the analysis of suitable local natural raw materials and parts to meet international standards or the standards of the importing countries, especially according to European Union regulations. Over time, more advanced product design has increasingly been executed locally. Nissan, for example, used to carry out only the mass production of final products in Thailand, but now, sophisticated activities like clay modelling and vehicle planning and simulation are also carried out in its technical centre.

As for parts suppliers, the College of Management, Mahidol University, Thailand (Mahidol University 2006) carried out comprehensive research based on the technological capability framework developed by Bell and Pavitt (1995). The study examined the technological capabilities of six groups of automotive component suppliers, namely: suspension and brakes, interior, exterior, engine, electronics and drive transmission. The results show that, on average, component suppliers in Thailand could be grouped into two categories based on their level of technological capabilities. Firms focusing on suspension and brakes, and on interiors and exteriors, had relatively higher capabilities, allowing them to compete regionally and globally. Those that focused on engines, electronics and drive transmission components had lesser capabilities as their principal technologies are more sophisticated, requiring the proprietary knowledge of the TNCs. Interestingly, the study illustrated that Thai-owned firms had higher capabilities than foreign-owned firms or joint ventures, in terms of making investment decisions, product development, linking up with customers and markets and linking up with supporting institutions, whereas foreign-owned firms had higher capabilities in project management, quality control and linking up with materials and technology suppliers. Thai-owned firms had higher technological capabilities than their foreign counterparts in some areas because they needed to make their own investment decisions; they carried out product development activities by themselves and collaborated more with local research and supporting institutions in order to be able to compete with foreign competitors. Unlike foreign-owned makers or joint ventures, they could not rely on technology supply and technical assistance from parent companies. This can be demonstrated in the cases of Daisin and the Somboon Group.

Daisin

Daisin is a majority Thai-owned supplier, which has managed to stay on as a first-tier supplier for several decades. The company was founded in 1979 to produce aluminium casting parts for the automotive industry as a joint venture with Nissin Kogyo (Nisshin Kōgyō) Co., Ltd, with the Thai partner being a larger shareholder with 67 per cent ownership. The company employed a retired Japanese engineer who assisted the firm in upgrading its production capability and negotiating with Nissin to considerably lower its royalty fees. Subsequently, the firm also accessed external knowledge besides its partnership with Nissin by employing other Japanese technical consultants to assist in upgrading its design capability. The firm was eventually able to suggest a new handbrake design and a new lighting system to its customers (Japanese car manufacturers). However, their foreign part makers' investment strategies had to be in accordance with the parent company's strategies, and so most product development activities were done within parent companies or at headquarters (Intarakumnerd and Techakanont 2016).

Somboon Group

The Somboon Group was founded in 1962 by a local Chinese Thai family and is considered the pioneer in manufacturing springs for motor vehicles in Thailand. It has 2,900 full-time employees based in Bangkok (40 per cent) and Rayong (60 per cent). Its main customer is Japanese OEM companies, which accounted for 89 per cent in 2012. The group's customers are Toyota and Hino (forming 30 per cent of total sales), Mitsubishi (forming 20 per cent), Kubota (forming 18–20 per cent) and Isuzu, Honda, Nissan, General Motors, Ford, Mazda, as well as others. In the beginning, since the company had limited knowledge and skills, OEM customers requested Somboon to make use of technical assistance (TA) for their key manufacturing processes. Toyota, for example, requested that the company have Japanese partners and TA from Japan, and use the Toyota Production System (TPS). TA provided technical support and technical training for Somboon's engineers. In 2009, the company established an R&D centre to carry out product design, testing and raw material development. With this R&D capability, the company started to be more self-reliant, reducing its use of TA, establishing its own technical team. It relied on TA only for troubleshooting, technical problem solving and the production of specific new parts. In 2010, it was able to design and patent new brake discs and half shafts for customers. For troubleshooting issues, the company requested the assistance of Japanese specialists on a short-term basis for any technical problems. In 2011, the company established a learning academy for process improvement training and human resource development (Intarakumnerd, Gerdsri and Teekasap 2012). In 2017, Somboon established a new joint venture with a German firm for spring development, from which further knowledge transfer was expected.

Seafood Sector

Thailand has attained position as one of the world's largest and most advanced producers and exporters of processed food products. Its agricultural traditions and abundance of natural resources, in conjunction with substantial investments in international quality standards, technology and food safety R&D have helped Thailand to become the only net food exporter in Asia. In 2019, Thailand's export-oriented food industry generated USD 32 billion (Bank of Thailand 2020).

In the seafood industry in particular, Thailand is one of the key players in the market. In 2019, the value of processed fish exports reached USD 3 billion, making Thailand one of the world's large fish exporters. During the 2000s, there was a substantial expansion in frozen shrimp and cephalopod processing, and tuna canneries. Thailand is now the world's largest producer and exporter of canned tuna and shrimp. The three levels of value chain of the seafood industry are:

1.   Upstream: sourcing and production of raw materials, which can come from the sea or farming;
2.   Midstream: post harvesting, sales, transportation and early processing; and
3.   Downstream: processing, product development, freezing and exporting.

Compared to chilled or frozen seafood, processed seafood has a higher value per kilogram. Over 90 per cent of Thai seafood products are exported, the major part of these being chilled or frozen shrimp. Over 90 per cent of Thai exports are OEMs for foreign customers, with Thai manufacturers being just subcontractors for foreign brands. Thai-owned brands, though on a significant increase, are still far fewer than OEMs. The ability to sell products under their own labels is still a major challenge for Thai seafood manufacturers. As Thai seafood products experience competition from lower-cost countries like Vietnam and Indonesia, future survival necessitates the progressive development of branded and more sophisticated products. Non-tariff barriers, in the form of increased food safety standards in developed countries, are also a major problem. Both the two main market segments in the Thai seafood industry—chilled or frozen shrimp and chilled or frozen fish—are labour intensive and utilise low technology. Over 85 per cent of raw materials in the shrimp industry are from farming, while most of the raw materials for the fish industry are drawn from waters inside and outside Thailand.

Unlike the electronics and automotive industries, the frozen seafood industry is led by two types of locally owned firms: large firms and SMEs. Large firms supply both the domestic and export markets. Most are still OEMs supplying under the brand names of large domestic supermarkets and foreign customers. Nonetheless, some of them have become own-brand manufacturers (OBMs), like the CP Group, Thai Union Frozen, Surapon Food, Pacific Fish Processing (PFP), S&P and Prantalay. The ratio of OBM to OEM products of these firms was around 1:1 in 2015 (Intarakumnerd, Chairatana and Kamondetdacha 2015). Many of the large firms have acquired know-hows from abroad through joint ventures, and large firms have full or partial vertical integration, accomplishing several activities in the value chain from farming to marketing and distribution. To guarantee that they will have sufficient high-quality raw materials, these companies either have their own farms or have established contract-farming with local farmers. These local farmers are provided with larvae, necessary materials and technical support. Some companies even have large fishing fleets for sea-catching.

In food processing, food technologists and engineers upgrade existing production processes and design new ones. Most companies have their own R&D departments to perform product and process innovations. Normally, personnel in the R&D departments have food science and food engineering education/ training. Since the 2010s, graduates in home economics, as well as chefs from both domestic and international educational institutes have been employed to work in these departments. In collaboration with food scientists and engineers, they develop new recipes for ready-to-eat and ready-to-cook products. Fascinatingly, fusion food, originating from the creative mixing of different cuisines, was also launched in the market. These new products were the outcome of a convergence between science—such as new freezing and chilling techniques, food packaging technologies and better food logistics—art—such as innovative and delicious recipes, artistic and nice-looking packaging, and appealing product storylines—and services, such as retailing practices in supermarkets and convenience stores, and advertising.

Some firms have extended their R&D undertakings by establishing culinary development centres to vigorously develop new processes and products with their customers, whom the companies consider as the most significant source of knowledge. Marketing departments also work closely with R&D departments, aiming to learn what new products customers need, and to convince them that the firm's new products meet those needs. Several companies have made product innovations in frozen or ready-to-eat food with various recipes created to please demanding customers' diverse tastes. There have also been process-innovations to enhance productivity, safety and traceability. The CP Group, to name just one, possesses several distribution outlets like Seven-Eleven and Lotus department stores in China. S&P, another firm, was initially a Thai-food chain-restaurant business which diversified to produce packaged, ready-to-eat food for ordinary customers under its own brand name.

Linking up with domestic and overseas customers are important channels for learning about preferred technologies, packaging styles, foreign-market regulations and of coure tastes. This is particularly significant for OEM products. Many firms have been able to export their products under their own brand names while some firms like the CP Group and Thai Union Frozen became TNCs. The CP Group invested in more than 20 countries, while Thai Union Frozen set up its own subsidiaries in Indonesia, Papua New Guinea and Vietnam, and took over leading food processing manufacturers in the US, Canada and France. Apart from market access, the reason for these two firms to invest in other developing countries was to exploit capabilities already developed at home. Investment in developed countries was aimed at tapping into advanced knowledge, international brands and extensive distribution networks.

Collaboration between large firms and universities has turned out to become increasingly significant since the 2000s. This collaboration has taken several forms, namely joint- or contract-research to develop new products, personnel training and student internships. The Faculty of Agro-Industry of Kasetsart University, Thailand, for instance, provides courses in production processes, product development and marketing. It has also undertaken contract research for large firms on raw materials analysis, production process improvement and product development. To elaborate on the proactive technological upgrading of a Thai-owned firm, let us examine the case of Charoen Pokphand Foods (CPF) and Thai Union Frozen (TUF)

Charoen Pokphand Foods

Charoen Pokphand Foods, which was established in 1978, is the leading agro-industrial and food conglomerate operating a vertically integrated business model. There are four core businesses, both locally and internationally, comprising feed, farm, food processing and retail food outlets. The company's operations are divided into two main areas: domestic operation (in Thailand)

and international operation. For its domestic operation, the company operates a vertically integrated agro-industrial and food business, both for domestic sale and export to more than 40 countries across five continents. On the international operation front, it operates and invests overseas through subsidiaries in 13 countries, which include China, Vietnam, Turkey and Laos, as well as through an associated company in Cambodia and jointly controlled entities. The company has a specialised R&D team to analyse customer behaviour in each country, with a view to meeting consumer demand and has signed a Memorandum of Understanding (MOU) with the National Science and Technology Development Agency (NSTDA) on R&D in food and agriculture. Further, CPF has also collaborated with universities on researching new knowledge and technology, as well as training students (Intarakumnerd, Chairatana and Kamondetdacha 2015).

Thai Union Frozen

Thai Union Frozen Products Public Company Limited (TUF) is a leading global processor and exporter of canned and frozen seafood. TUF was founded in 1977 and its core business is processing, distributing and exporting frozen and canned seafood domestically and internationally. TUF started as an OEM company, with its main markets in the US, Europe and Japan. Initially, its strength was in low-cost mass production, but it subsequently expanded its business globally, beginning with a strategic partnership in Japan with two Japanese companies in 1992. In 1997, TUF was able to acquire an American Company, Chicken of the Sea, which was the third largest producer in the US canned tuna market. It expanded its business to Indonesia in 2006 and Vietnam in 2008, and acquired the largest seafood processor in Europe in 2010. In developed countries, the company's focus was on acquiring leading companies with significant brand recognition and distribution channels, while its investments in developing countries was aimed at acquiring raw materials and markets. The company reported a sales volume of USD 40 million in 2012 and an employment headcount totalling 12,000 staff.

In the area of technology upgrading and innovation, TUF hired an American culinary director from the US to head up its newly established culinary R&D centre in Thailand to develop suitable products to meet the needs of consumers in various markets. Through its overseas acquisitions, TUF was able to launch new brands specifically for those markets. Product packaging was also improved to an easy-to-open can, which can itself be considered a new product innovation. TUF obtained new machinery, technology and automation techniques as a consequence of the knowledge transfer from operating abroad.

It also formed a new joint development project with Kasetsart University for new product development in Thailand (Intarakumnerd, Chairatana and Kamondetdacha 2015).

Like large firms, SMEs also produce for both domestic and foreign markets, but a majority of SMEs are family-owned firms relying on imported technologies. Technological development activities are limited to minor adaptations of imported machinery and equipment, while most SMEs lack efficient energy and waste management systems. Unlike large firms, which focus on continuous development, SMEs' quality control systems are executed only to the extent needed to pass minimum certification requirements. Their R&D activities are very limited. Product and process development is passive, that is, ambitions do not go beyond fulfilling the immediate needs of customers. Many SMEs only export early-stage, standardised, processed seafood, for example, unpeeled shrimps (particularly to Europe). Training is also limited as SMEs prefer to recruit experienced production personnel. Lastly, collaboration with universities and public research institutes is also quite limited because SMEs usually seek technical support from other manufacturers.

Contributions of Entrepreneurship to Social and Economic Development

One direct contribution of entrepreneurs to society has been through their activities in the name of corporate social responsibility (CSR). In 2016, Thailand was ranked highest among countries in Southeast Asia in a survey on CSR conducted by the National University of Singapore (NUS) and the ASEAN CSR Network. Leading Thai firms in CSR were Advanced Info, Intouch, True, PTT, Bangchak, PTTEP, Thai Oil, Charoen Pokphand, Delta Electronics and Electric Generating Company. Compared to firms in other countries in this region, Thai firms on average performed better. Thailand also ranked first in a corporate disclosure survey, which measured the steps taken by companies to be transparent and to discourage graft. In general, in this respect, large companies such as those that are listed on Thailand's Stock Exchange are well ahead of SMEs. Despite that, only 100 of Thailand's 600 listed companies participated fully in CSR activities. (*The Nation* 2016). Though Thailand ranked highest in Southeast Asia, the concept is still new, and there is no universally accepted definition of CSR, especially among SMEs, for whom the role models in CSR practice in Thailand are large, listed companies.

Interestingly, though, the concept of CSR came from the West. It was localised by the two largest cultural influences in Thailand: the royal family and Buddhism. CSR in Thailand was somewhat related to a local development concept—the philosophy of the "sufficiency economy", which was initiated by the late King Bhumibol Adulyadej [discussed in Chapter 8 (The Making of a Thai Consumer Goods Conglomerate: The Role of Dynamic Entrepreneurship and Social Capital)]. The main thrust of the philosophy is building a strong economic foundation and self-reliance at a local community level. CSR and this philosophy share many similar traits, for instance, community-based development, local networking, stakeholder participation, partnership and collaboration, and the importance of the community context and local wisdom. As a result, CSR practices have been strengthened and adapted to local conditions and a community-based lifestyle. Buddhism is another strong influence. The belief in the law of karma—the spiritual principle of cause and effect, where the intent and actions of an individual influence the future of that individual—is deeply rooted in Thai society, where 95 per cent of the population are Buddhists. Research has found that more and more businesses have been embracing Buddhist principles, and that acts of giving are socially appreciated, particularly when specific cases are made public in the media (Onozawa 2013).

A broader contribution of entrepreneurship in Thailand is related to gender equality. Thailand has an equal proportion of female and male entrepreneurs at all stages of business activity, from the initial intention to start a business through to starting up, to sustaining it, and finally becoming an established business owner. Nevertheless, the high rate of female entrepreneurship in Thailand is accompanied by the fact that more than 70 per cent of Thai female entrepreneurs operate as micro-business owners. While this illustrates the level and ability of Thai women in relation to self-employment, the contribution of these micro-businesses to job creation is quite limited (GEM, Bangkok University and BUSEM 2013).

Conclusion

The Thai manufacturing industry is in general technologically weak. Although a direct causal effect is hard to substantiate, the financial crisis in 1997, to some extent, contributed to changes in the atmosphere surrounding both government policies and the behaviour of firms. It was like a wake-up call—that doing things in the usual ways was no longer sustainable. Several large Thai-owned business groups, like the CP Group, expanded their R&D activities. A number of smaller companies increased their technological efforts by working with universities to improve their production efficiency and develop new products. Several subcontracting suppliers in the automobile and electronics industries were pressured by their TNC customers/partners to upgrade their product designs and improve production efficiency. Emerging young start-up companies exploited their own design and engineering and R&D activities. New government policy initiatives paid more attention to strengthening indigenous technological and innovative capabilities. Previous studies (Suehiro 1992; East Asian Analytical Unit 1995) stated that overseas Chinese entrepreneurship models had both positive and negative aspects on technological learning and the innovation of firms. A survey from Global Entrepreneurship Monitor (GEM, Bangkok University and BUSEM 2013) also showed that there are more necessity-based entrepreneurs than opportunity-based ones. This is because there is a lack of perception of opportunities and of perceived capability among potential entrepreneurs, even in comparison with neighbouring Southeast Asian countries.

The case studies of the three leading industries above illustrate the extent of technological upgrading and innovation by Thai-owned firms. Unlike the subsidiaries of TNCs, they cannot rely passively on their mother companies for knowledge transfer. The more successful ones have *proactively* enhanced their internal technological and innovative capabilities, as well as collaborated with external partners (like competitors, suppliers, customers, universities and public research institutes). They have made significant attempts to leverage external sources of knowledge through hiring foreign consultants, sending their engineers for external training, licensing foreign technology and know-hows, and even taking over foreign knowledge-intensive firms in advanced countries. In a nutshell, they have demonstrated the positive side of overseas Chinese businesses as they have dared to invest in risky and costly activities with the aim to upgrade their technological and innovative capabilities, and have at the same time leveraged the knowledge and resources of firms beyond their family business groups, overcoming the negative side of overseas Chinese business approaches. However, these more successful firms are still a minority. Most locally owned businesses still focus on trading and short-term profit and do not invest adequately in technological upgrading and innovation. What Thailand needs more is a critical mass of "opportunity-based" entrepreneurs who can leverage other resources and undertake risky but innovative businesses and activities similar to the firms in our case study.

When it comes to any broader contribution to economic and societal development, however, we do find that CSR practices are increasingly important, especially for large Thai firms, although SMEs are still lagging behind. As explained, the concept of CSR has been localised by two key societal influences— the royal family and Buddhism—and entrepreneurship has contributed to gender equality, although much of this is still limited to the level of micro-enterprises.

To summarise, entrepreneurship in Thailand is facing two major challenges. The first is developing opportunity-based entrepreneurship emphasising on enhancing innovation and technological upgrading. This type of entrepreneurship is imperative for the long-term survival and competitiveness of firms. The second is diffusing the concept of CSR to a larger number of firms, so as to make the concept an integral part of firms' entrepreneurship, as opposed to merely "adding on" charitable activities.

Note

[1] Meaning that economic and business outcomes are dependent on choices and outcomes in the past, and not just on present conditions.

References

Bank of Thailand. 2020. "Total Value and Quantity of Exports Classified by Product Group, Bank of Thailand, Bangkok, Thailand". Accessed 3 November 2020. https://www.bot.or.th/App/BTWS_STAT/statistics/ReportPage.aspx?reportID=747&language=eng.

Bell, Martin and Keith Pavitt. 1995. "The Development of Technological Capabilities". In *Trade, Technology and International Competitiveness*, ed. I. Haque, 67–101. Washington DC: World Bank.

College of Management, Mahidol University. 2003. "S&T Needs and Production of Manpower in the Manufacturing Sector". Raighan kwamtongkarn withayasart le technology le karnpalit kalangkon nai pak utsahakam [Final report submitted to the National Science and Technology Development Agency, Thailand, June].

East Asia Analytical Unit. *Overseas Chinese Business Networks in Asia*. Canberra Australia, Department of Foreign Affairs and Trade, 1995.

Global Entrepreneurship Monitor (GEM), Bangkok University and BUSEM. 2013. "Thailand Report 2013". Bangkok, Global Entrepreneurship Monitor. Accessed 22 July 2018. https://summeruniversitythailand.org/pdf/2013%20GEM%20Thailand%20Report.pdf.

Hobday, Michael and Howard Rush. 2007. "Upgrading the Technological Capabilities of Foreign Transnational Subsidiaries in Developing Countries: The Case of Electronics in Thailand". *Research Policy* 36 (9): 1335–6.

Intarakumnerd, Patarapong. 2000. "Thai Telecommunication Business Groups: An Analysis of the Factors Shaping the Direction of their Growth Paths". Unpublished DPhil thesis. Science Policy Research Unit, University of Sussex, Brighton, United Kingdom.

Intarakumnerd, Patarapong, P. Chairatana and T. Tangjitpiboon. 2002. "National Innovation System in Less Successful Developing Countries: The Case of Thailand". *Research Policy* 31 (8)/(9): 1445–57.

Intarakumnerd, Patarapong, P. Chairatana and R. Kamondetdacha. 2015. "Innovation System of the Seafood Industry in Thailand". *Asian Journal of Technology Innovation* 23 (2): 271–87.

Intarakumnerd, Patarapong, P. Chairatana and P. Chaiyanajit. 2016. "Global Production Networks and Host-site Industrial Upgrading: The Case of the Semiconductor Industry in Thailand". *Asia Pacific Business Review* 22 (2): 289–306.

Intarakumnerd, Patarapong and K. Techakanont. 2016. "Intra-industry Trade, Product Fragmentation and Technological Capability Development in Thai Automotive Industry". *Asia Pacific Business Review* 22 (1): 65–85.

Intarakumnerd, Patarapong, N. Gerdsri and P. Teekasap. 2012. "The Roles of External Knowledge Sources in Thailand's Automotive Industry". *Asian Journal of Technology Innovation* 20 (supp 1): 85–97.

Ministry of Labour, Bangkok, Thailand. 2018. "Sarub satanakran le naewnom dan ranghan nai deun kanyayont 2561" [Summary of Labour Situation and Trend in September 2018]. Accessed 3 November 2020. http://warning.mol.go.th/uploadFile/pdf/pdf-2019-01-04-1546575538.pdf.

National Economic and Social Development Board (NESDB), Bangkok, Thailand. 2020. "Gross Domestic Product Chain Volume Measures, National Economic and Social Development Board". Accessed 3 November 2020. https://www.nesdc.go.th/nesdb_en/ewt_news.php?nid=4426&filename=national_account.

Organisation for Economic Co-operation and Development (OECD). 2021. "OECD Investment Policy Reviews: Thailand". *OECD Investment Policy Reviews*. Paris: OECD Publishing. https://doi.org/10.1787/c4eeee1c-en.

Onozawa, N. 2013. "A Study of CSR in Thailand I: Awareness and Practice". *Bulletin of Tsukuba Gakuin University*, Volume 8, 13–24. Accessed 22 July 2018. https://www.tsukuba-g.ac.jp/library/kiyou/2013/02-onozawa.pdf.

Suehiro, A. 1992. "Capitalist Development in Post-war Thailand: Commercial Bankers, Industrial Elite, and Agribusiness Groups. In *Southeast Asian Capitalists*, ed. R. McVey, 35–64. New York: Cornell University Press.

Thailand Automotive Institute. 2019. "Kor saneunae cheng Nayobai sumrab utsahakam yanyon mai" [Report on Policy Recommendations for New Thai Automotive Industry]. Accessed 3 November 2020. http://www.thaiauto.or.th/2012/backoffice/file_upload/research/2812563848231.pdf.

Tan, Itthi C. 2016. "Thai Firms Top in Region for CSR Activities". *The Nation*, In Focus, 23 July 2016. Accessed 22 July 2018. https://www.nationthailand.com/in-focus/30291268.

Chapter 7

The Linkage between Stewardship, Competitive Advantage and Firm Performance: An Empirical Study of Indonesian Family Businesses

Sari Wahyuni and Sely Haudy

Introduction

Family businesses have long proven to be the engine of growth for many economies around the world, and Indonesia is no exception. More than 95 per cent of the country's businesses are family owned, generating millions of jobs while playing a pivotal role in the economy. Across the Asia Pacific, in 2016, the top 85 family businesses employed more than 3 million people and accounted for 4.3 per cent of the region's gross domestic product (GDP) (EY *Family Business Yearbook* 2016). However, family businesses often have short life spans, with only a mere 33 per cent surviving the departure of the founder and an astounding 95 per cent failing by the third generation. They often become victims of their own making, failing to prepare subsequent generations for the demands of a growing business (Sato 2004). Numerous studies have shown that good governance can help companies improve performance through better decision making, stronger risk management and enhanced efficiency. Effective governance can also boost the confidence levels of potential investors and business partners, resulting in improved access to capital. Many Indonesian firms, such as Medco and the Blue Bird Group, as well as others, have since realised the value extended to a business in raising governance standards and have taken steps to do so.

Indonesia has been undergoing rapid industrialisation at a current expected growth rate of around 5 per cent a year. It remains the largest Association of Southeast Asian Nations (ASEAN) economy. It is therefore not surprising that more and more foreign investment is pouring into the country. Foreign investors seek trustworthy business partners and good governance plays a crucial part in their decision making (Razook 2016). Investors look not only at the governance of the business but also at the family's role within it. They enquire on the background of the family; where their money comes from; how the family is involved in the business; and how it will be involved in the future. This is where family governance—and not just corporate governance—becomes a crucial part of the equation. The unique challenge for family businesses is one of sustainability; their long-term success is tied not only to the fundamentals of the business but also to the family behind the company. We need to consider the importance of them becoming what we call a stewardship corporation, and what this might mean.

Cossin and Hwee (2016) defined stewardship as the act of safeguarding and enhancing an organisation's capability to create economic and societal value over time. Three dimensions of stewardship are suggested: (1) leading with impact, (2) safeguarding the future and (3) driving social good. These three dimensions may be summarised as follows:

(1) Leading with impact

Steward leaders inspire their followers, thinking for the long-term future of the organisation and its contribution to society. They tend to have a transformational style of leadership, can engage at the emotional level with their followers, put trust in their subordinates and share a long-term view across the organisation. Steward leaders continuously create impact and are respected because of their vision, values and integrity; their work and care for others; and also their ability to deliver business results.

(2) Safeguarding the future

Well-stewarded organisations are built on corporate cultures where relationships are based on trust and employees are actively engaged in achieving a meaningful, lasting corporate purpose. Employees in a well-stewarded organisation have a long-term view of their career paths within the organisation. They also understand how they can best contribute their talents and energies to create value for the company.

(3) Driving social good

Well-stewarded organisations also want to play a constructive role in society. Profit is considered as the reward for their contribution to society, rather than their objective. Though important, profit maximisation is not the only objective of the business. Value creation is regarded as the main objective of the firm. By understanding and actively communicating with all stakeholders, the organisation has a positive and meaningful impact on them.

The concept of stewardship sees people as inherently trustworthy. The aim is to go beyond economic purpose to do good for the organisation's future and also for society. This is in line with Shibusawa Eiichi's advocacy of *gapponshugi*, the principle that emphasises developing the right business, with the right people, in service of the public good (Fridenson and Kikkawa 2017). Shibusawa formulated a historical perspective on morality and ethics in the business world which, unlike the concept of corporate social responsibility (CSR), concentrates on morality inside firms, industries and private-public partnerships. As a banker and creator of joint-stock companies, Shibusawa's conception of *gapponshugi* encouraged the general public to purchase stock in businesses openly, transparently participating in stockholder's meetings, with their names prominently displayed for public view. It was, in a nutshell, a form of economic democracy. Shibusawa's coupling of the commoner/transparency model of *gapponshugi*, with a moral imperative calling for virtuous community-oriented ethics, made his approach in some respects similar to the stewardship concept. Shibusawa believed that business could be carried on according to Confucian ethics; he was steadfast in asserting that capitalists could and should place a strong emphasis on righteousness and benevolence, eschewing greed-oriented profit despite engaging in competition. Adhering to degraded morals would drive out good morals; virtue is noble, and giving back to the community through philanthropy essential. Ethical, community-oriented, capitalism was not only possible but indispensable as well.

Many scholars argue that the concept of principal/agent conventionally applied to firm governance and the concept of a stewardship-approach to governance seek to achieve the same objectives but through different mechanisms, so it is reasonable to assume that both approaches can coexist within a single organisation (Madison, Kellermanns and Munyon 2017), and can even be complementary (James, Jennings and Jennings 2017). This complementarity is needed because managers in a firm may behave as either stewards or agents in different decision situations at different stages of the family firm's life, and at different stages of the family manager's life (Chrisman et al. 2007). Also, not everyone in an organisation is sufficiently trustworthy to be regarded as a steward (Barney 1994), and the market needs companies to have both perspectives. As Clarke (2004) points out, cycles in the market will influence a firm to offer more stewardship at one time, and more agency at another.

In this chapter, we empirically study the impact of the agency governance mechanism, together with stewardship, on firm reputation, competitive advantage and firm performance among family businesses in Indonesia. The reasons for this focus are as follows. Firstly, firm reputation highly correlates with stewardship and governance. A stewardship firm will actively undertake CSR, which enhances a firm's reputation (Saeidi et al. 2014). Secondly, a firm with good corporate governance (GCG) will attract investors, as it is regarded as more valuable and more professional when compared with firms lacking GCG. Lastly, competitive advantage is the key to firm performance, while performance is the common measure of success of a firm. This study therefore explores not only how family businesses in Indonesia think about their responsibilities towards stakeholders and society, but also the extent to which they may incorporate an ethical dimension into their operations, thereby offering a potential alternative to some of the prevailing models of shareholder capitalism.

Why the Family Business?

We choose the family business context because family businesses are known to have a higher emphasis on stewardship than non-family businesses (Dood and Dyck 2015, 313; Miller, Le Breton-Miller and Scholnick 2008), although Corbetta and Salvato (2004) argue that this will depend on the family that owns the business. Cossin and Hwee (2016, 78) also noted that in Indonesia, there is a preference for informal, vaguely defined relationships, and for leadership styles where trust is typically invested in the relationships. Around 95 per cent of businesses in Indonesia are family-owned (International Finance Corporation 2016).

Some studies show that family businesses appear to have the potential to contribute in numerous ways to overall socio-economic prosperity (Heck and Trent 1999). Another unique feature of the family business rests in the innate conflicts which arise when its members try to juggle issues such as family, business commitments, goals and resource requirements. Sundaramurthy and Kreiner (2008) discuss the overlapping nature of the family unit with the business, positing that organisational identity may provide the firm with a competitive advantage. This unique family identity within a family firm is extremely difficult for rival firms to copy and may be important for the company's ability in achieving competitive advantage. Utilising this identity in a way that supports the business may create and sustain an advantage. Having non-economic, as well as economic goals may result from the fact that the culture of a family business is often closely related to the family's values and goals. PricewaterhouseCoopers's research on family businesses shows that most family businesses in Indonesia are engaged in some form of philanthropic activity. In their survey in 2018, 56 per cent of Indonesian family businesses were engaged in activity beyond giving money to good causes and the local community (PricewaterhouseCoopers 2018). This study was based on 2,953 interviews in 53 countries. From Figure 7.1, we can see that philanthropy in Indonesian family businesses is relatively large compared to the global total.

Figure 7.1: Indonesian vs global philanthropic activities

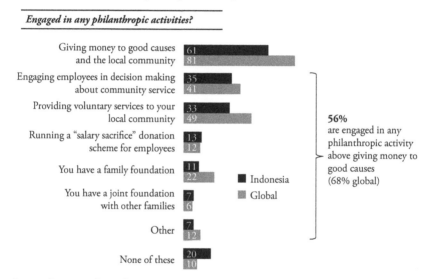

Source: PricewaterhouseCoopers, 2018.

Many family businesses define success not just in terms of financial wealth but in terms of the less tangible elements of personal growth/development, community/employee support and the upholding of core values. Continuity and endurance become key legacy hopes for long-term family business success. Table 7.1 (page 152) reflects opinions on balancing the ultimate goals of the family and the business.

Table 7.1: Stewardship: balancing family goals and the business

For the family/community	For the business
• To be a well-respected, honourable employer with happy and secure employees • To maintain family values/feeling, for example, honesty and reliability • To have benefitted society, not taken advantage of it. To have made a difference in a positive way, for example, engage in local projects • For children/family members and employees to have a good life and thrive (financially and in broader sense) as a result of the business • To leave a source of wealth and employment for family, employees, shareholders and the community	• To endure and remain a sustainable player in the market; to keep going and to keep growing. To leave behind a strong, profitable enterprise. • To face and overcome challenges and changes; to stand up to pressure • To have stewarded well, so as to pass the business to next generations in a better shape than it was inherited • To leave a legacy of quality products/ services • To have diversified and professionalised where appropriate

Examples of firms' responses from Indonesia

"To have built a successful business that has been able to provide good jobs, and to have given positive contributions to the society."	*"To have our business last for generations beyond the core family, continually existing, expanding, growing and evolving to meet market demands, being led by a team of professionals, and remaining as a source of blessing for the community."*
"That the value that the family instills continue to run, bringing positive benefits to the people of Indonesia as a whole."	*"To be known as a successful corporation that uses creativity and innovation to increase its value in bringing many opportunities to employees and society."*

Source: PricewaterhouseCoopers, 2018.

Research Model

The model that we have developed, based on our review of the literature on the topic, is shown in Figure 7.2 (page 153). Monitoring and incentives will increase a firm's reputation by preventing any observable unethical conduct by employees (Ertimur, Ferri and Maber 2012). Monitoring can also improve competitive advantage and a firm's performance by helping the firm to ensure that all members do as instructed by monitoring their progress to the agreed target (Jensen and Meckling 1976). Incentives also improve a firm's reputation by showing that the firm cares for employee welfare and values employee performance (Ertimur, Ferri and Maber 2012). Consequently, incentives will also directly improve a

Figure 7.2: Research model showing the links among the different variables

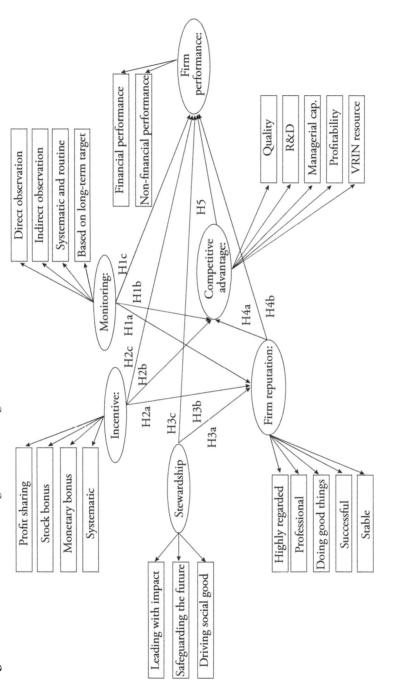

firm's competitive advantage and performance by aligning employee interests towards the firm's interests (Castellaneta 2016). Stewardship, on the other hand, improves a firm's reputation through its ethical approach, and because it cares about stakeholders outside the firm (Cossin and Hwee 2016). Stewardship firms will also aim to do their best for both customers and society, which will in turn positively affect a firm's competitive advantage and firm performance (Heuer 2010). Moreover, enhancing a firm's reputation will strengthen its ability to attract capital and new customers, further increasing its competitive advantage and performance (Gatzert 2015; Fombrun, Gardberg and Barnett 2000). Lastly, sustainable competitive advantage will lead to above-average performance in the long run (Porter 1985).

On the basis of this model, we put forward a number of hypotheses relating to the relationship between the variables, starting with the impact of monitoring. A firm monitors its employees to avoid the risk of higher agency costs, such as stealing, corruption and other unethical conduct. In practice this means that the organisation as a whole, as well as individual managers, monitor opportunistic behaviour and keep self-serving behaviour in check (Jensen and Meckling 1976). A company with good governance demonstrates its professionalism and is likely to attract corporate investors, while proper monitoring will ensure an effective and efficient business operation. It will also reduce the risk of strategic failure, and although more complex strategies generate higher monitoring costs (Zajac and Westphal 1994), this is essential for successful strategy implementation. A number of studies have shown that agency governance mechanisms such as monitoring and incentive systems contribute positively to firm performance (Andersen and Reeb 2003; Chrisman et al. 2007). This leads us to three hypotheses, namely that monitoring positively influences firm reputation; that monitoring positively influences competitive advantage; and that monitoring positively influences firm performance (H1a–H1c in Figure 7.2).

In relation to the impact of incentives, the main objective of incentives is to align employee behaviour with the firm's interest (Jensen and Meckling 1976). The firm provides compensation for agreed targets and covers any opportunistic behaviour that cannot be handled through monitoring. Employees in firms with good incentive systems may be motivated to achieve more, strengthening the positive impressions of stakeholders and further boosting the firm's reputation. In conjunction with monitoring, having incentives embedded in firm governance will help the firm maximise its resource potential in the face of competition. Well-planned incentives aligned with the firm's strategy will mean the entire organisation is united in its goals. In addition, Castellaneta (2016) has argued that even firms with many capabilities can under-perform. Managers may not be given proper incentives to pursue firm goals. Only when managers are given proper incentives does higher performance become possible. Such a "carrot-and-stick" approach is logical and practical in terms of increasing firm performance. Farley (1964) and Weinberg (1975), for example, found that a sales division incentive will maximise firm profits while also maximising the salesperson's income through commissions. This leads to three further hypotheses, namely that incentives positively influence firm reputation; that incentives positively influence competitive advantage; and that incentives positively influence firm performance (H2a–H2c in Figure 7.2).

Stewardship appears to have a number of positive impacts for a firm, and here, we focus on three possible variables. Firstly, we seek to test the influence of stewardship on firm reputation. A stewardship firm wanting to deliver social goods will pursue a range of actions to achieve that vision, most popularly CSR initiatives. Studies suggest that CSR is important for enhancing a firm's reputation among a broad range of stakeholders, including customers, suppliers, competitors, bankers and investors (Branco and Rodrigues 2006). Stewardship firms are no exception to this. This leads us to hypothesise that stewardship positively influences firm reputation (H3a in Figure 7.2).

Secondly, following Gardberg and Fombrun's (2006) argument that citizenship programmes are strategic investments comparable to R&D and advertising, Heuer (2010) suggested that stewardship could be a source of competitive advantage, also nurturing firm reputation, reputation capital, personal and organisational networks, social capital, trust and legitimacy. This strategy, Heuer suggested, "provides the greatest opportunity to achieve economic returns and gain competitive advantage" (2010, 36). This leads to a further hypothesis, namely that stewardship positively influences competitive advantage (H3b in Figure 7.2). The third variable is based on the work of Cossin and Hwee (2016), who argue that firms with high stewardship characteristics are known to possess a number of advantages, including a tendency to less debt, higher liquidity, higher returns on equity (ROE), higher shareholder returns and less stock volatility. They are also more likely to limit their downsizing in a crisis; a steward leader is known to have a positive influence on firm performance in a family business context (Wesley 2010). Our third hypothesis relating to stewardship is therefore that stewardship positively influences firm performance (H3c in Figure 7.2).

When it comes to firm reputation, scholars have agreed that a positive firm reputation can lead to a significant competitive advantage (Gatzert 2015; Fombrun, Gardberg and Barnett 2000; Fombrun and van Riel 2004). Reputation is important in the competition for talent, as in a highly competitive industry such as IT, in which human resources are the main source of competitive advantage, the most competent people will be attracted to firms with the highest reputations, further enhancing their competitiveness. We can therefore hypothesise that firm reputation positively influences competitive advantage (H4a in Figure 7.2). Firm reputation is also known to have a positive effect on financial performance and to facilitate the raising of capital (Gatzert 2015; Fombrun, Gardberg and Barnett 2000). New customers will be more willing to try a product from a highly regarded firm than risk buying from an unknown firm, especially when price is not an issue (Fombrun and van Riel 2004). We can therefore hypothesise that firm reputation positively influences firm performance (H4b in Figure 7.2).

When it comes to competitive advantage—defined as the relative performance of a firm compared with its competitors in the same product market (Peteraf and Barney 2003)—it has been suggested that the trust and reputation generated by a stewardship culture will enhance competitive advantage (Heuer 2010). Barney (1994) has noted the opportunities that arise from a high level of trust, whether from cost advantages due to the reduction or absence of governance costs in relation to a particular exchange, or the greater exchange of opportunities associated with higher trust levels. High levels of trust are therefore likely to generate competitive advantage for a firm. In line with this view, we highlight how a stewardship approach can nurture all human-related intangible resources, including reputation, in turn enhancing competitive advantage and ultimately increasing firm performance. This leads to a final hypothesis, namely that competitive advantage positively influences firm performance (H5 in Figure 7.2).

Methodology

We have undertaken quantitative research with the objective of measuring the relationship between the identified variables. Our sample is gathered from Indonesian family businesses and business groups. Following Chua, Chrisman and Sharma (1999), we define a family business as one that is managed by a highly dominant coalition consisting of members of the same family who seek to shape and pursue the vision of the business; thus, there is no "lone founder" business in our sample. We asked leaders in each firm (CEO or other top-level officers, directors, or the GM) to assess the level of stewardship, monitoring and incentives of their organisation; the reputation of the company in the eyes of customers; the firm's competitive advantage; and its performance over the previous three years. We then used a structural equation model to analyse the data using Lisrel 8.8. The operational variables are also shown in Figure 7.2, and in more detail in Table 7.2.

Table 7.2: Operationalisation of research variables

No	Variable	Definition	Dimension and number of items assessed	Reference
1.	Monitoring	Act of actively monitoring the opportunistic behaviour of agents	Monitoring (4)	Chrisman et al. (2007)
2.	Incentives	Existence of an internal incentive system in the organisation aligning agent behaviour to organisational direction	Incentive (4)	Chrisman et al. (2007)
3.	Stewardship	The practice of actively safeguarding and enhancing the organisation's ability to create economic and societal value over time, increasingly recognised as the best route to a company's long-term success	Leading with impact (8); safeguarding the future (7); driving social good (9)	Cossin and Hwee (2016)
4.	Firm reputation	Global perception of the extent to which an organisation is held in high esteem or regard	Highly regarded (1); professional (1); successful (2); stable (1); doing good things (1)	Weiss, Anderson and MacInnis (1999)
5.	Competitive advantage	Conditions under which competitors are unable to replicate a company's competitive strategies	Quality (1); R&D (1); managerial capability (2); profitability (1); valuable, rare, inimitable or non-substitutable resource (2)	Chang (2011); Barney (1991); Coyne (1986); Porter and van der Linde (1995)
6.	Firm performance	Ability of a firm to give returns to shareholders	Financial (2); non-financial (5)	Wiklund and Shepherd (2003); Delaney and Huselid (1996)

The control variables were education, gender and age, position, industry, tenure, firm age, organisation size and company sales. In total, 71 Indonesian firms participated in our study. For business groups with dozens of "child" (member) companies, we contacted one representative for each company and counted each "child" company as one of the sample. Our sample comprised 81.7 per cent men and 18.3 per cent women. Most participants were aged 41–50 (46.5 per cent of the sample), indicating that older people dominate top positions in firms. With most participants in their forties, that the dominant education level was a bachelor degree is unsurprising in view of the more limited opportunities for this generation to access higher education. Table 7.3 presents more detail on the gender, age and education level of participants.

Table 7.3: Gender, age and education level of participants

Criteria	Number	Percentage
Gender		
Male	58	81.7
Female	13	18.3
Age		
Below 30	5	7.0
31–40	13	18.3
41–50	33	46.5
51–60	19	26.8
Above 60	1	1.4
Education		
Bachelor/ vocational	43	60.6
Master degree	24	33.8
Doctorate	4	5.6

Our participants also had a balanced distribution in term of work tenure. The profiles of participants' positions and work tenure are shown in Figure 7.3.

Figure 7.3: Positions and work tenure

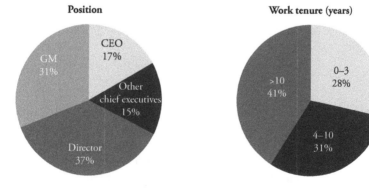

Our participants were spread unevenly across sectors. The largest group consisted of leaders in service and manufacturing firms. Table 7.4 shows participation by sector in descending order.

Table 7.4: Participants' sector profile

Sector	Number	Percentage of total
Service	25	35.2
Manufacturing	11	15.5
Finance, insurance and property	8	11.3
Mining	6	8.5
Retail	6	8.5
Construction	4	5.6
Transportation, communications, electricity and gas	4	5.6
Agriculture, plantation and fisheries	4	5.6
Pharmaceuticals	1	1.4
Media	1	1.4
Fast moving consumer goods (FMCG)	1	1.4

Results

The results of our study revealed that monitoring does not have a significant impact on firm reputation, competitive advantage and firm performance. Interestingly, incentives had a positive impact on firm reputation, but at the same time, had a significant negative impact on firm performance. By contrast, stewardship, like incentives, had a positive impact on firm reputation, but did not negatively impact firm performance. Lastly, our results also confirmed previous findings that firm reputation positively influences competitive advantage and vice versa. These results are represented in Figure 7.4 (page 160), with bold lines representing a positive significant effect and dashed lines indicating a significant and negative relationship between incentives and performance.

Our hypothesis regarding the positive impact of monitoring on firm reputation (H1a) was rejected, suggesting that monitoring schemes do not significantly influence firm reputation. A well-monitored organisation does not directly translate to an organisation of good repute. Monitoring may theoretically help to maintain a firm's reputation level—for example, by preventing employees from doing something bad or unethical which might damage the firm's reputation. However, monitoring cannot completely cover all possible unethical behaviour; once news of unethical conduct by a member of an organisation becomes public, monitoring can no longer help. Further, reputation does not come from the absence of bad news but the existence of good consistent actions. Neither did the findings support our hypothesis that monitoring supports competitive advantage (H1b). An adequately monitored firm is not necessarily a more competitive one that has better product quality, better profitability and better resources. A high monitoring level can suppress opportunistic behaviour and minimise agency costs, but does not itself deliver a competitive edge over other firms. In the long run, employees who are monitored will not necessarily work harder than those who are unmonitored.

Figure 7.4: Result of hypotheses

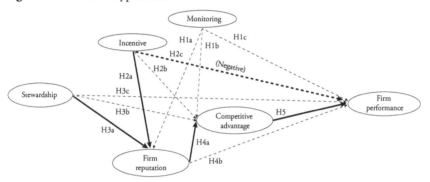

We also rejected the hypothesis that monitoring positively impacted firm performance (H1c). Monitoring might minimise the risk of agents undermining a firm's wealth, but it cannot deliver performance. Agents only "play the system" to maximise their own benefit. Monitoring one person's behaviour is hard enough, monitoring that of many is impossible. In an ideal world, managers preside over a hierarchical monitoring system, and it is also hoped that individuals in an organisation will monitor each other. However, unethical conduct among managers and subordinates is often collective, and monitoring mechanisms are ineffective against collective corrupt activity. Individuals will cover for each other and hide this from group-outsiders. Motives range from tangible things, such as money, to intangible psychological factors, such as acceptance by the group or threats from others involved. Such collective criminal behaviour will ultimately destroy performance from the inside.

We did find support for our hypothesis that incentives have a significant positive influence on firm reputation (H2a). People in a firm with a good incentive system in place may be motivated to do more. A positive atmosphere gives stakeholders a good impression. Real targets tied to real incentives mean employee satisfaction with company management, which in turn impacts positively on other stakeholders such as customers. Incentive systems also suggest that a company cares about employee performance, or even employees' economic welfare. Conversely, a firm with no incentive system is regarded as neglecting the welfare of employees. By contrast our hypothesis relating to the impact of incentives on competitive advantage (H2b) was rejected. A highly incentivised firm will not automatically succeed in competition. Given that any firm can follow the same practice of using money or other incentives to secure the commitment of employees, incentives cannot be regarded as directly increasing competitive advantage. As Zajac and Westphal (1994) have noted, "... linking [a] manager's compensation too closely to firm wealth might lead to risk-avoiding behavior on the part of the agent". In an environment in which incentives are closely related to firm performance, they may limit managers' creativity and boldness. Managers may focus on the short term rather than be willing to take risks for the longer-term future of the firm (for fear of failure). Changes that may risk their personal rewards, for example the amount of incentives, may be avoided.

Interestingly, our findings not only rejected the hypothesised relationship between incentives and firm performance (H2c) but also revealed that incentives had a significant negative impact on firm performance. Strong incentives may actually lower firm performance, posing a dilemma: that is, increasing incentives to minimise agency cost may also put pressure on firm performance. Since we included non-financial as well as financial indicators of firm performance, this suggests that incentives can damage both financial and non-financial performance. Our results indicate that most of the participants in our sample fail to use incentives wisely and effectively, perhaps only using them in "low return on investment" areas, or even seeing them as a waste of money. Incentives constitute a complex mechanism that needs careful planning to be useful. Zajac and Westphal (1994) argue that incentive (and monitoring) mechanisms may have diminishing returns; beyond a certain point, incentives may no longer be effective in aligning an agent's behavior with the interests of the firm, possibly damaging performance rather than enhancing it. Agents motivated only by rewards will not be effective workers in the long run as they will only work for rewards (despite already getting monthly wages).

When it comes to stewardship, our findings support our hypothesis that stewardship has a significant positive effect on firm reputation (H3a). Firms valuing a high level of stewardship impress stakeholders with visionary initiatives, trustworthy track records and a concern for society. In short, a stewardship firm which consistently practices CSR will also improve its reputation in the eyes of stakeholders (Branco and Rodrigues 2006). We did not find, however, that stewardship necessarily always translates to a higher level of competitiveness

(H3b). A stewardship firm may fail to appreciate the customer's point of view, where it is not aligned with its vision, and may fail to meet customers' demands despite delivering superior products or services in line with that vision. For example, green products may not always attract many customers due to high sale prices or a failure to meet the targeted customers' perceptions of taste and value. Likewise, our findings rejected the hypothesis that stewardship has a direct influence on firm performance (H3c). We found that stewardship affects performance only indirectly through firm reputation. Despite a tendency to less debt, higher liquidity, higher returns on equity, higher returns for shareholders, less stock volatility and less downsizing in crisis, stewardship in firms does not guarantee stronger firm performance. Following Ireland, Hitt and Sirmon (2003), we argue that a stewardship firm needs other capabilities as well to achieve competitive success.

We did find, however, that firm reputation has a significant positive effect on competitive advantage (H4a). This confirms previous findings that firms with better reputations are known to find it easier to raise capital and attract talent, and have greater bargaining power in relation to customers (Gatzert 2015; Fombrun and van Riel 2004; Morrison and Wilhelm 2004). By contrast, our results rejected the hypothesis that high firm reputation guarantees better firm performance (H4b). A product from a highly regarded firm may not be attractive if it is not perceived as offering better value or meeting customers' demands. For example, despite its great reputation in the luxury car segment, Ferrari will perform badly in poor rural areas. Finally, we did find that competitive advantage has a significant positive impact on firm performance (H5). A firm in a superior position to its competitors will deliver good performance. Firms with better products or service, and better R&D, profitability, managerial capability, or unique, valuable and rare resources will outperform their competitors.

Conclusions

Our results show that Indonesian family business leaders are unable to effectively monitor their employees in a way that has a significant effect on performance. This may be due to a number of reasons. Firstly, there may exist a bias towards family members. For example, the owner of the business may be reluctant to let a non-family member hold some strategic position (such as CEO), so a less competent family member is put in the position. Any future misconduct by a family member will be forgiven because he or she cannot be replaced by a non-family member. Top management or the Board are therefore unable to monitor the organisation objectively as shareholders favour family ties over competency.

This renders monitoring mechanisms ineffective and can trigger hostile behaviour by non-family managers who regard it as an unfair treatment of employees.

Secondly, families want to do things "their own way". As the majority owner, the family wields absolute power and authority over the firm and is able to do whatever it wants at any given time. Often, one family member may be too dominant, delegating insufficient authority to managers, instead claiming it him/herself. This monopolises control and undermines the role of managers; unprofessional action by the owner nullifies the organisation's monitoring mechanisms. Employees will naturally object to such conduct, but opposition may risk an employee's position in the company. They are left with only two choices: to keep silent about the issue or leave the company. If the dominant family member is left unchallenged by other family members, the problem only gets worse.

Our unfavourable findings regarding the impact of monitoring and incentives reflect the insufficient quality of monitoring and incentive practices in Indonesian family businesses. Not only do they fail to improve overall performance, but some of the agency governance mechanisms in our sample even made performance worse. We therefore conclude that both the level of stewardship and the implementation of agency governance mechanisms in family businesses in Indonesia remains low. Critically, this reinforces the need for both agency governance and stewardship. Without the proper monitoring of non-family employees *and* family members, family businesses will fail to suppress opportunistic behaviour, instead triggering it with the inequitable treatment of family and non-family members.

Finally, stewardship is imperative in a family business context. Only if family members pursue the interests of the organisation, rather than their own individual interests, can family businesses stop undermining their own performance. The ethical dimension of stewardship should encourage family members to see beyond their family circle. A family business learning to be a steward for society will begin to consider and prioritise the welfare of all those in the organisation, and of society, more than its own family welfare.

As we can see, an agency governance mechanism helps the firm to build a professional business organisation that is fair, makes sure no individual takes advantage of others and shows appreciation to those who work hard for the organisation. Stewardship, on the other hand, helps a firm to realise the importance of those outside the family. We believe this two-pronged approach to governance will produce a better outcome for all businesses, and for family businesses in particular.

Managerial Implications

Our study has shown that stewardship works through indirectly improving competitive advantage and firm performance. Managers wanting to benefit from this study should start by implanting stewardship values in their organisations. The process has to start from above; a visionary leader can lead the whole organisation towards becoming a steward-firm. Stewardship values such as doing the best for the organisation and society will begin to have impact if practised consistently.

Such top-level steward leaders need to communicate their vision to the whole organisation, creating more stewardship leaders from among their direct subordinates. The process will eventually reach the lower tiers of the organisation. Not all will become steward leaders, but stewardship in the organisation will keep growing because of mutual influences between those who are, reflecting Shibusawa's emphasis on developing the right business, with the right people, in service of the public good. By building a historical perspective on morality and ethics in the business world that—unlike CSR—concentrates on the morality within firms, industries and private-public partnerships (Fridenson and Kikkawa 2017), we may better understand our rapidly globalising world in which deregulation and lack of oversight risk repeating the financial, environmental and social catastrophes of the past.

If Indonesian organisations practice stewardship and *gapponshugi*-type policies consistently, their reputations will be enhanced, in turn helping to further develop competitive advantage. A strong reputation helps to attract high quality talent, new customers and additional capital. Also, workers within the firm who are satisfied with the incentive system and inspired by the firm's stewardship values and actions will encourage others to help the organisation achieve its goals. Even if a well-reputed company is small, it will do better than one with a poor reputation. A good reputation helps to attract capital, but how this capital is used to develop competitive advantage is crucial. Human, economic and social capital must be managed effectively to this end. If not, it will not translate into improved performance, and may even damage a firm's reputation. For example, we know that well-regarded firms may suffer more than firms with a lower reputation if talented individuals leave, or when a partnership is broken (Kwon and Rupp 2013; Morrison and Wilhelm 2004). Results depend on the firm's strategy and its execution. Here, a resource-based view can build a bridge between capital (resources), competitive advantage and wealth creation (Ireland, Hitt and Sirmon 2003), again analogous to Shibusawa's ability to establish trust in financial markets by popularising the joint-stock company and insisting on the importance of morality, transparency and professionalism. Such a strategy is extremely crucial for Indonesian family businesses to be able to survive and grow over the long term. Significantly, previous studies have shown that Indonesian family businesses that survived the 1997 financial crisis have good governance are run with professionalism, and emphasise morality as their business ethos (Adiperdana 2013).

We therefore conclude that, as shown in Figure 7.5, stewardship initiates a virtuous cycle by strengthening reputation, which in turn attracts capital into the firm. If that capital is used along the lines of stewardship for both the organisation and for society, this virtual cycle will be reinforced.

Figure 7.5: Virtuous cycle of stewardship

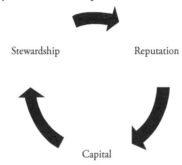

Stewardship   Reputation

Capital

References

Adiperdana, Ardan. 2013. *Pengaruh corporate governance mechanism dan organizational competence terhadap competitive advantage dan performance: Studi pada BUMN non perbankan dan anak perusahaannya* [The Influence of Corporate Governance Mechanisms and Organizational Competence on Competitive Advantage and Performance: A Study of State-owned Enterprises and their Subsidiaries]. Dissertation, Undergraduate Program in Management Science, Faculty of Economics and Business, University of Indonesia.

Anderson, R.C. and D.M Reeb. 2003. "Founding-family Ownership and Firm Performance: Evidence from the S&P 500". *Journal of Finance* 58: 1301–28.

Barney, J.B. 1991. "Firm Resources and Sustained Competitive Advantage". *Journal of Management* 17 (1): 99–120.

———. 1994. "Trustworthiness as a Source of Competitive Advantage". *Strategic Management Journal* 15: 175–90.

Branco, M. and L.L. Rodrigues. 2006. "Corporate Social Responsibility and Resource-based Perspectives". *Journal of Business Ethics* 69 (2): 111–32.

Castellaneta, F. 2016. "Building Firm Capability: Managerial Incentives for Top Performance". *Journal of Business Strategy* 37 (4): 41–6.

Chang, C.H. 2011. "The Influence of Corporate Environmental Ethics on Competitive Advantage: The Mediation Role of Green Innovation". *Journal of Business Ethics* 104 (3): 361–70.

Chrisman, J.J. et al. 2007. "Are Family Managers Agents or Stewards? An Exploratory Study in Privately Held Family Firms". *Journal of Business Research* 60: 1030–8.

Chua, J.H., J.J. Chrisman and P. Sharma. 1999. "Defining the Family Business by Behavior". *Entrepreneurship Theory and Practice* 23 (4): 19–39.

Clarke, T. 2004. "Cycles of Crisis and Regulation: The Enduring Agency and Stewardship Problems of Corporate Governance". *Corporate Governance: An International Review* 12 (2): 153–61.

Corbetta, G. and C. Salvato. 2004. "Self-Serving or Self-Actualizing? Models of Man and Agency Costs in Different Types of Family Firms: A Commentary on 'Comparing the Agency Costs of Family and Non-family Firms: Conceptual Issues and Exploratory Evidence'". *Entrepreneurship Theory and Practice* 28 (4): 355–62.

Cossin, D. and O.B. Hwee. 2016. *Inspiring Stewardship*. United Kingdom: John Wiley & Sons.

Coyne, K.P. 1986. "Sustainable Competitive Advantage—What it is, What it isn't". *Business Horizons* 29 (1): 54–61.

Delaney, J.T. and M.A. Huselid. 1996. "The Impact of Human Resource Management Practices on Perceptions of Organizational Performance". *Academy of Management Journal* 39 (4): 949–69.

Dood, S.D. and B. Dyck. 2015. "Agency, Stewardship, and the Universal-Family Firm: A Qualitative Historical Analysis:. *Family Business Review* 28 (4): 312–31.

EY. 2016. *EY Family Business Yearbook 2016*. https://familybusiness.ey-vx.com/pdfs/asiapac-facts.pdf.

Ertimur Y., F. Ferri and D.A. Maber. 2012. "Reputation Penalties for Poor Monitoring of Executive Pay: Evidence from Option Backdating". *Journal of Financial Economics* 104: 118–44.

Farley, J.U. 1964. "An Optimal Plan for Salesmen's Compensation". *Journal of Marketing Research* 1 (2): 39–43.

Fombrun, Charles J. and Cees B.M. van Riel. 2004. *Fame and Fortune (How Successful Companies Build Winning Reputations)*. New Jersey: Prentice Hall Publishing.

Fombrun, Charles J., Naomi A. Gardberg and Michael L. Barnett. 2000. "Opportunity Platforms and Safety Nets: Corporate Citizenship and Reputational Risk". *Business and Society Review* 105 (1): 85–106.

Fridenson, Patrick and Takeo Kikkawa. 2017. *Ethical Capitalism: Shibusawa Eiichi and Business Leadership in Global Perspective*. Toronto: University of Toronto Press.

Gardberg, Naomi A. and Charles J. Fombrun. 2006. "Corporate Citizenship: Creating Intangible Assets Across Institutional Environments". *Academy of Management Review* 31 (2): 329–46.

Gatzert, N. 2015. "The Impact of Corporate Reputation and Reputation Damaging Events on Financial Performance: Empirical Evidence from the Literature". *European Management Journal* 33 (6): 485–99.

Heck, Ramona K.Z. and Elizabeth Scannell Trent. 1999. "The Prevalence of Family Business from a Household Sample". *Family Business Review* 12 (3): 209–24.

Heuer, M. 2010. "Defining Stewardship: Towards an Organisational Culture of Sustainability". *Journal of Corporate Citizenship* 30: 31–41.

Ireland, R.D., Michael A. Hitt and D.G. Sirmon. 2003. "A Model of Strategic Entrepreneurship: The Construct and its Dimensions". *Journal of Management* 29 (6): 963–89.

International Finance Corporation. 2016. "IFC and Indonesia's Family Business Nusantara Foundation Help Family-Owned Enterprises Improve Corporate Governance". https://ifcext.ifc.org/ifcext/pressroom/ifcpressroom.nsf/0/191893606E133B9B8525 806600175903.

James, A.E., Jennifer E. Jennings and P.D. Jennings. 2017. "Is it Better to Govern Managers Via Agency or Stewardship? Examining Asymmetries by Family Versus Non-Family Affiliation". *Family Business Review* 30 (3): 262–83.

Jensen, M.C. and W.H. Meckling. 1976. "Theory of the Firm: Managerial Behavior, Agency Costs and Ownership Structure". *Journal of Financial Economics* 3 (4): 305–60.

Kwon, K. and D. Rupp. 2013. "High-performer Turnover and Firm Performance: The Moderating Role of Human Capital Investment and Firm Reputation". *Journal of Organizational Behavior* 34 (10): 129–50.

Madison, K., F.W. Kellermanns and T.P. Munyon. 2017. "Coexisting Agency and Stewardship Governance in Family Firms: An Empirical Investigation of Individual-level And Firm-level Effects". *Family Business Review* 30 (4): 347–68.

Miller, D., I. Le Breton-Miller and B. Scholnick. 2008. "Stewardship vs Stagnation: An Empirical Comparison of Small Family and Non-Family Businesses". *Journal of Management Studies* 45 (1): 51–78.

Morrison, D.A. and W.J. Jr. Wilhelm. 2004. "Partnership Firms, Reputation, and Human Capital". *The American Economic Review* 94 (5):1682–92.

Peteraf, M.A. and J.B. Barney. 2003. "Unraveling The Resource-based Tangle". *Managerial and Decision Economics* 24: 309–23.

Porter, M.E. 1985. *Competitive Advantage: Creating and Sustaining Superior Performance*. New York: Free Press.

Porter, M. E. and C. van der Linde. 1995. "Green and Competitive: Ending the Stalemate". *Harvard Business Review* 73 (5): 120–34.

PricewaterhouseCoopers. 2018. "Global Family Business Survey 2018". PwC Global, Services, Family Business. https://www.pwc.com/gx/en/services/family-business/family-business-survey-2018.html#:~:text=After%20surveying%20nearly%203%2C000%20family,pay%20off%20in%20real%20terms.

Razook, C. 2016. "Family Businesses Need Good Governance, Too". *Jakarta Post*, 16 November.

Saeidi, S. et al. 2014. "How does Corporate Social Responsibility Contribute to Firm Financial Performance? The Mediating Role of Competitive Advantage, Reputation, and Customer Satisfaction". *Journal of Business Research* 68: 341–50.

Sato, Yuri. 2004. "Corporate Governance in Indonesia: A Study on Governance of Business Groups". In *The Role of Governance in Asia*, ed. Yasutami Shimomura, 88–136. Singapore: Institute of Southeast Asian Studies, 2003 (copyrighted in 2003 by Japan Institute of International Affairs and ASEAN Foundation).

Sundaramurthy, C. and G.E. Kreiner. 2008. "Governing by Managing Identity Boundaries: The Case of Family Businesses". *Entrepreneurship Theory and Practice* 32 (3): 415–36.

Weinberg, C.B. 1975. "An Optimal Sales Commission Plan for Salesmen's Control Over Price". *Management Science* 21: 937–43.

Weiss, A.M., E. Anderson and D.J. MacInnis. 1999. "Reputation Management as a Motivation for Sales Structure Decisions". *Journal of Marketing* 63 (4): 74–89.

Wesley, C.L. 2010. "The Impact of Stewardship on Firm Performance: A Family Ownership and Internal Governance Perspective". Doctoral dissertation, Texas A&M University Texas, United States.

Wiklund, J. and D. Shepherd. 2003. "Knowledge-based Resources, Entrepreneurial Orientation, and the Performance of Small- and Medium-sized Businesses". *Strategic Management Journal* 24 (13): 1307–14.

Zajac, E.J. and J.D. Westphal. 1994. "The Costs and Benefits of Managerial Incentives and Monitoring in Large US Corporations: When is More not Better?" *Strategic Management Journal* 15 (Supplement 1): 121–42.

Chapter 8

The Making of a Thai Consumer Goods Conglomerate: The Role of Dynamic Entrepreneurship and Social Capital

Patnaree Srisuphaolarn and Motoi Ihara

Introduction

The objective of this chapter is to illustrate how Sahapat, a small importer and distributor in an emerging market like Thailand, has been able to turn into a consumer goods conglomerate in spite of various institutional voids, and in the presence of powerful foreign companies as its rivals on top of it. The time period in focus is from the 1950s to the 1990s, which is the period when Thailand started implementing the first National Economic Development Plan and also enjoyed double-digit economic growth for over four decades. Doing business in an economic take-off period has advantages in terms of market growth, but the absence of formal institutions forces businessmen to be creative in compensating for institutional voids like undeveloped capital markets or human resources training and development. Dynamic entrepreneurship is an important factor for success in emerging markets. In this study, the authors also seek to depict how an entrepreneur visualised and materialised business opportunities via exogenous social capital, that is, via foreign business partners. Such a study is therefore of value for studies on the business history of emerging markets. It also demonstrates the extent to which this particular Thai business drew on the Japanese way of doing business, in particular focusing on the value of goodwill and altruism and the societal responsibilities of a business through the construction of an internal market to nurture national champions.

The Business Landscape in Thailand in the 1950s

Although free trade and industrialisation were introduced to Thailand from the mid-19th century, it was not until the 1980s that indigenous Thai companies were able to develop into what might be identified as a "large business" (Suehiro 1986; Phongpaichit and Baker 2002). However, there was a turning point in the 1950s when the Thai Government adopted an import substitution approach as its economic development policy. Consequently, domestic production was promoted while imports were discouraged. Existing local manufacturers were small in scale and limited in number. Firms with experience in international business mostly focused their activities on finance and trade, importing consumer goods from port cities or earlier industrialising countries like Singapore, Hong Kong, Japan and Taiwan.

However, to turn an economy in which the basic economic activity had long been the export of natural resources and agricultural products into a more industrialised one needed tremendous changes in business infrastructure, such as roads and transportation facilities, new skill sets to run and manage manufacturing, and new ways of handling products and marketing. In sum, the country was in need of all kinds of capital, and all at once. On the one hand, industrial infrastructure such as dams and power plants, as well as highways, were built via loans from the World Bank. On the other hand, the Government opted to attract foreign capital to create jobs and transfer technology (Phongpaichit and Baker 2002). The most important sources of foreign investment at that time were the United States and Japan. US capital tended to insist on a wholly owned mode of entry, while Japanese capital was much keener to engage in joint ventures (Suehiro 1986).

Due to the fact that Thailand at that time was not well urbanised and the market for manufactured products was, therefore, limited, some wholly owned American firms asked the Government for protection as a condition for their investment. This protection took the form of the Thai Government not permitting the establishment of any company in the same area of production within the first 5 years of a US firm establishing its own Thai-affiliated company. Joint ventures with Japanese partners, in most cases, did not yield good results, leading to hostile takeovers of Thai stakes (Chokwatana 1991a). These multinational companies brought new products and new technologies to the market, but at the same time also created hurdles to competition from local Thai companies—in terms of brand power, scale of capital and the application of modern technology in manufacturing and management. Consequently, a natural "division of labour" was also seen. Foreign firms produced, while local firms helped these companies with distribution. Once the foreign firms gained local market knowledge, distributors were forced out of the market and had to look for new brands for which they could become a distributor.

Sahapat, Now and Then

Among firms that were active as traders in the 1950s, Sahapat was one of those that managed to survive, spin-off and eventually form a conglomerate. As of 2020, Sahapat and its affiliated companies, known as the Saha Group, have been doing business in three areas: consumer goods, food and beverage and industrial parks. Not all the companies in the group are listed in the stock market, but key companies like Sahapat are. Sahapat was listed in the market as early as 1978, 3 years after the Stock Exchange of Thailand (SET) started its operation. The official website states that it currently has a fully paid-in capital of USD 10 million. The 2019 financial statement shows the total assets of Sahapat as USD 1.093 billion, with an annual return on equity of 9.75 per cent. The company was among the 98 companies that were listed under the "Thailand Sustainability Investment" banner in 2019 by SET (Sahapat 2020).[1]

Sahapat, the core company of the Saha Group, was founded in 1942 as a grocery store in Sampeng,[2] which is a key distribution centre of the country and also home to Western and Japanese trading companies such as Borneo, Oriental Store, A.E. Nana, Mitsui and Anglo-oil (Saha Group 2020; Viriyapunditkul 2009a). It started to import and run a trading business in 1946, strengthening its overseas procurement channel in port cities such as Swatow in Guangdong Province, southeast China (now Shantou), Hong Kong and Singapore,[3] and by 1952, opened an affiliated company in Osaka, Japan, to explore potential products for import (Viriyapunditkul 2009a).

Thiam Chokwatana,[4] the founder of Sahapat, was born in 1916 to a Teochew Chinese[5] immigrant father and a Thai mother. At the age of 15, he decided to quit school because—in his words—he loved and respected his father and wished to become an apprentice in his family business. His father had founded a small grocery store, but his uncle was the manager. In the store, he started working as a handyman, running small errands and doing everything the others did not want to do. During his apprenticeship in the store, he learnt to master the key functions of a store owner. Eventually, he opened his own grocery store when he was 26 and had his own family, with three sons and a daughter. While his father was rather risk-averse, Thiam was more of a risk-taker. He insisted on transitioning from an ordinary grocery store that depended on the sale of staple goods (like sugar and rice) to become a wholesaler of broader product lines, such as T-shirts and the thermos, which suited people's new lifestyle after World War

II. His father did not agree with expanding the business by borrowing money from others, but Thiam insisted that paying a high interest rate was a rational choice in as far as it rendered a higher return.

With Thiam's positive attitude towards making changes, and a strong network through which he could procure a range of supplies from overseas, Sahapat earned a reputation as an influential importer of various brands of consumer products. But the one product that fast-tracked the company, being a really popular and lucrative product for Sahapat, was Lion powder shampoo from Japan. Powder shampoo was first introduced to Thailand by Kao Industrial (Thailand) and its sale became phenomenal, garnering monthly sales of 1.2 million units as its capacity to clean was far better than that of soap. Sahapat started ordering Lion powder shampoo in 1958, and learning of its huge potential from a market survey, Thiam decided to make this item the company's new cash cow. Lion powder shampoo competed neck and neck with Kao Feather. It was this item that triggered Sahapat to move down the value chain to manufacturing. When the Government, in 1959, implemented the import substitution policy, raising the import tax on finished goods from 50 per cent to 75 per cent, leaving no margin and incentive for importers to distribute imported goods, Thiam did not hesitate to revise his company's strategy by setting up his own plant[6] and importing powder shampoo in bulk to be repacked domestically (Viriyapunditkul 2009a; 2009b). Powder shampoo was the stepping-stone to the production of detergents in later years (Chokwatana 1991a). Lion Dentifrice (Thailand), the first joint venture with Lion Dentifrice Corporation, was completed in 1966 to focus on the marketing of toothpaste. One year later, Lion Fat and Oil (Thailand), later renamed Thai Lion, was set up as the second joint venture with the same Japanese partner to produce detergent and powder shampoo (Thai Lion 2009).

Despite the fact that Chinese merchants at that time were skeptical about investing with the Japanese, Thiam was certain that the Japanese way of doing business, which he saw as based on building goodwill, would lead to long-term prosperity. He had mentioned in his journal—where he recorded lessons on business or business practices—that Lion Fat and Oil had survived the financial crisis, but never once that it had opted to reduce the product quality as a way to survive. Instead, it strengthened its product quality and its relationship with distributors and sought better understanding of consumer behaviour via thorough surveys. On another occasion Thiam's analysis of Lion's success compared to the failure of rivals who started their businesses at the same time concluded that the firm's emphasis on goodwill was one of the keys to this success (Chokwatana 1991a).

While most importers running businesses at the same time were reluctant to move down the value chain to producing goods and had gone out of business, Thiam had envisioned that the import tax would one day be increased and was prepared to diversify into manufacturing. He planned to use the powder shampoo repacking plant as an experimental site where his staff could learn how to produce and become aware of the related issues that might emerge, so that when the time came to move into the full manufacturing of the product, there would be a firm foundation on which to run the business (Chokwatana 1991a). The joint venture with Lion Fat and Oil Corporation was a stepping-stone for Thiam and Sahapat to form a business group in later years.

Thiam passed away in 1990, when he was 74. By the time of his death, Sahapat had become an influential business group. Thiam's third son, Boonsithi, became the leader of the group (Viriyapunditkul 2009b). Thiam was regarded as a "role model" for businessmen, having built his business empire with "clean hands". Unlike most entrepreneurs in emerging countries who had built their businesses via concessions or links with key figures in the Government, Thiam made it clear that he would not engage in that kind of business. Many books on his business philosophies were published and the Sahapat story became the source of case studies for many MBA courses. Many regarded him as their business mentor.[7]

Entrepreneurial Process and Social Capital

A study of Thiam's business thoughts and philosophy is possible because, compared to most businessmen of his time, there is fairly rich information on him. He left two documented sources that can be used to trace his management ideas and the history of the company. The first is his "journal". He was keen on knowledge sharing, and so he would summarise into "lessons" and points to ponder, his thoughts on business talks he attended, company visits that he hosted and participated in (domestic and international) and what he read in the news, as well as his general observations—synchronised with his knowledge of Chinese and Buddhist literatures—as entries in his journal. He circulated these entries as memos to his staff. During the years 1971 to 1983, he circulated 301 journal pieces.[8] This twelve-year period was the period after the company had become engaged in the joint venture, when it was growing fast and facing various challenges in scaling up. Thiam wrote about everything he had learnt, as well as the lessons that needed to be learned from cases of both success and failure. He even copied down trade statistics to demonstrate world economic trends at the time. Later, these documents were published as a three-volume book series.

Another source of information is a thorough analysis of Sahapat's strategy—in effect a corporate history—by Somjai Viriyapunditkul, who got the opportunity to interview Thiam and key staff for her analysis in 1990. Written by the same author is a book on the work and life of Boonsithi, who was his right-hand man in moving from trade to manufacturing, and also a key link between Thiam and his Japanese partner. These five volumes together provide details of people and their contribution to the growth of the group, which the authors of this chapter have taken up in their analysis. In addition to the triangulation of this data with other printed materials, such as company anniversary booklets, news stories and articles in business papers, we also conducted four interviews to explore details not covered by the extant secondary data. Our interviewees included Boonsithi Chokwatana, the current Saha Group president; Boonyarit Mahamontri, the president of Thai Lion and one of the first batch of interns at Lion Corporation (Japan); Kobayashi Kazuo, who was among the first group of Japanese expatriates who came from Lion Corporation to Thailand; and Taira Naohito, the engineer who came to teach Thai staff about production techniques. The interviews took place in October 2013 to November 2014 in Bangkok and Tokyo, Japan.

To understand how Thiam has been successful in building his business group, we propose to divide his business development into three stages: the early stage of selling groceries; becoming a trader; and becoming an industrialist. At each stage, the necessary skills and knowledge needed to run the business were different. The same was true of the sources of his business opportunities and how they might have materialised, which was namely through his social network.

From Thiam's life and work, it is apparent that the Confucian values he learnt from his father and teacher in school had a strong influence on him. Among the various Chinese proverbs and sayings that he mentioned in his journal, one that was widely quoted was "fast and slow, hard and soft". This phrase summarised his approach to work: the quality of a person to make a right decision; when to act quickly; when to wait; when to work hard and make significant efforts; and when to let go. He also mentioned that his father had emphasised the virtue of reputation: goodwill rather than monetary benefit. Maintaining goodwill, at any cost, would deliver long-term benefit.[9]

As Thiam had quit school at an early age, he realised that he had to put more effort into learning on his own. His best way of learning was to ask questions, and to take action according to the answer he got. Everyone could be his teacher, young or old. He stressed that any individual should be naïve enough to ask any question so that he or she could learn. Pretending that one already knew something would be a hurdle to improving oneself (Prachachat Turakij 1989). During his apprentice years with his uncle, Thiam observed that the store was too passive in waiting for orders to come, so he offered to visit clients and take orders at their places. This later developed into a habit of visiting dealers and wholesalers to get first-hand feedback on consumer preference and market information.

At the age of 26, when Thiam opened his first business, which was a grocery store, he became exposed to international circles via Japanese and Western importers. He gained the trust of these merchants, which resulted in their consulting him regarding price setting, as well as asking him to be their distributor.[10] Thiam's business skills were so highly valued by these trading firms that the Mitsui company invited him on a business trip to Japan, and he was able to observe a range of business opportunities via these foreign business circles. Thiam was also known for his generosity and for being altruistic. He mentioned that there should be no rivals and helped others when he could. He once helped a Japanese man named Okuda, who had been left in Thailand during World War II, even offering him 20 per cent of the shares in his new firm in Osaka, Japan.[11] Overall, he had a wide personal and business network both domestically and internationally (Viriyapunditkul 2009a).

Due to increasing transactions with businesses outside Thailand, Thiam was exposed to the financial crisis due to the fluctuations in exchange rates. His Chinese school classmates who had pursued higher education and become lawyers—and in some cases later become active in Thailand's national politics and financial world—and officers at the Bank of Thailand introduced him to the concept of the "forward exchange rate". Hence, he learnt how to cope with risk when doing international business from the early years of the establishment of the company. He was also a friend of Chin Sophonpanich, founder of Bangkok Bank and a leading banker of the time. Chin helped him with cash flow management and financial capital when Thiam wanted to expand the business. These friends from his Chinese diaspora in Sampeng Market were important assets for the growth of Thiam's business.

When Thiam moved down the value chain to become an importer, he continued to learn from his Japanese business partners, mentioning from time to time the comments and advice he had received from businesses and individuals such as Wachol, Tanjo, YKK (Zipper) and Lion Corporation (Chokwatana 1991a; 1991b; 1991c.). These suppliers invited him to visit their companies in Japan and he also travelled to the US to understand more about the operation of modern businesses. Discussions with business partners were a key source of Thiam's business and management knowledge provided him with information on everything—from the job description of a salesman (including market surveys and competitor observation) to succession planning, and from the knowledge of new technologies and management to the impact of world trade on socio-economic trends. Thiam made frequent mention of how different Japanese and Thai companies organised their sales teams, or the importance of adopting an M-Form (multidivisional) structure in line with the product range to improve sales performance (Chokwatana 1991a). He emphasised that Thai executives should consider adopting Japanese methods of organising and managing teams, as well as the concept of continuous improvement. Human resources development and continuous improvement were the two key takeaway messages that Thiam would periodically remind his staff about in his "journal memos".

Money, Man, Manufacturing, and Quality Control

It was when he became an industrialist, however, that Thiam appears to have learnt the most on how to run a modern business. To move from being a trading firm to becoming a manufacturer, the company needed a huge amount of capital, as well as to upgrade its organisational capability in three areas: organisational culture, human resources and marketing. Regarding the working capital for the new venture, which required a registered capital of THB 4 million, Thiam obtained loans from Bangkok Bank and Mitsubishi Bank. As noted earlier, one of his close friends from his hometown played a leading role in Bangkok Bank (Viriyapunditkul 1991a), while Mitsubishi Bank was the main bank of Lion Corporation (Kazuo Kobayashi, personal communication with author, 2014). In total, Thiam secured access to more than THB 10 million to run his new venture. In an illustration of his philosophy of "fast, slow, hard and soft" Thiam normally used informal financing to run his business, reserving his bank credit for big business deals (Chokwatana 1991a).

It is essential to note here that the ethnic Chinese firms in those days were highly hierarchical structures with the owner at the apex of the company. In Thiam's words, they were "one-man-show" organisations (Chokwatana 1991c) with the company head as the ruler. Firms were organised in a paternalistic way, rather than according to the strict meritocracy applied by many Western/ modern businesses. This style of organisation may work when the business is small in scale, but a different method of organisation is likely to be necessary if it grows into a complex organisation with a large scale and scope.

Moreover, selling is also very different from producing. Selling needs persuasive negotiation skills and good communication abilities. Production, by contrast, needs a different set of complex skills, especially in production planning and quality control. In trading, the key activities had been procurement and redistribution; the operation could be flexible in terms of product selection, with products that proved not to be popular being crossed off the list of items ordered. A manufacturer's activities, however, start from the procurement of raw materials, and thus need precise planning and coordination. Agility and flexibility—the qualities that allow a business to excel in the selling process—were not what was required in managing the production line. Here, punctuality and precision were the key, and a set of formal production procedures was needed to ensure that standards were maintained. The manufacturing process also needed employees who could absorb new technologies in production and management. The skills needed to manage a production plant were thus very different from those needed to manage a sales operation, and also entailed the training of workers. At the same time, production departments needed to adjust production plans to correspond with the marketing strategy. Marketing surveys became the key to understanding the needs of consumers. New techniques had to be learnt and put into practice as existing practices using a rough rule of thumb or intuition were no longer sufficient. Systematic market research and data interpretation were also required, to reveal new potential products and markets.

Lion Corporation offered help in developing all of these three areas. Regarding improvements in human resource management, it sent capable engineers to teach Thai staff members how to run the production line, also making it a condition of the collaboration that Sahapat should send Thai staff members to train in Japan. On the marketing front, it worked hand in hand with Sahapat to carry out market surveys. To ensure product quality and sound management control, Lion Corporation transferred to Sahapat from Japan the most up-to-date management and quality control systems.

Educating employees was not a practice previously adopted by Chinese merchant enterprises. The core competences of a trading firm lay in its networks of suppliers and buyers. Supply sources and their list of buyers were kept as a trade secret, because if employees could gain access to this information, they might quit the company and open a store of their own. Thiam, however, held a different perspective; he was keen to empower the young. He made a young man in his early twenties a store manager. He sent groups of young managers— many of them university graduates—to train and to take apprenticeships in Japan. The first batch of these recruits was referred to as "the three musketeers" and consisted of Damri Darakanond (who later went off on his own to form the influential Saha Union Group, assuming the role of group president), Chalong Wittayanond and Pakun Tangchaisak (Viriyapunditkul 1991a). Thiam had mentioned from time to time that the world had changed in favour of the younger generation and new practices. When he himself had been a young boy, people then had learnt from old experiences, but later in the 1970s, those who were older had needed to constantly upgrade their knowledge or they would have been left behind. Thiam revealed that he used to teach Damri when the latter was an apprentice at Sahapat, but "at this age"—which was 55—it was he who had to learn from Damri (Chokwatana 1991a).

In his journal, Thiam also mentioned the human resource management style of Japanese companies a number of times. One example which he emphasised was the succession of the Lion Fat and Oil Company president in 1970. The president had died leaving no officially written will and no male successor. An executive with 53 years of experience at the company was made acting president but did not present good performance. Later, the former president's son-in-law, who was young and knowledgeable, was nominated as president (Chokwatana 1991a), demonstrating that Thiam tended to use meritocracy rather than the number of years of experience to assign people to their jobs. When it came to marketing, Thiam got to learn the importance of thorough research, especially research techniques. From the early years of the business, he was keen to get first hand data via wholesaler visits and personal observation. Systematic survey methods from Japan were therefore of interest to him. He often mentioned how salesmen could also help in market surveys by collecting data from consumers and competitors (Chokwatana 1991a; 1991b; 1991c).

When David Fought Goliath: Sahapat's Success in Building a Local Brand[12]

As a latecomer in the toiletries and cleaning product manufacturing sector— one in which two well-established market leaders were already sharing more than half of the market—it took Sahapat 13 years to outperform Colgate and become the second-largest producer in the Thai detergent market. It was Thiam's contribution in brand name selection and Lion Corporation's assistance in quality upgrading that helped to make the Thai brand Pao become, as it were, the talk of the town in 1976. In most emerging markets, Western names tended to be associated with superior quality (Austin, Davila and Jones 2017), so choosing a name in the local language was to many a rather odd idea, but in this case, it worked.[13]

Sahapat imported Top, one of Lion Corporation's detergent brands, into Thailand in 1950. Top performed well until Unilever and Colgate started to produce their own products locally in 1958. Importing detergent meant cost disadvantages as well as a product disadvantage because of the slower adjustment of the product to local market preferences. This included things such as scent, the amount of bubbles and the touch of it when dissolved in water, as washing machines were not yet diffused in the Thai market then. However, even when Sahapat and Lion Corporation were successful in producing detergent in Thailand in 1967 to address the cost disadvantage, other troubles remained, including marketing communication and product quality.

Sahapat's early strategy as a distributor of imported products had been its penetration strategy, namely using low prices as an incentive to buyers. Sahapat had been notorious for prioritising promotion over quality. Allowing some exaggeration, Thiam admitted this, mentioning in his journal that at a time when sales performance was not good, the responsibility must lie with the promotion team. Sahapat's sales promotions were in fact evaluated by song composers and market communicators as legendary (Vilaithong 2006). Sahapat would continuously come up with creative yet practical methods to communicate with its target market in rural areas, such as product-specific jingles, radio programmes, music and comedy bands, and caravan sales, in addition to its standard approach of showing films in conjunction with product demonstrations. However, when Sahapat launched Pao, Thiam tried to rebrand Sahapat products with a strong emphasis on quality. This strategy— pursued through thorough training and the implementation of quality-control circles—paid off when Pao qualified for certification by the Thailand Industrial Standards Institute. The company claimed that Pao was the first of its kind to receive this quality assurance stamp (B. Mahamontri, Thai Lion President, personal communication with author, 19 December 2013).

Pao was positioned in the market as a detergent with "an affordable price and precise quality". It was also fortunate in the timing of its launch, which was just about the time when the oil shock hit Thailand in early 1974. The product was well received, and the detergent became a household staple. Since the rising price of detergent meant increased living costs, detergent was listed as an item with a price tightly controlled by the Government. Moreover, aside from price fluctuations, cases of poor-quality detergent were reported almost on a daily basis, resulting in price and quality becoming critical purchasing criteria. The quality of Pao was developed by adding an "optical brightening agent", which made the powder look a shining-white compared to rival products. The chemical also worked well for washing white shirts. As part of its price strategy, Pao redesigned its package size and set its price at 20 baht, while rival products sold at 27 baht (Viriyapunditkul 2009a). Within four years, Pao was able to increase its market share to 24 per cent and has remained one of the three big manufacturers in the detergent market since then. By the time it celebrated its 20th anniversary, Thai Lion was exporting its products to Japan and the Middle East, as well as to other countries. It had also become an original equipment maker (OEM) for Henkel of Germany, producing detergents to be sold in Singapore and Hong Kong (Prachachat Turakij 1989). It was the success of Pao that ensured that Sahapat was able to establish a firm foothold as a quality manufacturer. Its successful joint venture with Lion Corporation also made Sahapat a prominent story in business news in Japan. As a result, more Japanese companies became inclined to co-invest with Sahapat. By 2009, Sahapat had joint ventures with 64 Japanese companies (Viriyapunditkul 2009a).

Apart from Pao detergent and consumer products that were under license from the Lion Corporation, Sahapat developed one more pillar: Mama instant noodles. This business was triggered by a member of the Bangkok Bank in the Chinese trading district, Rajawongse, where Sahapat's trading office was situated. This banker knew a textile manufacturer who had diversified into the production of instant noodles in Taiwan. Sahapat co-invested with Taiwan President Foods and Jen—the banker—at an equal ratio of 30 per cent each, awarding the remaining 10 per cent to a Taiwanese who liaised with the Taiwan manufacturer. The CEO who was nominated for Thai President Foods again revealed Thiam's focus on meritocracy. With the consent of his Taiwanese partner, Thiam nominated Pipat Paniangvait as CEO instead of Jen, based on Pipat's proficiency in Chinese and his business acumen. However, unlike in the Taiwanese market, instant noodles were not well received when they were first launched in Bangkok. Consumers could not see any price benefit compared to the products of street food vendors. It was the 1974 oil shock that in fact turned Mama into a popular product, as Sahapat insisted on maintaining its existing price despite increasing production costs. This act of "altruism" helped to make Mama a staple in Thai households.

The knowledge gained from managing its factories in Thailand enabled Sahapat to expand and strengthen its production network into Europe and America; its joint venture partners included Janome, Molten, Samsung and Nissin, just to name a few. The company engaged in many forms of internationalisation, including joint ventures, licensing, and foreign direct investment in China, Myanmar, Cambodia and Indonesia (Viriyapunditkul 1991a). It is also necessary to note here that Boonsithi, who was a key person in dealing with Japanese executives and in running the factory during the pre-production period, had worked for six years at Kyoko, a Sahapat-affiliated firm in Shinsaibashi, Osaka, Japan. While his other siblings had been sent to colleges in the US, Boonsithi had been asked by Tham to take an apprenticeship in Japan after finishing high school. Besides his job at Kyoko, Boonsithi also visited small manufacturers in the area, mastering the Japanese way of doing business (Viriyapunditkul 2009b). He became, as it were, the "cultural translator" for Thiam, in terms of both the Japanese-Thai working culture and the culture of trading and manufacturing. This was one reason why the joint venture with Lion Corporation was carried out smoothly.

Managing the Growth Strategy

Instead of combining all business units within a single organisational structure, Sahapat developed a strategy more similar to those of some Japanese business groups. As Boonsithi, the current President of the Saha Group, has emphasised, a business must be run by capable persons. Blood ties should not be the condition for taking charge of a business. (Viriyapunditkul 2009b). Thiam himself had eight children: six sons and two daughters. All, except for one daughter who chose to pursue her religious beliefs, built their own business empires. Employees of Sahapat were also able to start up their own businesses, something that Sahapat viewed as a new opportunity rather than looking upon them as rivals; Sahapat usually invested in such new ventures. Saha Union and Thai President Foods were two outstanding examples of this strategy. In Thiam's words, investing in different initiatives enabled him to talk with a board of directors who were young, and from different fields (Chokwatana 1991a). Board meetings served for him as a classroom for new business practices. There was another advantage too, namely that each company supported and competed with one another. In other words, Sahapat had created its own internal market to nurture national champions. This way, every party concerned could be active and continuously improve its performance, in turn improving the performance of the group as a whole. This strategy can be summarised in the phrase "grow up and spin off, yet spin off to grow up".

Under its business philosophy of "grow up and spin off", as of 2009, the group had expanded to cover ten product groups with 211 companies actively running their businesses under an affiliation to the Saha Group.[14] Its products have come to range from household products like toothpaste and detergents, to food (like instant noodles), textiles and apparel, electric appliances, and logistics and warehouse systems.[15] It can be said that the Thai population and Thai businesses have increasingly had to use the Saha Group's products or services one way or another. By the 2010s, the group was marketing more than 30,000 products under 1,000 brand names. By the end of 2018, the group owned three industrial parks and had created more than 100,000 jobs. The total annual sales of the core company alone was USD 1,090.5 million in 2018.[16] Sahapat's official website reported in 2020 that its total assets as of 2019 was USD 903.2 million and its liabilities USD 289.37 million. Return on assets was 6.49 per cent and return on equity 9.75 per cent. The company's liabilities to equity ratio was 0.47

(Sahapat 2020). It had, moreover, survived two oil shocks as well as economic crises, especially the 1997 Asian financial crisis that had crippled most Thai businesses founded in the 1950s. Thai Lion continued to contribute to Lion Corporation's international performance by actively continuing to launch new products, many of which were locally developed, and some of which actually allowed the group to engage in reverse exports to Japan (B. Mahamontri, Thai Lion President, personal communication with author, 19 December 2013). To summarise how Sahapat has grown, the key events in the development of the Saha Group are shown in Table 8.1 (page 183).

Conclusion

This paper has illustrated how Sahapat has grown into a business group. Encountering various institutional voids, for example in management education, human resources development, limited financial products and limited marketing intermediaries, as well as government policies that were favourable to foreign rivals and economic downturns due to oil shocks, Sahapat managed to fill these voids by utilising the founder's entrepreneurship and social capital, both domestic and international, and both personal and from business networks. It could be said that Thiam was able to take advantage of merchant circles in Sampeng, but it was his strong desire to become successful that led to his expanding his circle to include capable individuals from overseas.

Thiam was a risk taker and an avid learner. In all his conversations with any of his partners—be they bankers, wholesalers, consumers or business counterparts—he kept his eyes and ears open for any business opportunity. While others remained uncertain about taking a step further into joint-venturing with the Japanese, Thiam, after thorough observation, was willing to take the risk. Having a compatible organisational culture and growth strategy made a key contribution to the success of the venture, and this in turn resulted in goodwill towards it among Japanese business circles. Continuous upgrading of its organisational capability gave Sahapat a competitive advantage in the long run. Inspired by how profit should be managed, in conjunction with Thiam's personal character of being altruistic, the company's creative internal market system—"spin off and grow"—created a healthy environment for nurturing generations of entrepreneurs and enabled Sahapat to form a business entity that has remained influential up to the present day.

Table 8.1: Key events in the Saha Group 1940s–80s

[Compiled based on data on the Saha Group, 1991: *Anusorn Nai Ngan Prarajjathan Dinfangsob Naai Thiam Chokwatana* (In Memory of Mr Thiam Chokwatana's Funeral), 58–61; Chokwatana (2009); and *Sahapat Lae Borisat Naikrua: Chak Bantuk Kwamsongjam Dr Thiam Chokwatana* (Sahapat and Affiliated Companies: From Dr Thiam Chokwatana's Memo to Staff), 84–9.]

Year	Growth/organisation strategy	Motivation
1942	First grocery business founded	Market opportunity
1946	Import and trading business started	Insufficient goods due to World War II
1949	Started to import from Japan	Seeking greater variety of supplies to sell in the home market
1952	Set up a trading company to do business with Japanese partners	Business opportunity with the Japanese
1958	"Spin-off and grow" strategy (small businesses within the Saha Group)	Human resource retention in line with Confucian values and investment opportunities
1959	Invested in packaging Lion shampoo in Thailand	Market opportunity & reduction of cost disadvantage caused by increase of import tariffs. Preparation to full scale domestic production.
1961	Local production of toothpaste	Capability to upgrade to production.
1967	Local production of detergent and raw materials	Product development strategy
1972	Fully diversified from a trading firm to a manufacturer	Long-term survival and sustainability
1974	Completely changed from a "one-man-show" management style to a formal organisation	To respond to the company's expansion into a business group
1978	Founded Sahapattana Investment	Focus on diversification and investment, especially in manufacturing plants
1978	Invested in Sriracha Industrial Park	Rising price of land in Bangkok and metropolitan areas—location of Sriracha near eastern seaboard supports exports; Thiam chose Sriracha as the result of lessons learnt from Japanese land development
1978	Sahapat became a listed company on the Stock Exchange of Thailand	Wealth sharing through capital markets
1986	Founded the Dr Thiam Foundation	Funding of education and health promotion

Notes

[1] "Financial Information", Investor Relations, Sahapat, accessed 9 December 2020, www.sahapat.co.th/investor/financial.

[2] For more on the importance of Sampeng and neighboring areas as a distribution centre and home to Chinese merchants, some of whom became business tycoons, see Sukkhi (2006) and Endo (2013).

[3] Overseas Chinese trade networks were established and grew tremendously after the opening of ports in China 1842 onwards. Starting in the rice trade, these companies later diversified into insurance, trading and so forth. Their products expanded to consumer goods after World War II to substitute for products from Europe.

[4] In Thailand, calling people by their given name is considered very polite. This chapter will therefore refer to the founder of Sahapat as Thiam, rather than use his surname.

[5] Teochew Chinese, originating from eastern Guangdong, China, became more influential, especially in trade, the mid-18th century onwards. The number of Chinese immigrants into Thailand increased continuously during the period 1918–30, with more than 60,000 Chinese coming into the country annually. The highest number recorded is 154,600 people, in 1927.

[6] This plant was registered as Lion Plant (Thailand) Limited Partnership, later renamed Bangkok Lion. A few years after opening, it also began to produce toothpaste for Lion Dentifrice (Thailand). See Viriyapunditkul (1991b).

[7] One of these was the founder of the entertainment business group listed on the Stock Exchange of Thailand, Paiboon Damrongtham. See Damrongchaitham (2011). There are further examples in Subpaiboon (2000).

[8] The number of journal memos released in each of the first 8 years from 1971 was: 7, 59, 89, 70, 39, 26, 8 and 3 respectively.

[9] The emphasis on goodwill can be seen in Thiam's journal entries in several places. He also recorded his observations on how Lion Fat and Oil could grow rapidly. In his analysis, unlike Thai (Chinese merchant-based) firms that focused on their own benefit, Japanese firms tended to invest more in companies and their people, aiming for the long-term benefit of all stakeholders. He also mentioned the story of the YKK (Yoshida Kōgyō Kabushiki Kaisha) zipper business investment in the UK, where YKK contributed to local communities rather than simply focusing on reaping profits to send back to the company's head office in Japan (Chokwatana 1991a.) This idea was compatible with doing the right thing and the five key relationships of the Confucian value system.

[10] In his journal, Thiam mentioned the case of an Oriental Store manager who asked for his comments on how to sell canned condensed milk, and to whom he offered solutions. The sales performance surprised the manager and enhanced Thiam's reputation (Chokwatana 1991a).

[11] Okuda later on introduced Thiam to many Japanese producers, including Lion Corporation.

[12] Thiam wrote in his journal about his rivals from the US and Europe in relation to the detergent market: "... we [Sahapat] were like a child fighting a Giant. Thus, we need[ed] to get well prepared and move wisely" (Chokwatana 1991a). This again reflected his philosophy of "fast, slow, hard and soft".

[13] Pao is actually the name of a judge in Song dynasty, China, who was well-known for his integrity to his profession, and whose life story was made into a TV drama by a Taiwanese film maker, which gained popularity in Thailand in early 1975. In Thailand, people are quite used to Chinese brand names and have regarded them as local.

[14] Not all of these affiliated companies have been listed on the stock market, hence obtaining a recent update is rather difficult. A key executive in the group has admitted that it is difficult for them to figure out how many companies are actually within the group; although 242 companies had been founded under the Saha Group, 31 had gone out of business.

[15] The ten product groups include: (1) systems, logistics and warehouse systems; (2) cosmetics and toiletries; (3) electrical products; (4) food and beverages; (5) footwear; (6) household products; (7) garments; (8) textiles; (9) services; and (10) miscellaneous. Each of these respective product group has a number of affiliated companies as follows: 10; 15; 4; 11; 47; 5; 14; 11; 22; and 4, respectively. The footwear sector is more conspicuous among the rest for having 47 companies; this is because Sahapat has control over the whole value chain of footwear products.

[16] Based on US$1 = THB$30 (as of December 2020).

References

Austin, G., C. Dávila and G. Jones. 2017. "The Alternative Business History: Businesses in Emerging 'Countries'". *Business History Review* 91 (3): 537–69.

Chandler, A.D. 1995. *Strategy and Structure: Chapters in the History of the Industrial Enterprise*. Massachusetts: Massachusetts Institute of Technology.

Chokwatana, T. 1991a. *Bunthuk Kwamjam Por Sor 2514–2515* [A Journal A.D. 1971–1972]. Bangkok: Dokyar.

_____. 1991b. *Bunthuk Kwamjam Por Sor 2516* [A Journal A.D. 1973]. Bangkok: Dokyar.

_____. 1991c. *Bunthuk Kwamjam Por Sor 2517–2521* [A Journal A.D. 1974–1978]. Bangkok: Dokyar.

_____. 2009. *Sahapat Lae Borisat Naikrua: Chak Bantuk Kwamsongjam Dr Thiam Chokwatana* [Sahapat and Affiliated Companies: From Dr Thiam Chokwatana's Journal], ed. Sirina Paowaloranwittaya. Bangkok: Amarin Printing.

Damrongchaitham, P. 2011. "Paiboon Damrongchaitham Pood Thung Dr Thiam Chokwattana 1" [Mr. Paiboon Damrongchaitham's Reflection on Dr Thiam Chokwatana Part I]. Accessed 25 February 2013. www.youtube.com/watch7v=JDK0GEgCGH4.

Endo, G. 2013. *Diversifying Retail and Distribution in Thailand*. Chiang Mai: Silkworm Books.

Phongpaichit, Pasuk and C. Baker. 2002. *Thailand: Economy and Politics*. Selangor: Oxford University Press.

"Twentieth Anniversary of Thai Lion Corporation". *Prachachat Turakij*, Special issue, 1989.

Saha Group. 1991. *Anusorn Nai Ngan Prarajjathan Dinfangsob Naai Thiam Chokwatana* [In memory of Mr Thiam Chokwatana's Funeral]. Pamphlet distributed at Thiam's funeral.

_____. 2020. "Key Figures from Financial Report 2017–2019". Investor Relations. Accessed 9 December 2020. www.sahapat.co.th/investor/financial.

Subpaiboon, T. 2000. *55 Trakul Dang Pak 1* [55 Famous Families: Part I]. Bangkok: Nation Multimedia Group.

Sukkhi, C. 2006. "Sampeng: laengroam settakij laengroam kwambunthueng" [Sampeng: Business Centre Entertainment Centre]. In *Sampeng Prawatsat Chumchon Chaojiin nai Krungthep* [Sampeng the History of Chinese Community in Bangkok], ed. Suphang Chantawanich, 93–121. Bangkok: Chinese Study Centre of Chulalongkorn University.

Viriyapunditkul, S. 2009a. *Sahapat Toh Laew Taek Lae Taek Laew Toh* [Sahapat, Spin-off to Grow and Grow to Spin-off]. Bangkok: People Media Books.

————. 2009b. *Boonsithi Chokwatana: Chiwit Nii Pen Arai Koh Dai Tae Tong Pen Nueng* [Boonsithi Chokwatana: Whatever I am, I Must be the Number One]. Bangkok: People Media Books.

Vilaithong, V. 2006. "A Cultural History of Hygiene Advertising in Thailand, 1940s–early 1980s". Unpublished PhD thesis, Australian National University, Canberra, Australia.

Chapter 9

Antecedents of Corporate Social Responsibility in Indonesia, 1900s–1950s

Pierre van der Eng

Introduction

Chapter 12 will discuss how Indonesia's 2007 company law made commitments to corporate social responsibility (CSR) compulsory for registered companies. Scholarships on CSR in Indonesia generally assume that the concept is entirely new to the country (see for example Waagstein 2011). However, until 1958, Dutch-owned companies were among the largest in Indonesia, and the findings of Sluyterman (2012) suggest that several Dutch entrepreneurs and companies perceived their obligations to society in the early 20th century in ways similar to what now motivates CSR. This chapter does not intend to argue that Dutch firms were motivated by CSR. Rather, it seeks to establish whether practices now associated with CSR were part of the ways in which the largest enterprises in the country carried out their business before the 2000s. The chapter focuses on the 1900s to the 1950s, when the total number of incorporated firms in Indonesia increased from 1,000 in 1900 to 2,200 in 1940 (Lindblad 2008, 22–3). The largest were registered in The Netherlands, but other large firms were registered in Indonesia.[1] The chapter ends in the late1950s, when the Indonesian Government nationalised most foreign-owned firms in Indonesia and continued them as State-owned enterprises.

The next section elaborates the definition of CSR used in this chapter. The section "Legal Requirements" explains the changes in the minimum legal obligations on companies to provide social benefits and amenities to stakeholders, particularly employees. The section "CSR-type Practices" discusses the provisions made by firms beyond this minimum, which can be regarded as equivalent to CSR.

A CSR Definition—Implications for Historical Research

A commonly used definition of CSR is as follows: "... actions that appear to further some social good, beyond the interests of the firm and that which is required by law" (McWilliams and Siegel 2001). This definition is ambiguous, because actions to advance a social good beyond the legal minimum may not be in the direct interest of a firm, but may still benefit a firm. For example, such actions may enhance a firm's public reputation and, therefore, increase sales and/ or shareholder value, but it would be difficult to establish conclusively that this is the intended effect of any company action. For the purpose of this chapter, the most practical understanding of CSR is assumed, in that it comprises a company's actions that create social goods beyond legal obligations and that benefit the company's stakeholders.

However, a few complications arise when applying this definition of CSR to an analysis of the past:

1. Social legislation and the legal obligations on firms have been in constant flux around the world since the late 19th century, including in Indonesia. Voluntary actions of benevolence that met the CSR definition ceased to do so once they became legislated.

2. Some parts of colonial Indonesia were under the rule of sultans and princely rulers. Legal plurality meant that not all government legislation applied throughout the country. Even if companies implemented relevant legislation consistently, the same actions might amount to CSR in some parts of the country, but not in areas under colonial law.

3. Legislation established the minimum of benefits and amenities that employers were obliged to provide to workers. There was scope to provide benefits and amenities voluntarily to a greater and/or qualitatively higher degree at higher expense. Depending on the degree that employers did this, it could be regarded as CSR.

4. CSR-related actions by firms coincided with the expansion of public amenities. In some cases, local or national governments provided subsidies to encourage firms to provide amenities as a public good, even though there was no legal requirement to do so. In such instances, the lines between public and private actions were blurred.

5. In some cases, firms responded to increasing labour union activity and the legal right of workers to withhold their labour during disputes. Consequently, companies created social goods, not necessarily due to a moral stance of company owners or managers, but to evade the potential costs of strikes. After 1918, labour unions in Indonesia became very vocal in demanding improvements in the freedom of association, the right to strike, minimum wages, maximum hours of work, restrictions on child and female

labour, social insurance—such as old age pensions—and unemployment pay. To different degrees, companies agreed to such demands.

6. Actions of firms generally targeted their employees. However, in many cases, firms found it difficult or ethically untenable to exclude other stakeholders, especially in rural areas. Their amenities were conceived as social goods.

7. There are few comprehensive tallies of all "CSR-related" actions in which firms engaged; just indications of what individual firms did.

Legal Requirements

Point (1) above is particularly significant in Indonesia's historical context and needs further discussion in order to differentiate legal obligations from voluntary CSR-like commitments. Defining the legal entitlements of workers and introducing social legislation were slow processes. Both related to the gradual expansion of employment opportunities outside farm agriculture, particularly from the 1870s. They also related to developments in the international economy after World War I and the responses of firms to changing economic conditions during the 1920s and 1930s, mitigated by an understanding that the impact of new social legislation would be limited as it could not be enforced in the informal sector of the economy. Changes were shaped by expectations in Indonesian society during the 1940s and 1950s, that imposing new social legislation on companies would resolve and prevent social ills.

The expansion of employment at companies operating agricultural estates and mining ventures in sparsely populated and remote rural areas from the 1870s depended on migrant labour, which firms recruited overseas or in Indonesia's core island, Java, with formal labour contracts. To attract contract workers, employers had to establish amenities. Poor facilities at some ventures caused the abuse of workers, which the colonial government, after 1880, sought to remedy by making labour contracts subject to regulation. This led to a system of "coolie ordinances" for different regions in the outer islands of Indonesia (Heijting 1925, 27–78, 188–90). Details of the ordinances varied, but the 1889 Coolie Ordinance for North Sumatra, for example, specified that an employer was required to treat contract workers well, pay their wages regularly, and provide them with "suitable housing" and "reasonable medical care" (Houben and Lindblad 1999, 14). Similar legislation did not apply to Java, where labour protection in private firms took the form of health and safety regulations and a decentralised system of casual supervision by regional colonial officials of labour conditions at companies.

Later legislation augmented the details of the coolie ordinances, but did not specify the quality of the amenities that companies had to provide. Whether the employer-provided amenities were up to legal expectations remained a matter of interpretation for the Labour Inspectorate established in 1908. In addition, minimum standards applied only to contract labourers in the outer islands. Like in Java, it was up to employers to decide what further amenities they provided to all wage labourers and to employees in supervisory and administrative positions.

In the 1920s, standards provided for by social legislation in Indonesia exceeded these minimum standards for contract labourers in the outer islands. The Netherlands became a member of the International Labour Organization (ILO) of the League of Nations after World War I. It was not immediately clear whether colonial Indonesia would also be covered by the ILO's 1919 International Labour Conventions, which dealt with hours of work in industry, unemployment, maternity leave, female night work, and child labour and night work. The new Labour Office (Kantoor van Arbeid) in colonial Indonesia started the development of relevant new legislation. For example, the Government passed a 1925 ordinance prohibiting the employment of children under the age of 12 and of women at night. Colonial Indonesia became an ILO member in its own right in 1926 (Tjoeng 1948, 129).

This coincided with two developments, the first of which was an increase in labour union activity and a spate of strikes, especially during 1920 to 1921. An important reason was the rapid rise in the cost of living during the late 1910s due to high international rice prices that was not matched by wage increases. There was also the increasing politicisation of Indonesian nationalism, while high international commodity prices caused estate and mining companies to pay high dividends to shareholders. This led the Volksraad, the parliament of colonial Indonesia, to call for legislation making "profit sharing" between firms and communities compulsory. Secondly, the Volksraad urged the Government to investigate labour conditions in the Java sugar industry. In 1919, the Government appointed a Labour Commission (Arbeidscommissie) to investigate the introduction of minimum wage legislation and arbitration in wage conflicts. The Sugar Investigation Commission (Suiker-Enquêtecommissie) was to study the reasons for increased labour militancy in the sugar industry and the possibility of sugar companies sharing their profits with employees in Java. Both commissions proposed new social legislation.

During the early 1920s, several items of social legislation were publicly discussed in Indonesia, including minimum wages, compulsory unemployment insurance, the establishment of regional labour councils to mediate labour conflicts and profit sharing in the sugar industry (Van der Mandere 1922). In the course of the 1920s, commodity prices decreased, company profits fell, government tax revenues shrank, and the realisation sank in that several policy proposals were impractical. Nevertheless, the Labour Office used its mandate to research labour conditions in Indonesia and the outcomes of this research informed the drafting of further social and industrial relations legislation. This was partly a response to increasing nationalist and labour union advocacy in Indonesia in the 1920s, and partly an expression of the view that improving labour conditions through regulation was socially justified.

Further social legislation included the 1931 amalgamation of coolie ordinances, the 1938 additional planters regulation, the 1939 compulsory workplace accident insurance, the 1941 regulation of work in the manufacturing industry, the 1941 repeal of coolie ordinances and the 1941 general pension fund. Enforcement of the laws by the Labour Inspectorate determined their effectiveness. The first comprehensive item of labour regulation was the 1940 government ordinance establishing a tripartite Commission for Labour Affairs (Commissie voor Arbeidsaangelegenheden). It had regulatory power over private employers. Companies employing more than 20 people could no longer dismiss large groups, decrease wages or cut pension rights without the Commission's approval (IOB 1940; Ingleson 2014, 327–8).

Following independence, the Government of the Republic of Indonesia sought to improve labour conditions through new legislation. For example, Law No. 12 of 1948 regulated the employment of children, young people and women, hours of work, rest periods, maternity leave and vacations and holidays. It came into force throughout the country in 1951 (Thiis-Evensen 1954, 2). Each new law regulating labour conditions was accompanied by an implementing regulation that spelled out enforcement provisions (Wit 1961, 38–41). The 1950s saw an accumulation of increasingly restrictive labour market regulations. However, the limited number of labour inspectors could only hold large companies to the rules. Informal and/or small- and medium-scale enterprises generally evaded them, exacerbating the labour market dichotomy between formal and informal sector workers.

New legislation raised minimum labour conditions for workers in companies that were held to account. However, there were ample opportunities for companies to provide additional benefits for their employees. Public service enterprises (like postal service, railways and so on), State-owned enterprises and large private companies offered their employees labour conditions well beyond the legal minimum, particularly where they competed against each other for skilled workers. This development also increased the labour market dichotomy.

Both before and after the war, the amenities that companies provided benefited both employees and local communities. Especially in distant rural areas, where public services remained minimal, private firms included local communities in their provision of healthcare and education facilities. That estate or plant managers believed that it was part of their commitment to the local population to include them was noted in Volksraad discussions during the 1920s and 1930s, on proposals for legislation to provide universal coverage on areas such as accident insurance (Drooglever 1980, 255–64). Companies often distinguished different categories of employees to whom they provided benefits and amenities. Most arrangements, such as company pensions, were extended to employees who had full-time and continuing employment rather than to part-time and temporary employees, and/or to employees who had been with a company for a minimum number of years.

The provision of benefits and amenities was generally not related to the ethnic origin of employees. The 1920s marked the start of a process of "indigenisation" of employment. Initially, it was in 1925 that the colonial government started to replace European employees with native Indonesians. The purpose was to save on labour costs at a time when public revenues were under pressure, because the salaries and prerequisites of expatriate Europeans exceeded those of Indonesians (Ingleson 2014, 70, 150–6, 265–71; Lindblad 2008, 35–6). This process accelerated during the 1930s economic crisis, when private firms also indigenised their work forces to save on labour costs.

Following independence, the Indonesian Government forced foreign-owned enterprises to increase the employment of Indonesians. Among a range of policies, it gradually decreased the number of work permits for foreign nationals at companies, reduced the number of permits for foreign staff replacements to enter the country, reduced the number of employees permitted to remit earnings overseas and also banned foreigners from certain occupations at a time when many foreign nationals left Indonesia (White 2012, 1282–4). In response, companies indigenised their work forces further. They offered better employment conditions for experienced and skilled Indonesian workers in efforts to poach workers from each other, and/or invested in company-specific training and education facilities.

Foreign-owned firms took active steps to indigenise their lower and middle management positions, but encountered difficulties in attracting well-educated and capable Indonesian managers into higher management positions (Van de Kerkhof 2005, 2009; Lindblad 2008, 149–76; White 2012, 1282–4). A 1951 survey found that on average, the share of Indonesian staff members increased from 1.5 per cent in 1950 to 12 per cent in 1951, and in Java, from 25 to 41 per cent (Ochsendorf 2015, 22–3). During the 1950s, the outflow of foreign nationals accelerated due to a lack of safety in rural areas, erosion of salaries by inflation, limits on foreign transfers of personal savings and limited education facilities for the children of expatriates.

CSR-type Practices

This section discusses the benefits and amenities firms provided to their employees without legal obligations, or beyond the minimum required levels noted in the section above. It is difficult to generalise this, as there were no comprehensive surveys until the 1950s. Generally, large companies operating agricultural estates, sugar factories, and mining and manufacturing ventures offered their employees benefits and amenities that exceeded those of small- and medium-sized firms. Size was not necessarily an issue, as smaller firms were in principle able to pool their resources. For example, in some regions, firms producing batik established cooperatives that maintained amenities for employees, such as polyclinics.

Health Care

A prime concern of both employers and employees was health care, especially in remote parts of the country where few public health facilities existed. Without legal obligation, companies operating sugar factories and estates in Java had already, in the late 19th century, started to retain local doctors. They also established clinics where a local doctor would visit a few days per week and there was an attendant (*mantri*) to dress wounds, provid immunisations, treat parasites and dispense malaria prophylactics and so on to workers and their family members. They also established infirmaries, where injured or ill workers could recuperate. In the outer islands, basic medical facilities were required under the coolie ordinances after 1880. Companies operating mines and agricultural estates generally established infirmaries and clinics. Companies operating several estates created central hospitals if distances and transportation made that feasible.

Depending on the size of the company's operations and the number of employees, companies expanded polyclinics, established hygiene amenities, employed a medical practitioner and nursing staff, and eventually established their own company hospitals that combined a polyclinic, infirmary, treatment facility and basic laboratory.[2] Over time, firms pooled small company hospitals in the same area into larger ones, where more specialised and full-time medical personnel could be employed, and where doctors trained support staff, like attendants, nurses, analysts and such, and where indigenous medical students could take internships. They then converted small hospitals into relief hospitals or polyclinics that referred patients to larger hospitals. Joint medical facilities not only offered medical care, but also laboratories for medical analysis and research.

By 1935, there were 103 company hospitals in Indonesia compared to 199 public hospitals, and 129 hospitals run by missionaries (Zondervan 2016). Of the company hospitals, only 20 per cent were located in Java, reflecting that the coolie ordinances required companies outside Java to provide medical services, and that most public hospitals were already located in Java. One third of all company hospitals were established during each of the decades: 1900 to 1909, 1910 to 1919 and 1920 to 1929. Clearly, most companies did not have their own hospital, although many maintained a polyclinic, while financially supporting a central company hospital to which patients could be dispatched.[3] Other companies provided financial support to clinics and relief hospitals run by missionaries, in return for the treatment of their employees.

In Java, the Jatiroto sugar factory of the Handelsvereeniging Amsterdam in Jember established the largest company hospital (*Indische Courant*, 2 March 1928). Like other large enterprises operating in remote areas, it operated several auxiliary hospitals and a supporting network of polyclinics to benefit all company operations (Penris 1930, 19–74). The Deli Planters Association in North Sumatra maintained the largest medical care system in the outer islands, with central hospital and research facilities in Medan, and polyclinics on tobacco and rubber estates.

In the outer islands, employers could legally compel contract labourers on estates and mines to attend medical services, but in Java, employees attended company medical facilities voluntarily (Penris 1930, 8–9). The purpose of the medical facilities of companies was not just to treat the injured and the sick, but also to improve hygiene practices, reduce incidences of infectious diseases and increase labour productivity. It is difficult to be specific about the effectiveness of company-provided medical facilities. For example, on agricultural estates in North Sumatra, there was just one medical practitioner per 5,900 workers in 1929, excluding trained medical support and nursing staff; annual mortality rates among contract labourers decreased from 11 per cent in 1904 to 7 per cent in 1931 (Van Driel, 1931; *Het Vaderland*, 4 June 1932).

Company hospitals in remote areas not only provided medical services to employees and their families, but also to people in the vicinity as a social service (De Moor 1930, 190–1; Penris 1948, 1441–3). The Government expected firms in Java to provide medical care as a "moral obligation" (*Bataviaasch Nieuwsblad*, 29 November 1928). The local population was also included in hygiene measures, such as malaria and plague eradication campaigns organised by estates.

During the 1930s crisis, several firms had to close medical facilities. In the 1940s, many hospitals in remote areas were destroyed during the war of independence. The reconstruction and rehiring of medical personnel often had to wait until estate or mine managers returned. In the 1950s, it became increasingly difficult for firms to sustain medical facilities because expatriate doctors and nurses either opted for repatriation or faced difficulties getting re-entry permits, and few local replacements were available (*Java Bode*, 27 January 1955).

An ILO survey in 1951–52 showed that of a total of 1,364 firms with 354,000 employees, 58 per cent provided medical examinations for workers, 62 per cent provided treatment and 52 per cent hospitalisation facilities (Van Hoey 1953, 62–71). And in 1953–54 the ILO found that 16 per cent of the largest 1,065 manufacturing and mining ventures—with 77 per cent of all employees in the formal sector—had medical services at the plant, including nurses, part-time doctors, hospitals and clinics (Thiis-Evensen 1954, 20–1). In 50 per cent of these firms—with 16 per cent of employment—medical facilities were provided outside the plant. Thirty-three per cent of firms—with 7 per cent of employment—did not provide medical facilities. Agricultural estates with long-established medical facilities were not included in the survey. The survey noted a great discrepancy in medical care and health facilities between large and small ventures. Good industrial hygiene conditions generally only existed at large, foreign-owned companies (Wit et al., 1961, 54–5), for example companies operating in remote areas, such as oil companies Stanvac and Caltex (Higgins 1957, 81–2; *De Nieuwsgier*, 14 December 1953). Following the nationalisation of Dutch-owned enterprises in 1957–58, medical facilities deteriorated due to the increasing employment of unqualified staff and neglect of facilities (De Reus, 1963; *Nieuwsblad van het Noorden*, 25 February 1958).

Housing

In remote parts of Indonesia, housing was a concern for both employers and employees. In Java, agricultural estates were expected to recruit employees from the population living locally. In practice, estates and sugar factories recruited migrant workers who did not live in the region, for whom they provided basic accommodation on company land. Regular workers in supervisory positions often lived in detached housing, while migrant workers used shared accommodation during planting and harvesting.[4]

In the outer islands, mining and agricultural ventures initially relied on male Chinese contract labour. The coolie ordinances required companies to provide basic housing. In the late 19th century, this often took the form of large dormitories (*pondok*) made of wood and bamboo. At a West Sumatra coal mine, they housed 100–120 workers each (Houben and Lindblad 1999, 188–9). Bathrooms and kitchens were in separate outhouses. After 1904, married coolies and spouses lived in a subdivided dormitory, or in detached houses on company land. In 1926, individual family housing became a requirement for married labourers with 5 years of service.

These facilities were gradually improved following inspections by the Labour Inspectorate, results of medical and hygiene research and company decisions to fund improvements. For example, without legal obligation, the Deli Maatschappij, in 1906, extended the provision of company housing facilities to non-contract labour migrants and their families (*Het Vaderland*, 4 June 1932). By the 1910s, improved dormitories were constructed with brick and wood. The sugar industry in Banyumas (Central Java) provided company housing for all workers and their families, with pumped and piped supplies of potable water, bathrooms, toilets, sanitation and drainage, and such improvements were also extended to non-company houses in nearby villages (Kievits 1921, 289–90). Similar facilities existed in other sugar cane areas in Java (Van der Mandere 1928, 133–4).

By that time, companies had also started to provide individual housing on company land to supervisory staff and their families that were arranged as villages and organised as village communities. The creation of such company villages followed developments in Java, where companies in remote areas had from the outset arranged company housing for employees (not migrant workers) as villages. For example, the Jatiroto sugar factory constructed 25 villages with housing and amenities for workers, and in the following years improved cooking and sanitation facilities (Penris 1948, 1440, 1443–4). In its oil concession in South Sumatra, oil company BPM likewise built a village for workers in 1911 (Heijting 1925, 108). Some companies in the outer islands established agricultural estates with villages, intending to encourage non-contract migration from Java, and for migrants to colonise vacant land.

The extent to which companies provided company housing cannot be generalised. As an example, tea estate Pasir Nangka in Priangan (Java) had 1,100 company houses that were destroyed during the revolution that had to be rebuilt in 1948 before tea production could resume (*Het Dagblad*, 27 September 1948). This estate operated 5,000 hectares. The total tea area in Java was 180,000 hectares, so the tea industry in Java alone may have provided up to 40,000 company houses. During the 1950s, recovery of company housing was difficult. Companies with military protection, such as Caltex and Stanvac in South Sumatra built houses for many employees.[5] In other large companies, management and other regular employees were provided with housing, but where housing facilities for labourers were insufficient, non-housed workers received allowances to rent accommodation (Wit et al. 1961, 56).

Village Amenities

Companies in the outer islands not only provided housing to their workers, but also a range of village amenities, even though the coolie ordinances did not require this. Companies providing housing in Java did the same. One reason was self-interest, as improper sanitation would have increased the prevalence of disease and, therefore, worker absenteeism. But humanitarian concern about living conditions was also a part of it. Some measures flowed from the medical and housing amenities that companies provided. For example, enterprises with hospitals also ran preventative sanitation programmes to purify drinking water, arrange clean bathing water and proper sewage disposal, and spray against malaria.[6] In 1905, the Deli Maatschappij constructed 38 kilometres of water mains to deliver potable spring water to tobacco estates in North Sumatra, a provision that also benefited water supply in Medan city (Ochsendorf 2015).

Firms providing company housing increasingly also supplied drinking and bathing water, waste water drainage, sanitation facilities, sewage disposal, garbage collection, village roads, electricity for lighting, as well as village facilities such as a telephone connection, market places (*pasar*), hygienic slaughter houses, places of worship (*musholla*, sometimes a mosque) and for Muslim burial, and facilities for entertainment, such as parks, cinemas, stages for *wayang* and *gamelan* performances and football fields (Penris 1930, 84–95).[7] It is not possible to generalise these commitments. Their establishment may have depended on the non-availability of public facilities and the importance that company management attached to these amenities.

Improved company housing sometimes spilled over to local communities, either because the local community could not be excluded, or because estates and their companies considered it a part of their mandate to provide amenities to villages in the vicinity. In particular, anti-malaria campaigns and pest and plague control measures in company villages had to involve nearby villages to be effective (Penris 1948, 1443–4). Sugar factories in Banyumas invested in the improvement of water supply and stormwater and swamp drainage, on both factory land and surrounding farmland (Kievits 1921, 290).

Just like company housing, many facilities were subject to neglect, destruction and robberies during the 1940s and 1950s. Recovery was incomplete. In the 1950s, during collective bargaining about labour conditions with the largest firms, trade unions frequently raised issues of housing and electric lighting in company villages. The largest firms generally invested in establishing such facilities and other amenities (Wit et al. 1961, 56).

Education for Children

Primary education was not compulsory in Indonesia until 1950. The Government supported the establishment of basic vernacular village schools, and the brightest students could attend European-style public education. There was no obligation on companies to provide education facilities for the children of workers and employees, but many did, especially companies with operations in distant regions.[8] For example, the Koloniale Bank financed the construction of a school and the salary of teaching staff at its sugar factory in Maron (East Java) in 1906. The school was initially for the children of workers, but subsequently extended to also include children in the vicinity. The bank later financed schools at seven of its other sugar factories (OMW 1914, 5–6). In 1906, companies in North Sumatra maintained 28 schools for the children of workers, and there were companies elsewhere that did the same (Heijting 1925, 103–4). Sugar factories in Banyumas provided village school education to workers and to people in the vicinity, while one factory offered European-style primary education (Kievits 1921, 289–90).

Like village schools, company schools had difficulties retaining students. The main reasons were the indifference among parents, and children having to take on household tasks. By the 1920s, child labour hardly existed at large formal companies, but it was rife in the informal sector. Industry associations had banned child labour, at times even well ahead of the 1925 prohibition by the government ordinance.[9]

Low school attendance was a concern for companies in sparsely populated North Sumatra intending to recruit students for further education and training, and ultimately employment on their estates. In 1919 the Deli Maatschappij reinvigorated its support for primary schools, aiming to encourage regular school attendance. It started with schools at its large Senembah estate, which provided general education and basic agricultural education (*Sumatra Post*, 8 December 1936). As there was little public primary education in the region, the Government subsidised half of the operating cost of these company schools on the condition that a government school inspector would supervise and ensure quality in the school's education standards and operation (*Sumatra Post*, 13 August 1919).

School attendance in the estates of the members of the Deli Planters Association in North Sumatra increased to 2,500 students in 1923 (*Bataviaasch Nieuwsblad*, 16 May 1924); by 1926, 3,514 students at 71 schools were using 115 company libraries (*Sumatra Post*, 3 June 1927),[10] which increased to 4,843 students in 74 schools in 1928 (*Sumatra Post*, 11 June 1929). In 1928, the association supported teacher training courses for trainee teachers at company schools. However, the problem of parents not sending children to school continued. Only about 7 per cent of all children of workers on estates attended school in 1938.[11] But attendance was higher than that across the outer islands as a whole, which was about 2 per cent of all children.

Company schools were among the first amenities that companies reconstructed after they reoccupied estates in the late 1940s and 1950s (*De Locomotief*, 7 April 1948; *De Preangerbode*, 25 August 1950; 19 March 1952).

The purpose was to encourage the return of workers to estates in remote and unsafe areas. Public school attendance increased quickly during the 1950s, but large companies in distant areas continued the company schools for the children of workers and children in villages in the vicinity. For example, the BPM-Shell oil plant in South Sumatra offered primary education facilities to 4,600 children in 1952 (*Java Bode*, 24 January 1952).

Education and Training for Workers

Although not legally obliged to do so, many large companies or associations of companies provided education to workers. These were not just opportunities for on-the-job learning and occasional skills training, but also fulltime courses (*bedrijfsscholen, sekolah perusahaan*) that took at least one year to complete. The sugar industry in Java began a range of staff training programmes from the late 1880s on (Knight 2013, 82–6). From 1926, the large Deli Maatschappij established a technical high school at its Belawan estate for the purpose of training technicians with an all-expenses paid two-year course, in return for a three-year contract for graduates to work at the company (*Nieuws van den Dag voor Nederlandsch-Indië*, 20 September 1926; *Sumatra Post*, 11 May 1931).

In the 1950s, the urgency increased for companies to formalise the training and education they offered, following the repatriation of foreign workers and the increasing transience of skilled Indonesian employees. The numbers of graduates from commercial or vocational schools increased during the 1950s, but many students still required specialised training before being job-ready. Companies in expanding industries had to provide such education themselves. For example, oil company BPM-Shell established a school for technical training in 1950 (*Nieuwe Courant*, 2 November 1950; Lindblad 2008, 162–3). It also offered a variety of other education opportunities (*Java Bode*, 24 January 1952), as well as scholarships for employees to study elsewhere and overseas (*De Preangerbode*, 27 September 1957). Stanvac did the same (Higgins 1957, 70–80). Caltex offered courses in English, administration and typewriting at its expanding company school, as well as education opportunities for supervisory personnel (*De Nieuwsgier*, 14 December 1953). Companies in established industries did the same. For example, printing company Kolff had a 1-year course in graphic techniques (*Java Bode*, 11 July 1951), and Borsumij and Bank Negara collaborated to offer a 2-year programme in commerce (*Java Bode*, 3 June 1952). Nevertheless, a 1956 survey found that of the 2,101 medium-large firms surveyed, only 10 per cent had training facilities that ranged from venues for on-the-job training to full-time school attendance for different age groups and grades (DTK 1958, 18–19).

A problem with the indigenisation of the workforce through providing training and education was that employees who had completed courses would often capitalise on their qualifications by leaving for better paying or more prestigious positions, particularly in the public service (Sinninghe Damsté 1952, 259; Lindblad 2008, 167). Consequently, many firms were reluctant to invest in training and education as companies poached each other's employees. Given the growing shortages of skilled personnel and open discrimination against ethnic Eurasians and Chinese in public service positions, many foreign-owned companies increased their indigenisation rate by employing more Eurasians with Indonesian citizenship in mid-level and senior management positions (Van der Veur 1961, 49–50, 54), or promoting mid-level employees—generally ethnic Chinese—to senior management positions (White 2012, 1294).

In 1957, labour unions occupied all Dutch-owned companies with support of the local military. These companies were nationalised in 1958. Ethnic Chinese business operations were banned from rural areas of Indonesia in 1959, and cooperatives expected to take over their role. Repatriations of Dutch nationals and ethnic Chinese increased the urgency of indigenising supervisory and management personnel. In plantation agriculture alone, no fewer than 2,300 managers on 400 Dutch estates had to be replaced during 1957–58 (Hawkins 1971, 225) and the urgency for firms to establish training facilities increased.

Pension Funds

Until the 1930s, companies were not legally obliged to provide insurance for old age, sickness, disability, death and/or unemployment. Although labour unions included some or all of these in their enterprise bargaining claims, it was up to individual firms to provide them. Many companies provided pensions to their senior and supervisory personnel, depending on the years of service, regardless of ethnicity. Some also had arrangements for ordinary workers. The retirement age in Indonesia was generally 55. In the early 1920s, more large agricultural enterprises in Sumatra started to pay pensions to labourers with a minimum number of years of service—15 or 25 years (Heijting 1925, 97–100). Depending on years worked, retirees received a specified amount per month, or a lump sum if they retired and returned to China or Java (Houben and Lindblad 1999, 134).

Companies had pension arrangements with very different specifications. Large firms offered good pension schemes (Ingleson 2014, 66, 81), as did State-owned enterprises such as the railways, that matched public service pension entitlements (Ingleson 2014, 155–6). Smaller firms generally did not offer their employees pensions. Medium-sized firms in specific industries, and/or organised in large industry associations, would pool pension arrangements, and also invite association members to join on behalf of their employees, in order to save on overhead costs and maximise the return on investments. For example, the Association of Employers in the Java Sugar Industry established a joint pension fund for employees of its member firms in 1927 to minimise significant variations in pension schemes across members (Levert 1934, 257–60). The scheme was open for continuing employees, and also for day labourers, if they were team supervisors, as well as day labourers who had worked for a company 30 years or more. Pension arrangements took the form of either a growing pool of premiums paid by companies and managed on behalf of workers, or companies paying pensions in return for reduced labour services, and/or after retirement. Pension arrangements were generally not restricted to European employees; employees of other ethnicities participated as well (Hoedt 1930, 118–9).

During 1933 to 1938, the Government prepared a pension ordinance (*pensioenordonnantie*) to make it compulsory for companies to establish and pay into pension funds on behalf of their employees. A final report was submitted in 1938, but the plan did not come to fruition. Consequently, a myriad of company pension funds continued to grow (*De Telegraaf*, 4 June 1938). The only significant change was the establishment of a government-run General Pension Fund for Trade and Industry (Algemeen Pensioenfonds van Handel en Industrie) in 1941 for medium and higher-level personnel (*Bataviaasche Courant*, 29 October 1941). Without regard to ethnicity, any employee who was not yet contributing to an existing pension fund could buy a policy. Employers were not required to contribute to the fund. This situation continued into the 1950s, with many individual companies establishing new company-based pension funds (Wit et al. 1961, 73–4). However, due to minimal government supervision, newspaper reports about the misuse of pension deposits by fund managers increased, or seemed to have. Generally, only large companies continued to provide relatively generous pensions (Tedjasukmana 1961, 497).

Already, before World War II, some companies paid invalid pensions and offered support for widows and orphans although there was no legal obligation. Generally, such payments were made after accidents and on a casual basis, depending on the merits of the case. Labour unions were active in establishing mutual funds for death benefits or pensions, with or without the cooperation and payments of employers (Ingleson 2014, 174–6). Increasingly, unions claimed for death, invalidity, unemployment and pension benefits to be included in collective bargaining rounds with employers (Ingleson 2014, 250–1). Such benefits were not a standard part of labour conditions until after 1949 when the unions of European employees insisted that companies also provide them (see for example *Nieuwsblad voor Sumatra*, 24 April 1950; *Nieuwe Courant*, 16 February 1951).

Lastly, many companies donated funds to families for funeral costs and provided support for widows and orphans for up to a year after the death of a worker. This happened both before World War II and during the 1950s (Levert 1934, 339; Wit et al. 1961, 74).

Disability Insurance

By the early 1920s, several firms in the outer islands provided disability insurance, which covered the incomes of employees during illness and recuperation from injury, even though this was not required by law (Heijting 1925, 97–9). In Java, the members of the Association of Employers in the Sugar Industry paid disability pensions for physical or mental incapacity after injury, although until 1927 it was not standardised across member companies and the disability pension only applied to employees who had been with the company a minimum of 20 years (Levert 1934, 257–8). In 1927, 41 per cent of the people on a disability pension had been employed at sugar companies for less than 20 years of service; this was because payments were at the discretion of their company.

During 1929 to 1930, the Volksraad discussed accident insurance legislation based on investigations by the Labour Office, but the introduction of a law was postponed due to the early 1930s crisis (Penris, 1939). It took until May 1939 when the introduction of the law made accident insurance compulsory with the introduction of a government Accidents Regulation (Ongevallenregeling) which marked the implementation of the ILO's 1925 International Convention on Workmen's Compensation. The regulation, which provided benefits for workers who sustained injuries at work, became active in 1940 and was the first compulsory type of social insurance.

The Industrial Accident Law—Law No. 33 of 1947 and Law No. 2 of 1951— required companies to pay compensation in case of industrial accidents in certain dangerous industries. This insurance covered injuries and industrial diseases, as well as the cost of transportation home or to the hospital, medical care and medicines, funeral allowances, survivor and temporary/partial or permanent/ full disability allowances and cash allowances, depending on the severity of the accident (Thiis-Evensen 1954, 2–3).

Health Insurance

Many companies had implicit health insurance as they allowed time off with pay and medical care when regular employees were injured or sick. Employees on casual and daily contracts were often only entitled to medical care, but not continued pay. Nevertheless, formal health insurance remained at the discretion of companies. Several companies took out health insurance on behalf of their employees, or individual employees themselves took out insurance for medical costs and income support (Winckel 1933). The coolie ordinances in the outer islands required employers to provide income support to contract workers who were temporarily deprived of income (*onderstandsregelingen*) (Houben and Lindblad 1999, 134). Employers were also obliged to support the families of workers who were hospitalised. For example, rubber estates in North Sumatra that were members of the AVROS industry association gave pregnant female employees rice for 2 months before and after delivery; by 1925 all employers had similar arrangements.

Despite the relevant ILO conventions of 1927 and 1936, Indonesia did not have compulsory health insurance for workers (Thiis-Evensen 1954, 5). Arrangements were at the discretion of employers and remained so into the 1950s. A 1951–52 survey found that only a mere 38 out of 1,300 surveyed companies had a health insurance scheme (Wit et al. 1961, 74–6). During the 1950s, labour unions added employer-provided health insurance to their collective bargaining claims. Given that health insurance only covered large-scale companies, the Government considered ways to increase coverage. The Ministry of Labour experimented with subsidies to existing private health funds and clinics in major cities—Bandung, Yogyakarta, Palembang, Tegal and Jakarta— to encourage them to take on more policy holders. The Ministry also offered supervision and guidance. In 1957, the Government trialed the Workers Social Security Foundation (Yayasan Jaminan Sosial Buruh). The foundation paid benefits in case of sickness, pregnancy, confinement, death, any accident and old age and also extended other social security plans on the basis of contributions from employers and employees and subsidies from the Ministry of Labour (Craig 1958). However, the trial was not scaled up and accelerating inflation soon eroded the Foundation's funds.

Unemployment Benefits

There were no government-provided unemployment benefits in Indonesia. The 1930s economic crisis quickly increased unemployment, but employers did not consider it their task to care for the unemployed and their families. Such care was taken on by local private organisations made up of volunteers, and depended on occasional donations from the public. These local organisations formed a national Central Support Committee (Centraal Steuncomite). Companies and business associations did make large donations to the Committee, which also raised funds through lotteries, fairs and such. It distributed funds to local organisations, which also raised funds locally, and it organised financial support for the unemployed—in principle regardless of ethnicity (*Sumatra Post*, 20 March 1935; Cool 1938; Ingleson 2015).

During 1933 to 1935, company incomes and company donations to the Committee decreased while unemployment increased further. Only in 1935 did the Government include a modest amount for unemployment support in its supplementary budget (*Bataviaasch Nieuwsblad*, 8 June 1935). That year, the economy started to recover and unemployment decreased. After World War II, the same arrangements remained in place during the 1950s, with private companies on occasion making donations to regional organisations that supported the unemployed (Craig 1958).

Other Benefits

Individual companies provided other benefits and amenities, some of which went to local communities, like contributions to the health and quality of livestock through donations of thoroughbred buffaloes and cows, supplies of superior seeds and support for agricultural extension efforts to improve farm productivity. Other activities were initially focused on company workers but spilled over to villages and communities in the vicinity. A common benefit during periods of high food prices was the procurement of food products, particularly rice, which was distributed at below-market prices to workers and local communities. Food supply was not a legal requirement of labour contracts according to the coolie ordinances in the outer islands (Heijting 1925, 92–7), nevertheless, agricultural estates and mines purchased and distributed subsidised food to workers.

Sugar factories in Java also purchased rice and supplied it below cost, especially during the years of rice shortage (around 1919–22) (Levert 1934, 255). For example, in Banyumas, some sugar factories sought to prevent usury in neighbouring villages by buying and storing paddy after the harvest and selling it to workers and villagers at below-market prices during lean months (Kievits 1921, 290). Some companies also sold other goods, such as textiles, earthenware and lamps, which they purchased from wholesalers in bulk and sold at below-market prices in factory shops. Other companies in Java topped up salaries of employees with food allowances (Ingleson 2014, 66). In the 1950s, companies resumed the distribution of food to their workers, particularly at State-owned enterprises in crucial industries, in order to augment the cash salaries of workers. Several companies employed a commissary to provide workers with basic food packages and other goods (Wit et al.1956, 56).

Conclusion

Social legislation was relatively minimal for a long time in Indonesia and the supply of public goods was constrained by available funds. Consequently, private companies internalised the supply of a range of social benefits and amenities to workers and local communities. By definition, many of these have to be regarded as what we now consider to be CSR. The provision of such amenities or benefits started in the 1900s and continued into the 1950s. There are few aggregated statistics that allow us to indicate conclusively to what extent companies provided them. Not all firms arranged for such benefits or amenities, as there was generally no legal obligation on them to do so. Particularly, it was large, foreign-owned firms located in rural areas that provided them. It is difficult to say whether smaller firms in Indonesia duplicated these quasi-CSR practices. Starting in 1958, most foreign firms were nationalised and converted to State-owned enterprises. It is possible that reduced profitability and increased dependence on budgetary subventions impinged on the ability of nationalised firms to continue activities that sustained this form of CSR. Either way, it is obvious that CSR, entering at around the 2000s, may have been new to Indonesia as a concept, but it was hardly new as a management practice.

Notes

[1] Until Indonesia became an entirely separate jurisdiction in 1949, corporate law required firms operating in Indonesia to be registered in either The Netherlands or in the Netherlands Indies.

[2] There are many accounts of companies providing health care at hospitals and polyclinics, as well as hygiene facilities to employees, their families and the local population. For example, Van Gulik (1930); Heijting (1925, 62–6); Snijders (1920, 1921); Kievits (1921, 287–8); Van de Velde (1918); Van der Heijden (1916; 1918); Tichelaar (1927, 196–200); Van der Mandere (1928, 131–3); De Moor (1930); Hoedt (1930, 120–3); Penris (1930, 19–66; 1948); and more recent studies, such as Gooszen (1999, 200–205); Hesselink (2011, 287–90); Houben and Lindblad (1999, 190–2, 222–3); Van Bergen (2007, 39–43); Knight (2013, 176); and Zondervan (2016).

[3] In the Java sugar industry in 1929, 41 factories were associated with 8 central hospitals; 16 had 12 auxiliary hospitals, 8 had clinics, 60 had polyclinics and 85 subsidised other medical facilities where workers and family members were treated (Penris 1948, 1439, 1445).

[4] On company housing, see for example Knight (2013, 74, 175); Penris (1930, 84–94); Snijders (1921); Heijting (1925, 60–2); Tichelaar (1926, 200–2); Hoedt (1930, 113–7); and *Soerabaijasch Handelsblad* (6 February 1930; 1–2 July 1930; 28 December 1940).

[5] Higgins (1957, 83–90) noted that Stanvac could only house 2,500 of 9,800 employees. Caltex housed all its employees (*De Nieuwsgier*, 14 December 1953).

[6] Jacometti (1925) explains how water supply benefited workers on estates and neighbouring villages.

[7] Hoedt (1930, 117) mentions that such facilities existed at almost all enterprises in South Sumatra. *Het Vaderland* (4 June 1932) noted that they also existed throughout East Java. Heijting (1925, 100–2) gives an overview of companies with entertainment facilities for workers.

[8] There are many descriptions of company schools, but no aggregated statistics. See for example Heijting (1925, 103–4); Hoedt (1930, 118); *Sumatra Post* (13 August 1919; 3 June 1926; 9 February 1928); and *De Indische Courant* (15 March 1923; 25 May 1934).

[9] For example, the Java Sugar Employers Association banned the employment of children under 12 years of age in 1924 (Levert 1934, 193).

[10] The education inspector counted 4,966 children in company schools in all of North Sumatra in 1926 (*Sumatra Post*, 9 February 1928).

[11] Ochsendorf (2015) mentions that 3,300 out of a total of 50,000 children of workers on the estates of the Deli Maatschappij attended the company's primary schools.

References

Craig, Isabel. 1958. "Report to the Government of Indonesia on Social Security". *Report No. ILO/TAP/Indonesia/R.10*. Geneva: International Labour Office.

Cool, F.M.J. 1938. "De bestrijding der werkloosheidsgevolgen in Nederlandsch-Indie gedurende 1930-1936" [Combating the Consequences for Employment in the Netherlands Indies during 1930–1936]. *De Economist* [The Economist] 87: 135–47, 217–43.

De Moor, C.E. 1930. "Sanitaire organisatie en landbouwindustrie in Nederlandsch-Indië" [Organisation of Sanitation and the Agricultural Industry in Netherlands Indies]. *Nederlandsch Tijdschrift voor Geneeskunde* [Netherlands Medical Journal] 74: 188–92.

De Reus, Tj. 1963. "Enige aspecten van naveltetanus in Deli (Indonesië)" [Some Aspects of Navel Tetanus in Deli (Indonesia)]. *Nederlands Tijdschrift voor Geneeskunde* [Netherlands Medical Journal] 107: 1265–7.

Drooglever, Pieter. 1980. *De Vaderlandse Club 1929–1942: Totoks in De Indische Politiek* [The Patriotic Club 1929–1942: Totoks in Politics in Colonial Indonesia]. Franeker: Wever.

Direktorat Tenaga Kerja (DTK) (Labour Force Directorate). 1958. "Laporan penjelidikan tenaga kerja ('manpower survey') tahun 1956" [Report on Labour Force Research ('Manpower Survey') in 1956]. *Ekonomi dan Keuangan Indonesia* [Economics and Finance in Indonesia] 11 (1): 2–46.

Gooszen, A.J.A. 1999. *Demographic History of the Indonesian Archipelago, 1880–1942*. Singapore: Institute of Southeast Asian Studies.

Hawkins, Everett D. 1971. "Labor in Developing Countries: Indonesia". In *The Economy of Indonesia: Selected Readings*, ed. Bruce Glassburner, 196–250. New York: Cornell University Press.

Hesselink, Liesbeth 2011. *Healers on the Colonial Market: Native Doctors and Midwives in the Dutch East Indies*. Leiden: KITLV Press.

Heijting, Herman George. 1925. *De Koelie-Wetgeving voor de Buitengewesten van Nederlandsch-Indië* [The Coolie Legislation in the Outer Islands of the Netherlands Indies]. The Hague: Van Stockum

Higgins, Benjamin. 1957. *Stanvac in Indonesia.* Washington DC: National Planning Association.

Hoedt, Theophile George Emil. 1930. *Indische Bergcultuurondernemingen voornamelijk in Zuid Sumatra: Gegevens en Beschouwingen* [Upland Agricultural Enterprises in the Netherlands Indies, Particularly in South Sumatra: Data and Analysis]. The Netherlands: H. Veenman & Zonen.

Houben, Vincent J.H. and J. Thomas Lindblad. 1999. *Coolie Labour in Colonial Indonesia: A Study of Labour Relations in the Outer Islands, c.1900–1940.* Wiesbaden: Harrassowitz Verlag.

Ingleson, John. 2014. *Workers, Unions and Politics: Indonesia in the 1920s and 1930s.* Leiden/ Boston: Brill.

_____. 2015. "Race, Class and the Deserving Poor: Charities and the 1930s Depression in Java". *Journal of Southeast Asian Studies* 46 (2): 205–26.

Indische Ondernemersbond (IOB) (Employers Association of the Netherlands Indies). *De Ordonnantie tot Instelling van Een Bijzonder Overheidstoezicht op de Rechtsverhouding tusschen Werkgevers en Arbeiders* [The Ordinance to Establish Special Government Supervision of the Legal Interactions between Employers and Workers]. Batavia: Indische Ondernemersbond, 1940.

Jacometti, A.W.A. 1925. "Bad-en drinkwatervoorziening op cultuurondernemingen" [Bath and Potable Water Supply on Agricultural Estates]. *Archief voor de Suikerindustrie in Nederlandsch-Indië* [Archive for the Sugar Industry in the Netherlands Indies] 33: 1010–7.

Kievits, D.B.J. 1921. "Behartiging der volksbelangen, door de suikerondernemingen in de residentie Banjoemas" [Advancing the People's Interests by Sugar Enterprises in Banyumas Residency]. *Archief voor de Suikerindustrie in Nederlandsch-Indië* [Archive for the Sugar Industry in the Netherlands Indies] 29, Bijblad [supplement]: 287–90.

Knight, G. Roger. 2013. *Commodities and Colonialism: The Story of Big Sugar in Indonesia, 1880–1942.* Leiden/Boston: Brill.

Levert, Philip. 1934. *Inheemsche Arbeid in de Java-Suikerindustrie* [Indonesian Labour in the Java Sugar Industry]. Wageningen: H. Veenman & Zonen.

Lindblad, J. Thomas. 2008. *Bridges to New Business: The Economic Decolonization of Indonesia.* Leiden: KITLV Press.

McWilliams, Abagail and Donald Siegel. 2001. "Corporate Social Responsibility: A Theory of the Firm Perspective". *Academy of Management Review* 26 (1): 117–27.

Ochsendorf, Frank. 2015. "Gains from Foreign Investment for Indigenous Society in North Sumatra, 1860–1960". Paper presented at the 17th World Economic History Congress, Kyoto, 3–7 August 2015.

OMW. 1914. *Onderzoek naar de Mindere Welvaart de Inlandsche Bevolking op Java en Madoera, VIe: Overzicht van de Uitkomsten de Gewestelijke Onderzoekingen (half 1904/1905) naar den Niet-Inlandschen Handel en Nijverheid en Daaruit Gemaakte Gevolgtrekkingen* [Investigation into the Decreasing Prosperity of the Native Population of Java and

Madura, Volume: Overview of the Outcomes of Regional Surveys (mid-1904–1905) into the Non-native Trade and Industry and the Conclusions Flowing from it]. Batavia: Papyrus Publishing.

Penris, Peter W. L. 1930. *Geneeskundige Verzorging van Arbeiders bij Landbouwondernemingen op Java* [Health Care of Labourers on Agricultural Enterprises in Java]. Amsterdam: H.J. Paris.

_____. 1939. "Wettelijke ongevallenregeling voor Ned.Indië" [Legal Arrangement of Accident Insurance for the Netherlands Indies]. *Nederlands Tijdschrift voor Geneeskunde* [Netherlands Medical Journal] 38: 436–8.

_____. 1948. "Het aandeel der landbouwondernemingen op Java in de geneeskundige voorzieningen van Nederlandsch-Indië" [The Contribution of Agricultural Enterprises in Providing Medical Services in the Netherlands Indies]. *Nederlands Tijdschrift voor Geneeskunde* [Netherlands Medical Journal] 92 (2): 1438–45.

Sinninghe Damsté, J.S. 1952. "De positie van de ondernemer in Indonesië" [The Position of the Entrepreneur in Indonesia]. *Maatschappijbelangen* [Social Interests] 116: 257–61.

Sluyterman, Keetie. 2012. "Corporate Social Responsibility of Dutch Entrepreneurs in the 20th Century". *Enterprise & Society* 13 (2): 313–49.

Snijders, Emilius Paulus. 1920. *Rubbercultuur in Nederlandsch-Indië: Bedrijfshygiëne* [Rubber Industry in the Netherlands Indies: Industrial Hygiene]. Amsterdam: De Bussy.

_____. 1921. *Koeliehuisvesting en Geneeskundige Dienst op Rubberondernemingen* [Coolie Housing and Medical Service on Rubber Estates]. Amsterdam: De Bussy.

Tedjasukmana, Iskandar. 1961. "The Development of Labor Policy and Legislation in the Republic of Indonesia". PhD Thesis, Cornell University, New York, United States.

Thiis-Evensen, E. 1954. "Report to the Government of Indonesia on Occupational Health". *Report No. ILO/TAP/Indonesia/R.6.* Geneva: International Labour Office.

Tichelaar, J.J. 1927. *De Java-Suikerindustrie en hare Betekenis voor Land en Volk* [The Java Sugar Industry and its Significance for Java and its Population]. Surabaya: Algemeen Syndicaat van Suikerfabrikanten in Nederlandsch-Indië (General Syndicate of Sugar Manufacturers in The Netherlands Indies).

Tjoeng, Tin Fong. 1948. *Arbeidstoestanden en Arbeidsbescherming in Indonesië* [Labour Conditions and Labour Protection in Indonesia]. The Hague: Van Stockum.

Van Bergen, Leo. 2007. *Van Koloniale Geneeskunde tot Internationale Gezondheidszorg: Een Geschiedenis van Honderd Jaar Nederlandse Vereniging voor Tropische Geneeskunde* [From Colonial Medicine to International Health Care: A History of 100 Years of the Netherlands Association for Tropical Medicine]. Amsterdam: KIT Publishers.

Van de Kerkhof, Jasper. 2005. "*Indonesianisasi* of Dutch Economic Interests, 1930–1960: The Case of Internatio". *Journal of the Humanities and Social Sciences of Southeast Asia* 161 (2)/3): 181–209.

_____. (2009). "'Colonial' Enterprise and the Indigenization of Management in Independent Indonesia and Malaysia". In *Indonesian Economic Decolonization in Regional and International Perspective*, ed. J. Thomas Lindblad and Peter Post, 175–96. Leiden: KITLV Press.

Van der Heijden, H.N. 1916. *De Arbeidersverzorging en het Hospitaalwezen in de Bovenlanden van Benkoelen* [Medical and Hospital Care for Labourers in Upper Bengkulu]. Surabaya: Nederlandsch-Indisch Landbouw Syndicaat (Agricultural Syndicate of The Netherlands Indies).

————. 1918. "De hygienische verzorging der arbeiders-immigranten in de Buitenbezittingen" [The Hygienic Care for Migrant Labourers in the Outer Islands]. *Koloniale Studiën* [Colonial Studies] 2: 44–84.

Van der Mandere, H.Ch.G.J. 1922. "Sociale wetgeving in Nederlan[d]sch Oost-Indië" [Social Legislation in The Netherlands Indies]. *Vragen van den Dag* [Current Issues] 36: 801–18.

————. 1928. *De Javasuikerindustrie in Heden en Verleden Gezien in het Bijzonder in Hare Sociaal-Economische Beteekenis* [The Java Sugar Industry in Present and Past, Considered with Particular Reference to its Social and Economic Significance]. Amsterdam: Bureau Industria.

Van der Veur, Paul W. 1961. "Eurasian Dilemma in Indonesia". *Journal of Asian Studies* 20 (1): 45–60

Van Driel, B.M. 1931. "De sterfte der ondernemingsarbeiders ter Oostkust van Sumatra en in Atjeh in 1929" [The Mortality of Estate Labourers in East Sumatra and Aceh in 1929]. *Nederlandsch Tijdschrift voor Geneeskunde* [Netherlands Medical Journal] 75: 3959–70.

Van Hoey, F. 1953. "Report to the Government of Indonesia on Social Security". *Report No. ILO/TAP/Indonesia/R.3*. Geneva: International Labour Office, 1953.

Waagstein, Patricia Rinwigati. 2011. "The Mandatory Corporate Social Responsibility in Indonesia: Problems and Implications". *Journal of Business Ethics* 98 (3): 455–66.

White, Nicholas, J. 2012. "Surviving Sukarno: British Business in Post-Colonial Indonesia, 1950–1967". *Modern Asian Studies* 46 (5): 1277–1315.

Winckel, I.W.F. 1933. "Ziekfondsen in Nederlandsch-Indië" [Health Insurance in the Netherlands Indies]. *Nederlands Tijdschrift voor Geneeskunde* [Netherlands Medical Journal] 77: 3275–83.

Wit, Daniel et al. (1961). *Indonesian Labor: A Management Survey*. Washington DC: Governmental Affairs Institute.

Zondervan, Sjoerd. 2016. "Patients of the Colonial State: The Rise of a Hospital System in the Netherlands Indies, 1890–1940". PhD thesis, Maastricht University, Maastricht, The Netherlands.

Chapter 10

Reconstructing Business Ethics through Egodocuments: Non-Western Perceptions of Business Ethics in Indonesia, 1950s–2000s

Farabi Fakih

This chapter will interrogate ethical values as a discourse through reading published egodocuments (in particular biographical and autobiographical writings) of prominent Indonesian capitalists in the New Order (1966–98) and post-New Order (1998–present) periods. The objective is to determine if there is a common perception of a shared national culture and ideology, and how that impacts two things: the perceived ethical stance of businessmen and their behaviour or strategies in business. This is achieved by analysing such documents and how they present the ethical position of the businessmen in question. Denzau and North (1994) have pointed out the importance of how institutions like values and ideologies serve as shared mental models and affect the behaviours of agents in an economy. A key question is whether there exists a common mental model that is shared by everyone, or whether there is no such commonality. The idea of ethics as guiding capitalist development (Fridenson and Kikkawa 2017) is fundamental to the focus of this volume, but such an idea becomes more complex in multicultural societies in which businessmen come from various groups, both racially and culturally. Is it possible, therefore, to identify groupings based on ethical stance through a reading of these egodocuments?

The chapter's main goal, therefore, is to read the egodocuments and establish groupings which can potentially allow us to see the multiple ethical or mental models that exist within a limited group of businessmen in Indonesia (Bagdasaroy et al. 2016). The objective is not to determine any effect on decision making, but instead to locate these groups within the development of Indonesian society. These groupings tell us a lot, not only about how ethics determine the actions of particular people, but also about how the conditions in which people find themselves in determine the particular ethics to which they choose to subscribe. If there is no common mental model, there may be multiple mental models that are somehow interconnected to form multiple, national models. Yet how do we go about analysing such a construction? This chapter undertakes this challenge of analysing multiple models and their interactions within one national "cultural system". In pursuit of this objective, the first part of the chapter offers an overview of Indonesian business history in the 20th century and its multicultural roots. I show that Indonesia's colonial legacy has resulted in a strong antagonism towards the business elite, and that changes in attitudes toward businessmen and entrepreneurs can actually be traced in the changing nature of published egodocuments. I then go on to discuss the biographies of group members. This will serve to provide a more in-depth analysis of the various mental models, using individual biographies as case studies. After this biographical discussion, the chapter then offers a preliminary analysis of the documents, focusing on an attempt to map the mental models of the various groups. Conducting the analysis through a reading of the egodocuments allows us to understand the mental model as understood by the businessman himself/herself. These published egodocuments are often personal statements on identity and ethics and involve the shaping of a narrative identity, thus potentially comprising the idealised ethical models of businessmen rather than their real life behaviour and strategy. Consequently, although the analysis of biographies, autobiographies and personal narratives is an established methodology in business history and the study of entrepreneurship, users of the methodology have to remain aware of the potential that an entrepreneur's crafting of a narrative identity may cause divergences between self-description and any independent analysis (Reveley 2010; Hulsink and Rauch 2021). This is particularly relevant to this chapter in light of significant changes in Indonesia's political regime since the late 1990s.

Colonial Roots of Negative Perception of Business

Indonesia's deep-seated anti-business sentiment was rooted in the colonial period and in the growth of Indonesian nationalism during the early 20th century. One of the first nationalist mass organisations growing out of the business competition between indigenous Muslim merchants and Chinese merchants (Azra 1994), the Sarekat Islam, was founded in 1912 and subsequently represented an amalgamation of the forces of the Muslim merchant class with Marxist elements that had been growing since 1914. While the organisation was initially supported by the Muslim merchant class, its ideas took on a strong anti-capitalist position (Lin 2018). Marxism served as a tool for criticising Dutch colonialism and its paternalistic developmentalist ideology, embodied in the so-called Ethical Policy (McVey 1990). The Dutch argued that Indonesians were incapable of independent development and required the technical assistance of the Dutch.

Marxist critics turned this viewpoint on its head, arguing that Dutch colonialism primarily served the purposes of large Western capitalist enterprises and that colonialism extracted the wealth of the Indonesians to pay for the development of The Netherlands. It was argued that while the Ethical Policy inaugurated in 1901 did promote developmentalist policies aiming to nurture the entrepreneurial spirit of the Indonesians through programmes such as micro-credits, agricultural extensions and small industry workshops, because these initiatives were operating in the context of a Dutch colonial ideology that saw Indonesians as lacking a business sense, they only resulted in confirming the position of the Indonesian in the lower rungs of society. The expansion of micro-credit, for instance, did not affect the difficulties experienced by Indonesians in accessing bank credits.

Although most businesses in the colony were run by Indonesians, they were dominant only in the small-scale business sectors. Large businesses were almost bereft of Indonesian participation, with only a few cases such as the sugar mills of the Mangkunegaran Palace of Surakarta (Wasino and Nawiyanto 2019). While the majority of large businesses were in the hands of Dutch and other Europeans, there was also a sizeable number of Chinese businesses. Large Chinese businesses, such as the Oei Tiong Ham (OTH) Concern or business group. (The OTH Concern ceased to exist in the 1950s and no longer exists today.) Although indigenous Indonesian merchants did develop banks in order to provide credit for their members, there is little evidence of the formal colonial banking sector providing any meaningful credit to develop Indonesian business. As a result, the absence of Indonesians in the middle- to large-scale sectors had become more pronounced by the end of the colonial period.

Middle- to small-scale Chinese businesses competed directly with mid- to small-scale indigenous Indonesian business sectors. The Chinese were thus the primary competitors to Indonesian businessmen. As the case of Sarekat Islam has shown, this led to animosity and a nationalist perspective which saw Indonesian economic independence as independence from both Western and Chinese business control. Yet, unlike the Dutch who were to be repatriated from the country in the 1950s, Chinese-Indonesians continued to play a major role in the national and economic life of the country. Postcolonial national identity in Indonesia was thus often ambivalent about the position of the Chinese-Indonesian population, whose members were persistently seen as an alien component of society.

Post-Independence Tumult (1945–65)

Independent Indonesia nurtured an economic nationalism that was defined as the creation of an independent, *Indonesian* (that is, non-Chinese) national capitalist class. In the 1950s, much of the economy was still in the hands of Dutch and Chinese firms. Dutch businesses would eventually be nationalised by the end of the 1950s, yet unlike the situation of the introduction of Malaysia's New Economic Policy, Indonesia never formulated a comprehensive policy regarding Chinese-Indonesian businesses. This was a result of the fragmented nature of the Indonesian political elite, which made it difficult to develop a coherent policy (Thee 2006). Efforts were mainly focused on supporting the development of a modern indigenous entrepreneurial class. One of the first postcolonial efforts in this direction was the Benteng Program, under which indigenous businesses were given preferential treatment in the form of import licence and credit facilities. Access to these facilities was abused by many indigenous businesses, which became a front for Chinese-Indonesian companies, something referred to as the Ali-Baba strategy. The programme was terminated by 1956 and was seen as a failure. Nevertheless, it did spur the development of the Indonesian elite and Chinese businesses, as well as a rise in Indonesian businesses in the 1950s, including those supported by the Benteng Program, which were characterised by good personal relationships with political elites (Lindblad 2008, 129–36; Robison 1986, 36–65). These relationships were seen as corrupt, and thus Chinese businesses tended to be associated with the nurturing of political and economic corruption.

Increased anti-Chinese sentiments were stoked by nationalists like the former acting president, President Assaat Datuk Mudo. The "Assaat movement" targeted Chinese businesses, supporting what it called the indigenisation of the economy. In 1957, the remaining Dutch population was repatriated and all Dutch-owned enterprises taken over by labour unions; the army then also nationalised all of these companies for fear of their being taken over by Communists. Anti-Chinese sentiment also drove over 100,000 Chinese-Indonesians to leave the country by 1960 and the banning of Chinese businesses in rural areas of the country. The nationalisation of Dutch-owned businesses resulted in an expansion of the role of the army in the economy and the strengthening of elite army/civilian and Chinese business networks in comparison to indigenous businesses (Brown 2006; Muhaimin 1990, 91–7).

President Sukarno enacted an economic policy that focused on self-sufficiency and the decoupling of the Indonesian economy from the global economy. This proved to be a failure, especially during the 1960s, as Indonesia's economy contracted and many businesses went bankrupt. Yet, under Sukarno's regime, preferential treatment and access to credit and projects were given to so-called "palace businessmen" (Muhaimin 1990, 179–80). This was a continuation of the model through which the administrator class had developed business patronage in relation to either Chinese or Indonesian businessmen. Many of Sukarno's business clients were Indonesian nationalist businessmen hailing from outside of Java (Robison 1986, 89–93). In the 1960s, economic mismanagement, rampant inflation and Sukarno's antagonism toward the Western world saw an erosion of confidence in business. The nationalisation of foreign assets continued in the 1960s, with British interests getting taken over in 1963 during the *Konfrontasi*[1] (or Borneo conflict) with Malaysia. With a negative growth rate during the first half of the 1960s, business growth in the country was limited (Robison 1986, 85–98). The collapse of Sukarno's regime in late 1965 resulted in an army takeover of the country under President Soeharto who would rule the country for over 30 years after.

Normalisation of Businessmen under the New Order

During the New Order (1966–98), several major changes occurred. First, the Indonesian business world became a more "normal" place, with the Government committed to market capitalism and the integration of Indonesia into the global economy. Two major phases showed the gradually increasing strength of the business class. The first was the result of the resentment towards Japanese business expansion in the early 1970s felt by indigenous Indonesian businesses that felt neglected by the Government. A series of public meetings and publications criticising the Government, and a riot by students in Jakarta in early 1974 during the visit of Japanese premier Tanaka Kakuei, resulted in a shift of government policy towards an Import Substitution Strategy. Flush with oil money from the oil boom (1974–82), the Government expanded the subsidies going into Indonesian businesses (Thee 2002, 207–10). The main beneficiaries of this were Indonesian and Chinese-Indonesian businesses that had patronage relations with the Government and army officers. The biggest loser was the Muslim merchant class whose main patrons—the social democrats and Muslim parties—lost control of a government that was now dominated by army officers and members of the Javanese nobility.

The second, more important, phase was the deregulation and liberalisation from the early 1980s until the 1990s following the failure of import substitution. This phase started after the end of the oil boom (1982) and was the outcome of a strategic relationship between business tycoons, liberal economists, parts of the political elite and major press groups like *Kompas* and *Tempo* magazine. The result was support for policy makers pushing for deregulation and the liberalisation of the economy. This was what Rizal Mallarangeng (1992, 127–58) refers to as an epistemic community in which Indonesian's public opinion was swayed through public meetings and publications. The state conducted what Shin Yoon Hwan has termed an ideological project to change the mindset of the regular Indonesian towards businessmen, capitalists and capitalism. Through seminars, conferences and other public means, terms such as "entrepreneurs", "businessmen" and "capitalists" were aired and became common in public discourse. The rise of the term "national businessmen" changed the dynamic through the assumption that both indigenous people, and Chinese-Indonesians were part of the same group (Shin 1991). The inclusion of both Chinese and Indonesian in the reference "national businessmen" was implemented not only through partnership and mixed business ownership, but also through the employment of indigenous Indonesians as managers. Business-specific newspapers such as *Bisnis Indonesia* began to be published. Popular culture mimicked this trend by normalising, and then fetishizing, the image of the young business executive. During this period, the distinction between Indonesian and Chinese-Indonesian businesses became blurred as more joint ventures and integrated companies arose from the relationships that were being built in organisations such as the Indonesian Chamber of Commerce or from the various industry-specific organisations that had been set up much earlier during Sukarno's Guided Democracy. A truly national business class had begun to emerge by the 1990s.

The Rise of Businessmen Memoirs

This "normalisation" of business and Indonesian capitalism may have allowed for the normalisation of the businessman as an integral part of the national elite, but one major caveat to this can be seen in the publication of personal memoirs. Personal memoirs had been the domain of nationalist politicians, and their narratives were often intended to locate a personal narrative within the larger context of the national historiography. The reason for writing a biography was to add to the national narrative, while at the same time emphasise the importance of a person's action within that historiography. It was seen as benefiting both national and personal narratives. Indonesian biographies were "performance designed to promote a desired image to the outside world" (van Klinken 2007, 199). Obviously, the national historiography was inherently one-sided, that is, it was the story of the nationalists who had successfully conducted the national revolution (van Klinken 1945–49) and brought about the independence of the nation. From this perspective, the position of those outside of the national narrative became irrelevant. Even more significant was the fact that the position of those who were deemed antagonistic to the national narrative had no place within it.

The normalisation of business from the early 1980s ultimately created a new space within which the voice of the Indonesian businessman had a place in the public narrative by means of a personal memoir. The number of published personal memoirs of businessmen increased and their nature began to change. As a public document, a memoir no longer required an individual's participation in the revolution or the independence movement in order for it to be deemed adequate. Personal memoirs meant to be read by few—for instance for family members only—had probably been published for much longer, but the idea of a public memoir that would be sold openly in bookshops had a rather different threshold in terms of its components.

Figure 10.1 (page 219) shows that businessmen's memoirs were quite rare before the mid-1980s. In fact, it was only starting from 1987 that the number of business memoirs produced grew significantly, some years after the start of the ideological normalisation of business had begun. It also shows that only in the 1990s and especially in the 2000s, after the fall of Soeharto, did memoirs and other egodocuments of businessmen become much more common. Gerry van Klinken (2007, 209) has pointed out that interest in the biographies of businessmen was related to middle-class interest in character traits that make up a successful entrepreneur. This was thus associated with an increasing interest in entrepreneurialism. The rise of the professional manager is also related to this shift in ideas relating to businessmen. Instead of bloodsucking capitalists, the image of the manager, along with the modern term *eksekutif muda* (young executive), obtained an alluring, almost modern fetish amongst the new and growing middle class (Raillon 1991, 89–90). This can be seen in various movies from the period, where the protagonists were often young executives working in an office skyscraper in Jakarta (Hanan 2008, 54–69). Management books appeared on the shelves of bookstores, filled with the writings of Western management gurus and their tips and tricks. Chinese-Indonesian businessmen gained respectability as masterful managers and some—like Mochtar Riady for instance—would go on to write prolifically on the issues and problems of management (Riady 1999; 2004; 2008).

The 1990s saw the further entrenchment of the businessman within the public narrative in Indonesia. After the signing of the Plaza Accord in 1985, and with the successful series of deregulation conducted throughout the 1980s and 1990s, Indonesia began experiencing significant foreign direct investment (FDI) towards the end of the 1980s. This resulted in high growth rates in manufacturing and a speedy integration into the global economy. Indonesia was considered one of the Asian Tigers in the 1990s, with the World Bank publishing the *Asian Miracle* report praising its high growth and high equality (World Bank 1993). Skyscrapers mushroomed in Jakarta, indicating its integration with the global capitalist economy. The image of the Indonesian businessman was someone who should be emulated instead of reviled. The acceptance within the national discourse, of businessmen as possible leaders and part of the national elite was a significant development, especially in relation to the post-Soeharto period. However, Indonesia's fast-growing economy of the 1990s was built on a rash and ill-regulated financial sector that gave way under the pressure of a failing rupiah currency. The collapse of the rupiah and the national financial sector resulted in the collapse of the New Order government.

Post-Soeharto Period: The Normalisation of Chinese-Indonesian

Although many businesses in Indonesia went bankrupt during the 1997–98 crisis, most showed resilience by bouncing back with vigour. Many had holdings and investment portfolios that extended to other countries and were thus shielded from the economic downturn in Indonesia. Many had also stashed funds in anonymous offshore accounts. Banks, along with their assets, were taken over by the Government's Indonesian Bank Restructuring Agency (IBRA). In some cases, the former owners of bankrupt companies were able to get their companies back at only a fraction of the amount the State had put into it. This caused great outcry from the general public, but it also showed how well-connected businessmen were able to restructure their relationship with the changing elites (Chua 2008, 97–113). The deregulation of various sectors pushed by the International Monetary Fund (IMF) resulted in the rise of new businessmen and capitalist families operating in a range of sectors, from aviation—as shown by Lion Air (1999) and its founder, Rusdi Kirana—to the media—in the instance of Chairul Tanjung and Hary Tanoesoedibjo. Aside from these newcomers, many old business tycoons survived and thrived in the post-Soeharto era (Fukuoka 2012, 80–100). This may indicate that the capitalist class had achieved greater independence from the State's elite, but it may also mean that the oligarchy had been successful in reorganising itself.

In relation to the production of memoirs and other egodocuments, the current period is the most productive in Indonesian history. One important difference compared to earlier periods is that more Chinese-Indonesian businessmen have published egodocuments now compared to in the past. There are several possible reasons for this. One is that the end of the New Order significantly reduced the primacy of the elite's interpretation of the national narrative. The loss of State and elite monopoly over the national historiography has seen the rise of other competing narratives, including the rise of a leftist anti-globalisation narrative echoing Sukarnian ideas and Sukarno's deep distrust of the Western-dominated world. Another narrative to have emerged is an Islamist revisionist one that tries to rewrite Indonesian history by centering it on and seeing it through the gaze of the Muslim actor (Fakih 2015). This opening space for the reimagining of the Indonesian narrative has allowed for new spaces in which personal stories do not have to be included within the national context. As noted, this started earlier in the New Order as part of its plan to shift Indonesia into an FDI-based industrialisation model.

Another reason relates to the politicisation of society. While the New Order strictly limited political participation by members of society—seeing it as something potentially negative, citing the 1950s as proof of the problems it could cause—the democratisation and decentralisation of society, as well as the fall of the New Order unleashed the potential for the politicisation of society. Instead of the concept of "bureaucratic polity" articulated by Karl Jackson (1978), which envisioned a State cut off from society, the post-Soeharto State is more in line with Joel Migdal's (2004) "state in society", where the State itself is seen not as a single hegemonic organisation but as a series of vested interests and their relations with different groups in society. In this context, one of the most visible changes to the body politic of Indonesia has been the increasingly assertive and participatory actions of its businessmen. The head of Partai Golongan Karya (The Party of Functional Groups), or Golkar, is the tycoon heading the old Bakrie family. We also find new parties, like the National Democratic Party, created by media mogul Surya Paloh, and the Perindo Party, headed by another media mogul and Chinese-Indonesian, Hary Tanoesoedibjo. The number of businessmen and tycoons that have been currently participating in the political process has been unprecedented in Indonesian history (Tapsell 2015).

Egodocuments

The biographical materials that are analysed in this chapter have been confined to the published books written by, or with the support of, Indonesia's 200 most successful businessmen as listed in the 1992 Data Consult edition (PT Data Consult 1992). This list contains some duplication, as there are many families with multiple entries, and of the 200 businessmen listed, only 36 have produced public egodocuments in the form of either books or biographies and autobiographies. Sources available at the Asia Library of Leiden University, The Netherlands, have been used to construct a preliminary grouping of businessmen from the list of books produced by individuals in the Data Consult list. As can be seen in Figure 10.1, prior to the mid-1980s, few egodocuments were produced by Indonesian businessmen. The increase in these egodocuments since the mid-1980s is probably related to the deregulation of Indonesia's economy after 1982, which contributed to the expansion of private enterprise and media interest in business issues, including the rise of published egodocuments (Soesastro 1989).

Figure 10.1: Annual publications (memoirs/biographies/books) by Indonesian and Chinese-Indonesian businessmen during 1969–2015 that were named in the 1992 Data Consult list

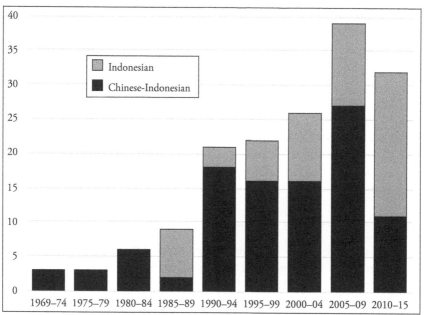

Aside from a general rise in the number of publications, there was also an increase in the number of publications by Chinese-Indonesian businessmen, especially in the post-Soeharto era, that is from 1998. This was especially the case in the 2000s. If the 1980s to the1990s represented the normalisation of business, then the 2000s represented the normalisation of the Chinese-Indonesians. During the *reformasi* period following the resignation of Soeharto in 1998, Chinese-Indonesians felt less inhibited to express their ethnicity. In that context, more (auto)biographies of Chinese-Indonesian entrepreneurs were published. As noted earlier, another reason for the increase in such publications may be the breaking of the dominance of Indonesia's earlier national narrative, which may have been something that may have started in the 1980s, but which was definitely completed in the 2000s.

Tropes in the Biographies of Indonesian Businessmen

As mentioned above, the phenomenon of businessmen biographies began mainly in the early 1980s and truly exploded after the fall of Soeharto. It thus occurred in conjunction with the gradual normalisation of business and the democratisation of Indonesian society. The chart above also demonstrates the gradually growing participation of Chinese-Indonesian businessmen, especially in the late 1990s and the 2000s. So how do the biographies published during this period show the changing ideas of business ethics amongst the various businessmen? The published biographies analysed for this chapter suggest three broad tropes: (1) businessmen as nationalists or freedom fighters; (2) businessmen as activists and humanitarian philanthropists; and (3) businessmen as individuals. Each of these tropes represents a different moral position that a businessman in that trope assumes within his societal context: within these tropes, particular moral strategies are enunciated that provide a glimpse into the business ethics professed by a particular group. These moral positions appear to be chosen in relation to the definition of the "society" within which each biography places itself.

Businessmen as Freedom Fighters

The first of these tropes was mostly enunciated by indigenous Indonesian businessmen and was prominent during the early period of the biography publication trend in the 1980s. Many of the famous Indonesian businessmen who published biographies during this period hailed from the 1950s during the time of Sukarno's Presidency. Soedarpo Sastrosatomo, for example, a shipping magnate and close confidant of Sutan Sjahrir, former socialist prime minister of Indonesia and founder of the Indonesian Socialist Party, survived in the New Order despite pressure from some members of the military elite, especially in the 1970s. One of Sukarno's old palace businessmen, Hasjim Ning, also survived and thrived after the fall of President Sukarno, unlike many of his colleagues, for example Teuku Markam, Mohamad Aslam and Agus Musin Dasaad, who had their businesses confiscated; some of them were also taken to jail.

Figure 10.2: Mara Karma's 1979 biography of Ibnu Sutowo shows a photo of Sutowo in military clothing, displaying his legitimacy as a freedom fighter

The need to provide legitimacy was one of the main reasons behind the trope of freedom fighters for national independence.[2] This can be seen in the titles of some of the biographies; for instance, the biography of Tumpal Dorianus "T.D." Pardede, with its subtitle *Pejuang Patriot* (Fighter Patriot), or that of Hasjim Ning, entitled *Pasang Surut Pengusaha Pejuang* (The Ebb and Flow of a Fighter Businessman). The use of the word *pejuang* is instructive here, because it denotes a fighter for national independence, representing the most sacred figures in the Indonesian national pantheon. This dogmatic patriotism is sometimes also reflected on the book cover imagery. For example, in Mara Karma's biography of the businessman Ibnu Sutowo (shown in Figure 10.2), Ibnu Sutowo is presented in his military uniform, signifying his relationship to the nationalist cause.

In Hasjim Ning's biography, his identity as a nationalist freedom fighter is positioned as superseding his more prominent identity as a nationalist businessman. The moral guidance he offers is thus based not on a particular form of business ethics, but on his nationalist commitment.

If I were to exploit my friendship with the then head and the ministers of the [S]tate, it would not have been that difficult to do. Particularly during the autocratic rule of President Sukarno. A true entrepreneur in reality should take every opportunity to develop his business or to enrich himself. There would have been many means at my disposal for such a plan. Yet I did not do so. First, for moral reasons. The moral of a freedom fighter absolutely denies gluttony and the view that the Republic of Indonesia was created in order to enrich the interests of those individuals on the back of the misery of the people. Second, because basing your strategy for growth on the back of a political relationship is something a speculator would do, not a true entrepreneur (Ning and Navis, 1986, 358).

In his biography, Hasjim Ning explained that often, his business decisions were "illogical": he chose "wrongful" policies not as a result of an illogical mind but because of his moral position as a nationalist. Another of the old indigenous businessmen of the 1950s was T.D. Pardede. His biographies, published in 1981—with the title *Pengusaha Mandiri Pejuang Berani* (The Face of an Entrepreneurial Fighter)—and in 1987, commemorating his 70th birthday— again under the heading *Pejuang Patriot* (Fighter Patriot)—showcases the legitimating function of nationalism and the individual's contribution in the fight for independence during the late 1940s (Pardede 1987; 1991).

Figure 10.3: Hasjim Ning's autobiography with its explicit title *Pengusaha Pejuang* (Businessman Fighter), alluding to the fighters or *pejuang* who won Indonesia's independence from the Dutch

The articulation of the businessman as a nationalist fighter is especially present in the biographies of politicians-cum-businessmen. These include the 1991 autobiography of Sebastian Tanamas, who was involved in political rebellion in the 1950s, and who later became a successful furniture exporter (Tanamas and Yusra 1998), and Oene "R.H.O." Djoenaidi, who had been involved in the independence movement during the colonial period in the Aceh region (Boesyairi 1982). As in the case of Hasjim Ning, the moral imperative of the group of politician (nationalist-Indonesian) businessmen was to realise the economic independence of Indonesians from the domination of "foreigners", and this eclipsed business efficiency. This emphasis on nationalist sacrifice as opposed to business success may in fact have been a way of deflecting attention from the failure of Indonesian businessmen to grow successfully by comparison with their Chinese-Indonesian business counterparts.

Businessmen as Political and Humanitarian Activists

One of the earliest Chinese-Indonesian businessmen to have published a national biography was Tjio Wie Tay or Masagung, the owner of the publishing company and book store Gunung Agung. He was close to President Sukarno in the 1960s and had converted to Islam in the 1970s, his position as a convert reducing his Chinese "otherness". Masagung was not only a convert but quite religious in his writings. In 1982, he published his autobiography titled *Masagung: Sukaduka Anak Jalanan* (Masagung: The Travails of a Street Child), with the sub-subtitle *Sukses Karena Allah S.w.t.* (Because of Allah, Glorified and Exalted); another biography was published in 1983 (Pitoko 1982; Masagung 1983). Although not himself a freedom fighter, Masagung was able to place himself within the national discourse because of his unusual position as a Chinese-Muslim, and has used this as a platform to preach on Islamic values in relation to business. This was the prelude to a rising interest in Islamic business ethics that arose in the 1990s, with the appearance of books such as *Etika Bisnis dari Sudut Pandang Islam* (Business Ethics in Accordance with Islam) (Masagung 1990).

For some individuals like Sofjan Wanandi (born Lim Bian Khoen), who was not only a major businessman but also a student activist and an important member of the influential Chinese-Catholic think tank of the New Order, the Center for Strategic and International Studies (CSIS), it has been possible to give his status as activist or politician greater emphasis than his status as a businessman. Sofjan Wanandi published his biography entitled *Aktivis Sejati* (True Activist) in 2011 with a view to emphasising his role during the transition to and development of the New Order (Sanda 2011). His brother, Jusuf Wanandi, published his own memoir in both Jakarta and Singapore titled *Shades of Grey: A Political Memoir of Modern Indonesia, 1965–1998* (Wanandi 2012), in which he too emphasised his political role in the shaping of modern Indonesia. This was an approach shared by many indigenous Indonesian businessmen who highlighted their non-business activities, or their role in the national struggle as opposed to their economic role. Soedarpo's biography, published in 2001, pointed out his role in the diplomatic struggle for Indonesian independence, in fact calling him a diplomat—a position that he had not held since the early 1950s (Anwar 2003). Ibnu Sutowo, the notorious head of the State oil and gas company who had allegedly bankrupted the company in the mid-1970s as a result of corruption published a biography written by Mara Karma in 1979 entitled *Ibnu Sutowo: Pelopor Sistem Bagi Hasil di Bidang Perminyakan* (Ibnu Sutowo: Pioneer of the Profit-sharing System in the Petroleum Sector), extolling his virtues in developing a more equitable arrangement of oil investment between Indonesia and large multinational oil companies (Karma 1979).

Figure 10.4: Sofjan Wanandi's biography, titled *Activis Sejati*, depicts his role not as a businessman, but as that of a nationalist activist who works tirelessly for the betterment of the nation

In the post-New Order period, an emphasis on humanitarian activism came to the fore, seen for instance in the biography of Dr Tahir (born Ang Tjoen Ming),

Living Sacrifice. Tahir was the founder of the Mayapada Group and dedicated his biography to his nation: "My country, a country in which all of my movement is sourced and which has become the goal of my endeavor. I work and pray for Indonesia. There are many things that I continue to hope from this nation [*sic*]. The rise of its people, the growth of its economy and the increasing strength of the belief in ourselves" (Tahir 2015, 27). The biography of Tay Juhana (born Tay Jui Chuan), the agribusiness magnate of PT Pulau Sambu, also reflects a similar identification with the nation. "Although of Chinese ethnicity and born in Singapore, the spirit of Tay Juhana is for Indonesia. His empathy is closely aligned with the trajectory of the nation. He is concerned with the poverty it endures, he hates knowing when the nation is fooled by other nations and he is anxious when the nation is incapable of exploiting its own natural resources for the benefit and welfare of the nation" (Tay 2018, 332). These kinds of biographies emphasise the roles of businessmen as multifaceted; the role in the political and humanitarian development of the nation is celebrated, and this is the root of any ethical position. The businessman cares about the nation, expresses sympathy with it, and emphasises his relationship with the nation as an integral part of that nation. His ethical position is considered a personal sacrifice based on his emotional and moral relationship with the society of which he is a part.

Figure 10.5: Dr Tahir's biography, *Living Sacrifice*, celebrates his role as an international humanitarian, rather than his role as a businessman

Success Rooted in Individual Character

The last trope is represented in the biographies of businessmen who position themselves as individuals. In this case, the nation or wider society does not come to the fore, but remains as the background against which an individual businessman and his business/es can grow. The relationship of the businessman with the wider nation is often ambivalent. Competing normative contexts in these cases include regional societies, often the overseas Chinese community or general "Western" business society, and the family. Their business values and ethics are based on teachings founded in philosophy and religion, such as in Confucianism or Islam, or is based on something often attributed to their fathers or elders; to lessons learnt during the formative period of their business careers; or to their time as teenagers during periods of political and social turbulence, including the period of the Indonesian Revolution or the tumultuous 1950s. Often, during these troubled times, a personal guide was reported to have come along to provide the businessman with moral teachings that strengthened his ethical stance during his early career; this guide might appear in the form of a friend, a teacher or even another businessman, such as a Japanese or Western business mentor. The business values articulated by these men are based on their own individual inclinations. Personal values such as keeping one's word, paying back debt, gratitude, and being honest are deemed essential, but these ethics and morals are not necessarily contextualised within wider society. The reward for such moral values is success in life, but without the articulation of any greater societal goal; wider political or societal goals play no part in the expansion of the business strategies of these individuals. If such philanthropic or humanitarian gestures occur, they are tangential to their business philosophy rather than being central to it. This is different from the other two other groups whose members— at least in their published writings—highlight their political and humanitarian position as a prominent part of their identity. Another important point is the fact that many of these "individual" biographies are published not just in the national media, but internationally, and written either in English or Mandarin for a Chinese audience in China. Some are published with the family in mind, as a sort of family history.

Hadi Budiman (born Ang Kok Ha) of PT Prospek Motor assembly of Honda motors and cars started his life in misery and tragedy with the Japanese Occupation and the Indonesian Revolution. He noted the importance of his father's teaching of Confucian values in shaping his ethical worldview. This related to "issues of gratitude and the importance of giving to others instead of receiving from others, so that it is of the utmost importance to repay someone's kindness". Several years later, Kok Ha obtained the books of the philosopher

Confucius. "These books convinced the little boy of the goodness of applying these ethical values to his life" (Sumarsono 2003, 14). Hardship during the war also molded his character to have gratitude for the help he received from those around him. He thus valued the Chinese community's sense of solidarity. His biography stated: "Do not look at Hadi Budiman as an Indonesian lacking in nationalism only because he had previously wanted to become a citizen of another country. Every person has the right to receive a sense of safety and protection. Every person also must look for this safety and protection.... In the end, didn't Hadi Budiman choose Indonesia as his country? And isn't it true that his wish to become a citizen of another country, namely Brazil, disappeared when the certainty of his choice became apparent—when he obtained his citizenship of Indonesia" (Sumarsono 2003, 123). The identities of many Chinese-Indonesian businessmen were determined through the lens of the family and the individual. It was familial and individual virtues that determined their ethics—even in business—and not any overarching sense of belonging to a nation.

Carlo Hein Tabalujan (born Tan Tjin Hin), of the conglomerate PT Sumber Selatan Nusa, recalled the importance of his travails from being stranded in Batavia in 1942, away from his family in Manado during his school years; in particular in the years of the Indonesian Revolution in the late 1940s and the early independence period. This period was formative to his ethical worldview: "I began, and have continued, my business career on the basic principle that one of the most valuable assets any businessman can have is a well-founded reputation for absolute reliability and trustworthiness". He reiterated: "... looking back on those early years, I am absolutely certain that the reason I succeeded where so many failed was that I managed to build a good reputation with bankers as well as a wide range of commercial companies" (Tabulajan and Tallboys 1995, 89). Yet, unlike Hadi Budiman's acknowledgement of his ethical roots in the Confucian values taught by his father, Carlo Tabalujan emphasised his education at the Anglo-English College near Xiamen in China, which he had attended early in life, and which "retained many of the moral values that [he] had experienced and valued" (Tabulajan and Tallboys 1995, 78).

Julius Tahija's autobiography, entitled *Horizon Beyond* and published in 1995 (Tahija 1995), was a celebration of his life. In this autobiography, he recounts his role in Indonesia's history, but identifies himself as both an Indonesian and an international businessman. As in the case of Carlo Tabalujan with his Anglo-Chinese upbringing, Julius Tahija focuses on the relationships he built as a Moluccan with strong ties to Dutch colonial society. He recounts his multicultural upbringing as part of the "cosmopolitan" society of the elite of the Dutch East Indies, rubbing shoulders with Dutch and Chinese pupils. In the early 1950s, he joined Caltex and would continue as a manager in Western multinationals, working in Indonesia and acting as a liaison to Indonesian elites. Julius Tahija's business ethics are decidedly Western, and he later married an Australian. Like Carlo Tabalujan and Hadi Budiman, his ethical views are both international and individual in context. He often adopts Western ethical viewpoints, such as a concern for the environment; some of his biggest influences have been other Western managers.

Religion in Indonesian Business Ethics

One recurring trope in many of these biographies and autobiographies has been the role of religion and religious values. As we have seen above, this was apparent in the case of Masagung and others like Bob Hassan (born The Kian Seng), a major *cukong* and timber magnate under President Soeharto;[3] a religious dimension was perhaps a necessary qualification for one of the first Chinese-Indonesian businessmen to publish a biography in the early 1980s. Islam was a gateway through which Chinese-Indonesians gained legitimacy. Yet, by the 1990s, and certainly after the fall of the New Order, many Chinese-Indonesian businessmen published biographies which espoused Christian or Confucian ethics. An outward show of being religious became more widespread, with some businessmen in the later post-New Order period manifesting a more religious persona. This can be seen, for instance, in the changing persona of Sukamdani Sahid Gitosarjono, a prolific writer and indigenous businessman close to Soeharto, who subsequently donned religious garb and published religious-inspired biographies and books on business ethics.[4] This tendency mirrored the increasing religiosity in Indonesian society itself.

Burhan Uray (born Bong Swan An), a timber magnate, said in his autobiography that "God will help his flock that work hard. If God wills it, then it will come true" (Uray 2012, 61). Dr Tahir, in his biography, *Living Sacrifice*, wrote: "... whatever I do can never be separated from my faith. I want to live a life in accordance with God's wishes. As a result, if some of my actions are considered not so logical by my business colleagues, this is probably the result of my faith taking action" (Tahir 2015, 25). Mochtar Riady (born Lie Mo Tie) was well-known as an evangelical Christian who had made donations to create elite Christian schools in Indonesia. Like many Chinese-Indonesian businessmen, Mochtar Riady identified personal virtues as central to his understanding of ethics. He also saw ancient Chinese philosophies, such as Confucianism, as valuable in relation to the shaping of behaviours and personal values. Like Hadi Budiman, Mochtar Riady emphasised the role of his father in transmitting these values: "Besides, father often strictly reminded us not to receive gifts from other

Figure 10.6: Sukamdani Sahid Gitosuhardjo's later biographies published in the post-New Order period had a decidedly religious image of the businessman in comparison to his earlier biographies published during the New Order

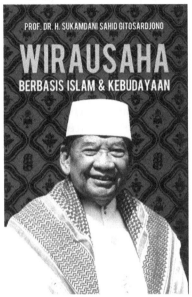

people without reason. It will stifle you, make it easy for you to be controlled. We must live with no attachments and must appreciate and love ourselves. He taught us that 'to give is more rewarding than to receive'.... Through these lessons, father taught us Chinese culture and philosophy" (Riady 2015, 9).

In the post-New Order period, religion replaced the nationalist fighter as one of the most important tropes for indigenous businessmen. In this respect, a biography of a businessman like Chairul Tanjung (owner of CT Corporation, with interests in media and banking), with a book cover showing him in a *peci*, a nationalist-cum-religious symbol (Tanjung 2012), is perhaps less direct than Sukamdani Sahid's cover of himself looking like an Islamic preacher. Yet, these religious symbols are of similar importance to the military uniforms an earlier generation of businessmen displayed on their book cover. In the post-New Order period, many Indonesian businessmen increasingly became directly involved in national politics. The rise of many Muslim merchant-class families to become part of the government elite or enter into parliament has been shown in the appointment of Vice President Jusuf Kalla from the Kalla Family of South Sulawesi as the head of the Golkar party, and through the appointment of Aburizal Bakrie from the Bakrie family of Lampung as Minister of Economic Coordination. Fahmi Idris, a member of the indigenous business association, Himpunan Pengusaha Muda Indonesia (HIPMI), and parliament member for the Golkar party, published a book titled *Saudagar dalam Lintasan Sejarah Politik Indonesia* (Businessmen in Indonesian Political History). He used the term *saudagar*, which is often translated as "traders", to denote origins deep within Indonesia's trading history. Fahmi Idris blamed the brainwashing by the bureaucratic class for the negative perception held by Indonesians of businessmen entering politics. "In the post-reform period, although the Mataraman[5] political culture has faded in the political reality of the Republic, there are still people who hold these beliefs, even if subconsciously. They see the marriage of economic and political forces as poisoning power" (Idris 2015, xxxi). This amounted to criticism of the Javanese bureaucratic control that had prevailed under both President Sukarno and President Soeharto. Overall, we can say that the rise of the indigenous Muslim business community to power has shifted legitimacy away from the military nationalism supported by many Javanese bureaucrats towards more multicultural forms of expression, with an emphasis on Islamic or other religious business ethics.

Conclusion

Reading into the biographies above shows the complicated and interconnected nature of ethics and identities constructed in the context of the modern Indonesian nation-state. Modern nation-states embody imagined societies whose boundaries have been created and recreated by the othering of specific groups. In colonial societies, the collapse of the colonial order radically reshaped the border and legitimacy of specific groups, changing their relationships with both the wider society and the State itself. In Indonesia's case, the position of businessmen was fragmented into several group identities based on racial or religious groupings. These identities determined the relationship with the State, which in the postcolonial period became one of the pre-eminent criteria determining business success. Significantly, the group that contributed the largest number of businessmen, the Chinese-Indonesian, was put in the category of "other" in the new nation-state. Yet, this position of "other" was extended to practically all Indonesian businessmen because of the way in which Indonesian national identity was framed within predominantly Marxist parameters that viewed capitalism as an extension of imperialism, and hence colonialism as being rooted in the capitalist drive of businessmen. Indonesian businessmen were thus all "others" within the context of Indonesian national identity. The postcolonial period can be seen as a process of normalisation and de-"othering" of the various business groups as part of Indonesian society. This process resulted in the greater integration of the narratives and life stories of Indonesian businessmen, starting from the late 1970s/early 1980s. These narratives were couched within tropes that engaged in forms of the legitimisation of businessmen: older period businessmen used the trope of national fighters, while later businessmen claimed national activism and—especially in the post-New Order period—religious identities. Some Chinese-Indonesian businessmen opted not to engage with national identity in their narratives, but instead engaged with a more international audience, including ethnic Chinese societies in other parts of the world and in China, which had increasingly opened up to the Chinese diaspora from the 1990s. Many of those who have engaged with this wider audience have a tendency to place emphasis on individual character based on personal trials, strength of the family and the teachings of Chinese philosophies. Some non-Chinese businessmen, such as Julius Tahija, have also engaged in this more liberal and individual approach in seeking to address a more Western audience. Reading through Indonesian business biographies thus complicates the narrative of business history, but at the same time, it also opens up the ways in which business ethics have engaged with different social structures and experience, and the borders of the various levels of imagined identities.

As noted earlier, we need to be cautious about taking the statements in these personal narratives at face value. In many cases, destined for public consumption, they are bound to offer justification for earlier actions and decisions, and to draw on concepts that are seen to be politically and socially appropriate. It is clear, however, that the importance of the discourses articulated in these accounts goes beyond simple justification and public image. As a result, these narratives also exhibit a diversity borne out of the business context outlined in the first half of this chapter, which results in turn in a range of stated approaches to issues of ethics and morality in relation to the conduct of business. This complexity suggests that Indonesia is still somewhat removed from the emergence of any consensus on possible alternatives to Anglo-American capitalism.

Notes

[1] The Indonesia–Malaysia confrontation or *Konfrontasi* was an armed conflict from 1963 to 1966 that arised out of Indonesia's opposition to the creation of the state of Malaysia from the Federation of Malaya.

[2] This particular form of Indonesian biographical discourse is discussed in more detail in Van Klinken (2007, 197–214).

[3] *Cukong* is a term of the New Order and denotes Chinese businessmen who had developed a clientelist relationship with President Soeharto.

⁴ For instance, his books on the Islamic educational institutions that he himself had built (Gitosardjono 2003; 2013).
⁵ Mataraman meaning bureaucratic or feudal, referring to the Javanese kingdoms which had provided the bulk of indigenous bureaucrats during the colonial period.

References

Anwar, Rosihan. 2003. *Against the Current: A Biography of Soedarpo Sastrosamo*. Jakarta: Pustaka Sinar Harapan.

Azra, Azyumardi. 1994. "The Indies Chinese and the Sarekat Islam: An account of the Anti-Chinese Riots in Colonial Indonesia". *Studia Islamika* [Islamic Studies] 1 (1): 25–54.

Boesyairi, Badroezaman. 1982. *R.H.O. Djoenaidi: Pejuang Pengusaha dan Perintis Pers* [R.H.O. Djoenaidi: Entrepreneur and Press Pioneer]. Jakarta: Yayasan RHO Djoenaidi Manondjaya (Djoeniadi Foundation).

Brown, Rajeswary Ampalavar. 2006. "Indonesian Corporations, Cronyism and Corruption". *Modern Asian Studies* 40 (4): 953–92.

Chua, Christian. 2008. *Chinese Big Business in Indonesia: The State of Capital*. London: Routledge.

Denzau, Arthur and Douglass North. 1994. "Shared Mental Models: Ideologies and Institutions". *Kyklos* 41 (1): 3–31.

Fakih, Farabi. 2015. "Reading Ideology in Indonesia Today". *Journal of the Humanities and Social Sciences of Southeast Asia* 171 (2)/(3): 347–63.

Fridenson, Patrick, and Takeo Kikkawa. 2017. *Ethical Capitalism: Shibusawa Eiichi and Business Leadership in Global Perspectives*. Toronto: University of Toronto Press.

Fukuoka, Yuki. 2012. "Politics, Business and the State in Post-Soeharto Indonesia". *Contemporary Southeast Asia: A Journal of International and Strategic Affairs* 34 (1): 80-100.

Gitosardjono, Sukamdani Sahid. 2003. *Pantulan cahaya Islam dari Gunung Menyan: Kisah Inspiratif Membangun Kader Bangsa unggul, Berbudaya dan Islami Melalui Pondok Pesantren Modern dan Pendidikan Tinggi Islam Sahid* [Reflections of Islamic Light from Mount Menyan: An Inspiring Story of Building Superior, Cultured and Islamic National Cadres through Modern Islamic Boarding Schools and Sahid Islamic Higher Education]. Jakarta: Pustaka Bisnis Indonesia.

———. 2013. *Wirausaha berbasis Islam dan Kebudayaan* [Entrepreneurship Based on Islam and Culture]. Jakarta: PT Aksara Grafika Utama.

Hanan, David. 2008. "Changing Social Formations in Indonesian and Thai Teen Movies". In *Popular Culture in Indonesia. Fluid Identities in Post-Authoritarian Politics*, ed. Ariel Heryanto. London: Routledge.

Hulsink, Willem and Andreas Rauch. 2021. "About the Lives and Times of Extraordinary Entrepreneurs: The Methodological Contribution of Autobiographies to the Life Course Theory of Entrepreneurship". *Journal of Small Business Management* 59 (5): 913–45.

Idris, Fahmi. 2015. *Saudagar dalam Lintasan Sejarah Politik Indonesia* [Businessmen in Indonesian Political History]. Jakarta: Masyarakat Bangga Politik Indonesia.

Jackson, Karl. 1979. "Bureaucratic Polity: A Theoretical Framework for the Analysis of Power and Communications in Indonesia". In *Political Power and Communications in Indonesia*, ed. Karl Jackson and Lucien Pye. Berkeley CA: University of California Press.

Karma, Mara. 1979. *Ibnu Sutowo: Pelopor Sistem Bagi Hasil di Bidang Perminyakan* [Ibnu Sutowo: Pioneer of the Profit-Sharing System in the Petroleum Sector]. Jakarta: Gunung Agung.

Lin, Hongxuan. 2018. "Sickle as Crescent: Islam and Communism in the Netherlands East Indies, 1915–1927". *Studia Islamika* [Islamic Studies] 25 (2): 309–50.

Lindblad, Thomas. 2008. *Bridges to New Business: The Economic Decolonization of Indonesia*. Leiden: KITLV Press.

Mallarangeng, Rizal. 1992. *Mendobrak Sentralisme Ekonomi 1986–1992* [Breaking Economic Centralism 1986–1992]. Jakarta: Gramedia.

Masagung. 1983. *Kilasan Riwayat Pribadi Masagung* [A Look at Masagung's Personal History]. Jakarta: Yayasan Idayu.

_____. 1990. *Etika Bisnis dari Sudut Pandang Islam* [Business Ethics in Accordance with Islam]. Jakarta: Yayasan Idayu.

McVey, Ruth. 1990. "Teaching Modernity: The PKI as an Educational Institution". *Indonesia* 50: 5–27.

Migdal, Joel S. 2004. "State Building and the Non-Nation-State". *Journal of International Affairs* 58 (1): 17–46.

Muhaimin, Yahya. 1990. *Bisnis dan Politik: Kebijaksanaan Ekonomi Indonesia 1950–1980* [Business and Politics: Indonesian Economic Policy 1950–1980]. Jakarta: Institute for Social and Economic Research, Education and information (LP3ES).

Ning, Hasjim and A.A. Navis. 1986. *Pasang Surut Pengusaha Pejuang: Otobiografi Hashyim Ning* [The Ups and Downs of a Warrior Entrepreneur: The Autobiography of Hashyim Ning]. Jakarta: Grafitipers.

Pardede, T. Dorianus. 1987. *Dr. T.D. Pardede 70 Tahun: Pejuang, Patriot* [Dr. T.D. Pardede 70 Years: Fighter, Patriot]. Jakarta: H. Masagung.

_____. 1991. *Pengusaha Mandiri Pejuang Berani: 75 Tahun Dr. T.D. Pardede* [The Face of an Entrepreneurial Fighter: 75th Anniversary of Dr. T.D. Pardede]. Medan: Universitas Darma Agung.

PT Data Consult. 1992. *Anatomy of Indonesian Conglomerates*. Jakarta: PT Data Consult.

Pitoko. 1982. *Masagung: Sukaduka Anak Jalan* [Masagung: The Travails of a Street Child]. Jakarta: Yayasan Idayu.

Raillon, Francois. 1991. "How to Become a National Entrepreneur. The Rise of Indonesian Capitalists". *Archipel* 41: 89–116.

Reveley, James. 2010. "Using Autobiographies in Business History". *Australian Economic History Review* 50 (3): 284–305.

Riady, Mochtar. 1999. *Mencari Peluang Ditengah Krisis* [Looking for Opportunities in the Middle of a Crisis]. Jakarta: Universitas Pelita Harapan Press.

_____. 2004. *Nanotechnology Management Style: Bagaimana Menyehatkan Penyakit Ketuaan Pada Perusahaan dan Menyelamatkan Perusahaan Keluarga* [Nanotechnology Management Style: How to Overcome the Old Age Disease in Companies and Save the Family Business]. Jakarta: Fakultas Ekonomi dan Bisnis Universitas Indonesia (FEUI) (Faculty of Economics and Business, University of Indonesia, Jakarta, Indonesia).

_____. 2008. *Filsafat Kuno dan Manajemen Modern* [Ancient Philosophy and Modern Management]. Jakarta: PT Bhuana Ilmu Populer.

_____. 2015. *Manusia Ide di Mata Sahabat dan Kerabat* [The Man of Ideas in the Eyes of Friends and Relatives]. Jakarta: Kompas.

Robison, Richard. 1986. *Indonesia: The Rise of Capital*. Sydney: Allen & Unwin.

Sanda, Abun. 2011. *Sofjan Wanandi: Aktivis Sejati* [Sofjan Wanandi: True Activist]. Jakarta: Gramedia.

Shin, Yoon Hwan. 1991. "The Role of Elites in Creating Capitalist Hegemony in Post-Oil Boom Indonesia". *Indonesia*, Special Issue on the Role of the Indonesian Chinese in Shaping Modern Indonesian Life: 127–43.

Soesastro, M. Hadi. 1989. "The Political Economy of Deregulation in Indonesia". *Asian Survey* 29 (9): 853–69.

Sumarsono. 2003. *Dari Pakuhaji sampai P. Jayakarta: Mencari Hikmah dari Perjalanan Hidup dan Usaha Hadi Budiman* [From Pakuhaji to P. Jayakarta: Looking for Wisdom from the Life and Business Journey of Hadi Budiman]. Jakarta: PT Budiman Kencana Lestari.

Tabalujan, Carlos Hein and Richard Tallboys. 1995. *Fifty Years of Business in Indonesia: An Autobiography*. Edinburgh: Pentland Press.

Tahija, Julius. 1995. *Horizons Beyond*. New York: Times Books International.

Tahir (Weng Junmin, Alberthiene Endah and Dr Tahir). 2015. *Living Sacrifice: Dato' Sri Prof. DR. Tahir*. Jakarta: Gramedia Pustaka Utama.

Tanamas, Sebastian and Abrar Yusra. 1998. *Tak Menggantang Asap: Otobiografi Seorang Pejuang dan Pengusaha Industri Kerajinan* [No Smoke Emissions: Autobiography of a Fighter and Craft Industry Entrepreneur]. Jakarta: Gramedia Pustaka Utama.

Tanjung, Chairul. 2012. *Si Anak Singkong* [The Cassava Child]. Jakarta: Kompas.

Tapsell, Ross. 2015. "Indonesia's Media Oligarchy and the 'Jokowi Phenomenon'". *Indonesia* 99: 29–50.

Tay, Ciaying. 2018. *Tay Juhana: Pelopor Industri Kelapa* [Tay Juhana: Pioneer of the Coconut Industry]. Jakarta: Kompas.

Thee, Kian Wie. 2006. "The Indonesian Government Economic Policy Toward the Chinese: Beyond Economic Nationalism?" In *Southeast Asia's Chinese Businesses in an Era of Globalization: Coping with the Rise of China*, ed. Leo Suryadinata. Singapore: Institute of Southeast Asian Studies.

_____. 2002. "The Suharto Era and After: Stability, Development and Crisis, 1966–2000". In *The Emergence of a National Economy: An Economic History of Indonesia, 1800–2000*, ed. Howard Dick. New South Wales: Allen and Unwin.

Uray, Burhan. 2012. *Berbakti untuk Indonesia* [Dedicated to Indonesia]. Jakarta: Universitas Al Azhar Indonesia.

Van Klinken, Gerry. 2007. "The Combative 'I': State Domination and Indonesian Self-Writing". *Journal of Life Writing* 4 (2): 197–214.

Wanandi, Jusuf. 2012. *Shades of Grey: A Political Memoir of Modern Indonesia, 1965–1998.* Jakarta: Equinox.

Wasino, Hartati E.S. and Nawiyanto. 2019. "From Royal Family-based Ownership to State Business Management: Mangkunegara's Sugar Industry in Java from the Middle of the 19th Century to Early 20th Century". *Management and Organizational History* 14 (2): 167–83.

World Bank. 1993. *The East Asian Economic Miracle: Economic Growth and Public Policy.* Washington DC: World Bank.

Chapter 11

The Essence and Mechanism of Transformation to a "Sufficiency Economy"

Patnaree Srisuphaolarn and Nuttapol Assarut

In this chapter, the authors seek to introduce the concept and practice of what is referred to in Thailand as "Sufficiency Economy". The main question behind the concept is this: How can we help small producers in general, and farmers in particular, benefit from economic development that is based on industrialisation, mass production and a free market ideology? It argues that the essence of a Sufficiency Economy is centreed on problem-solving skills: How do we develop critical and analytical skills so that the root causes of problems can be identified and sustainable solutions attained? The logic of the Sufficiency Economy results in the different management of economic resources. Social capital is highly utilised so that the members of society who apply the ideas of the Sufficiency Economy can enjoy both economic independence and social inclusivity—the ultimate goals of economic development. This entails nurturing entrepreneurship at both the personal and the collective levels, especially among those with less formal education and are in, but are not limited to, the agricultural sector.

This study therefore focuses on the agricultural sector as the majority of the Thai population is in this sector and they are on average poorer than people in other sectors. Based on two case studies, the authors aim to systematically test the concept of the Sufficiency Economy and to clarify the process, such that economic actors transform themselves from an ordinary tiny part of the broader economic system as a whole to a Sufficiency Economy practitioner. The Sufficiency Economy, we would contend, constitutes just one of many possible alternatives—or complements—to existing models of shareholder capitalism and demonstrates the diverse ways in which economic actors and businesses can think about their responsibilities towards society as a whole.

Introduction

The merits of Washington Consensus-based free-market capitalism have been increasingly questioned since the eruption of a series of economic crises—especially the one of 2008—in the United States, with growing inequality being observed in almost every economy. Even though the existence of a fair income redistribution mechanism is regarded as one of the necessary conditions to support a free-market ideology, there appears to be missing links in the process that might enable efficient income redistribution measures (Bresser-Pereira 2010; Hope 2011). This chapter therefore focuses on the concept of the Sufficiency Economy as an alternative to existing methods of resource and wealth distribution (Piboolsravut 2004). The concept itself can be said to have deep roots in the historical and cultural backgrounds of countries with a high percentage of economic activity in the agriculture sector, as well as a very recent history of industrialisation. In other words, its roots are in societies in which collectivist values predominate, and where social harmony and cooperation, rather than competition, are the norm. The concept was effectively "reintroduced" in Thailand in response to the Asian financial crisis in 1997, which largely hit newly industrialised economies like Thailand, Indonesia and Korea, 9 years prior to the 2008 crisis that hit developed economies. However, despite a number of scholars seeking to explain the essence of the Sufficiency Economy, little attention has been paid to its mechanisms, such that the Sufficiency Economy might be adopted to transform an economy. Understanding the process of rethinking the ways in which small farmers might manage their resources may contribute to a better understanding of how to prevent people from falling below the poverty line and experiencing unpleasant circumstances like hardship and hunger.

The key cause of poverty in Thailand's agricultural sector is farmers' incomplete knowledge about the value chain and how it works. This was the starting point to that understanding. Thai farmers are generally regarded as having a low level of general education, not to mention a low level of financial literacy. They also tend to accept any supporting options that are offered by the Government and/or middlemen rather than making their own independent choices. The two agricultural communities investigated in this paper, however, represent cases in which farmers have been successful in making their own choices in designing production and dealing with the market. Moreover, as the world becomes rapidly globalised, each individual and each company becomes a tinier part of the whole global production and marketing process. This implies that we are all in some respects in the same situation as farmers who cannot see how their work impacts others and vice versa. Thus, we would also suggest that practising the Sufficiency Economy concept may be instructive for any economy in which many businesses are encountering "crisis". It may trigger some thoughts on how we might design our lives, our work and our happiness, which is, after all, the real purpose of any economic or self-development.

Origin and Philosophy of the Sufficiency Economy

The Sufficiency Economy is the product of the summed up four decades of experiences of King Bhumibol (Rama IX) of Thailand, who ascended the throne in 1946, right after World War II ended (and as the Cold War was beginning). Situated in a strategic location with the potential to block the diffusion of communism from China and Indochina, Thailand secured economic and military aid from the US and international organisations, with the aim of fighting communism by reducing poverty. The construction of industrial infrastructure, such as dams for electricity production, roads and highways started in the mid-1950s. However, Thailand consists of four regions, each with a distinctive geographical and cultural setting. The economic development plans drawn up by the Economic Development Bureau in central Bangkok, which were implemented by highly centralised government agencies, therefore did not effectively function to increase the standard of living of the population in remote areas as urbanisation was limited to Bangkok.

King Bhumibol sought to fill this gap via various projects. Firstly, he aimed to help the hill tribe people in the northern region turn from growing opium to growing fruit. His fundamental idea was to develop arable land and a secure water supply so that people could undertake farming to feed their families. Visiting almost every remote village in these hazardous areas, which were characterised by high mountains and deep forests, the king formulated a concept of financial governing within which individuals could attain and maintain a "sufficiently" good-enough life. This was the Sufficiency Economy concept which was made public right after the 1997 financial crisis in Thailand. The Government thus made the concept of the Sufficiency Economy part of its national agenda as a counter-crisis measure. Economic analysts, at the time, asserted that the causes of the financial crisis were rooted in speculative investment and an overdependence on foreign technologies. On the one hand, they suggested that Thais had focused on what they could earn without considering what they might lose in so doing. On the other hand, they also exerted that Thais were prone to "buy" rather than to "make". Investments had been made based on the assumption that double-digit economic growth would continue, and with minimal concern paid to risk management. Investments were made even though debt-to-equity ratios were exceptionally high. In this context, in contrast to the assumption of stable economic growth that characterises neo-classical economics, the Sufficiency Economy concept assumes an uncertain environment in which growth and recession are much less predictable. This is not a risk-aversed idea, but rather a risk-aware one. As such, the concept has come to be seriously considered by many individuals in both the business and non-business worlds.

Learning from the experience of newly industrialised economies, development economists have proposed a focus on the development of human capital and the qualitative aspects of development, such as health, social and economic freedom and cultural affluence (Sen 1988). The Sufficiency Economy operates along exactly the same lines as these ideas. Though the term itself implies the humble lifestyle of a monk, it is in practice less humble than such an extreme. Rather, it is about how individuals rationally design their production, consumption and investment in both the short term and the long term. Being rational in the Sufficiency Economy sense is a bit different from what we think of as the behaviour of a "rational economic actor". "Being rational" here means thinking thoroughly about the causes and consequences of any action. In accordance with the Sufficiency Economy, a rational actor would run his or her economic activities based not on monetary motivations alone, but on a holistic calculation of the trade-offs these activities entail: costs and benefits, money and health, wealth and relationships, and so forth.

The Sufficiency Economy and Free-Market Capitalism

Existing studies on the Sufficiency Economy and free-market capitalism suggest to us three key differences. First, is the basic assumption of how an economic system operates. Free-market capitalism is premised on an assumption that the division of labour and standardisation—an equilibrium set by price signals and perfect information—will lead to better wealth creation. It further assumes that there will exist appropriate mechanisms of wealth distribution to ensure the welfare of society as a whole. These assumptions appear theoretically sound, and are attractive, provided the requisite institutions, including the Government, labour market, education and culture work well. Free-market capitalism is essentially an institutional approach to development, and much of the work related to it is concerned with structural reform (Singsuriya 2017; Unger 2009). Producers do not know consumers; the two parties are connected by middlemen who generally hold information from both sides. In this respect, it is an a-social and impersonalised system that pays little attention to interpersonal relationships among players in the system. The Sufficiency Economy makes more organic assumptions about the creation and distribution of wealth, emphasising not the role of an invisible hand in allocating resources and wealth, but the visible hands of people in the community. Production is not determined by price but by the needs of producers and the capacity of the resources they possess. The system will be sustainable as long as its members bear in mind the importance of moderation, the need for the optimisation of existing resources, rational thinking, knowledgeability in their economic actions (that is, production, value chain and so on), good ethics, harmony and sharing (Piboolsravut 2004). The Sufficiency Economy can be considered a cultural approach to development that is most concerned with transforming people's thoughts and behaviours (Singsuriya 2017; Unger 2009).

The second key difference lies in the ultimate goal of economic activities, or more specifically, in the route to happiness, and perhaps, the definition of happiness *per se*. The mechanisms of free-market capitalism prioritise the material dimension and the psychological dimension is excluded. The basic concept is the sale of products in return for some medium like money, which is in turn used to buy the things that the producer wants. Wealth is accumulated when the production price is lower than the consumption price. If the product being exchanged is basic, then a division of labour seems to lead to better working conditions and living standards, but if the producers of the basic product wish to consume more complicated products—which may have a higher price due to there being a chain of multiple producers involved—they will need to produce more of the basic product to be able to afford these more complicated products. However, increased output causes the price of the basic product to fall, leading basic producers into a vicious circle of lower incomes compared to producers of complicated final products. The system, almost by default, produces inequality, meaning that the wealth distribution mechanism is critical to keeping the system running smoothly. Moreover, the price mechanism means the existence of a time lag between production and consumption, making accurate planning essential. This time lag means that tremendous waste may already have been incurred by the time there is any realisation that a product may not meet the needs of the market.

By contrast, the Sufficiency Economy mechanism is more concerned with the psychological aspects of relationships. It suggests that an individual must first fulfill his and his family members' basic needs, exchanging what remains by barter or through market mechanisms. The producer must be knowledgeable about what he will produce and what he wishes to consume, which in turn determines his production capacity. He can reach a basic level of income and security as he knows that he is likely to survive regardless of fluctuations in market prices. Being assured by this "sufficiency" fulfilling of his basic needs, he would have no more fear, stress or anxiety. He would then have time and energy for other economic activities. At the macro level, there will be no waste out there in the market. In order to achieve basic sufficiency, a producer must by definition rely on more than one crop or product; farmers must produce the vegetables, rice and other crops that will enable them to achieve food security. In the king's terminology, this is a "new theory of agriculture", in which a single plot of land is allocated between rice paddies, fruit orchards and fields for other crops, instead of the whole plot of land being allocated to a mono-crop. On top of that, in order to have sufficient water to ensure a robust, healthy yield, a certain proportion of the land needs to be allocated to a private reservoir; by also housing fishes or other water-dwelling livestock, the reservoir can also serve as an extended food source of protein for the family. All this entails a lot of calculation and analytical thinking about how to design the utilisation of the land to render the best possible "sufficiency" outcome for the individual unit.

The third key difference is the meaning of "limited resources". If the free-market mechanism is a structure-based view, the Sufficiency Economy is rather a resource-based view of production strategies. In the former case, production is maximised to earn a margin, while in the latter, production increases only up to the level of actual consumption. The free-market mechanism assumes that the aggregate supply of resources is limited, but that individuals are able to buy and consume as far as they can afford to do so. In this sense, those with a higher income can seize the share of those with a lower income, driving people to increase their income to be able to enjoy the world's resources. The Sufficiency Economy assumes that "my share" of resources is limited and should be used rationally and smartly to ensure that there is no waste. No one should use resources beyond their own share merely because they can afford to do so.

Sample and Data Collecting Methods

We selected rural communities whose main economic activity is farming, and which had been suffering from chronic debts but were able to gain economic independence after a dramatic change in concepts and attitude towards production, keeping in mind the question: What makes a good life? Both communities were located in the north of Thailand and started to experiment before the Sufficiency Economy concept was widely introduced to a Thai audience. Thus, neither were influenced by the concept at the time when they decided to look for alternatives to their existing way of production. They have nevertheless proved their ability to achieve economic independence, as well as social well-being, still existing after decades of operation. In addition, both communities consist of different generations in the villages and actively engage in community work, indicating the healthy demographic structure of the community. This evidence suggests that the communities need not make social sacrifices in pursuit of the economic benefit derived from sending young people to work in the big cities.

In order to understand the context and process of the changes that have occurred in each case, we collected primary data through interviews and observation. In the interviews, we asked our key informants whether they believed that the current direction of economic development based on the free-market paradigm works in the context of developing countries, and, if not, what did they feel was an alternative approach? From raw data, we conducted selective coding to extract the main concept and understand the process the key informants have gone through to achieve economic independence. We then compared what we got from the data and the concept of Sufficiency Economy with general practices based on free-market ideology.

Background of Case Study 1: MT Organic Farming Village

MT is a district in Lampoon Province, located approximately 50 kilometers south of Chiang Mai, Thailand. This area used to be a fertile teak forest. However, the forest had become degraded due to the activities of the forestry and tobacco industries in the late 19th century, as well as the introduction of industrialisation by the British (Ongla 2017). After the decline of the tobacco industry, people earned their living by growing vegetables, rice and other crops using traditional methods, including producing their own organic fertilizers and growing different crops on a single plot of land.

During the 1960s, Thai agricultural policies were influenced by the green revolution concept, which aimed to prevent world food shortage. Farmers were advised to turn to mono-crop farming in order to increase productivity. Seeds, chemical fertilizers and insecticides were promoted to further enhance productivity. This meant farmers were induced to pursue the mass production of a single crop that was in high demand in the market. Money was needed to invest in new equipment and for other overhead costs for the first few years. Farmers could sell their products at a good price and they gained a good income. This was because the crop was still new on the market and facing limited competition, and the use of agrochemicals generated high productivity. Farmers did not have to pay for transportation costs themselves because middlemen would come to pick up their product from the place of production—although, they were usually unaware that transportation costs had been implicitly deducted from the price offered by the middlemen.

However, the high prices of the new crops attracted competitors. As more farmers switched to the same crop, market prices fell due to oversupply. This led to more new crops being introduced, necessitating new fertilizers and insecticides and the reformulating of soil composition and irrigation. Farmers had to make new investments in search of higher income to cover losses from the previous year. They switched from one crop to another in the hope of increasing income only to find themselves burdened by ever bigger debts. Over time, the overuse of agrichemicals damaged the soil and over decades, productivity continuously declined. Thirty years later, farmers were suffering from heavy debts and losing ownership of their land which they had put up as collateral on their loans. Many farmers all over the country organised protests against the Government asking for measures to address their chronic debts but the response amounted to little more than lip service.

Background of Case Study 2: PH Coffee Plantation Village

PH Village is an Akha village located on the Thai-Myanmar border in the Mae Sai district of Chiang Rai Province. The Akha were one of the hill tribes who migrated to the Thai border during periods of political instability in Mainland China in the 1940s. Hill tribes are well known for moving the plots they cultivate year after year, and for opium production. This farming style was harmful to the environment as it encroached on forests, as well as harmful to national security as opium could be traded for arms on the black market. Coffee cultivation was introduced to move these farmers away from growing opium. The king's patronage organisation, generally known in Thailand as the Royal project, introduced the contract farming of coffee to this village, providing coffee seeds, teaching techniques and guaranteeing a market. On top of that, in advance of the coffee crop, villagers were paid to act as forest guardians, guaranteeing them a steady income. In return, land allocation in the village was redesigned. An appropriate ratio between forestry, residential areas, and farming was agreed and had to be maintained if the village was to continue to receive economic aid from the Government. However, these villagers never drank coffee, only tea. Consequently, they were also not sophisticated coffee growers, merely picking the cherries and selling them to the processor, which put them at the mercy of the market price.

The Path Towards Sufficiency Economy

Our two case studies differ in terms of both the production sectors and historical background. We nevertheless found a similar development pattern in both cases.

Both have gone through three development processes: (1) questioning the status quo, (2) expanding new ideas and (3) upgrading quality.

Stage I: Questioning the Status Quo

The first step concerns re-evaluating the current situation and the desired situation. At MT Village, at the most critical point, farmer P raised this question: What would be the benefits of growing mono-crops and being dependent on the market—represented by the middlemen—in terms of both production factors and harvest prices? He started to calculate the total cost of production, which he had never thought of doing before and was surprised to find that the cost of agrochemicals amounted to nearly 40 per cent of his income; seeds, farming materials and tools also had to be paid for. This left only 10 per cent of the annual income for his household expenses—equivalent to less than the minimum day's wage of an urban labourer. Further, the farmer had to invest a substantial amount of money 3 to 6 months prior to the harvest without knowing in advance at what price he could sell his produce. He needed to wait for the middlemen, who would take the produce from the farm and come back 2 to 4 weeks later to give him whatever amount remained following deductions for equipment, insecticides, fertilizers and other items that the farmer had bought on credit at the beginning of the season. Farmer P realised that he had no bargaining power and no control over the outcome of his hard work. The more crop he produced, the more he was going into debt. He would not survive if he were to follow this pattern forever. Farmer P recalled how his parents had worked before this green revolution and decided that the first thing he had to do was to reduce his costs as much as possible—both production and his living cost. He started an experiment, going back to the traditional way of growing crops using homemade organic fertilizers and found that productivity became satisfactory and the quality of the land was improved. He was able, firstly, to avoid further increasing his debt; he was then able to write off all his debts within 3 years.

In the case of PH Village, the limited knowledge of coffee processing meant that the income came mainly from selling fermented coffee cherries which were priced at approximately US$0.11 per kilogram.[1] Then, around 1994 to 1995, the village head bought a coffee cherry processing machine, allowing the primary processing of coffee, adding value to the product. At the time, parchment coffee—cleaned coffee that retains its parchment covering—could be sold at US$2.5 per kilogram, but in 2001, the price of parchment coffee began to drop by 25 per cent and was subject to fluctuations due to competition in the world market. Given the limited land area of the village (240 hectares), increasing the production capacity was impossible. The only solution appeared to be rethinking coffee production, in particular whether to produce it as a basic commodity or as a specialty. Eventually, farmers M and D decided to add value to their product by expanding their downstream operations. They started to seriously study the whole coffee production process from growing to brewing. They became more active in selecting the right strains for their mountainous area, and considered the roasting and brewing processes, as well as how the product could be marketed to tourists. They started to outsource the roasting process to experts in 2003, and to establish a community enterprise to access bank loans in 2007. By 2012, they had begun to learn how to take on the roasting process and complete it in-house, two years later investing in a coffee roasting machine with the help of a Japanese friend.[2] The value of the roasted coffee reached around US$8.5 per 250 grams,[3] approximately 20 times higher than the basic coffee cherry price.

It is clear that at this stage, only one or two persons out of the many villagers had managed to figure out new and different ways of dealing with difficult situations. These individuals possessed some of the qualities of sustainable entrepreneurs, in that they were able to recognise risk, to critically analyse the root cause of their poverty, and possess the capability and vision to address the problem (Belz and Binder 2017; Bullough, Renko and Myatt 2014). Normally, when individuals realise that they are in trouble, they will try and get out of it, either by taking the situation as it is or by searching for a new equilibrium. Further decisions also have to be made about whether to prioritise economic benefit over social benefit—that is, whether to leave the village for the city to find a job that pays more than being a small farmer, or stay and come up with new farming methods.

Stage II: Diffusing New Ideas

After a process of trial and error, farmers P, D and M found an appropriate solution to help them get out of their respective crisis. Others then became curious about this new way of getting rid of debts and looked up to these leaders as success stories, and learnt and followed their new methods. As a result, the network expanded; informal rules and a transparent system were established. All members in the network knew their respective shares of both effort and gains.

In the case of MT Village, farmer P's success in growing a range of organic crops made other villagers curious about the key to his success and they would come and ask him for advice, indicating had that he gained trust and respect among them. By following his advice, villagers were able to write-off their debts and buy their land back from the money lenders. Convinced that this was a promising solution, they became more inclined to cooperating and thought actively about what was good for the community, further sustaining this new prosperity. Realising the importance of fertile soil and a good water supply—and the fact that healthy forests were the source of these—villagers offered to care for forest restoration as well as making organic other farming activities in the village, such as the rearing of livestock. Without debts, there was no need to sell land. Further, the environment had improved and the village became a desirable place in which to work and live, with land prices making a climb. On top of that, the villagers no longer sold their products to middlemen in bulk, instead selling small quantities of many items in nearby markets, which guaranteed freshness and in turn awarded the village and the farmers the reputation of being quality-product producers, creating leverage for the village name to thus become an organic brand trusted by customers, even in the absence of any certification by global certifying bodies.

Similarly, villagers at PH Village started to notice the different yield and success levels of farmers D and M and asked to learn their methods. Trust was thereby developed between these farmers and their neighbours. Later on, when the two farmers needed to procure coffee cherries for the roasting process, the other farmers became steady suppliers of good quality cherries. Farmer M realised that the villagers could not contribute to quality upgrading if they did not know what good quality coffee tasted like, so he started a coffee shop and homestay business in the village. Villagers could try a cup of "PH Coffee" for free at the coffee shop at any time, allowing them to relate the quality of the cherries to the final taste of the beverage. At the same time, the homestay business created awareness of PH Coffee and allowed customers to experience life in the village. The way that the production process chain of PH Coffee interacted with the villagers stimulated their trust and support, in turn guaranteeing the supply of the raw material. As the coffee became more famous, more middlemen came to buy parchment coffee from the villagers. Although villagers continued to sell some parchment coffee to middlemen because of the price incentives, they still retained some parchment coffee to supply PH Village's own coffee operations.

To summarise, the key driver at this stage is the diffusion of new ideas among the network or "social web" of the community leaders. By social web we mean the entrepreneurs' families and friends, or other members of the community who shared and supported the ideas of the leaders, enabling them to go through the trial and error process (Cornwall 1998). As knowledge is shared and the network grows, trust and engagement are built among members. Informal rules and agreements are established, resulting in a system that is transparent to all those within it.

Unlike in the normal market system, in which middlemen intervene between producers and consumers, the key decision makers in both case studies act more like coordinators connecting the members of a supply chain. This system has been sustained based on the transparency that results from trust which—we would argue—is a distinctive characteristic of a traditional Thai village. A clear understanding of the role of each member in the value chain leads to a mutual agreement on how income is distributed, satisfying all members in the system. The system is not run by the invisible hand of the price mechanism alone, but rather by a cultural approach based on relationships. When an opportunistic middleman offers higher prices at times of high demand, villagers usually sell only if they have a surplus over and above what has been promised to the community. Strong relationships between the villagers protect the system from threats posed by a short-run rush to produce large quantities to benefit from higher market prices. Good quality products are sustained, as well as the village's reputation as a quality producer of specific items—in these two cases, coffee and organic vegetables.

Stage III Upgrading Quality

From their past experiences, the farmers learnt that markets are dynamic. They better understand the importance of continuous improvement to survive possible competition in the long run. The two case studies show how leaders and other villagers worked together to pre-empt this threat. In the case of MT Village, farmer P realised that "everyone faces limitations in resources and capability. The key to gaining more income is not to increase production, but to increase the value added in the product. Because if we try to produce more, it means we have to borrow money for investment in the production process".[4] Based on this idea, farmer P and his network opted to continuously increase quality rather than quantity, so as to maintain a steady income. Two decades on, their children who have furthered their studies in big cities and who work there at present have started to realise the bonds that tie them to their hometown. Many have chosen to move back to the village, where they try to add value to their products, differentiating them from other organic produce by applying for official recognition, like organic certification, or through brand creation and opting to make processed products.

At PH Village, farmers M and D realised that the key resource of their village is land, which cannot be increased, so they had to maximise their product value instead. As noted earlier, they have improved the production process and tried to move further down the value chain, for example by investing in a coffee roasting machine and starting to sell roasted coffee directly to consumers via an online platform, and by opening a homestay business to create brand awareness and knowledge of PH Coffee among consumers. Aware of the high level of imports of low-quality coffee from neighbouring countries, they opted to position their coffee as a speciality product. In 2011, PH Coffee received the "Best Coffee" award at the World Horticultural Exposition.

The key characteristic of the Sufficiency Economy highlighted in this stage is the direction of growth. The farmers chose quality over quantity. Based on the idea that resources are scarce, instead of expanding their production quantity—which might have resulted in a drop in quality and a fall in the sale price—both communities made the best use of their resources by continuously learning to improve their product quality and create added value in their product. Once the product gained traction in the market and became more well-known, they expanded both their producer and consumer networks. The more they understood the market, the more they knew how to serve the end-consumer better—that is, end-users whom they had never had a chance to come in contact with in the previous system of the middleman intervention.

The Essence of the Sufficiency Economy

In reviewing the transformation process discussed above towards a Sufficiency Economy, we were able to identify the roles of the key elements of the Sufficiency Economy that drove the communities forward towards its adoption. When people realised that they were in crisis and decided to make attempts to get out of the situation, they had two alternatives: they could either choose to continue with mainstream capitalism or could go down the alternative route of the Sufficiency Economy, as did the villages in the case studies discussed in this chapter. It is therefore instructive here to revisit and compare the core elements of mainstream capitalism and the Sufficiency Economy. These elements relate to their assumptions about the overall system, goals and resources, as summarised in Table 11.1. We will consider each of these sets of assumptions in turn.

Table 11.1: Comparison of mainstream capitalism and the Sufficiency Economy

	Mainstream capitalism	Sufficiency Economy
System	A-social	Social
Goal	Wealth accumulation	Well-being and healthy social network
Resource	Mobility	Stability

System

Any community sustains itself based on assumptions about the operation of the overall system, in particular the ways in which individuals within the system interact with each other. Mainstream capitalism assumes an a-social system with individuals' roles and responsibilities identified by formal rules and agreements. However, with regards to the Sufficiency Economy, the two case studies suggest that individuals interacted with each other based on trust and human relations. Informal rules prevailed. Everyone respected individual differences, and individuals had the freedom to make their own decisions as long as they did not impact the overall system negatively. It is a transparent system in which every individual understands their role and that of others, as well as their and others' contributions to the system, thus achieving a fair distribution of income. Once the system had been established on the basis of trust and individual engagement, this interdependency protected it from outside investors and the overuse of resources, resulting in its sustainability.

Goals

Another basic assumption relates to the ultimate goal of undertaking economic activities. Mainstream capitalism assumes steady and continuous growth in the economy, in other words, uncertainty needs to be controlled. Hence, firms tend to invest more in order to expand their business and increase their productivity whenever the opportunity presents itself. The ultimate goal is individual wealth accumulation to achieve a high standard of living. However, the ultimate goal of the Sufficiency Economy is to achieve collective well-being. Healthy social networks are hence the key, serving as a safety net when crises happen. Uncertainty is accepted as a built-in component of the system. Economic growth and downturns are taken into consideration and economic activities planned with flexible adjustment mechanisms. People are careful not to overinvest purely for profit maximisation. Instead, they engage in critical and thorough analysis prior to any decision. Hence, though the economy may fluctuate, a steady income and standard of living can be maintained, shielding those involved from crises. The belief is in manageable risk and acceptable returns.

Resources—Sufficiency and Capability

The last element relates to how resources are defined. Resources here include money, land, time and manpower. Mainstream capitalism assumes that resources are scarce but mobile. When businesses exhaust their existing resources, they can procure resources from elsewhere, for example through importing materials, raising money via loans and the capital market or outsourcing labor. However, the Sufficiency Economy treats resources as stable and limited to those that are available within immediate proximity and availability. The emphasis is on the sufficient and rational use of resources in business activities, not in a monetary sense, but in the sense of undertaking only a manageable level of risk.

Summary and Conclusions

This chapter has aimed to investigate the mechanisms that have moved agricultural communities in Thailand towards becoming a Sufficiency Economy. Our case studies suggest that although at different times and places, these communities each encountered their individual crisis and struggled to address their problems; their paths to economic and social freedom was paved along the concept of the Sufficiency Economy proposed by King Bhumibol. The interviewees themselves, too, also mentioned on several occasions that the solutions from the crisis solving process that they had come up with were similar to those suggested by the king.

The essence of the Sufficiency Economy can be summarised into three points. Firstly, an individual should optimise the usage of his existing resources. If the existing resources are able to provide a safety net for basic needs, then the individual can take the next step to expand. For example, one should secure food supplies by fully utilising the resources at hand before seeking resources in the market where the cost is higher and the quality unknown. Secondly, our findings suggest that a practitioner of the Sufficiency Economy approach can experience poverty reduction, secure economic and social freedom, and have personal and social health, as well as restore degraded environments—all of which are listed as sustainable development goals by the United Nations (2018). Thirdly, the Sufficiency Economy also implies inclusiveness, in that it does not let anyone be cut off from society. Altruism, trust building and inter-dependency are the key assumptions behind the concept. Individuals do not benefit by negatively affecting the rest of the community. It is important to note, of course, that the objective of the Sufficiency Economy is not to replace the mainstream market mechanism and the free-market ideology. Rather, it is complementary, especially for those seeking an alternative. King Bhumibol also asserted clearly that even if only 40 per cent of the farming population embraces the Sufficiency Economy approach, the whole nation would achieve food security in both qualitative and quantitative terms.[5]

While our two case studies have shed light on the essence of the Sufficiency Economy in the agricultural sector, further research is needed to see how far the concept is applicable to businesses in other sectors of the economy. Companies that have recently been questioned about business ethics and their adherence to various international standards are increasingly monitoring their own behavior. Corporate social responsibility (CSR) has also been catching the interest of consumers and communities more broadly. In an era in which changes are rapid, there is an ongoing need to search for more effective ways of managing businesses sustainably. Our case studies have been focused on cases from a single country. Further study would of course be needed to confirm whether, given the shared characteristics of many developing economies, this concept of Sufficiency Economy can be more broadly applicable.

Notes

[1] The exchange rate before 1997 was roughly ฿25 to US$1.

[2] This Japanese friend also helped them design appropriate packaging marked with the PH Coffee logo, that would preserve the original aroma of the coffee.

[3] The exchange rate in 2012 was roughly ฿30 to US$1.

[4] Farmer P, interview with author, 5 January 2018.

[5] This is because Thailand is known as one of the world's biggest importers of dangerous insecticides, some of which are prohibited in developed countries. There are various studies on how chemicals used in the agricultural sectors may affect wider public health (Panuwet et al. 2012; Plianbangchang, Jetiyanon and Wittaya-Areekul 2009).

References

Belz, F.M. and J.K. Binder. 2017. "Sustainable Entrepreneurship: A Convergent Process Model". *Business Strategy and the Environment* 26 (1): 1–17.

Bresser-Pereira, L.C. 2010. "The Global Financial Crisis and a New Capitalism?" *Journal of Post Keynesian Economics* 32 (4): 499–534.

Bullough, A., M. Renko and T. Myatt 2014. "Danger Zone Entrepreneurs: The Importance of Resilience and Self-efficacy for Entrepreneurial Intentions". *Entrepreneurship Theory and Practice* 38 (3): 473–99.

Cornwall, J.R. 1998. "The Entrepreneur as a Building Block for Community". *Journal of Developmental Entrepreneurship* 3 (2): 141–8.

Hope, W. 2011. "Crisis of Temporalities: Global Capitalism after the 2007-08 Financial Collapse". *Time & Society* 20 (1): 94-118.

Ongla, O. 2017. "People's Movements and Decentralization for Forest and Land Management in Tha Neua Sub-District, Mae On District, Chiang Mai Province". Proceedings of the 16th Conference of Thailand's Sociology and Anthropology Graduate Student Network. 29–30 June 2017.

Panuwet, P. et al. 2012. "Agricultural Pesticide Management in Thailand: Status and Population Health Risk". *Environmental Science & Policy* 17: 72–81.

Piboolsravut, P. 2004. "Sufficiency Economy". *ASEAN Economic Bulletin* 21 (1):127–34.

Plianbangchang, P., K. Jetiyanon and S. Wittaya-Areekul. 2009. "Pesticide Use Patterns Among Small-Scale Farmers: A Case Study from Phitsanulok, Thailand". *Southeast Asian Journal of Tropical Medicine and Public Health* 40 (2): 401–10.

Sen, A. 1988. "The Concept of Development". In *Handbook of Development Economics*, Volume I, ed. H. Chenery and T.N. Srinivasarn. Elsevier Science Publisher B.V.

Singsuriya, P. 2017. "Sufficiency Economy and Backdated Claims of its Application: Phooyai (Headman) Wiboon's Agroforestry and Self-narrative", *Journal of Asian and African Studies* 52 (6): 794–806.

Unger, D. 2009. "Sufficiency Economy and the Bourgeois Virtues". *Asian Affairs: An American Review* 36 (3):139–56.

United Nations. 2018. *Transforming our World: The 2030 Agenda on Sustainable Development*. Pamphlet on sustainable development goals. Accessed 25 April 2018. www.sustainabledevelopment.un.org.

Chapter 12

Business in Indonesia since *Reformasi*: New Opportunities for CSR and Ethical Capitalism

Pierre van der Eng

Introduction

Since President Soeharto resigned in 1998, Indonesia has experienced waves of significant political and social changes known in the country as *reformasi*. Many earlier changes had since been crystallised, while others continued to be added since a 2004 stock-take of Indonesia's business system (Van der Eng 2004). This chapter assesses whether these changes help to explain why Indonesia became strongly predisposed to corporate social responsibility (CSR) and to public discussion about aspects of "ethical capitalism".

One obvious reason for this change is Indonesia's 2007 Law on the Limited Liability Company which made CSR compulsory. The law defied the common, accepted and known definitions of CSR as the voluntary act of enterprises (Sheehy 2015). The terms CSR and its Indonesian equivalent *Tanggung jawab Sosial Perusahaan* have since become part of Indonesia's vocabulary and public discussion. Much of the discussion is superficial, expressing approval of companies putting their best foot forward, while some of the discussion is more profound—largely about intricacies, such as the definition of CSR, the minutiae of the rules and regulations that companies should abide by and the public relations aspect of company commitments to CSR.

This chapter discusses several salient features of Indonesia's business system to put this growing interest in CSR into context. Its ultimate purpose is to assess the viability of public discussion in Indonesia about "ethical capitalism", which is the view that the operations of companies not only serve the direct objective of generating financial returns for shareholders, but also have a duty of creating long-term economic and social value for all their stakeholders. There is potentially great interest in Indonesia in such a discussion, because firstly, according to Google Scholar, the number of academic publications with "CSR" and "Indonesia" in their titles has increased enormously from just 4 20 years ago to, on average, over 800 per year today. CSR is also the subject of regular media coverage in Indonesia. Secondly, key business practitioners are taking greater interest. For example, a 2014 survey of Indonesian high-wealth investors revealed that 89 per cent expect their investments to be used to achieve "social impact" (Capgemini 2014, 26–7). The 2016 version of this survey found that 46 per cent of the investment portfolio of these investors was allocated to projects intended to drive "social benefit" in Indonesia; this number was higher than in all other Asia-Pacific countries surveyed (Capgemini 2016, 8–9).

To provide context, the sections of this chapter discuss several key features of Indonesia's business system, starting with its origins, the role of the financial sector and the related issue of corporate governance reform. Also significant are the fact that business groups continue to dominate the business landscape, the role of corruption and the rise of services companies. All these aspects help to put the current CSR "revolution" in context and identify the degree to which this revolution builds on the existing norms and values in Indonesian society, which may nurture public interest in discussing the merits of ethical capitalism.

Origins of Indonesia's Business System

Various elements of Indonesia's business system were carried over from a distant past. One of these elements of continuity is in the legal sphere. Several aspects of civil law in Indonesia hark back to the Dutch colonial era and the Dutch legal principles of codification. For example, the 1847 Law on Commerce remained Indonesia's main company law until the introduction of a new company law in 1995, which actually sustained many components of previous legislation. However, the way in which business unfolds in Indonesia is also based on non-codified social norms and values, as well as other historically determined institutions.

One important historical aspect was the fact that foreign-owned enterprises, mostly controlled by parent companies in The Netherlands, were predominant at independence in the 1940s. There was also a large number of formal and informal ventures owned and operated by Chinese-Indonesians, some of which were of considerable size (Van der Eng 2022). Dutch-owned companies were nationalised in 1958, followed by UK and US enterprises in 1964–65. Several enterprises of Chinese-Indonesian business families were also nationalised in 1960, but most continued operations and increasingly filled voids in the private sector.

During the 1960s and 1970s, Indonesia's business system was dominated by State-owned enterprises (SOEs). Most continued operating the nationalised assets of foreign and Chinese companies in a wide range of industries: agriculture, mining, manufacturing, finance, trade, transport and so on. Many were managed by former military officers and served to funnel off-budget income to the military to pay for salaries and hardware purchases (Purwanto 2009). SOEs were major beneficiaries of Indonesia's 1967 to 1985 oil and gas export boom. Part of the increased public revenues was invested in upgrading SOE assets and expanding their operations. Shielded by increasing trade protection, new SOEs were established in manufacturing and services to produce for growing domestic markets. Many turned into business groups by spinning-off associated ventures as suppliers.

The end of the oil boom in the mid-1980s limited public subsidies for SOEs. Further economic growth took the form of the expansion of the private enterprise. As Indonesia opened up to foreign direct investment (FDI) and reduced trade protection, inflows of FDI found their way into export-oriented industries as well as import-protected industries producing for growing domestic markets. In both cases, foreign firms were required to have domestic joint venture (JV) partners. They often preferred Chinese-Indonesian entrepreneurs who had survived the 1960s and risen to prominence in the still small but thriving private sector. Their business experience and political connections made them suitable JV partners. Other well-connected entrepreneurs also diversified their business interests as JV partners.

As JV partners, the business interests of Indonesian entrepreneurs expanded rapidly in the 1990s, allowing them to nurture highly diversified conglomerate business groups. Some groups grew well beyond their core competencies and developed their own ambitions with funds borrowed from domestic private banks and in international capital markets by selling company bonds overseas that were listed on foreign stock exchanges. When the Indonesian currency depreciated rapidly during the 1997–98 Asian financial crisis, many were unable to service these debts. Several groups were forced to sell prized assets, though some others emerged from the crisis largely intact.

By the early 2000s, Indonesia's business system was still dominated by two types of companies: those associated with the business groups that surrounded large SOEs and those that were part of sprawling privately controlled business groups. There was also a large number of small- and medium-sized formal ventures and an even greater number of very small informal enterprises. However, their accumulated assets were modest compared to large companies in the formal sector.

Indonesia's economy recovered from the 1997–98 crisis by 2002. Economic growth after the 1999 nadir was over 5 per cent per year until 2020. While lower than the 7 per cent that economic planners expected, this growth was uninterrupted for almost two decades. In the long run, uninterrupted growth may be more important than the stop-go growth Indonesia experienced in the past (Van der Eng 2010; Broadberry and Wallis 2018). During the 2000s, economic growth benefited from the China-related commodity boom that boosted export revenues, but most growth was carried by steadily increasing domestic demand. New investment and increasing consumption were spurred by higher average incomes and advancing market integration across Indonesia, and increasing savings. Steady growth was indicative of expanding business opportunities in the country and a thriving business sector comprising foreign and domestically owned private firms, as well as SOEs.

Privatisations of SOEs in the wake of the Asian financial crisis reduced their number to about 140, although several SOEs have received a new lease of life in recent years under Indonesia's 4-stage National Long Term Development Plan (RPJPN 2005–25). This is an ambitious effort to reduce the country's significant "infrastructure deficit". Having failed to mobilise sufficient private sector investment in planned infrastructure projects, the Government looked to SOEs involved in operating facilities such as power stations, toll roads and ports to take the lead in commissioning contractors and attracting loans for new projects. Consortia of companies from China took a prominent role in answering the call, bringing soft loans from Chinese State-owned banks and bolstering the assets of Indonesia's SOEs in the process.

Changes in the Modest Financial Sector

The expansion of domestic business activity from 2000 was partially financed with historically high inflows of foreign investment, but mainly with increased domestic savings. Both triggered increasing financial intermediation and a significant growth of equity capitalisation. Indonesia's financial market remains small and shallow by international standards (Azis 2018), but has since 2000 experienced increasing competition among companies for funds through banks, non-bank financial institutions and equity markets, which resulted in higher company awareness of investor interests beyond financial returns.

This had not been the case for a long time though. From their nationalisations in 1958, Indonesia's largest banks were State-owned. Monetary policies had cut them off from international capital markets for 30 years, limiting their assets and lending abilities. Experience with debilitating hyperinflation in the 1960s caused Indonesia's authorities to pursue conservative monetary and financial policies after 1968, which cemented the prominence of State-owned banks. In the context of capital scarcity during the 1970s to 80s, banks essentially followed government directions by lending to Indonesia's SOEs and to some well-connected private enterprises. Other private firms were forced to finance expansion by reinvesting earnings and/or inter-firm lending of surplus cash on the basis of their ties within business groups.

As part of deregulation since the mid-1980s, Indonesia lifted controls on the operations of banks and licensed new private banks often associated with sprawling business groups. But by 1997 many State-owned and private banks were overly risk-exposed due to excessive lending without proper due diligence and overseas borrowing. When Indonesia's currency depreciated quickly in 1997–98, many import-dependent borrowers defaulted on their debts and banks reneged on servicing dollar-denominated loans. During the crisis, banking was weighed down by non-performing loans. Monetary authorities forced State-owned banks to amalgamate and absorb near-bankrupt private banks, thus nationalising most non-performing loans and the private banks holding them (Van der Eng 2004, 7–9). Authorities placed banks on a workout programme to reduce their non-performing loans by writing debts off against assets. Former private banks were nurtured to health and sold to foreign and domestic investors. Nevertheless, most financial assets remained with large State-owned banks that dominated Indonesia's financial sector. Although down from 91 per cent in 2003, banks still held 70 per cent of assets of all financial institutions in 2018 (Bank Indonesia 2003–18).

This is important because State-control and relatively conservative monetary policies have since 1997–98 imposed limitations on the role of banks in business finance. Nevertheless, the expansion of Indonesia's economy at over 5 per cent per year implies that other capital market institutions have become more significant in financing business expansion. For example, equity capitalisation on the Indonesia Stock Exchange (ISE) has increased significantly as more companies have sold stocks and bonds through public offerings. Since 2000, closer supervision by Bank Indonesia has made banks more prudent in their lending practices. Details are confidential, but it appears that borrowers are required to be much more truthful in declaring investment intentions, and banks more active in exercising due diligence. At the same time, monetary stability and increasing economic growth have encouraged increased public savings in the form of bank deposits, increasing their role as mediators between savers and investors.

Increased equity capitalisation, growing mediation by banks, and the fact that in 2018, 30 per cent of financial assets were handled by non-bank financial institutions all indicate increasingly active and competitive capital markets. Consequently, firms are now required to be much more open about their operations and management decisions with lenders and minority investors than was the case in the 1990s. In all, this may have benefited the corporate governance (CG) practices of Indonesia's companies. On the other hand, Indonesia's financial market remains relatively small and shallow and bank lending continues to dominate the external finance accessed by most companies. Internal and inter-firm lending remain significant forms of business finance, which is one rationale sustaining the prominence of business groups. Both factors also put an upper limit on the degree to which firms feel obliged to "open up" to lenders, minority shareholders and stakeholders in general.

The Good Corporate Governance Drive

These limitations on the urgency for companies to "open up" imply that CG reforms in Indonesia since 2000 have had partial results. Following the 1997–98 Asian financial crisis, Indonesia and other Asian countries seemed imbued with the need to change the CG practices that had contributed to the crisis and subsequent financial sector problems. Comparative research demonstrated how opaque, devoid of outside scrutiny and lacking due diligence corporate decision making had been in many large Asian companies. This had allowed "insiders" such as business families with controlling interests in companies to take advantage of minority shareholders (see for example Claessens et al. 2000). Based on changes in relevant regulations and information campaigns to raise awareness of the need for greater openness in corporate decision making, improved CG practices were expected to take hold after the early 2000s.

Several initiatives were pursued in Indonesia (Siregar 2017). In terms of voluntary regulatory change, Indonesia's accounting fraternity prescribed new accounting and auditing rules that aimed for greater conformity with the International Generally Accepted Accounting Principles and which would ultimately improve transparency in the annual reports of companies. In 1999, the Government encouraged the formation of the National Committee for Corporate Governance, with participants from the public sector, business sector and academia. It published Indonesia's Code of Good Corporate Governance. This document informed Indonesian's new corporate law, Law No. 40 of 2007 on the Limited Liability Company, which incorporated elements of good CG aimed at protecting shareholders. Further specification of relevant rules had to wait until after the establishment of the long-awaited Otoritas Jasa Keuangan (OJK) or Financial Services Authority in 2011, which regulates and supervises the financial services sector, including the ISE.

The OJK tightened the ISE rules and required listed companies to observe good CG practices. In 2014, it issued two documents to that end. The *Indonesia Corporate Governance Manual*, prepared in collaboration with the International Finance Corporation of the World Bank, provides an overview of the CG regulations applying to listed companies and clarifies OJK's intentions. The *Roadmap Tata Kelola Perusahaan Indonesia* (*Indonesia Good Corporate Governance Roadmap*) contains detailed instructions for executives of Indonesia's listed companies. OJK also introduced the "comply and explain principle" requiring firms to explain any deviation from the *Roadmap*'s details.

A reason for OJK's CG advocacy is that, despite efforts to the contrary, Indonesia was at the bottom end in the two rankings of Asian countries on their CG practices based on the annual survey and perceptions-based ranking of the Asian Corporate Governance Association (since 2003) and a ranking by the Asian Development Bank based on the scrutiny of practices within the 100 largest listed companies, which was published as the *ASEAN Corporate Governance Scorecard 2012–2015*. In combination, these rankings suggest that Indonesia's largest companies are increasingly committed to good CG practices, but that the majority of firms do not share that urge to the same degree. Publicity (created through press releases and reports in the Indonesian media) in 2014 indicated that OJK released the documents above to prepare Indonesian firms for the ASEAN Economic Community (AEC), which came into force in 2015, and which freed up some financial services trade across countries part of the Association of Southeast Asian Nations (ASEAN). OJK's expectations were that improved CG practices would enhance the competitiveness of Indonesia's firms in attracting cross-ASEAN finance, as well as the competitiveness of its financial firms in AEC's more integrated financial markets.

Increased activity on the ISE underpins the significance of these changes. Indonesia had an active stock exchange—1898 to 1942 and 1952 to 1957—but it collapsed into oblivion after 1957, before a revival in 1977. Securities trading increased, but a significant expansion in activity did not occur until after 2002 (Kung et al. 2010, 333). Between 2002 and 2020, the number of listed companies increased from 331 to 721, and total market capitalisation grew from 15 to 45 per cent of gross domestic product (GDP), but still somewhat modest in international perspective. These developments have been in the interest of minority shareholders. Maximising information on which equity investors can base their perceptions of risk and their expectations of returns in principle mobilises equity investment. In addition, good CG also allows shareholders to articulate their views on the purposes that listed companies should pursue, whether it is for just maximising shareholder value or also for building brand value through good stakeholder relations.

Both OJK documents contain many references to the role of stakeholders and ethical behaviour, but detailed references to a key aspect of stakeholder engagement—CSR—are missing. In fact, the 2014 version of the *Roadmap* document warns against conflating CG and CSR. It argues that the two are different concepts, even though good CG is likely to reinforce a firm's commitments to CSR (OJK 2014, 40, 190). The 2018 version no longer contains this warning. It states that Indonesia's 1999 CG Code offers guidance for CG implementation to "stimulate the company's awareness of social responsibilities, in particular the environmental and societal interests of local communities" (OJK 2018, 78), placing the obligation of fulfilling the company's social responsibilities with the board of directors (OJK 2018, 208). Both documents essentially rephrase the CSR clause in the 2007 Law on the Limited Liability Company, but unlike the 2014 version, the 2018 one sees commitments to good CG and CSR as conjoint rather than separate. Hence, it now appears that discussion in Indonesia about good CG has been joined with that about CSR. Together, they may be a starting point for public debate about "ethical capitalism", although there is no evidence that this is materialising in Indonesia.

Two reasons dampen the likelihood that such debate will materialise soon. Firstly, the 721 listed companies are only a fraction of the total number of privately owned registered companies and the even greater number of informal ventures in Indonesia. As the comparison of the two rankings of CG practices in Asian countries indicates, the majority of unlisted firms in Indonesia do not consider better CG a matter of urgency. Secondly, many listed companies are part of business groups that continue to be controlled in various ways, such as through cross-shareholdings, holding company structures and the executive board positions of the business' family members. For example, majority shares in many listed companies in Indonesia are still held by holding companies that are themselves controlled by unlisted private companies, some of which are a little more than post office boxes in tax havens like the British Virgin Islands and Mauritius.

Sustained Role for Business Groups

The existence of business groups is nothing new for Indonesia. Colonial-era firms shared financial interests in new business ventures, and both Dutch and Chinese firms grew to become a part of business groups (Van der Eng

2022). While the role of Dutch groups ended in 1958, the diversified business interests of many Chinese entrepreneurs grew, especially from the 1970s. Other conglomerations of firms associated with key SOEs, regional military interests, Arab-Indonesian or *pribumi* Indonesian business interests also developed (Sato 1994). By the mid-1990s, corporate ownership in Indonesia was the most highly concentrated in East Asia (Claessens et al. 1999). Chinese-Indonesian business families and/or entrepreneurs who were members and friends of the Soeharto family dominated. Conglomerations of firms generally took the form of webs of cross-shareholdings, often with a pyramid structure (Habir 1999; Husnan 2001, 17–36). Popular resentment against this aspect of the business system spilled out into the streets of Indonesia during 1998, when offices of the companies of Soeharto's friends and family, and of Chinese-Indonesians, were targeted during protests and riots.

The 1997–98 crisis and its aftermath caused the de-concentration of company ownership in two ways. Many groups returned to core competencies, selling interests in non-core, often loss-making firms. In addition, many groups sold equity in order to attract funds, pay debts and stem the falling credit ratings of their core companies on which loan guarantees often depended. Some were more successful than others, while yet other groups expanded through acquisitions of new ventures at relatively low prices.

Sato (2003; 2004a; 2004b; 2005) studied the initial changes in the configuration of business groups and analysed the top 100 non-financial public firms (2004a), establishing that ownership was still highly concentrated in 2000—albeit less so than in 1996—and that ownership and management were still entwined. She also found that concentrated ownership and non-separation of ownership and management did not by themselves predict poor company performance. Firms associated with long-established business groups showed better performance than firms associated with groups that had grown rapidly during the 1990s, such as those associated with President Soeharto's children, and also firms not part of a business group.

The reconfiguration of business groups continued for several years, while further deregulation, new business opportunities, and the establishment, growth and listing of new firms also influenced their composition. Carney & Hamilton-Hart (2015) took stock of the reconfigurations, analysing 1996 and 2008 data for the 200 largest listed companies, supplemented with information about unlisted firms. They established that family ownership remained the most prevalent form of company ownership although there had been considerable churn in the identities of the most prominent business families compared to 1996.

Carney & Hamilton-Hart (2015) also found that listed SOEs were more prominent than before 1996; that the wealth funds controlled by the Governments of Singapore and Malaysia had come to hold substantial ownership stakes in many of Indonesia's largest corporations; and—not surprisingly, given the observations above—that in 2008, banking assets were no longer at the centre of most business groups. One element of continuity was the proportion of large listed firms with political links, which was similar in 2008 and 1996, even though there had been a reconfiguration of political ties away from the Soeharto-era pattern of captive patronage relationships towards a more varied range of political patrons and modes of political engagement (Chong 2015; Aspinall & Berenschot 2019).

These are significant findings if we combine them with other research outcomes. For example, analysing pre-crisis data on listed firms, Lukviarman (2004) found that large family-controlled firms and their business groups disenfranchised minority shareholders, misappropriated company funds and had contributed to the 1997–98 crisis. Other studies using firm-level data found a continued negative relationship between family control and firm performance in Indonesia (Ahmad et al. 2009; Prabowo and Simpson 2011; Siagian 2011; Basyith et al. 2015). Together, these studies suggest that the continuing high level of concentrated control places an upper limit on efforts to improve CG, as noted earlier, and is an additional reason why improvements in CG by firms themselves seem unlikely to make inroads on a major blight on Indonesia's business system: corruption.

The Continuing Blight of Corruption

Since 1995, Transparency International's ranking of countries according to perceived corruption has placed Indonesia towards the bottom of the ranking—according to a ranking scale of 0 marks for "highly corrupt" and 100 marks for "very clean". Corruption started to blight Indonesia's business system in the 1950s, when public service employment grew fast, public revenues to pay public service salaries were increasingly insufficient and accelerating inflation eroded public service salaries. Using public office for private gain was often the only way for poorly paid public servants to augment their incomes. A further factor was the constrained capacity of the guardians against corrupt behaviour since the colonial years—that is, an activist free press and an active and well-resourced public sector audit board like Badan Pemeriksa Keuangan Republik Indonesia (BPK) (or the Audit Board of the Republic of Indonesia).

Corruption became rampant during the troubled 1960s. Efforts to stamp it out largely focused on judicial means—that is, creating rules and regulations rather than addressing the heart of the issue, which was the underpayment of public servants, under-resourcing of agencies tasked with anti-corruption enforcement and underequipping these agencies by only giving them the ability to research and report, and not the authority to prosecute. As a consequence, corruption in the public sector became entrenched during the 1970s to the1980s. It was informally sanctioned and institutionalised by the Soeharto regime through cronyism and nepotism in relation to political and official appointments and business relations (McLeod 2011). This established the norms of captive patronage relationships between businesses, politicians and public administrators, with which Indonesia entered *reformasi* after 1997–98.

High expectations that corruption would soon be dealt with had to wait until the new Komisi Pemberantasan Korupsi (KPK) (or Corruption Eradication Commission) assumed duties in 2004. KPK was granted wide-ranging authority to investigate and prosecute those involved in major corruption cases (Van der Eng 2004, 10–12). KPK has in the years since brought various eye-watering corruption cases to light and also secured prominent convictions, sometimes against entrenched obstruction, stretching even to Indonesia's High Court (Butt 2011; 2015). Indonesia has gradually risen in Transparency International's ranking, but there are limits to the cases that KPK can research, prove and prosecute. Those it brought to light were well-researched and prominent, generally in the context of central government administration and politics in Jakarta. KPK has not had the resources to research and prosecute all of the more frequent forms of petty corruption at regional levels.

Despite various measures to achieve deregulation and lighten the administrative burdens that regulation imposes on entrepreneurs—creating opportunities for corrupt behaviour—many entrepreneurs are still dependent on central and local politicians and administrators for approvals and support related to their business projects. And despite the deterrence of KPK activity and the fact that OJK is now able to hold the 721 listed enterprises to the high ethical standards of good CG, many entrepreneurs still feel they have to seek political and administrative patronage and identify modes of political engagement that will be conducive to their enterprises. This includes establishing their own political parties and entering regional or national politics in their own right.

Increasing Space for Agile Services Companies

As mentioned, economic growth in Indonesia since 2000 has been lower than planners expected. On the output side of the economy, one significant phenomenon that became widely discussed was the concern with "premature deindustrialisation". In 2018, this concern spurred the Government's "Making Indonesia 4.0" initiative, which aimed for a "fourth industrial revolution" in Indonesia's manufacturing sector based on innovations in digital technology, biology and automation. It can be good to aim high. However, in many ways, Indonesia can still benefit from industrialisation 3.0 (entailing communication technologies and renewable energy sources) and even 2.0 (entailing factory electrification and production line mechanisation). In fact, rather than cutting-edge innovation, Indonesia continues to be in need of the more mundane, like just simply proper repair and maintenance of existing infrastructure (OECD 2016, 39–40, 69–70, 116). It also requires massive further investment in new basic infrastructure, so as to ensure that it can continue to function.

The evidence for "deindustrialisation" is the decreasing share of manufacturing in the GDP since 2012. In truth, the volume of manufacturing output is not falling, it is actually growing, and continues to grow. It is just growing at a lower rate than the services production. In part, this significant growth of services production is a consequence of underinvestment in services in the past. Many service sectors used to be heavily regulated and dominated by SOEs. For example, the deregulation of sections of the telecommunications sector increased the number of providers and competition and lowered prices (Lee and Findlay 2005). Output in the "communications" sector grew by an average of 17 per cent per year over years 2000 to 2019, which was three times higher than GDP growth. Another factor that explains the growth of the services output is the international trend of slicing the supply chain, which also takes place within countries as the cost of communications decreases, legal security of transactions improves and opportunities for outsourcing offer themselves. There are many examples of manufacturing and mining firms in Indonesia hiving off specific services as notionally separate companies. They also increased the outsourcing of a variety of business services.

One problem in analysing the role of service sector companies is that they are very heterogeneous and generally smaller than companies producing goods. It is therefore difficult to capture their activities and establish the impact of those activities. Macro-economic data, such as the growth of the services output, help. Another relevant macro-economic statistic is the contribution of productivity to economic growth, generally captured by total factor productivity (TFP). Van der Eng (2010) established that Indonesia during the Soeharto years experienced 0 per cent TFP growth, such that the mobilisation of capital and labour explained all economic growth. In contrast, during 2000 to 2015, Indonesia experienced an unprecedented sustained period of positive TFP growth, which explained the 29 per cent of GDP growth (Van der Eng 2016). Despite continued infrastructure shortcomings and gloomy perceptions of low growth and "de-industrialisation", this indicates increased macro-economic efficiency coinciding with the significantly greater role of services in the economy.

Findlay & Pangestu (2016) dissected the current trends in the service industries in Indonesia in order to identify the remaining obstacles to further growth. They also noted the significant growth of output in services, contrasting it with the low level of Indonesia's services exports compared to other ASEAN countries. They established that Indonesia's restrictive policies contribute to the sector's poor relative performance, despite its development in absolute terms. They called for appropriate reforms of regulatory frameworks—for example with a view to facilitating further developments in Indonesia's information and communications technology to allow businesses to capture the opportunities offered by e-commerce.

The relevant issue for this chapter is that the new generation of service companies in Indonesia is more likely to consist of agile start-ups that produce for end-users rather than intermediaries. The traditional person-to-person characteristic of services delivery, as well as higher online visibility, requires these companies to nurture relations with a wider range of stakeholders than traditionally necessary for manufacturing firms. Nurturing relations is important for the new services companies in order to build reputation as well as brand and shareholder value. In other words, this new generation of services companies may, by their nature, be more inclined to live up to the expectations associated with good GC and CSR.

The CSR Revolution Since 2007

While the 1997–98 crisis drew attention in Indonesia to issues of CG, interest in CSR was minimal before 2007. For example, Chapple & Moon (2005, 428–9) investigated the annual reports of samples of listed companies across Asian countries on their reporting of aspects of CSR and placed Indonesia at the bottom of their ranking. This may be related to the high degree of family control over Indonesia's largest companies and business groups. For example, in a multi-country study, using 2002–12 firm-level data, Rees & Rodionova (2015) found a negative relationship between family control and the environmental, social and governance rankings of listed companies.

Nevertheless, a considerable change took root after the 2007 Law on the Limited Liability Company (Article 74) and the 2007 Law on Capital Investment (Article 15) made it mandatory for companies to implement corporate social and environmental responsibility (Rosser and Edwin 2010; Waagstein 2011; Hofland 2012). The law extended a legal principle that had already applied to SOEs since 1995. Kamar Dagang dan Industri Indonesia (KADIN) (or the Indonesian Chamber of Commerce and Industry) and other business associations protested that compulsion violated the principles of good governance as CSR is by definition expected to be voluntary (*Jakarta Post*, 21 July 2007). KADIN appealed to the Constitutional Court, arguing that the CSR requirement without further clarification increased legal uncertainty and was an additional burden on businesses with negative consequences for the economy at large. After these claims were rejected in 2009, KADIN, other business associations and individual companies engaged in constructive discussions about implementing CSR strategies, which were at the heart of efforts by Indonesia Business Links (IBL) in Jakarta to advance ethical business practices among companies.

There was initial confusion about the minimum CSR requirements that firms would have to meet, what activities would count as CSR, the CSR reporting obligations, and the penalties that firms would face if they were found to be non-compliant. Government regulation No. 47 (2012) on Corporate Social and Environmental Responsibility contained further details on CSR but did not provide much clarity, except to state that companies had to base CSR activities on "propriety and fairness", that their boards of directors were responsible and that they had to record CSR expenditure as part of business costs. In practice, any confusion was resolved by local provincial, district or city authorities, which mostly issued their own clarifications. Details differ, but local regulations essentially stipulate that local authorities should prescribe a company's expected CSR expenditure relative to its income. Consequently, there is now a wide range of regional interpretations of the minimum level of CSR commitments expected of companies.

Despite the initial confusion, it appears that many entrepreneurs and companies in Indonesia have embraced CSR as an integral part of their operations. One reason for the apparent enthusiasm is the opportunity for firms to showcase themselves in an expectation of free publicity and a better reputation and increased brand value. News about CSR commitments frequently reaches the public through the media. *CSR Indonesia*, a dedicated magazine, as well as a variety of books on CSR are available in book shops; and local and national business associations award annual CSR prizes. The projects featured in the media vary significantly. They include company donations of funding and/or building materials for school restorations, company housing, the restoration of mosques and musholllas, the construction of more sanitary facilities, providing seedlings to local farmers and providing free medical services for local communities.

Newspapers also continued to report cases on the lacklustre uptake of CSR, companies found to be engaging in "fake" projects and the unaccounted spending of CSR funds pledged by companies. The enormous diversity of CSR practices led a parliamentary committee to draft a law in 2016 to regulate CSR, including the clarification and standardisation of the use of CSR funds and an applicable tax treatment. The reason for seeking clarification amounts to the fact that, under current tax legislation, only company expenses for the development of social infrastructure, training, education and research are tax deductible, which excludes other CSR-related commitments. Despite this effort, parliament did not proceed with the draft.

Consequently, it remains difficult to generalise the degree and nature of the CSR commitments of Indonesian companies, and motivations in general remain unclear. Stated motivations in public media and small surveys range from legal requirement through to expressions of sincere commitment to social investment and sustainable development. Nevertheless, the general impression is that companies are making commitments to what they understand CSR to be, and that they are aware of the opportunities CSR affords to strengthen their reputation and build brand value. In addition, activist media and outspoken academics continue to draw attention to CSR issues and raise general awareness.

From Philanthropy and Paternalism to Stakeholder Engagement

It seems that CSR galvanised Indonesia's society beginning 2007. The history of CSR in Indonesia still has to be written, but even before 2007, several companies were already well-known for their commitment to principles and activities that are now considered CSR activities, particularly the Astra automotive company established in 1957 (Sato 1996). In addition, some observers have argued that CSR caught on so quickly in Indonesia because it echoes long-held norms and values in Indonesian society.

One popular notion is that CSR perpetuates the concept of *gotong royong* (mutual reciprocal assistance) (see for example Sharma 2013). This might be a relevant rationalisation, were it not for the fact that *gotong royong* is a mythologised concept (Bowen 1986). During the colonial years, observers of rural communities in Java identified the existence of arrangements referred to as *tolong menolong* or *bantu membantu* (or the widely used Dutch term *zelfwerkzaamheid*): reciprocal efforts in building and maintaining structures and village amenities. The concept became part of efforts to foster rural development, in particular by encouraging the establishment of producer and consumer cooperatives known as *gotong royong* in Java in the 1930s. Also, in the 1930s, Indonesian nationalism absorbed and propagated the term *gotong royong*. During the 1950s, rural sociologists of Indonesia mythologised it as a core concept for rural development efforts, particularly through cooperatives (Grader 1952; Jaspan 1959, 35). The term also became a key feature of official propaganda after President Sukarno seized power in 1957, installed a "*gotong royong* cabinet", and popularised the term as part of his home-grown blend of nationalism and socialism. The term was perpetuated in official rural development propaganda after Soeharto succeeded Sukarno in 1967.

Due to this elevated and sustained use of the term, the reasons for its original use seem to have disappeared from collective memory. Today, it is generally used to express an almost nostalgic hankering for the uncomplicated, timeless, tranquil, homogenous and collectivist rural village society that thrived on sharing, harmony and a collective work effort in subsistence agriculture in an unspecified past. This romanticised vision of rural Indonesia persists despite many studies having established the existence of very significant social frictions and hierarchies in village communities past and present rather than perpetual harmony. Nevertheless, the myth of *gotong royong* is widely believed to be the foundation of "traditional society", including among academics and policy makers seeking to rationalise Indonesia's newfound attachment to CSR. Either way, it is difficult to see how either the original concept of self-help among rural villagers or the romanticised version of a harmonious village society is of direct use in defining relations between commercially oriented private firms and their stakeholders today. Its only practical use appears to be its ability to rally support for CSR through appealing to perceived traditional values.

A further explanation for the adherence to CSR in Indonesia is that it is in line with Islamic expectations. The Quran and Islamic teachings offer ethical guidance in business in several ways (Abeng 1997). For example, faithful Muslims are expected to engage in self-help through *ta'awun* (mutual co-operation) and *takaful* (cooperative pooling of funds), as well as philanthropy through *tabarru'* or *sedekah* (voluntary donations and gifts) and *zakat* (giving alms). They are also expected to participate in the establishment of *waqf* (pious charitable foundations).

Since the 16th century, the majority of Indonesians has been Muslim. Indonesia is currently experiencing increased piety and a growing popular desire to live according to Islamic principles. There is also a growing public and academic discussion about Islamic business ethics, and how its elements can be usefully applied. Muslims are familiar with the concepts above, even if superficially. The concepts are easily translated into the expectations that Muslim stakeholders have of the companies with which they interact. Increasingly, they also inform the strategic decisions that the Muslim board members of companies are willing to initiate and support.

This may appear to be a new development. The common perception is that Indonesia's economy has long been dominated by foreign and Chinese-owned enterprises, and that ethnic Indonesians are only now asserting their presence in business. In fact, ethnic Indonesians have long played an integral but under-researched role in business. For example, a 1920 incomplete listing counted 4,479 industrial business ventures run by ethnic Indonesians, of which 864 employed more than 5 people (Vleming 1926, 280–7). Post (1996, 2009) detailed the growing business interests of a generation of prominent ethnic Indonesian businessmen during the 1920s to the 1950s.

This significant activity of Indonesian entrepreneurs is consistent with an historical overview of Muslim charity by Fauzia (2013), which demonstrates an active role by Muslim businessmen in philanthropy in Indonesia since the 19th century. This took the form of contributions to the national Muslim organisation Muhammadiyah, as well as integrating philanthropic and business activities, for example in Sarekat Islam since 1911. Fauzia (2013) also identified increasing CSR-related company support for *zakat* agencies. These are philanthropic non-government organisations, such as the well-known Rumah Zakat (established 1998), which emerged well before 2007 to collect and disburse charitable *zakat* donations of companies in an accountable manner. Such agencies are currently thriving in Indonesia (Latief 2013; Osili and Ökten 2015).

Muslim businessmen have since the 1960s also articulated in other ways that their success in business should benefit Indonesian society. For example, entrepreneur Nurcholish Madjid, in 1986, established Yayasan Wakaf Paramadina, a non-profit organisation that fosters the understanding of Islamic philosophy and which functions as a think tank on Islamic modernism. It founded Paramadina University in 1998. In all, Islamic values have a longstanding association with business activities in Indonesia and a clear relationship with the philanthropic activities now considered part of CSR. Enthusiasm for CSR is so great that many are advocating a subset. Termed "Islamic Social Responsibility", it has already found practical applications in Indonesia's *shari'ah* banks.

A third notion that is relevant to explaining interest in CSR relates to the significant role of Chinese-Indonesians in business development. During the colonial years, many leading Chinese entrepreneurs were imbued with a strong sense of civic duty and reciprocity that led to their assuming leadership roles in their local communities. Mobilising business wealth to support philanthropic causes, such as establishing schools, was part of that role. Chinese-Indonesian businessmen continued to make philanthropic contributions. An example is the Pelita Harapan Education Foundation associated with the Lippo business group of the Riady family. It established Pelita Harapan University in 1994, partly as a business proposition, but also as a philanthropic commitment to education. The Chinese-Indonesian business families in charge of the largest business groups have established philanthropic foundations, such as the Tanoto Foundation (established 1981) and the Putera Sampoerna Foundation (established 2001).

Hoon (2010) analysed the reasons for Chinese-Indonesian entrepreneurs to engage in philanthropy. He noted, *inter alia*, reasons including "buying face" and social status; expressing religiosity; the urge to polish up a reputation tarnished by the association with the discredited Soeharto regime and being targeted during the 1998 riots; seeking tax relief; establishing a good family name; and an innate desire to support worthy causes.

Discounting the vague and impractical motivation of *gotong royong*, it appears that religious expectations and piety are prime drivers for Muslim entrepreneurs and their companies to be enthusiastic about CSR; a similar enthusiasm among Chinese entrepreneurs is based on their individual mix of pragmatic and personal reasons.

During the Soeharto era, domestic and foreign companies engaged in CSR-like paternalistic philanthropy in the form of health campaigns and community development initiatives, and also through donations to tax-exempt *yayasan* (charitable foundations) (Sasongko 2004; Ibrahim 2005). Since 2000, the number of philanthropic organisations and the assets they control have increased significantly in Indonesia (Anand and Hayling 2014, 16–31). They are essentially paternalistic as they turn the recipients of largesse into passive partakers for the gratification of donors and elevate donors to a position of perceived moral superiority, not least because givers can arbitrarily withhold favours from recipients.

Recent company surveys found that most Indonesian companies and their executives still associate CSR primarily with philanthropy (see for example Fauzi 2014; Gunawan 2016). Only foreign-owned and some large companies, particularly SOEs, have integrated CSR into their strategies and value chains, often in order to seize the opportunity for further interactions with their stakeholders (Hofland 2012; Gunawan 2016; Gunawan et al. 2014; Park et al. 2015; Famiola and Adiwoso 2016; Bhinekawati 2017). Paternalism and philanthropy are within the CSR concept, which is generally defined as "actions that appear to further some social good, beyond the interests of the firm and that which is required by law" (McWilliams and Siegel 2001). However, other definitions of CSR emphasise that companies' actions should, as a matter of course, benefit all stakeholders. In other words, CSR is not a matter of giving and receiving, but a matter of a company engaging with the interests of all its constituencies: shareholders and investors, and also employees, customers, suppliers and society. This interpretation of CSR comes closer to "ethical capitalism", a concept that involves companies pursuing the creation of long-term economic and social value by making a commitment to act as a steward in the interests of all stakeholders. Consequently, Indonesia's corporations still have quite some ground to cover before meeting such expectations.

Conclusion

The purpose of this chapter has been to review the changes in Indonesia's business system with the aims of explaining why Indonesia has become so strongly predisposed to CSR and establish the viability of public discussion about "ethical capitalism" in Indonesia today. The chapter could not discuss several factors that are also relevant, such as the high proportion of young people in Indonesia's population. Compared to their parents, these young people are better educated, much better connected to each other and the world, and more interested in the ideas shaping their perceptions of Indonesia's future, including those that relate to the role of private enterprise in Indonesian society.

The chapter has identified relevant changes and continuity. In essence, Indonesia's small financial sector is likely to sustain a continued role for business groups controlled by leading business families and SOEs as inter-firm lending remains important. Listed group companies are now challenged by new regulations that advance good CG, but they are a minority of all businesses. In addition, controlling business families may seek to evade the challenge of CG regulations as long as they can use ways other than shared ownership to control group companies. On the other hand, there are growing imperatives for all companies to yield to this challenge. Anti-corruption efforts have gained ground and are affecting the ways in which relations between business, administrators and politicians have long played out. The growth of the formal services sector increases the need for firms to communicate directly with stakeholders to build brand value. Both these changes have supported the wave of company and public interest in CSR since 2007.

The growing interest in CSR in Indonesia is also related to conceptual similarities between elements of Islamic teachings and CSR, and to the motivations of Chinese business families to engage in forms of paternalistic philanthropy. This differs from the intention underlying the CSR concept, namely that companies are automatically imbued with advancing stakeholder interests. Nevertheless, the increasing interest in CSR indicates a growing interest in public and academic discussion about the role of private enterprise in Indonesian society. This debate is currently influenced by strong, popular and academic interest in the aspects of Islamic Social Responsibility. The strands of ethical capitalism are not yet part of the debate. Consequently, attempts to elevate the concept's relevance to these debates in Indonesia will require concerted steps to draw attention to the motivations that support it and the potential outcomes to which it aspires. It will also require concrete proposals for Indonesia-specific arrangements that advance such expected outcomes.

References

Abeng, Tanri. 1997. "Business Ethics in Islamic context: Perspectives of a Muslim Business Leader". *Business Ethics Quarterly* 7 (3): 47–54.

Ahmad, Tarmizi et al. 2009. "The Iniquitous Influence of Family Ownership Structures on Corporate Performance". *Journal of Global Business Issues* 3 (1): 41–8.

Anand, Prapti Upadhyay and Crystal Hayling. 2014. "Levers for Change: Philanthropy in Select South East Asian Countries". In *Lien Centre for Social Innovation Social Insight Research Series, No.1-2014*. Singapore: Singapore Management University.

Aspinall, Edward and Ward Berenschot. 2019. *Democracy for Sale: Elections, Clientelism, and the State in Indonesia*. New York: Cornell University Press.

Aziz, Iwan. 2018. "Development and Shortcomings of Indonesia's Financial Sector". In *Routledge Handbook of Banking and Finance in Asia*, ed. Ulrich Volz et al., 76–88. London: Routledge.

Basyith, Abdul, Fitriya Fauzi and Muhammad Idris. 2015. "The Impact of Board Structure and Ownership Structure on Firm Performance: An Evidence from Blue Chip Firms Listed in Indonesian Stock Exchange". *Corporate Control and Ownership* 12 (3)/(4): 344–51.

Bhinekawati, Risa. 2017. *Corporate Social Responsibility and Sustainable Development: Social Capital and Corporate Development in Developing Economies*. London/New York: Routledge.

Bank Indonesia. *Financial Stability Review* (released bi-yearly). Jakarta: Bank Indonesia, 2003–18.

Bowen, John R. 1986. "On the Political Construction of Tradition: *Gotong Royong* in Indonesia". *Journal of Asian Studies* 45 (3): 545–61.

Broadberry, Stephen and John Wallis. 2018. "Growing, Shrinking and Long Run Economic Performance: Historical Perspectives on Economic Development". Working Paper No. 2018–14, Center for Economic Institutions, Hitotsubashi University, Tokyo, Japan.

Butt, Simon. 2011. "Anti-corruption Reform in Indonesia: An obituary?" *Bulletin of Indonesian Economic Studies* 47 (3): 381–94.

_____. 2015. "The Rule of Law and Anti-Corruption Reforms Under Yudhoyono: The Rise of the KPK and the Constitutional Court". In *The Yudhoyono Presidency: Indonesia's Decade of Stability and Stagnation*, ed. Edward Aspinall, Marcus Mietzner and Dirk Tomsa, 175–95. Singapore: Institute of Southeast Asian Studies.

Capgemini. *World Wealth Report 2014*. Paris: Capgemini, 2014.

_____. *Asia-Pacific Wealth Report 2016*. Paris: Capgemini, 2016.

Carney, Richard W. and Natasha Hamilton-Hart. 2015. "What Do Changes in Corporate Ownership in Indonesia Tell Us?" *Bulletin of Indonesian Economic Studies* 51 (1): 123–45.

Chapple, Wendy and Jeremy Moon. 2005. "Corporate Social Responsibility (CSR) in Asia: A Seven-Country Study of CSR Web Site Reporting". *Business and Society* 44 (4): 415–41.

Chong, Wu-Ling. 2015. "Local Politics and Chinese Indonesian Business in Post-Suharto Era". *Southeast Asian Studies* 4 (3): 487–532.

Claessens, Stijn et al. 1999. "Who Controls East Asian Corporations?" World Bank Policy Research Working Paper No. 2088. Washington DC: World Bank, 1999.

————. 2000. "Expropriation of Minority Shareholders in East Asia". Center for Economic Institutions Working Paper No. 2000-4. Tokyo: Hitotsubashi University, 2000.

Famiola, Melia and Siti Adiprigandari Adiwoso. 2016. "Corporate Social Responsibility Diffusion by Multinational Subsidiaries in Indonesia: Organisational Dynamic and Institutional Effect". *Social Responsibility Journal* 12 (1): 117–29.

Fauzi, Hasan. 2014. "The Indonesian Executive's Perspective of CSR Practices". *Issues in Social and Environmental Accounting* 8 (3): 171–81.

Fauzia, Amelia. 2013. *Faith and the State: A History of Islamic Philanthropy in Indonesia.* Leiden: Brill.

Findlay, Christopher and Mari Pangestu. 2016. "The Services Sector as a Driver of Change: Indonesia's Experience in the ASEAN Context". *Bulletin of Indonesian Economic Studies* 52 (1): 27–53.

Grader, Christian J. 1952. *Rural Organization and Village Revival in Indonesia.* New York: Cornell University, Department of Far Eastern Studies.

Gunawan, Janti et al. 2014. "Corporate Social Responsibility Practices in Indonesia: Intermediary Matters, Case Studies from Indonesia". In *Corporate Social Responsibility and Local Community in Asia*, ed. Kyoko Fukukawa, 128–38. London: Routledge.

Gunawan, Juniati. 2016. "Corporate Social Responsibility Initiatives in a Regulated and Emerging Country: An Indonesia Perspective". In *Key Initiatives in Corporate Social Responsibility: Global Dimension of CSR in Corporate Entities*, ed. Samuel O. Idowu, 325–40. Springer Publishing.

Habir, Ahmad Derry. 1999. "Conglomerates: All in the Family?" In *Indonesia Beyond Suharto: Polity, Economy, Society and Transition*, ed. Donald K. Emmerson, 168–202. London: M. E. Sharpe.

Hofland, Irene. 2012. "The Relationship between CSR and Competitiveness: The Indonesian Case". MSc thesis, School of Management and Government, University of Twente, Enschede, The Netherlands.

Hoon, Chang-Yau. 2010. "Face, Faith, and Forgiveness: Elite Chinese Philanthropy in Indonesia". *Journal of Asian Business* 24 (1)/(2): 51–67.

Husnan, Suad. 2001. "Indonesia". In *Corporate Governance and Finance in East Asia, Volume II*, ed. Ma Virginita Capulong, David Edwards and Zhuang Juzhong, 1–51. Manila: Asian Development Bank.

Ibrahim, Rustam. 2005. *Bukan Sekadar Berbisnis: Keterlibatan Perusahaan dalam Pemberdayaan Masyarakat, Studi Kasus Bogasari Flour Mills, Citibank, Coca-Cola Indonesia, Riau Andalan Pulp and Paper, dan Rio Tinto* [Not just Doing Business: Corporate Engagement in Community Empowerment]. Depok: Piramedia.

Jaspan, Mervin A. 1959. "Rural Sociology in Indonesia". *Current Sociology* 8 (1): 33–8.

Kemp, Melody. 2001. "Corporate Social Responsibility in Indonesia: Quixotic Dream or Confident Expectation?" UNRISD Technology, Business and Society Programme Paper No. 6. Geneva: United Nations Research Institute for Social Development, 2001.

Kung, James J., Andrew P. Carverhill and Ross H. McLeod. 2010. "Indonesia's Stock Market: Evolving Role, Growing Efficiency". *Bulletin of Indonesian Economic Studies* 46 (3): 329–46.

Latief, Hilman. 2013. "Islamic Philanthropy and the Private Sector in Indonesia". *Indonesian Journal of Islam and Muslim Societies* 3 (2): 175–201.

Lee, Roy Chun and Christopher Findlay. 2005. "Telecommunications Reform in Indonesia: Achievements and Challenges". *Bulletin of Indonesian Economic Studies* 41 (3): 341–65.

Lukviarman, Niki. 2004. "Ownership Structure and Firm Performance: The Case of Indonesia". PhD thesis, Curtin University of Technology, Perth, Australia.

McLeod, Ross H. 2011. "Institutionalized Public Sector Corruption: A Legacy of the Suharto Franchise". In *The State and Illegality in Indonesia*, ed. Edward Aspinall and Gerry Van Klinken, 45–64. Leiden: KITLV Press.

McWilliams, Abagail and Donald Siegel. 2001. "Corporate Social Responsibility: A Theory of the Firm Perspective". *Academy of Management Review* 26 (1): 117–27.

Organisation for Economic Co-operation and Development (OECD). *OECD Economic Surveys: Indonesia*. Paris: OECD, 2016.

Osili, Una and Cagla Ökten. 2015. "Giving in Indonesia: A Culture of Philanthropy Rooted in Islamic Tradition". In *The Palgrave Handbook of Global Philanthropy*, ed. Pamala Wiepken and Femida Handy, 388–403. London: Palgrave Macmillan.

Otoritas Jasa Keuangan (OJK). 2014; 2018. *The Indonesia Corporate Governance Manual*. Jakarta: Otoritas Jasa Keuangan.

Park, Young-Ryeol et al. 2015. "Corporate Social Responsibility in International Business: Illustrations from Korean and Japanese Electronics MNEs in Indonesia". *Journal of Business Ethics* 129: 747–61.

Post, Peter. 1996. "The Formation of the *Pribumi* Business Élite in Indonesia, 1930s–1940s". *Journal of the Humanities and Social Sciences of Southeast Asia* 152 (4): 609–32.

_____. 2009) "*Indonesianisasi* and Japanization: The Japanese and the Shifting Fortunes of *Pribumi* Entrepreneurship". In *Indonesian Economic Decolonization in Regional and International Perspective*, ed. Thomas J. Lindblad and Peter Post, 61–86. Leiden: KITLV Press.

Prabowo, Muhammad and John Simpson. 2011. "Independent Directors and Firm Performance in Family Controlled Firms: Evidence from Indonesia". *Asian-Pacific Economic Literature* 25 (1): 121–32.

Purwanto, Bambang. 2009. "Economic Decolonization and the Rise of Indonesian Military Business". In *Indonesian Economic Decolonization in Regional and International Perspective*, ed. Thomas J. Lindblad and Peter Post, 39–58. Leiden: KITLV Press.

Rees, William and Tatiana Rodionova. 2015. "The Influence of Family Ownership on Corporate Social Responsibility: An International Analysis of Publicly Listed Companies". *Corporate Governance: An International Review* 23 (3). 184–202.

Rosser, Andrew and Donni Edwin. 2010. "The Politics of Corporate Social Responsibility in Indonesia". *The Pacific Review* 23 (1): 1–22.

Sasongko, Adi. 2004. "Collaboration of NGOs and Private Sector in Improving the Health of Primary School Children in Jakarta, Indonesia (1987–2004)". In *Corporate Social Responsibility in the Promotion of Social Development: Experiences from Asia and Latin America*, ed. Manuel E. Contreras, 37–52. Washington DC: Inter-American Development Bank.

Sato, Yuri. 1994. "The Development of Business Groups in Indonesia: 1967–1989". In *Approaching Suharto's Indonesia From the Margins*, ed. Takashi Shiraishi, 101–53. New York: Cornell University Press.

_____. 1996. "The Astra Group: A Pioneer of Management Modernization". *Developing Economies* 34 (3): 247–80.

_____. 2004a. "Corporate Ownership and Management in Indonesia: Does it Change?" In *Business in Indonesia: New Challenges, Old Problems*, ed. Muhammad Chatib Basri and Pierre van der Eng, 158–77. Singapore: Institute of Southeast Asian Studies.

_____. 2004b. "Corporate Governance in Indonesia: A Study on Governance of Business Groups". In *Asian Development Experience Volume. 2: The Role of Governance in Asia*, ed. Yasutami Shimomura, 88–136. Singapore: Institute of Southeast Asian Studies.

_____. 2005. "Indoneshia no Kigyō Tōchi to Kigyō Hōsei Kaikaku" [Corporate Governance in Indonesia and Corporate Legal System Reform]. In *Higashi Ajia no Kigyō Tōchi to Kigyō Hōsei Kaikaku* [Corporate Governance in East Asia and Corporate Legal Reform], ed. Shinya Imaizumi and Makoto Abe, 229–74. Tokyo: Institute of Developing Economies (IDE).

Sharma, Bindu. 2013. "Indonesia: A *Gotong Royong* CSR". In *Contextualising CSR in Asia: Corporate Social Responsibility in Asian Economies and the Drivers that Influence its Practice*, 110–25. Singapore: Lien Centre for Social Innovation.

Sheehy, Benjamin. 2015. "Defining CSR: Problems and Solutions". *Journal of Business Ethics* 131 (3): 625–48.

Siagian, Ferdinand T. 2011. "Ownership Structure and Governance Implementation: Evidence from Indonesia". *International Journal of Business, Humanities and Technology* 1 (3): 187–202.

Siregar, Sylvia Veronica. 2017. "Corporate Governance in Indonesia". In *Corporate Governance in Developing and Emerging Markets*, ed. Franklin N. Ngwu, Onyeka K. Osuji and Frank H. Stephen, 160–72. London: Routledge.

Van der Eng, Pierre. 2004. "Business in Indonesia: Old Problems and New Challenges". In *Business in Indonesia: New Challenges, Old Problems*, ed. Muhammad Chatib Basri and Pierre van der Eng, 1–20. Singapore: Institute of Southeast Asian Studies.

_____. 2010. "The Sources of Long-term Economic Growth in Indonesia, 1880–2008". *Explorations in Economic History* 47 (3): 294–309.

_____. 2016. "Indonesia's Unprecedented Productivity Growth". *The Jakarta Post*, 24 June 2016.

_____. 2022. "Chinese Entrepreneurship in Indonesia, 1890–1940: A Business Demography Approach". *Business History* 64 (4): 682–703.

Vleming, Johannes L. 1926. *Het Chineesche Zakenleven in Nederlandsch-Indië* [Chinese Business in the Netherlands Indies]. Batavia: Volkslectuur.

Waagstein, Patricia Rinwigati. 2011. "The Mandatory Corporate Social Responsibility in Indonesia: Problems and Implications". *Journal of Business Ethics* 98 (3): 455–66.

Wijaya, Yahya. 2007. "The Prospect of Familism in the Global Era: A Study of the Recent Development of the Ethnic-Chinese Business, with Particular Attention to the Indonesian Context". *Journal of Business Ethics* 79 (2): 311–17.

Index